D1760140

"This book is designed simultaneously as a tribute one of the world's foremost scholars of prejudice, and as a 'state of the art' collection of essays delineating social psychology's contribution to the reduction of prejudice around the world. It succeeds admirably in both these aims. It is a fitting celebration of Pettigrew's career, both as a pioneering social scientist and as a courageous activist in the cause of social justice. The essays, written by a veritable 'Who's Who' in the social psychology of intergroup relations, are admirably concise and well-written accounts of the key recent developments in the field. There can be few topics which deserve more of our attention than that of improving intergroup relations. In an increasingly fissured world, it is both timely and reassuring to know that so many of social psychology's leading minds are addressing themselves here to the cause of promoting tolerance and social harmony. Researchers and policy makers alike will profit greatly from a close study of this book."

Rupert Brown, University of Sussex

"This remarkable book brings together the world's leading scholars of intergroup relations to pay tribute to the seminal work of Thomas Pettigrew, and in so doing to derive essential lessons for academics, politicians, and the public in general."

Douglas S. Massey, Princeton University

"Tribute and treat, this exciting collection celebrates social psychologist Tom Pettigrew's great impact on our understandings of prejudice, discrimination, and intergoup contact. Highly readable articles integrate well, offering a well-etched portrait of Pettigrew's many contributions to research on racial emotions, intergroup adaptation, deprovincialization of ingroups, and context effects. Once expelled from school for standing up to a bigoted teacher, Pettigrew's scholar-activist commitments to eradicating racism have been influential and equal to those of any social scientist of the last half century."

Joe R. Feagin, Texas A & M University

"Tom Pettigrew's research and writing has had a major impact on our understanding of prejudice, its causes and cures. This remarkable volume is both a tribute to Pettigrew's influence and an extension of its reach. A must read for anyone interested in intergroup relations."

Elliot Aronson, author of *The Social Animal*,
Nobody Left to Hate, and *Mistakes were Made (But Not By Me)*

Social Issues and Interventions

This edited series of books examines the psychological study of social problems and social interventions. Each volume draws together newly commissioned chapters by experts in social psychology and related disciplines in order to provide a multifaceted analysis of a particular contemporary social issue. Utilizing both case studies and theory, this series presents readers with a comprehensive examination of complex social problems while concurrently advancing research in the field. Editors have been chosen for their expertise of the featured subjects, rendering *Social Issues and Social Interventions* an urgent and groundbreaking collection for scholars everywhere.

Series editor: Marilynn Brewer

Explaining the Breakdown of Ethnic Relations: Why Neighbors Kill, edited by Victoria M. Esses and Richard A. Vernon

Improving Intergroup Relations: Building on the Legacy of Thomas F. Pettigrew, edited by Ulrich Wagner, Linda R. Tropp, Gillian Finchilescu, and Colin Tredoux.

Improving Intergroup Relations

Building on the Legacy of Thomas F. Pettigrew

Edited by

Ulrich Wagner, Linda R. Tropp,
Gillian Finchilescu and Colin Tredoux

Blackwell
Publishing

BLACKWELL PUBLISHING
350 Main Street, Malden, MA 02148-5020, USA
9600 Garsington Road, Oxford OX4 2DQ, UK
550 Swanston Street, Carlton, Victoria 3053, Australia

The right of Ulrich Wagner, Linda R. Tropp, Gillian Finchilescu and Colin Tredoux
to be identified as the authors of the editorial material in this work has been asserted
in accordance with the UK Copyright, Designs, and Patents Act 1988.

First published 2008 by Blackwell Publishing Ltd

1   2008

Library of Congress Cataloging-in-Publication Data

Improving intergroup relations : building on the legacy of Thomas F. Pettigrew / edited by
Ulrich Wagner . . . [et al.].
    p. cm. — (Social issues and social interventions)
    Includes bibliographical references and index.
    ISBN 978-1-4051-6972-1 (hardcover : alk. paper) — ISBN 978-1-4051-6971-4 (pbk. : alk.
paper). 1. Intergroup relations. 2. Pettigrew, Thomas F. I. Wagner, Ulrich, 1951–

    HM1111.I46 2008
    302.3—dc22

                                                                              2008001973

A catalogue record for this title is available from the British Library.

Set in 10.5/12.5pt Galliard
by Graphicraft Limited, Hong Kong
Printed and bound in Singapore
by C.O.S. Printers Pte Ltd

The publisher's policy is to use permanent paper from mills that operate a sustainable forestry
policy, and which has been manufactured from pulp processed using acid-free and elementary
chlorine-free practices. Furthermore, the publisher ensures that the text paper and cover board
used have met acceptable environmental accreditation standards.

For further information on
Blackwell Publishing, please visit our website at
www.blackwellpublishing.com

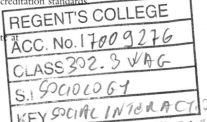

Contents

Notes on the Contributors

Arthur Aron is Professor of Psychology at the State University of New York at Stony Brook. His research centers on the self-expansion model of motivation and cognition in personal relationships, including the implications of the model for intergroup relations. His major current research programs focus on (a) the cognitive overlap of self and other in close relationships, (b) how shared participation in novel and arousing activities can enhance relationship quality, (c) the role of friendship with members of ethnic outgroups and knowledge of such friendships in reducing intergroup prejudice, and (d) identifying the neural circuits engaged by relationship-relevant cognitions and emotions. He is a Fellow of the American Psychological Association, the Association for Psychological Science, and the Society for the Psychological Study of Social Issues; he received the 2006 Distinguished Career Award for the International Association for Relationship Research.

Marilynn B. Brewer is Professor of Psychology and Eminent Scholar in Social Psychology at Ohio State University. Her primary areas of research include the study of social identity, collective decision making, and intergroup relations. She is the author of numerous research articles and books in these areas. Dr. Brewer was the recipient of the 1996 Lewin Award from SPSSI, the 1993 Donald T. Campbell award for Distinguished Contributions to Social Psychology from the Society for Personality and Social Psychology, and the 2003 Distinguished Scientist award from the Society of Experimental Social Psychology. In 2004 she was elected as a Fellow of the American Academy of Arts and Sciences and in 2007 she received the Distinguished Scientific Contribution award from the American Psychological Association.

Salena M. Brody received her Ph.D. in Social Psychology from the University of California, Santa Cruz. She is Assistant Professor of

Psychology at Collin College in Frisco, Texas. She is founder of the Cultivating Scholars research program that supports community college students conducting original research. Her research interests include intergroup relations, prejudice reduction, and service-learning.

Ed Cairns is Professor of Psychology in the School of Psychology at the University of Ulster in Coleraine, Northern Ireland. He has spent the last 30 years studying the psychological aspects of political violence in relation to the conflict in Northern Ireland. During this time he has been a visiting scholar at the Universities of Florida, Cape Town and Melbourne. He is a Fellow of the British Psychological Society and of the American Psychological Association and is a Past President of the Division of Peace Psychology of the American Psychological Association (Division 48).

Frances Cherry is Professor of Psychology at Carleton University, Ottawa, Canada. She holds a Ph.D. from Purdue University. In the mid-1980s, she turned her attention to the history and theory of social psychology, resulting in a book of critical research essays, *The "Stubborn Particulars" of social psychology: Essays on the research process* (1995). She continues to write about the history of social psychology at mid-20th century, with a particular focus on the multiple ways in which social psychologists have brought research and activism together.

Oliver Christ is a Lecturer in Psychological Methods at Philipps-University Marburg, Germany. Before, he was a Lecturer in Social Psychology at the University of Marburg and an advisor for survey methodology at the University of Bielefeld, Germany. He earned his Ph.D. in Social Psychology from Philipps-University Marburg, Germany in 2005. His research interests are in the field of intergroup relations, ethnic prejudice and social identity processes in organizations.

Mark D. Davis received his Ph.D. in psychology from New Mexico State University in 2004. He is currently an Assistant Professor at the University of West Alabama. His research interests include intergroup relations, emotion, and prejudice reduction. His primary focus is on the role that emotions play in intergroup relations.

John F. Dovidio received his Ph.D. from the University of Delaware, and is currently Professor of Psychology at Yale University, having been on the Faculty at Colgate University and at the University of Connecticut. At Colgate, he served as Provost and Dean of the Faculty. His research interests are in stereotyping, prejudice, and discrimination;

social power and nonverbal communication; and altruism and help-ing. Much of his scholarship has focused on "aversive racism," a subtle form of contemporary racism, and ways to reduce it in order to improve intergroup relations. He is currently Editor of the *Journal of Personality and Social Psychology—Interpersonal Relations and Group Processes* and Co-Editor of *Social Issues and Policy Review.*

Gillian Finchilescu is Professor and Chair of Psychology at the University of the Witwatersrand, South Africa. She received her first degrees from the University of Cape Town and her D.Phil. from Oxford University. Her research interests are in the broad field of intergroup relations. Gillian Finchilescu has published in a number of interna-tional journals on issues such as intergroup contact, race and gender prejudice, socio-political orientations of adolescents in times of rapid social change, HIV, and stigma and sexual harassment and violence.

Susan T. Fiske is Eugene Higgins Professor of Psychology, Princeton University. She received her Ph.D. from Harvard University. Dr. Fiske has authored over 200 articles and chapters, and edited many books and journal special issues. Notably, she edits the *Annual Review of Psychology* (with Schacter and Sternberg), and the *Handbook of Social Psychology* (with Gilbert and Lindzey). Currently, she investigates emotional prejudices (pity, contempt, envy, and pride) at cultural, inter-personal, and neural levels. She received the American Psychological Association's Early Career Award for Distinguished Contributions to Psychology in the Public Interest for anti-discrimination testimony, and the Society for the Psychological Study of Social Issues' Allport Intergroup Relations Award for ambivalent sexism theory (with Glick), as well as Harvard's Graduate Centennial Medal. She was elected President of the American Psychological Society and Fellow of the American Academy of Arts and Sciences.

Samuel L. Gaertner is Professor of Psychology at the University of Delaware. His research interests involve intergroup relations with a focus on understanding and reducing prejudice, discrimination and racism. He has served on the editorial boards of the *Journal of Personality and Social Psychology, Personality and Social Psychology Bulletin,* and *Group Processes and Intergroup Relations.* Professor Gaertner's research, in collaboration with John F. Dovidio, has been supported by grants from the Office of Naval Research, the National Institutes of Mental Health and currently, the National Science Foundation. Together with Dovidio, he shared the Gordon Allport Intergroup Relations Prize in 1985 and 1998, as well as the Kurt

Lewin Memorial Career Award from the Society for the Psychological Study of Social Issues, Division 9 of the American Psychological Association.

Samer Halabi obtained his Ph.D. in social psychology from the University of Haifa, Israel. His research interests are in intergroup relations, intergroup helping and prosocial behavior. Currently he is a faculty member in the Department of Behavioral Sciences, Zefat Academic College, Israel.

Jake Harwood is Professor of Communication at the University of Arizona. He is author of *Understanding Communication and Aging* (2007) and co-editor of *Intergroup Communication: Multiple Perspectives* (with Peter Lang, 2005). His recent publications have appeared in *Personality and Social Psychology Bulletin*, *Journal of Communication*, and *Communication Monographs*. He was editor of *Human Communication Research* from 2006–2009. In 2004, he was the recipient of the National Communication Association's Giles/Nussbaum Distinguished Scholar Award for outstanding teaching, scholarship, and service to the field of communication and aging.

Miles Hewstone is Professor of Social Psychology and Fellow of New College, Oxford University. He has published widely on the topics of attribution theory, social cognition, stereotyping, and intergroup relations. His current research focuses on the reduction of intergroup conflict. He is co-founding editor of the *European Review of Social Psychology*, and a former editor of the *British Journal of Social Psychology*. He is a Fellow of the British Academy and an Honorary Fellow of the British Psychological Society. He was the recipient of the British Psychological Society Presidents' Award for Distinguished Contributions to Psychological Knowledge in 2001, and the Kurt Lewin Award, for Distinguished Research Achievement, from the European Association for Experimental Social Psychology in 2005.

Kai J. Jonas is Assistant Professor at the University of Amsterdam, The Netherlands. He earned his doctoral degree in 2002 at the University of Goettingen, Germany, with a dissertation on stereotype consensus development. Since then he has held Post-Doctoral and Researcher positions at the University of Jena, Germany. His research interests include discrimination and prosocial behavior, addressed both within intergroup and social cognitive frameworks. Furthermore, he is developing, implementing, and evaluating social psychological intervention programs.

Herbert C. Kelman is Richard Clarke Cabot Professor of Social Ethics, Emeritus, and co-chair of the Middle East Seminar at Harvard University. A pioneer in the development of interactive problem solving—an unofficial third-party approach to the resolution of international and intercommunal conflict—he has been engaged for more than 30 years in efforts toward the resolution of the Israeli-Palestinian conflict. His writings on interactive problem solving received the Grawemeyer Award for Ideas Improving World Order in 1997. His major publications include *International Behavior: A Social-Psychological Analysis* (editor and co-author, 1965), *A Time to Speak: On Human Values and Social Research* (1968), and *Crimes of Obedience: Toward a Social Psychology of Authority and Responsibility* (with V. Lee Hamilton, 1989).

Shana Levin is Associate Professor of Psychology at Claremont McKenna College. She received her Ph.D. in social psychology from the University of California, Los Angeles. She has served on the governing councils of the Society for the Psychological Study of Social Issues, and the International Society of Political Psychology. She was a Visiting Scholar at the Russell Sage Foundation and received the 2007 Early Career Research Award from the Western Psychological Association. Her research examines ethnic identification, group dominance motives, ideologies of group inequality, perceived discrimination, diversity in higher education, and intergroup attitudes in the United States, Israel, Northern Ireland, and Lebanon.

Amélie Mummendey is Professor of Social Psychology and head of the International Graduate College on Conflict and Cooperation and of the Research Unit on Discrimination and Tolerance between social groups, established at the Friedrich-Schiller-University Jena. Her research interest is social identity and intergroup relations, discrimination and tolerance, cooperation and conflict, and aggressive behavior. She has published numerous articles and chapters in major social psychological journals and books, and received various awards for her work.

Stefania Paolini is a Lecturer in social psychology and statistics at the University of Newcastle, Australia. She completed her doctoral work in 2001 under the supervision of Miles Hewstone at Cardiff University, UK, and used models and methods of contact and social categorization research to explore "when" and "why" information about individual members of a social group affects the judgements of the group as a whole. She has published in, and has been regularly invited to act as reviewer for, leading social psychology journals on the topics of member-to-group generalization, intergroup contact, intergroup friendship, and intergroup emotions. She has recently taken a research fellowship position sponsored by the Australian Research Council to investigate the affective determinants of category salience during inter-ethnic and inter-generational contact, as part of an ongoing collaborative research project with Jake Harwood at the University of Arizona and Mark Rubin at the University of Newcastle.

Thomas F. Pettigrew is Research Professor of Social Psychology at the University of California, Santa Cruz. A Ph.D. graduate of Harvard University, he has taught at the Universities of North Carolina (1956–57), Harvard (1957–1980), and Amsterdam (1986–1991). He has been a Fellow at the Center for Advanced Study in the Behavioral Sciences, the Netherlands Institute for the Advanced Study of the Social Sciences, and Stanford University's Research Institute for the Comparative Study of Race and Ethnicity. Pettigrew has conducted intergroup research in Europe, and South Africa, in addition to North America. He has received the Kurt Lewin Award, twice the Gordon Allport Intergroup Relations Award, the Sydney Spivack Award for Race Relations Research, the Distinguished Scientist Award of the Society for Experimental Social Psychology, and the Lifetime Achievement Award of the International Academy for Intercultural Research.

C. Lausanne Renfro is a doctoral candidate in social psychology at New Mexico State University. She has taught at East Tennessee State University and is currently teaching at New Mexico State University. She was a co-author of the 1996 article that won the Allport Award for intergroup relations given by SPSSI. Her research focus is on intergroup relations with an emphasis on the integrated threat theory. She is also interested in the interplay between the affective and cognitive components of prejudice, as well as impression formation, trait inferences, and critical thinking in science.

Tamar Saguy is currently a Ph.D. candidate in Social Psychology at the University of Connecticut. She is studying social change and intergroup power relations including ethnic, racial and gender inequalities. Her dissertation examines how relative group power influences the way group members approach and experience intergroup interactions. She has extensive experience working as a facilitator of Jewish-Palestinian dialogue groups in Israel, and is committed to applying her research to field work.

Elmar Schlüter obtained his Ph.D. in the social sciences as a fellow of the DFG-Graduate School on Group-focused Enmity at the Universities of Marburg, Giessen and Bielefeld, Germany. His main research interests involve interethnic conflict, prejudice, and methods for longitudinal and cross-cultural data analysis.

Janet Ward Schofield holds a Ph.D. from Harvard University, and is Professor of Psychology and a Senior Scientist at the Learning Research and Development Center at the University of Pittsburgh. Her research interests include school desegregation, intergroup relations, and the social psychology of computer use. She has written over 100 articles and chapters as well as four books, one of which received the Gordon Allport Intergroup Relations Prize. She has served on numerous boards and committees at the National Academy of Sciences, as a visiting scholar in Singapore and Germany, and as a member of APA's Council of Representatives.

Jim Sidanius is Professor of Psychology and African and African American Studies at Harvard University. He received his Ph.D. at the University of Stockholm, Sweden and has taught at several universities in the United States and Europe, including Carnegie-Mellon University, the University of Texas at Austin, New York University, Princeton University, the University of Stockholm, Sweden, and the University of California, Los Angeles. His primary research interests include the political psychology of gender, group conflict, institutional discrimination, and the evolutionary psychology of intergroup prejudice. He has authored and published more than 100 scientific papers, and his most important theoretical contribution to date is the development of *social dominance theory*, a general model of the development and maintenance of group-based social hierarchy and social oppression.

Eliot R. Smith is Professor of Psychological and Brain Sciences, Indiana University, Bloomington. Much of his current research focuses on the role of emotions in prejudice and intergroup relations. He earned his Ph.D. under the direction of Thomas F. Pettigrew at Harvard University. From 2000–2005 he served as Editor of *Personality and Social Psychology Review*. Dr. Smith shared the Gordon Allport Intergroup Relations Prize from the Society for the Psychological Study of Social Issues in 1998, and has been honored with the Thomas M. Ostrom Award for distinguished contributions to social cognition in 2004 and the Theoretical Innovation Prize of the Society for Personality and Social Psychology in 2005.

Heather Smith is Professor of Psychology at Sonoma State University in California. She received her Ph.D. at the University of California, Santa Cruz. Her research interests include relative deprivation, social justice, group processes and intergroup relations.

Jost Stellmacher received his Ph.D. in 2004 and is now a post-doctoral researcher in the Department of Social Psychology at Philipps-University Marburg, Germany. His main research topics focus on ethnic intergroup conflict, juvenile delinquency and human rights.

Walter G. Stephan received his Ph.D. in psychology from the University of Minnesota in 1971. He taught at the University of Texas, Austin and at New Mexico State University where he currently holds the rank of Professor Emeritus. He has published numerous articles and book chapters on attribution processes, cognition and affect, intergroup relations, and intercultural relations. He has received the Otto Klineberg Award for research on intercultural relations (1996) and the Gordon Allport Award for research in intergroup relations (2002), both of which were awarded by the Society for the Psychological Study of Social Issues.

Tania Tam completed her Ph.D. in the psychology of intergroup conflict at the University of Oxford, UK, in 2005. She is currently a statistician and researcher at the Legal Services Research Centre in London, England. Her research focuses on policies related to the experience of civil problems and social justice. Her research interests also include intergroup forgiveness, trust, empathy, and well-being.

Nicole T. Tausch received her Ph.D. at the University of Oxford in 2006. She is currently a British Academy Postdoctoral Fellow at Cardiff University where she is working on a project examining predictors of support for terrorism. Her research interests lie broadly in the areas of social identity, intergroup relations, prejudice, and attribution. She has published work on intergroup contact, group-based threat, and trait attribution in journals such as the *Journal of Personality and Social Psychology, British Journal of Social Psychology*, and *Political Psychology*.

Colin Tredoux is Professor of Psychology at the University of Cape Town (UCT), South Africa. He obtained his Ph.D. degree in 1996, from UCT. His interests in social psychology include the micro-ecology and naturalistic study of intergroup contact, and classic contact theory.

Linda R. Tropp is Associate Professor of Psychology and Director of the Psychology of Peace and Violence Concentration at the University of Massachusetts Amherst. Her research concerns group members' experiences with intergroup contact, interpretations of intergroup relationships, and responses to prejudice and disadvantage. Together with Thomas F. Pettigrew, she has received the Gordon Allport Intergroup Relations Award for her research on intergroup contact. She has also served on the Governing Council of the Society for the Psychological Study of Social Issues, and she now serves on the editorial boards of Personality and Social Psychology Bulletin and Group Processes and Intergroup Relations. She has also worked on several state and national initiatives to reduce prejudice and improve race relations in schools.

Rhiannon N. Turner is a Lecturer in social psychology at the University of Leeds, UK. She holds an undergraduate degree from Cardiff University (2000), a master's degree from the University of Kent (2002), and a Ph.D. from the University of Oxford (2006). Her primary research interest is in intergroup relations, focusing specifically on dimensions, mediators and consequences of intergroup contact. She is currently conducting research on cross-group friendship and multiple categorization, funded by the British Academy and the Leverhulme Trust.

Rolf van Dick earned his Ph.D. from Philipps-Universität, Marburg, Germany. He is Professor of Social Psychology at the Department of Psychology, Johann Wolfgang Goethe-Universität Frankfurt. His primary research interests involve the application of social identity theory in organizational settings (diversity, leadership, mergers). He has published seven books and more than 50 papers in international journals. He is Associate Editor of the *European Journal of Work and Organisational Psychology* and Editor-in-chief of the *British Journal of Management.*

Colette van Laar is a faculty member in Social and Organizational Psychology at Leiden University in the Netherlands. She attended graduate school at the University of California, Los Angeles as a Fulbright Scholar, and obtained a Ph.D. in social psychology there. She was a Visiting Scholar at the Russell Sage Foundation and is a member of the governing council of the Society for the Psychological Study of Social Issues. Her research addresses the consequences of stigma for cognition, affect, and motivation in members of low status or disadvantaged groups. Her current work includes social identity and stereotype threat; the function of positive ingroup domains for maintaining motivation and performance in low status groups; and the social psychological aspects of the battle over the (Islamic) veil in Europe.

Alberto Voci is Associate Professor of Social Psychology at the University of Padova, Italy. He completed his Ph.D. at the same institution in 2000. His research concerns the field of prejudice reduction, in particular intergroup contact and empathy, the perceptions of group variability and, more broadly, the relation between motivational and cognitive processes in the dynamic between personal and social identity. He is member of the editorial board of the *European Review of Social Psychology*.

Christiana Vonofakou received her Ph.D. in social psychology at University of Oxford, UK, and she is currently a Research Associate at Renovata Partners, a board-level executive search firm. Her current research interests center around effective leadership styles at different stages of a company's growth. Her prior research focused on the beneficial effects of cross-group friendships, especially on the effects of attitude strength. She has recently published in the *Journal of Personality and Social Psychology*, with Miles Hewstone and Alberto Voci.

Ulrich Wagner is Professor of Social Psychology and Director of the Center for Conflict Studies at Philipps-University Marburg in Germany. Wagner heads the special graduate school addressing Group Focused Enmity, sponsored by the Deutsche Forschungsgemeinschaft [German Science Foundation]. For the academic year 2003–2004, Wagner was a Senior Fellow at the Research Institute of Comparative Studies in Race and Ethnicity at Stanford University. Wagner's reseach interests include intergroup relations, ethnic prejudice and intergroup aggression.

Iain Walker is Professor of Psychology in the School of Psychology at Murdoch University in Perth, Western Australia, and is currently also the Executive Dean of Health Sciences. He joined the faculty at Murdoch in 1986, directly following his graduate studies at the University of California Santa Cruz where Pettigrew was his advisor. His research falls primarily in the areas of stereotyping, prejudice, and intergroup conflict. His work has been funded by the Australian Research Council and through consultancies with agencies such as the Human Rights and Equal Opportunity Commission, the Office of Multicultural Interests, and the Department of Education and Training. He is the co-author of *Social cognition: An integrated introduction* (Sage, 2006), and co-editor with Heather Smith of *Relative* *deprivation theory: Specification, development, integration* (CUP, 2002) and with Gail Moloney of *Social representations and identity: Content, process, and power* (Palgrave Macmillan, 2007).

Hinna Wolf has been a post-graduate student in the graduate college of *Group-focused Enmity* at Philipps University in Marburg, Germany since 2004. Her research interests focus on intergroup relations, particularly in the areas of prejudice and intergroup contact.

Stephen C. Wright is Professor and Canada Research Chair in Social Psychology at Simon Fraser University, Canada. He received his Ph.D. degree from McGill University. He was on faculty at the University of California, Santa Cruz from 1991 to 2003. His research focuses broadly on intergroup relations, with specific interests in: the consequences of membership in stigmatized groups, antecedent and barriers to collective action, prejudice and its reduction, and issues of minority languages and cultures. His work has been published widely in scholarly volumes and major social, educational, and cross-cultural psychology journals. He is a fellow of the Society for the Psychological Study of Social Issues.

Andreas Zick is currently on leave from the University of Bielefeld to chair the professorship for social psychology at the University of Jena. Additionally, he manages the "Group-Focused Enmity in Europe" project. He received his Ph.D. at the University of Marburg in 1996, worked from 1998 to 2003 as Assistant Professor at the University of Wuppertal, from 2004 to 2006 at the University of Bielefeld, and headed the Chair of Social Psychology at the Unversity of Dresden from 2006 to 2007. His current research interests include migration as well as studies on prejudice, racism, and discrimination in Europe; right-wing extremism; social dominance and the self-concept in social identity.

Series Preface

The series of volumes on *Social Issues and Interventions* represents a joint effort of the Society for the Psychological Study of Social Issues (SPSSI) and Blackwell Publishing launched in 2006. Consistent with SPSSI's dual mission of encouraging systematic research on current social issues and bringing the findings of social psychological research to bear on public policy, the goal of the series is to help fill the gap between basic research on social issues and translation into social policy and program interventions. Each book in the series will be an edited volume devoted to a specific social issue-relevant theme, covering related theory, research, and application. Editors and contributors to each volume will be experts in social psychology and related disciplines in order to provide a multifaceted analysis of a particular contemporary social issue. Utilizing both case studies and theory, this series is intended to present readers with a comprehensive examination of complex social problems while concurrently advancing research in the field.

It is fitting that this second volume in the series should be a tribute to the work and contributions of Thomas Pettigrew. In many ways, Tom Pettigrew's career epitomizes SPSSI values in his commitment to issue relevant research and the link between social science research and social policy. His insights into the causes and consequences of racial antagonism and discrimination in the US (and later, Europe) have influenced public policy makers as well as generations of social psychologists. Beyond contributing to our basic understanding of racial attitudes, Pettigrew has made a lifetime commitment to resolving racial conflict and reducing social inequities. His dedication to finding effective interventions to promote intergroup contact and integration of schools, neighborhoods, and the workplace provides a model of how good empirical research and social values can go hand in hand to produce positive social change. The Pettigrew legacy infuses current theory and research on intergroup relations, as is well represented in the diverse contributions to the present volume.

Marilynn B. Brewer
Series Editor

Acknowledgments

The editors are grateful to Lana Brünges and Sarah Schönke for their careful work on references and indexes.

1

Editors' Introduction

Ulrich Wagner, Linda R. Tropp,
Gillian Finchilescu, and Colin Tredoux

Wherever humans assemble, we tend to differentiate ourselves into groups, on a wide range of ostensible differences. There are abundant historical and contemporaneous examples of intergroup differentiation along the lines of ethnic, racial, national, gender, and class dimensions, among others. In many cases it can easily be seen that groups are socially created, as in the case of political parties or religious groups. In other cases we consider ourselves to belong to groups that differ on some preexisting attribute or dimension, as in the case of gender groups.

Modern social psychological theories and research have described the basic mechanisms by which we perceive our social environment as composed of different groups. This includes our capacity to perceive and differentiate between social categories, as well as our tendency to identify with categories that are deemed as relevant by society, and which serve as the basis for defining our social identities.

Our everyday experience, as well as scientific documentation, informs us of the significance of these social categories, and how easily attention to categorical differences can breed conflict between groups. Upon distinguishing between members of our own ingroup and outgroups, outgroup members may be negatively stereotyped, devalued, avoided, discriminated against, or even physically attacked and killed. Daily, the news media abound with examples of such events—hate speech and attacks on people or property identified as belonging to "other groups" such as national, ethnic or religious groups; acts of intolerance ranging from avoidance to violence against members of stigmatized groups such as immigrants, homosexuals, and people known to be living with HIV/AIDS; numerous examples of discrimination against women, ethnic groups, and other underrepresented outgroups;

and genocide driven by differences in skin colour, religion, and cultural heritage. Although some of these cases can be explained by conflicts over material resources, social psychological perspectives suggest many other mechanisms and motivations that perpetuate intergroup conflict.

As such, social psychological research and theory on intergroup relations typically strives to understand the processes that can improve relations between groups, in order to make mutual images of the other less negative, to eradicate discrimination, and to find a basis for the elimination of intergroup violence. This emphasis was already evident in Robin Williams' (1947) monograph on *The Reductions of Intergroup Tensions* and Gordon Allport's (1954) influential book, *The Nature of Prejudice*. Following these writings, the contributions of social psychologists to the US civil rights movement (e.g. the impact of Kenneth and Mamie Clark's research in the case Brown vs. Board of Education), and their involvement in numerous court cases since that time, demonstrates an ongoing commitment to socially relevant research that can promote positive social change. Indeed, intergroup research is often closely connected to practical attempts at implementing appropriate interventions and procedures for combating intergroup conflict.

The present book follows in this tradition. It is a book about intergroup relations and the strategies by which these may be improved, based on recent theoretical and empirical advances. Development in science is on the one hand a matter of theory-driven accumulation of knowledge, but it is also influenced by central and outstanding scientific scholars. One of these scholars is Thomas Fraser Pettigrew, certainly one of the most influential social psychologists in the field of intergroup relations. Thus, this is also a book about Thomas F. Pettigrew, whose scientific contributions and influence have made recent developments possible, at the same time as he still actively contributes to them.

The present book is two-fold in character, concerning itself with recent developments in social psychology about the improvement of intergroup relations, and with Thomas F. Pettigrew's influence on this body of knowledge. It is fitting to his legacy that the book is written by many of his former doctoral students, academic colleagues, and scholars influenced by his research. Accordingly, we have asked the authors of the following chapters to describe the current state of their research, and to reflect on the ways in which Thomas F. Pettigrew has influenced their work on intergroup relations.

The book starts with two short introductory chapters. In this first chapter, we outline the organization of the book, and provide readers with an overview of topics to be addressed in later chapters. In the second, introductory chapter, Frances Cherry guides the reader through important milestones in Pettigrew's academic life and scholarly development.

Exploring the Causes of Prejudice and Discrimination

Attempts to improve negative intergroup relations through interventions need to be grounded in scientific theory and supported by empirical findings. Therefore, chapters in Part I involve the scientific exploration of the causes of prejudice and discrimination. Fiske, Smith, as well as Stephan, Renfro and Davis, focus on broad recent theoretical developments that enhance our understanding of the causes of negative intergroup attitudes and discriminatory behavior, along with identifying approaches by which they might be improved.

Susan T. Fiske starts this section with a review of her theoretical and empirical contributions to understanding the development of group stereotypes. She makes clear how the development of stereotypes depends on the relative power positions of the groups. This gives way to a focus on a special kind of intergroup stereotype, based on the relation of gender groups, and the conception of ambivalent sexism that she has developed together with Peter Glick. She extends this theme with a description of her latest theoretical contribution, the stereotype content model, which was developed together with Amy Cuddy, and which provides a comprehensive theoretical framework for understanding the emergence of stereotypes and the relation of stereotypes to intergroup behavior. Fiske explores the implications of these recent developments for practical interventions, giving examples from testimony against racial segregation that Pettigrew and she herself delivered.

Emerging intergroup research also shows that stereotyping, devaluation, discrimination and violence cannot be described comprehensively on the basis of cognitive processes alone. Eliot R. Smith, often in collaboration with Diane M. Mackie, has contributed substantially to this work, in line with Pettigrew's proposals regarding the significant role that emotions play in intergroup relations. As Smith shows, group members do not experience emotions only if they are affected individually, but also when a group they identify with is affected. Complementing the stereotype content model, individuals also connect distinct emotional experiences to outgroups that vary in terms of their relative power, which in turn allow for predictions of inter-group behavior.

Walter G. Stephan, C. Lausanne Renfro and Mark D. Davis consider a special kind of antecedent of intergroup emotions, namely intergroup threat. These authors present a number of theoretical considerations relevant to the development of their integrated threat theory, and their later revised threat theory. Together, these discussions show how, depending on a defined set of individual, intergroup, cultural and situational variables, different forms of threat vis à vis an outgroup are experienced, and these feelings of threat in turn explain the emergence of prejudice and intergroup rejection. The authors also combine threat theory with intergroup contact theory, thus adopting one of Pettigrew's major research themes, in which they discuss how threat can be both an antecedent and consequence of intergroup contact.

Functions of Intergroup Contact in Improving Intergroup Relations

Intergroup contact has repeatedly been shown to be one of the most effective means of reducing intergroup bias. Pettigrew has in many papers described a number of potential mediators in the process of changing intergroup attitudes and behavior, suggesting that changes in both the cognitive representation and the emotional relation to the outgroup might be of relevance. Part II thus focuses on the functions of intergroup contact in intergroup relations and includes contributions by Dovidio, Gaertner, Saguy and Halabi, Tropp, and by Vonofakou, Hewstone, Voci, Paolini, Turner, Tausch, Tam, Harwood and Cairns.

John F. Dovidio, Samuel L. Gaertner, Tamar Saguy and Samer Halabi describe a number of mechanisms that help us understand *why* contact works. Summarizing much of their work, these authors demonstrate how the different processes of de- and recategorization can mediate the effects of intergroup contact on intergroup attitudes and behavior. Adopting one of Pettigrew's models, they also argue that intergroup contact may be most effective in reducing intergroup biases when these kinds of categorization are activated in a sequential order. In addition, they present evidence showing that members of powerful and powerless groups may be differentially affected by these processes due to their differing interests in maintaining or changing the intergroup power status quo.

Extending this focus, Linda R. Tropp also examines the question of why intergroup contact works, and how contact can have different effects for members of different status groups. Related to Dovidio et al., Tropp emphasizes that it is often more difficult for low status minorities, as opposed to high status majorities to develop a feeling of trust in relation to the outgroup, and this might explain the asymmetrical effect of intergroup contact on minorities and majorities. She then discusses trust as a key mechanism underlying Pettigrew's concept of "friendship potential" and explores how close cross-group friendships help to establish a willingness to trust, which in turn can promote broader shifts in relations between groups.

Christiana Vonofakou, Miles Hewstone, Alberto Voci, Stefania Paolini, Rhiannon Turner, Nicole Tausch, Tania Tam, Jake Harwood and Ed Cairns focus on the effects of both direct and indirect contact for improving intergroup relations. They analyze data from multiple settings, using different indicators of intergroup attitudes ranging from paper and pencil measures to implicit measures of attitudes and attitude strength. They show that empathy with outgroup members, self-disclosure, intergroup trust, and anxiety reduction mediate the positive effects that direct and indirect contacts have on intergroup relations. In line with the views of Wright et al., these authors also emphasize the role of indirect contact in improving intergroup relations, especially where there is limited opportunity for direct contact.

Intergroup Relations and Reflections on One's Own Group Membership

Typically, research on intergroup relations analyzes the attitudes, emotions, and behavior that people experience as group members in relation to an outgroup. Thus, it is not the attitudes or behavior of single and isolated individuals that is of interest in intergroup research, but rather the psychology of the person acting as a group member. Growing from this view, Thomas Pettigrew has long emphasized that we must focus not only on the outgroup, but also need to reevaluate our own groups in our attempts to improve intergroup relations. Thus, the following three chapters, written by van Laar, Levin and Sidanius, Wright, Aron and Brody, as well as by Brewer, explore the dynamics of intergroup relations in terms of reflections on our own group memberships.

Colette van Laar, Shana Levin and Jim Sidanius present results of a longitudinal study on contact at a large multi-ethnic US university.

They found strong support for the basic assumption that contact between ethnic groups has a positive causal influence on ethnic intergroup attitudes. However, these authors also show that interactions with ingroup members, and especially interactions of white students with ingroup friends, can have a negative effect on individuals' attitudes toward other ethnic groups. They discuss their findings in terms of normative influences, such that greater interactions with ingroup members makes ingroup standards salient, thereby presenting norms and customs that may interfere with outgroup acceptance.

Whereas most research on intergroup contact has focused on the effects of direct contact experiences (i.e., face-to-face contact with an outgroup member), Stephen C. Wright, Arthur Aron and Salena M. Brody show convincingly how knowing that another ingroup member has a close relation with an outgroup member reduces intergroup prejudice. In their extended intergroup contact hypothesis they nominate a number of explanations for this effect: reduction of anxiety; perceived changes in group norms; and inclusion of the outgroup member in the self. Wright and his coauthors present empirical findings from a number of studies suggesting that inclusion of outgroup members in the self and the ingroup explains much of the extended contact effect.

In a 1998 contribution to the *Annual Review of Psychology* Pettigrew proposed that an important precondition of improving intergroup relations is the "deprovincialization" of one's ingroup. Marilynn B. Brewer takes this idea as a starting point for her discussion of how social identity complexity can improve intergroup relations. She explains how complexity of a social identity is negatively related to the perceived overlap between the different groups to which an individual belongs, and how it depends on cognitive abilities and values. As Brewer demonstrates across a range of studies, social identity complexity correlates with reduced intergroup tension and outgroup devaluation. Brewer then hints at a practical intervention by suggesting that negative intergroup relations may be reduced or prevented by increasing social identity complexity.

Focusing on Social Context in Improving Intergroup Relations

At the very beginning of his academic career as a social psychologist in the mid 1950s, Pettigrew compared the role of authoritarianism in understanding hostile intergroup relations in South Africa and in the

Southern US. With this paper he made one of the first contributions in social psychology to the analysis of context effects and cross-level interactions. He has persistently asked for a contextualized social psychology that allows focusing on the social context in improving intergroup relations. The chapters in Part IV, written by Finchilescu and Tredoux, Wagner, Christ, Wolf, van Dick, Stellmacher, Schlüter, and Zick, and Jonas and Mummendey, therefore concentrate on the relevance of contextual dimensions when attempting to improve intergroup relations.

Gillian Finchilescu and Colin Tredoux describe the phenomenology and effects of intergroup contact under unfavorable conditions, namely contact between ethnic groups in South Africa. The few available studies conducted during the Apartheid period show only weak effects of contact on outgroup attitudes, ostensibly due to the extremely negative social and political context of that period. But the situation seems to have changed very slowly, despite the dissolution of Apartheid and the installation of a democratic government. Finchilescu and Tredoux provide evidence showing that modern South Africa remains highly segregated. The research they cite and describe makes clear that being copresent in schools, universities, on beaches or in clubs does not necessarily imply intergroup contact, and ethnic groups typically self-segregate under those conditions. They point to survey data from contemporary South Africa that show that self-rated contact is negatively correlated with prejudice, and while this is grounds for optimism, they argue that it is important to understand the strong tendency to avoid contact.

Ulrich Wagner, Oliver Christ, Hinna Wolf, Rolf van Dick, Jost Stellmacher, Elmar Schlüter, and Andreas Zick also analyze the effect of coexistence of ethnic groups in the same geographical context. Based on results of large-scale survey data from Europe and Germany, they show that the immigrant percentage of the population has different effects on their acceptance by the autochthonous population, depending on the size of the geographical region under consideration. In smaller units such as districts, a higher percentage of immigrants is associated with a reduction in prejudice. By contrast, a higher immigrant percentage at the level of the national state is associated with higher prejudice. Wagner et al. show that this difference can be explained by different mediators, namely, on the one hand, intergroup contact and, on the other, intergroup threat. An increase in intergroup threat is assumed to depend on nationwide negative political propaganda about immigrants.

Kai J. Jonas and Amelie Mummendey point out that most intergroup research focuses on intergroup relations that are conflictual and negative. Similarly, intergroup programs that are intended to promote intergroup relations are typically designed to "reduce conflict," or "reduce prejudice," or in some way ameliorate a state of negative interaction. A different focus would be to consider, and develop explanatory models of positive intergroup relations. They present some considerations for such a model, and identify the significance of a superordinate joint group categorization as central, as well as some specific modes of interaction that can promote positive relations. They end their chapter by urging researchers in the field to consider widening the limited perspective in intergroup relations on levels of categorization, arguing that we should incorporate multilevel categorization into our theories. Such a widening, they suggest, may allow joint recognition of positive and negative instances of intergroup relations.

Intergroup Relations as a Commitment to Social Change

Interventions aimed at improving societal conditions and the lives of individuals should be based on systematic scientific knowledge and controlled empirical findings. Throughout his work, Thomas Pettigrew has demonstrated an unwavering commitment to rigorous scientific research that can be used to address social problems. He has always understood intergroup research as a commitment to social change, and he has served as an important example to researchers who wish to maintain high scientific standards while conducting socially relevant work. In Part V, Smith and Walker, Kelman, and Schofield, discuss the broader implications of intergroup research for the promotion of social change.

Heather Smith and Iain Walker focus on the roles of relative deprivation, perceived injustice and emotions for the emergence of collective action. They emphasize the importance of distinguishing between deprivation experienced at the personal and group levels, and they discuss the range of emotions that people may experience upon perceiving themselves to be disadvantaged. Citing from their own research and related work of their colleagues, these authors document how an individual's readiness to participate in social protest as a means of changing group relations depends on both rational decisions about cost–benefit probabilities and on emotional processes, especially anger.

With a shift in focus on relations between national groups, Herbert C. Kelman describes a series of interactive problem-solving workshops designed to help Israeli and Palestinian people find a way to peace.

The workshops Kelman organized are based on social psychological mechanisms known to help participants gain a feeling for their different perspectives, and to promote discussions of commonalities and differences in basic needs. The workshops were not developed to improve intergroup relations between participants only. Kelman and his coworkers usually selected politicians, state advisers, and opinion leaders as participants. Through this selection process, the effects of the workshop were expected to generalize more broadly, to have a positive impact on relations between the Palestinian and Israeli states.

The question of interrelationships between science and politics is also at the heart of Janet Ward Schofield's contribution. Stemming from social psychological perspectives on contact theory, she analyzes the effects of school desegregation in the US on ethnic intergroup relations over the past 50 years. She takes school desegregation as a case to discuss the complicated communication between social psychological scientists working in the field of intergroup relations and political decision makers. In particular, her list of constraints and sources of difficulty are extremely helpful for all who feel committed to using the scientific results presented in the foregoing chapters as a means for improving intergroup relations in everyday life.

Final Reflections

Taken together, the chapters in this book present recent theoretical analyses and empirical results regarding the many ways in which intergroup relations may be improved. It is also a book about one of the most prominent and influential promoters of research on intergroup relations and their improvement, Thomas F. Pettigrew. This book would not be complete without the voice of Thomas Pettigrew himself. In response to our request, he has written the final chapter, in which he reflects on the many new research directions that have emerged from his contributions to the study of intergroup relations and which are brought together in this book.

We hope that this book will be enjoyed by all those interested in the field of intergroup relations. But, above all, this book is a call for social psychologists and allied researchers to consider the broader implications of their work. Pettigrew's legacy lies in the demand that social psychology not remain simply an intellectual, academic discipline, but that it serves the quest for societal advancement, governed by principles of social justice. As such, we hope this volume will not only encourage future generations of research and theory development, but that it will inspire its readers to renew their commitment to achieving positive intergroup relations around the world.

References

Allport, G. W. (1954). *The nature of prejudice.* Reading, MA: Addison-Wesley.
Williams, R. M., Jr. (1947). *The reduction of intergroup tensions.* New York: Social Science Research Council.

2

Thomas F. Pettigrew

Building on the Scholar-Activist Tradition in Social Psychology

Frances Cherry

In a recent article, espousing the advantages of multilevel approaches to social issues, Thomas Pettigrew (2006, p. 616) wrote, "multilevel approaches are complex: but 'the real world' *is* complex." I would argue that this statement has guided his work in intergroup relations work for over five decades. It allows us to understand how Pettigrew has framed his scientific research on race/ethnic group conflicts and the ways in which he has unapologetically maintained a close connection between research and practice in "the real world" of race relations.

To understand what has shaped Pettigrew's work as a social psychologist, there are several early experiences that offer some insight. Thomas Pettigrew grew up under legal racial segregation in the United States of the 1930s and 1940s, in a social reality that "sensitized everyone to race as a primary social category" (Pettigrew, 1993, p. 159). However, he came to see both sides of that divide at a very young age. Pettigrew recounts a deep connection to his family's African-American housekeeper, Miss Mildred Adams, who he says "fired me early with indignation over racial injustice" (p. 160). It was through Miss Adams that the world of Richmond, Virginia's African American residents was made accessible to the young Pettigrew. He remembers spending time in Miss Adams' home and in her community and recounts that: "By the time I was 10 years old, the many psychological and cultural defenses that blind most white Americans to the racial injustice that surrounds them were no longer available to me" (p. 160).

It was not long after that Pettigrew took the first of many stands against racial injustice as well as the consequences that followed: in seventh grade, he stood up to a bigoted teacher and was summarily expelled from school. Fortunately, Pettigrew recounts, there was family support for standing up to racial injustice, particularly from his maternal grandmother and mother, Scottish immigrants who were quite skeptical about the prevailing American social order. These early experiences nurtured a capacity for probing beneath the surface of powerful normative structures holding injustice in place.

Social psychology has been Pettigrew's life-long terrain for bringing his early experiences together with political convictions and professional expertise. What follows is a very brief glimpse of the several ways in which this has materialized for more than five decades.

In Place of Psychological and Cultural Defenses

Pettigrew received his B.A. in Psychology from the University of Virginia in 1952. He had discovered a year earlier, in a social psychology course, that he could bring his political engagement with American racial inequality together with a career goal. He stated, "the idea that you could actually study, conduct research, even make a living specializing in race relations was an exciting revelation to me" (Pettigrew, 1993, p. 160).

When Pettigrew began graduate school at Harvard University in 1952, a major shift had already taken place in American social science. The study of fixed biological "races" had been eclipsed by the study of prejudice and race relations. An earlier generation of social scientists had found a way to engage with social issues such as the severe impact of the Depression, domestic labor unrest and the rise of Fascism in Europe through their founding, in 1936, of the *Society for the Psychological Study of Social Issues* (SPSSI) (see Kimmel 1997; Society for the Psychological Study of Social Issues website). The 1930s and 1940s was an era of foundational texts, in sociological and psychological social psychology, all of which were on Harvard's Department of Social Relations' course lists: Alfred McClung Lee's (1943) *Race Riot*, Gunnar Myrdal's (1944) *An American Dilemma*, and Theodore Adorno and colleagues' (1950) *The Authoritarian Personality*. These texts set a moral and intellectual tone fueling the belief that racism—as attitude, personality, norm, legal doctrine, and social policy—was an outrage, a paradox, a disease to be cured—in a liberal democratic and culturally pluralistic society. Throughout

World War II, social scientists honed their research expertise and professional networks (Capshew, 1999). As Jackson (2001, p. 215) succinctly put it: "Social scientists emerged from the war with two things: first, an overriding concern with racial prejudice, and second, the confidence that they could do something about it."

Pettigrew entered the Ph.D. program in Social Psychology amidst this charged atmosphere. Gordon Allport's war-time seminar on civilian morale had changed its focus to domestic racial prejudice, and was institutionalized in the Department of Social Relations' curriculum as *Social Relations 284: Intergroup Conflict and Prejudice* (Cherry, 2000). The Department had opened its doors in 1946 as a multidisciplinary unit, bringing together sociology, social and clinical psychology, and anthropology. It was Pettigrew's good fortune to be a part of this seminar[1] in a program where courses in each of the four sub-fields of the Department were required, and where students did not have to choose a single disciplinary loyalty.[2] He was part of the first generation of students who both contributed to and were shaped by Allport's seminars and his classic text, *The Nature of Prejudice* (1954).[3] That multiple levels of analysis were necessary in research-ing racism and effecting social change was an approach that had its roots in Pettigrew's graduate school environment and can be found in a variety of later more formal conceptualizations (Pettigrew, 1996, 1997; Stephan, Stephan, & Pettigrew, 1991).[4]

Pettigrew's immediate mentors were psychologist Gordon Allport and sociologist Samuel Stouffer, both of whom were instrumental in helping him shape his doctoral research (Pettigrew, 1957, 1959). Allport set an overall standard of excellence but encouraged students to pursue their own direction. Whereas Allport's work on prejudice had drawn Pettigrew to Harvard in the first place, he credits Stouffer with fostering his love of survey data that has also carried forward to the present[5] and expanded internationally (see for example Pettigrew & Meertens, 1995; Wagner, Van Dick, Pettigrew, & Christ, 2003).

Pettigrew arrived in graduate school at a time of collaboration among social science researchers, the legal profession, community field workers and activists. He recalls that, while his graduate student peers were pessimistic about his choice to pursue a career in race relations, several of the leading social psychologists of the day had become involved in civil rights research. While the landmark Supreme Court desegregation decision in *Brown v. Topeka Board of Education* (1954) was cause for their optimism, the *Brown v. Board of Educa-tion II* (1955) ruling slowed the implementation of desegregation and gave segregationists, particularly in the Southern United States, hope for their cause.[6] Undeterred by legal setbacks, in the summer of 1955, Pettigrew (1957, 1959) set out to gather his dissertation data in which he would show that Southern antipathy to desegregation was somewhat more complex. Pettigrew found that while white Southerners opposed desegregation, they did see it as inevitable. He had already observed that the progress of desegregation was uneven throughout the country and his thesis research was intended to probe both psychological and sociocultural factors sustaining these patterns. In his dissertation research, one can find several of the elements that appear in later more elaborate work: an intuitive sense of patterns in analyzing macro and micro levels of racism (the meso level followed later with intergroup contact theory and research) and a keen sense of the important questions to ask and how to ask them without setting off defensive reactions.

Traveling to small Southern towns with his undergraduate assistant and friend, Charles LaMonte (switching Northern license plates for Southern ones for their safety), Pettigrew interviewed people about the most important issues of the day. Stouffer had taught him one of the tricks of the survey researcher's trade—rather than directly asking about desegregation, he was advised to let it arise naturally, as it generally did in the South at that time. Interviews then went along uninterrupted by any defensiveness on the interviewees' part. Pettigrew recalls that his Southern accent helped out as well!

The importance of levels of analysis was also confirmed in his dissertation research. Contrary to the psychodynamic framework of the day, Pettigrew's northerners and southerners were no different in their levels of authoritarianism, and the F-scale was an equally valid predictor of racial prejudice for both regions. An individual-level psychological framework was, therefore, not sufficient for understanding the intensity of white Southern antipathy to African Americans. For this, Pettigrew argued for socially contextualized levels of understanding focusing on the role of societal norms and social conformity. Pettigrew's earliest research into Southern race relations confirmed for him that macro sociocultural factors of religion, ratios of White: Black Americans, and conformity pressures were important constraints on the success of social change. It was these variations that could better explain why desegregation was proceeding smoothly in some parts of the United States and not in others and why even within the South, a more nuanced view than individual bigotry had to be appreciated.

South Africa: "A Mind Shaping Experience"

Gordon Allport had been invited as a Visiting Consultant to the Institute for Social Research at the University of Natal (now Kwa-Zulu Natal) in Durban, South Africa for a 6-month period (Cherry, 2007). Allport arranged for Thomas Pettigrew to join him as a research associate and Pettigrew, dissertation research completed, left for South Africa in early March of 1956 for "half a year's stay in that troubled land" (Pettigrew, 1993, p. 163). In retrospect, Pettigrew has written that "this adventure proved a mind-shaping experience" (p. 163). Not only was it his first chance to conduct research outside the United States, but it was a chance to put to the test his central ideas about the psychological and sociocultural influences shaping race relations.[7]

While in South Africa, Pettigrew was involved in several research studies (Allport & Pettigrew, 1957; Pettigrew, 1958, 1960; Pettigrew, Allport, & Barnett, 1958). In the study of South African attitudes of those with British and Afrikaans backgrounds, he was able to draw similar conclusions as with the attitudes of Northern and Southern Americans. There are a number of ideas that were central in this early research that have been maintained in subsequent work. For example, racism is often held in place by social conformity; citizens can decry social change and still grasp its inevitability, particularly if strong leaders advocate for social change. He argued that action research programs were more successful when they worked towards "changing a person's relation to his culture" by restructuring the mores to which the intolerant person conforms than by "changing his basic personality structure" (Pettigrew, 1958, p. 40).

Allport and Pettigrew's visit has been credited with increasing the interest in mainstream American social psychology among South African researchers continuing to the mid 1980s (Louw, 2004; Louw & Foster, 1992). Legislation such as the Population Registration Act and the Group Areas Act that categorized South Africans by "race" and separated them accordingly focused attention on a variety of American lines of inquiry such as "authoritarianism and its relation to race attitudes, the contact hypothesis, and the concept of marginal personality" (Louw & Foster, 1992, p. 653).

Pettigrew's early activities in race relations and civil rights work did not go unnoted by authorities at home and abroad. In South Africa he attended meetings of the African National Congress (ANC) with sociologist, Hamish Dickie-Clark and traveled to parts of South Africa forbidden to Whites. There is a story he recounts about leaving South Africa *the first time*. Arriving at Customs, he was told by an official that he was no longer a welcome visitor. Indeed, he had been under surveillance by South African police and followed to African National Congress (ANC) meetings during his entire six-month stay. Keeping in mind that the grip of the apartheid government was tightening in 1956, the Passport officer looked at Pettigrew, then at his passport, and stamped it, "Banned from South Africa." Pettigrew recounts what happened next. He grabbed the officer by the lapels and said, with gusto, "Sir, you have paid me the highest honor!" Not surprisingly, when Pettigrew was invited by Jack Mann to address the South African Psychological Association in 1982, he was denied an entry visa.[8] There are many more times that followed when Pettigrew would voice his views on social injustice, earning him a file with the American FBI. He has obtained his file through the Freedom of Information Act, however, 90% of it is blacked out and provides mainly verification that he was under surveillance.

"I Wanted a Factual Orientation, but I Wanted to be an Activist too . . ."

Pettigrew has always articulated the need for a scholar-activist model with which social scientists could engage and make explicit their values. For that reason, he joined the Society for the Psychological Study of Social Issues in 1958, citing it as an organization whose mission was consistent with his belief that social justice values were an integral part of scientific research. There are many examples in Pettigrew's career of the scholar-activist tradition at work. In 1960, a grant to interview white Southern liberals took him to North Carolina just as the student protest movement was getting underway. Instead of studying attitudes, Pettigrew studied action in the form of the lunch counter sit-in movement, reflecting later on the young Black people involved in the 1960 sit-in process:

> None had taken a course yet . . . in either sociology or social psychology. And it was better that they had not done so, for the social science of the time, ensnared in its micro frame of analysis, would have provided the students with reasons that direct-action protest would have little chance of success. The white South "was not ready yet" . . . Bottom-up causal paths predominated in the thinking of the time; attitude change was thought to be essential before institutional change was possible. (Pettigrew, 1993, p. 165)

The year, 1967, was particularly significant for Pettigrew's scholar-activist approach to social psychology. As incoming President of SPSSI, and with the help of longtime colleague and friend, Kenneth B. Clark, the organization extended an invitation to bring Martin Luther King, Jr. to the American Psychological Association (APA) annual meeting to address the Society on "The Role of the Behavioral Scientist in the Civil Rights Movement" (King, 1968). Pettigrew (in Pickren & Tomes, 2002, p. 52) recalls the reaction of the APA: "The idea was bitterly opposed by many in the leadership of APA at the time—even to the point of at first (under great pressure, they finally relented) refusing us a large enough room (in the end, APA members not only filled the largest hall at the Washington Hilton but they had to open another large room equipped with a television feed)."

The years of setbacks that followed *Brown II* resulted in pessimism for many of those most dedicated to racial integration. Throughout these years, Pettigrew continued with civil rights work. He collaborated with Clark in the latter's newly established consulting organization, the Metropolitan Applied Research Center (MARC), to sponsor joint projects with SPSSI and to nurture the liaison work of SPSSI's Committee on Civil Rights, chaired by Robert Chin. In his Presidential Message for the SPSSI Newsletter (Pettigrew, 1967) Pettigrew articulated the "honest broker" model that would act as a two-way communication channel between policy makers and social psychologists. And in that regard, he suggested opening "a small SPSSI office in Washington, perhaps jointly with a similar organization. Definitely not a lobbying office . . ." (p. 6) where an SPSSI "honest broker" might reside (p. 6). As many readers will know, in 2001, SPSSI moved its Central Office to Washington, DC where its staff and members are actively engaged in policy work.

Throughout the 1960s and 1970s, Pettigrew provided his research expertise and expert testimony to various civil rights projects. He was a consultant to the United States Office of Education (1966–8) and the United States Commission on Civil Rights (1966–71), served as an expert witness before government bodies concerned with equal opportunity and testified in public school desegregation cases (see Pettigrew, 1979, 2004). In many instances, his efforts lent considerable support to cases that threatened to turn around the gains of the civil rights legislation of 1954 and the 1964 Civil Rights Act. In fact, Pettigrew credits participation in civil rights cases with his growing interest in contact theory and research (Pettigrew, 1998), which, while a part of his graduate training with Allport, became increasingly important with the recognized need for understanding the mechanisms operating in prejudice and conflict reduction.

Desegregation: Not If, Only When and How

Over the years since the *Brown v. Topeka Board of Education* and *Brown II* decisions in the 1950s, Pettigrew (1961, 1965, 1985, 2004) has often reflected on the course of desegregation in the United States. Furthermore, he has made his voice heard in both scholarly and public debates on desegregation. In 1975, at the beginning of the resegregation era (1974–present), James Coleman published a widely publicized study showing "white flight" to the suburbs was a natural consequence of residential and educational desegregation. Pettigrew argued against this interpretation and is well known for his critique of the Coleman Report, both its flawed science and the recommendations that ensued. While "white flight" was neither universal nor as damaging as thought, it provided judges with an acceptable reason for opposing urban school desegregation, thereby turning back the gains of the desegregation era (1930–73) and dismissing effective metropolitan solutions.

In the late 1970s, Pettigrew challenged the claim that race was declining in its significance relative to the rising role of social class, a claim put forward by sociologist William Julius Wilson. Pettigrew drew attention to the importance of the interaction of race and class, making racial discrimination only a matter of greater subtlety for better off African Americans. On the 50th anniversary of the Supreme Court's landmark ruling in *Brown v. Board of Education*, Pettigrew (2004) argued for a rededication to efforts for preventing further resegregation in American society. By combining the best research with political and historical analyses, Pettigrew has demystified legal arguments for segregation showing instead that separate educational facilities are inherently unequal. Furthermore, he has long held the view that intense residential segregation is a key and much overlooked element in resistance to integrated schooling (Pettigrew, 1963, 1973, 2004).

Pettigrew continues to be outraged by many white Americans' belief that problems of racism have been solved, and particularly by those in the part of the United States that is resegregating most quickly— the South. Equally, he rejects conservative African-American views, such as those held by Supreme Court Justice Clarence Thomas, that desegregation is premised on a belief in Black inferiority. With equal conviction, he has debated African-American civil rights lawyer,

Derrick Bell, whose contention it is that racism is necessarily a permanent feature of American society (Bell, 1992). Pettigrew acknowledges his privileged position as a white American, yet, he advances a more hopeful vision for American society, based on an underutilized reading of the evidence and increasing scholarship that is contesting the fashionable myth that racial problems have been solved (Pettigrew, 1999, 2004). The unrecognized positive impacts of desegregation over the long-term—as shown in high quality research—argue for a rededication to twenty-first-century racial justice rather than a return to nineteenth-century race relations. Pettigrew is a strategist and a pragmatist when it comes to his moral and intellectual conviction that an ethnically integrated society is a better society (Pettigrew, 2004). There is no arguing with him on that point, only working with him on matters of when and how. In this regard, it was probably Pettigrew's mentor, Gordon Allport, who acknowledged the earliest expressions of Pettigrew's lifelong commitment to scholarship and activism. Writing on behalf of his former student, Allport (1963) had this to say about Pettigrew's engagement with research and social issues:

> One might object that his work lies too close to the practical needs of society, that he is a reformer, a crusader, a "politician." Yes, he is all these things: his zeal for racial justice is intense. He may tomorrow be found in a picket line. It would, however, be completely false to say that his commitment affects adversely his scientific integrity or the objectivity of his own research.

At present, Pettigrew is focused on drawing attention to little-known successes in school desegregation's history (Pettigrew, 2004) and on researching the powerful effects of cross-group relationships in reducing prejudice (Pettigrew & Tropp, 2006). He continues to serve as an exemplar of the possible, namely, that in one social psychological lifetime it is possible to combine sound scientific research, social policy work, and political activism in the pursuit of social justice.

Acknowledgment

This chapter is based, in part, on the published writings of Thomas Pettigrew as well as my conversations with him (email and face-to face). I am further indebted to the SPSSI Historian, Alexandra Rutherford for making available an oral history she conducted with him (June, 2006).

Notes

1   Pettigrew assisted in, co-taught and later taught this course at Harvard University. He was an assistant professor at the University of North Carolina (1956–57) returning to Harvard in 1957 until his departure for the University of California, Santa Cruz (1980–present). He also held an appointment at the University of Amsterdam (1986–91) as Chair of the Department of Psychology.

2   Psychological social psychology and sociological social psychology were going in separate directions in terms of methods and subject matter in the 1950s, with interdisciplinary units increasingly rare by the late 1960s (Collier, Minton, & Reynolds, 1991; Hilgard, 1987; Morawski & Bayer, 2003). The Department of Social Relations closed its doors in 1972 against the protests of ardent supporters Robert Freed Bales, Herbert Kelman, and Thomas Pettigrew, among others.

3   Allport (1950) first published the multiple lens model for the etiology of prejudice as part of his Kurt Lewin Memorial Award address. It was subsequently incorporated as a chapter in *The Nature of Prejudice* (Allport, 1954).

4   Pettigrew co-taught a required sociology graduate course with Talcott Parsons for four years and humbly refers to his own writings on macro-, meso- and micro-level analyses of racism as "a poor man's interpretation of Parsons'" theory.

5   Pettigrew attributes much of his success in research to his own graduate students (he has mentored 74 doctoral students over five decades) and their capacity for obsession with detail (which he claims he lacks).

6   Social psychologists' expertise was brought to bear in both the 1954 and 1955 rulings. For a fuller treatment of the various U.S. Supreme Court decisions affecting desegregation and the role of social science research see Jackson (2001) and Pettigrew (2004).

7   Pettigrew has often drawn historical parallels between South Africa and the American South, writing, for example, that, "In 1956, South African race relations were like what race relations must have been in my native South about a decade before my birth" (Pettigrew, 1993, p. 163).

8   Thomas and Ann Pettigrew were newlyweds on their first trip to South Africa. Ann Pettigrew (B.A., M.D., M.P.H.) assisted with research in South Africa and has been an integral part of his work for five decades. Their second trip to South Africa marked their 50th wedding anniversary. They have a son, Mark Fraser Pettigrew, Ph.D. in Near Eastern Studies and lecturer in Islamic Studies at Columbia University.

References

Adorno, T. W., Frenkel-Brunswik, E., Levinson, D. J., & Sanford, R. N. (1950). *The authoritarian personality.* New York: W. Norton & Co.

Allport, G. W. (1950). Prejudice: A problem in psychological and social causation. *Journal of Social Issues, (Suppl. 4)*, 1–26.

Allport, G. W. (1954). *The nature of prejudice*. Reading, MA: Addison-Wesley.

Allport, G. W. (1963, December 5). Letter to Roger W. Brown, Acting Chair, Department of Social Relations. *Gordon W. Allport Papers*. Harvard, MA: Harvard University.

Allport, G. W., & Pettigrew, T. F. (1957). Cultural influence on the perception of movement: The trapezoidal illusion among Zulus. *Journal of Abnormal and Social Psychology*, 55, 104–113.

Bell, D. (1992). *Faces at the bottom of the well: The permanence of racism*. New York: Basic Books.

Capshew, J. H. (1999). *Psychologists on the march: Science, practice and professional identity in American, 1929–1969*. Cambridge: Cambridge University Press.

Cherry, F. (2000). The nature of "The nature of prejudice." *Journal of the History of the Behavioral Sciences*, 36, 489–498.

Cherry, F. (2007). South Africa through the lens of Gordon Allport. In V. van Deventer, M. Terre Blanche, E. Fourie, & P. Segalo (Eds.), *Citizen city: Between constructing agent and constructed agency* (pp. 59–69). Toronto: Captus Press.

Collier, G., Minton, H. L., & Reynolds, G. (1991). *Currents of thought in American social psychology*. New York: Oxford University Press.

Hilgard, E. R. (1987). *Psychology in America: A historical survey*. San Diego, CA: Harcourt Brace Jovanovich.

Jackson, J. P. Jr. (2001). *Social scientists for social justice: Making the case against segregation*. New York: New York University Press.

Kimmel, P. (1997). A history of Division 9 (Society for the Psychological Study of Social Issues). In D. A. Dewsbury (Ed.), *Unification through division: Histories of the divisions of the American Psychological Association: Vol. 2* (pp. 9–53). Washington, DC: American Psychological Association.

King, M. L. (1968). The role of the behavioral scientist in the civil rights movement. In J. M. Notterman (Ed.) (1997) *The evolution of psychology: Fifty years of the American Psychologist* (pp. 565–757). Washington, DC: American Psychological Association.

Lee, A. M. (1943). *Race riot*. New York: Dryden Press.

Louw, J. (2004). Race and psychology in South Africa. In: A. S. Winston (Ed.), *Defining difference: Race and racism in the history of psychology* (pp. 171–197). Washington, DC: American Psychological Association.

Louw, J., & Foster, D. (1992). Intergroup relations and South African social psychology: Historical ties. *Canadian Psychology*, 33, 651–656.

Morawski, J. G., & Bayer, B. M. (2003). Social psychology. In I. B. Weiner (Ed.), *Handbook of Psychology: History of Psychology: Vol. 1.* (pp. 223–247). New York: Wiley & Sons, Inc.

Myrdal, G. (1944). *An American dilemma: The Negro problem and modern democracy*. New York: Harper & Brothers.

Pettigrew, T. F. (1957). Desegregation and its chances for success: Northern and southern views. *Social Forces*, *35*, 339–344.

Pettigrew, T. F. (1958). Personality and sociocultural factors in intergroup attitudes: A cross-national comparison. *The Journal of Conflict Resolution*, *2*, 29–42.

Pettigrew, T. F. (1959). Regional differences in anti-Negro prejudice. *Journal of Abnormal and Social Psychology*, *59*, 28–36.

Pettigrew, T. F. (1960). Social distance attitudes of South African students. *Social Forces*, *38*, 246–253.

Pettigrew, T. F. (1961). Social psychology and desegregation research. *American Psychologist*, *16*, 105–112.

Pettigrew, T. F. (1963). *De facto* segregation, southern style. *Integrated Education*, *1*, 14–18.

Pettigrew, T. F. (1965). Continuing barriers to desegregated education in the South. *Sociology of Education*, *36*, 99–111.

Pettigrew, T. F. (1967). SPSSI as honest broker—a presidential message. *Newsletter of the Society for the Psychological Study of Social Issues*, *117*, 1–6.

Pettigrew, T. F. (1973). Black and white attitudes toward race and housing. In E. A. Hawley & V. P. Rock (Eds.), *Segregation in residential areas* (pp. 21–84). Washington, DC: National Academy of Sciences. (Reprinted in T. F. Pettigrew (Ed.) (1975). *Racial Discrimination in the United States* (pp. 92–126) New York: Harper & Row.)

Pettigrew, T. F. (1979). Tensions between the law and social science: An expert witness view. In *Schools and the courts: Vol 1. Desegregation* (pp. 23–44). Eugene, OR: ERIC Clearinghouse for Educational Management.

Pettigrew, T. F. (1985). New Black-White patterns: How best to conceptualize them? *Annual Review of Sociology*, *11*, 329–346.

Pettigrew, T. F. (1993). How events shape theoretical frames: A personal statement. In: J. H. Stanfield II (Ed.), *A history of race relations research: First-generation recollections* (pp. 159–178). Newbury Park, CA: Sage.

Pettigrew, T. F. (1996). *How to think like a social scientist*. New York: HarperCollins.

Pettigrew, T. F. (1997). Personality and social structure: Social psychological contributions. In R. Hogan, J. A. Johnson, & S. R. Briggs (Eds.), *Handbook of Personality Psychology* (pp. 417–438). New York: Academic Press.

Pettigrew, T. F. (1998). Intergroup contact theory. *Annual Review of Psychology*, *49*, 65–85.

Pettigrew, T. F. (1999). Review: Sociological analyses confront fashionable racial fallacies. *Sociological Forum*, *14*, 177–184.

Pettigrew, T. F. (2004). Justice deferred: A half century after *Brown v. Board of Education*. *American Psychologist*, *59*, 521–529.

Pettigrew, T. F. (2006). The advantages of multi-level approaches. *Journal of Social Issues*, *62*, 615–620.

Pettigrew, T. F., & Meertens, R. (1995). Subtle and blatant prejudice in Western Europe. *European Journal of Social Psychology*, *57*, 57–75.

Pettigrew, T. F., & Tropp, L. R. (2006). A meta-analytic test of intergroup contact theory. *Journal of Personality and Social Psychology, 90,* 1–33.

Pettigrew, T. F., Allport, G. W., & Barnett, E. O. (1958). Binocular resolution and perception of race in South Africa, *British Journal of Psychology, 49,* 265–278.

Pickren, W. E., & Tomes, H. (2002). The legacy of Kenneth B. Clark to the APA: The Board of Social and Ethical Responsibility for Psychology. *American Psychologist, 57,* 51–59.

Rutherford, A. (2006, June 22). Interview with Thomas Pettigrew. *Oral history collection of The Society for the Psychological Study for Social Issues.* Unpublished transcript.

Stephan, C. W., Stephan, W. G., & Pettigrew, T. F. (1991). *The future of social psychology: Defining the relationship between sociology and psychology.* New York: Springer.

Society for the Psychological Study of Social Issues website. History of the SPSSI. Retrieved January 24, 2008 from http://www.spssi.org

Wagner, U., van Dick, R., Pettigrew, T. F., & Christ, O. (2003). Ethnic prejudice in East and West Germany: The explanatory power of intergroup contact. *Group Processes and Intergroup Relations, 6,* 22–36.

Part I

Exploring the Causes of Prejudice and Discrimination

3

From Lewin and Allport to Pettigrew

Modern Practical Theories

Susan T. Fiske

When I was a graduate student, Thomas Pettigrew was not only conducting research on racism, integration, and relative deprivation, he was also testifying against the racial segregation of the Boston public schools. We heard that he received bomb threats for his evidence-based stands on these social issues. Even more than his specific stands, his blend of action-oriented research and research-based political action inspired us.

As this chapter will show, my initial work on outcome dependency (see Fiske, 2000, for a review) and then power relations (Fiske, 1993), both in the context of intergroup relations, followed in part from Pettigrew, but also Allport and Lewin. My willingness to use this work as an expert witness doubtless reflected their inspiration (Fiske, Bersoff, Borgida, Deaux, & Heilman, 1991). Subsequently, my work with Glick on Ambivalent (Hostile and Benevolent) Sexism (Glick & Fiske, 1996) and then on the Stereotype Content Model (SCM) with Cuddy (Fiske, Cuddy, Glick, & Xu, 2002) was influenced by both Allport's and Pettigrew's understanding of the subtlety, nuances, and textures of intergroup bias. Our current and future work bears Pettigrew's traces as well. Our SCM extension to the realm of discrimination, the Behavior from Intergroup Affect and Stereotypes (BIAS) map (Cuddy, Fiske, & Glick, 2007, shows that discrimination is predicted far better by affect than stereotypes, consistent with Pettigrew's current views (Tropp & Pettigrew, 2005; see also Talaska, Fiske, & Chaiken, in press). My student Harris and I are concentrating on neural indicators of immediate emotional responses to certain extreme outgroups, as measures of immediate affect (Harris & Fiske, 2006). Building on cross-cultural extensions of ambivalent sexism and of the SCM, another current student, Lee, and I are comparing across cultures people's expectations about friendship (Lee, Fiske, & Miyamoto, 2007), the main means for constructive intergroup contact interventions (Pettigrew & Tropp, 2006).

Outcome Dependency and Category-Based Impressions

Social cognition was just a scent in the air at Harvard in the late 1970s, as it was in other places, but at Harvard at that time, it also blew in the breezes from sociology. Sociological perspectives combined with the cognitive revolution to inspire my concerns with the ways that power relations affect cognitive processes in stereotyping.

No one can escape the hierarchical qualities of a private university, especially Harvard. But it was not until I reached Carnegie-Mellon University as an assistant professor that I became fully conscious of the impact of hierarchies on how people think about each other. Attention moves up every organization, in these cases from the undergraduates to their graduate teaching assistants to the junior faculty to the senior faculty to the department chair to the dean to the provost to the president to the trustees. Each level is contingent on the one above it, and people attend accordingly to those who control their outcomes.

This informal insight meshed with a concurrent problem in the social cognition of stereotyping, one that remained unresolved at that time. Research on person memory had assembled an impressive array of evidence that people preferentially recall expectancy-inconsistent information (see Fiske & Taylor, 1984, for a contemporary review). This finding flew in the face of stereotyping research, which indicated that people are biased to confirm their stereotypes. It also contradicted my own observation that stereotypes are difficult to contradict. And of course Pettigrew's mentor Gordon Allport (1954) wrote beautifully on the cognitive confirmation of stereotypes, as did Pettigrew in his (1979) work on the Ultimate Attribution Error. How to reconcile these findings?

Our own work on how people deal with stereotype-inconsistent information relied on three premises:

First, on-line attention would be a more sensitive indicator than recall of people's information-processing strategies. My graduate work had focused with Taylor on attentional processes (Fiske, Kenny, & Taylor, 1982; Langer, Taylor, Fiske, & Chanowitz, 1976; Taylor & Fiske, 1975, 1978; Taylor, Crocker, Fiske, Sprinzen, & Winkler, 1979), so I had come to believe in the power of these on-line impression formation processes.

Second, social categories influence impressions more powerfully than does individuating information (unless people are motivated to go beyond their categories). This perspective started in my graduate work with Taylor on social categorization (Taylor, Fiske, Etcoff, & Ruderman, 1978) and developed in my empirical work (e.g., Fiske, Neuberg, Beattie, & Milberg, 1987) that later culminated in the continuum model of impression formation (Fiske & Neuberg, 1990).

Third, people could be motivated to attend to stereotype-inconsistent information by making the interaction more involving than the typical social cognition paradigm: a hypothetical paper person or a purposeless getting-acquainted conversation. This last was the key insight that connected to Allport's and Pettigrew's work on the contact hypothesis: People have to be interdependent, in order to overcome their stereotypes. Armed with these hunches, we conducted a series of laboratory studies to examine the effects of outcome dependency on interpersonal impressions.

In our initial studies, students expected to work with another student, often creating educational games with wind-up toys, and they could win a prize for their performance, either separate (independent) or joint (interdependent). They had positive or negative expectations about the other person's aptitude for this task (e.g., self-reported experience and confidence). Then they received a series of practice-teaching evaluations, some of which were consistent and others inconsistent with their expectations. We timed their attention to each kind of information (with stop-watches in our pockets, no less). Outcome-dependent people reliably attend more to inconsistent information, make more dispositional inferences about it, and form more idiosyncratic impressions, as a result (Erber & Fiske, 1984; Neuberg & Fiske, 1987). It is interdependence per se, not cooperation, that causes these effects, for one-on-one competition works the same way (Ruscher & Fiske, 1990).

However, because all the studies had so far used symmetrical interdependence, we had to separate the effect of one's own outcome-dependency from one's responsibility for one's partner. For example, we designed a study in which people were trying to concentrate on a task that could win them points toward a lottery. A group of low- or high-power distracters (described as similar to noisy roommates) could interfere and reward them in trivial or serious ways. We used stereotypes about college majors (art and math) that were outgroups for psychology students, and we communicated mixed images of the distracter students. As it turned out, people's focus on stereotype-inconsistency was due to their own dependency on the other person (not that person's dependency on them): This became clear because asymmetrical outcome dependency had the same effects as symmetrical interdependence (Dépret & Fiske, 1999; Stevens & Fiske, 2000). In all this program of research, we felt we were identifying the micro mechanisms for successful intergroup contact; that is, attention to stereotype-inconsistent results from interdependence, thereby undermining prejudice. This supports Pettigrew and Tropp's (2006) meta-analysis of intergroup contact studies.

In our complex social environments, coming full circle to explaining the person memory work, we found that under control (independent) conditions, people did indeed concentrate on stereotype-consistent information, as a default, which would tend to perpetuate stereotypes. In the whole range of studies, it turns out that various factors (expectancy simplicity and novelty, lack of distraction, and a generally sterile environment) allow people to recall consistent or inconsistent information. In that same time period, Pettigrew reached a similar conclusion, via meta-analysis, in his case (Rojahn & Pettigrew, 1992; see also Stangor & McMillan, 1992).

The importance of interdependence to intergroup contact has clear applicability to real-world intergroup relations. When people need each other to obtain desired outcomes, they attend to each other, think hard about each other, and can go beyond their prejudices.

Power and Stereotyping

After examining asymmetrical outcome dependency from the perspective of the powerless, we naturally wanted to examine it from the perspective of the powerful. Logically, if people attend to others on whom their outcomes depend, then those whose outcomes depend less on others should not attend as much to other people. The lack of outcome dependency comes along with individual proclivities toward power, and the sheer numbers problem of looking down the power pyramid toward more people, instead of looking up at fewer people (Fiske, 1993). This theory laid the foundation both for our empirical work, and for more recent theories of power (Keltner, Gruenfeld, & Anderson, 2003). Our own work identified, on the one hand, the power-as-control framework, whereby supervisors might fail to individuate their supervisees, stereotyping by default. But it also identified motives to maintain one's powerful position, whereby supervisors might confirm their stereotypes about their supervisees, stereotyping by design (Goodwin, Gubin, Fiske, & Yzerbyt, 2000).

Randomly empowering undergraduates turns out to be difficult. At a large state university, students feel small and resist taking power over another students. At an elite private university, students resist being told another student has power over them. Nevertheless, we hit on some workable methods. For example, we gave students power to recommend high-school students for summer internships (Goodwin et al. 2000). Powerful decision-makers not only neglect stereotype disconfirming information, but they also over-attend to stereotype confirming information.

Again, the applicability of these results is clear. Powerful people in organizations can use their control over desired resources for good or for ill (Fiske & Berdahl, 2007). Our research shows that powerful people may be vulnerable to bias because they have few checks on their choices, so it matters to have structural monitoring of their decisions. That is, organizations need to be aware of the patterns and practices of powerful decision-makers, or face the potential legal consequences.

Expert Witnessing

Pettigrew and Lewin are right. Good theory aids practical application and vice versa. My background in social categorization and in power asymmetries both reinforced and developed from my expert testimony in discrimination cases. When first approached in the mid 1980s, I felt obligated to get our research out of the journals into the trench warfare of adversarial legal proceedings. The legal innovation was dual: Research on racial stereotyping had previously made a famous court appearance in the 1954 *Brown v. Board of Education* school desegregation decision, drawing on social psychologist Dr Kenneth Clark. But research on gender stereotyping had made no inroads into the courts. What's more, the new cognitive focus had not appeared in evidence. Social cognitive approaches have the benefit of not requiring us to psychoanalyze the motives of the defendants, but merely to summarize the relevant literature to explain how otherwise decent, ordinary people can stereotype other people by use of their spontaneous categories, and illustrate applications to the case.

Our field has much to say about the social contexts that encourage stereotyping; after giving a quick course in Social Cognitive Psychology 101, one then explains how the principles might apply to the current case (Fiske, 1995). Who knew that it would be appealed and upheld all the way to the U.S. Supreme Court (Fiske et al., 1991)? This became known as social framework analysis, an altogether new type of expert testimony (Fiske & Borgida, 1999). Social framework analysis provides the court with knowledge about the context in which, for example, people make decisions about other people. It provides the court with information about the social science consensus on the antecedent conditions, the indicators, and the consequences of, for example, stereotyping. Social framework analysis was sorely needed (Krieger & Fiske, 2006). A number of social psychologists have been confronting the question of how our field goes beyond common knowledge, to educate the court about social psychological matters from polygraphs to eyewitness testimony to media exposure and aggression (Borgida & Fiske, 2008).

Expert witnessing made me realize that peers are only one problem in the workplace (e.g., sexual harassment, Borgida & Fiske, 1995). Powerful decision-makers are an even bigger problem, both when they operate in biased manners and when they deny that their supervisees operate in a biased manner. This perspective contributed to my interest in issues of power. But it also contributed to my observations of the complexities of sexism.

Ambivalent (Hostile and Benevolent) Sexism

Our work on expert testimony had drawn on Peter Glick's analyses of masculine and feminine jobs (Glick, Wilk, & Perreault, 1995; Glick, Zion, & Nelson, 1988). So, when he proposed that we collaborate, I was delighted. The complexities of sexism had not yet been addressed; prior work had focused predominantly on blatant, hostile forms (e.g., Spence & Helmreich, 1972). Simultaneously with our effort, other scales appeared to take the modern sexism approach of more subtle forms of sexism (Swim, Aikin, Hall, & Hunter, 1995; Tougas, Brown, Beaton, & Joly, 1995).

Our take on this problem focused on the ambivalence inherent in male–female relationships. Men and women are the strangest of mutual outgroups: intimately interdependent yet defined by male societal power. Our analyses identified three domains for this interplay of interdependence and power: heterosexual intimacy, gender roles, power relations (Glick & Fiske, 1996). And the resulting biases included not only hostility toward nontraditional women but subjective benevolence toward traditional women. Prejudice against men, too, fits this analysis (Glick & Fiske, 1999). These principles generalize across the globe, correlating with UN indices of gender development and gender empowerment for both men and women (Glick et al., 2000; Glick et al., 2004).

Again, the theory was practical and useful. Organizations and the legal system need to be realistic about the role of subjectively benevolent sexism in particular. Seemingly benign, it instead constitutes part of an ideology that disempowers women and prevents their development. In the course of this work, I also discovered Thomas Pettigrew's long-standing role in advising women's studies at Princeton.

Stereotype Content Model

Another practical theory emerged after this time, and in retrospect seems closely related, though it was unconscious associations, not conscious parallels that drove the new approach. Both Allport's and Pettigrew's understanding of the subtlety, nuances, and textures of intergroup bias informed this approach. Allport (1954) noted the inverse stereotypes of American Jews and "Negroes": the one clever but allegedly obnoxious, the other socially warm but allegedly stupid. My own exhausting and exhaustive review of the literature (Fiske, 1998) convinced me that this was a general principle (Fiske, Xu, Cuddy, & Glick, 1999; Fiske et al., 2002).

According to the Stereotype Content Model (SCM), people first need to know whether another group is on their side (cooperatively inclined) or not (competitively inclined). If cooperative or neural, the other group is warm: trustworthy and nice. If competitive, the other group is not warm: hostile and untrustworthy. After learning the other's intent, one needs to know whether they can enact their intent: competent or not. These structural variables, thus, provide the trait inferences for a variety of groups, a structure–stereotype link that works both in correllational analyses for naturally occurring groups (Fiske et al. 2002) and in experimental manipulations of unfamiliar groups (Caprariello, Cuddy, & Fiske, 2007). (My Pettigrewian sociological roots show here.)

In this SCM view, then, we have the usual ingroups and outgroups: The societal reference groups (in the US, middle-class people,

Americans) are viewed as both warm and competent, being cooperative and high-status. Societal extreme outgroups are seen as neither warm nor competent, being competitive/exploitative and low-status (poor people, homeless people, drug addicts).

The unique contribution of the SCM adds two ambivalent groups: One is warm but incompetent, being cooperative but low-status (older people, disabled people). The other is competent but not nice, being competitive but high-status (rich people, Asians, Jews). These two ambivalent combinations not only place these groups in the warmth × competence space relative to other groups, but also inform detailed analyses of prejudice against each kind of group, for example a focused understanding of ageism (Cuddy, Norton, & Fiske, 2005) or anti-Asian prejudice (Lin, Kwan, Cheung, & Fiske, 2005).

The SCM clusters turn out to occur in comparable form across European and East Asian samples (Cuddy et al., in press). For example, rich people, poor people, and old people end up in the identical quadrants everywhere. The warmth × competence space also explains perceptions of heterogeneous groups, such as immigrants (Lee & Fiske, 2006) and gay men (Clausell & Fiske, 2005). That is, subgroups within these overall categories spread out across the space in useful ways. Overall, the warmth and competence dimensions appear to be universal principles that apply to both intergroup and interpersonal perception (Fiske, Cuddy, & Glick, 2007). For example, manipulating the relative status and cooperative/competitive relationship of two individuals has the same impact on their trait expectancies as the intergroup situations do (Russell & Fiske, 2007).

What's more, the warmth-competence dimensions result in reliable clusters of emotional prejudices (Cuddy et al., 2007; Fiske et al., 2002). The societal reference groups elicit pride and admiration; the lowest of the low elicit disgust and contempt. These unambivalent combinations elicit strongly valenced emotional prejudices. In parallel, the two ambivalent combinations elicit mixed emotions. The warm-but-incompetent groups elicit pity and sympathy, benign but paternalistic emotions. The competent-but-cold groups elicit envy and jealousy, emotions that resentfully admit that the other possesses some value.

Consistent with Pettigrew's meta-analysis (Tropp & Pettigrew, 2005) and our own (Talaska et al., in press), the emotions drive discriminatory behavior, more than the stereotypes do (Cuddy et al. in press). Our SCM extension to the realm of behavior, Behavior from Intergroup Affect and Stereotypes (the BIAS map) identifies behaviors predicted for each cluster (Cuddy et al., in press). The warmth dimension, being primary, predicts active help and harm.

The competence dimension, being secondary, predicts passive help and harm. Thus, the societal reference groups receive both active and passive help (e.g., both active help and passive association), and the low-low groups receive both active and passive harm (e.g., both active attack and passive neglect). The pitied groups receive both active help and passive neglect; consider the institutionalization of disabled or older people as examples. Finally, the envied groups receive a volatile mix of both passive association (going along to get along with them, e.g., shopping at their stores) and active harm (attack, when social order breaks down).

Thus, the SCM posits two dimensions of stereotype content: warmth and competence (intentions and the ability to enact them). These follow respectively from perceived competition and status. The warmth-competence combinations lead to specific emotions (pride, pity, envy, and contempt) for specific clusters of groups. And the emotions predict specific combinations of active and passive, helpful and harmful behaviors. The SCM has important applied implications, in that discrimination is not one-type-fits-all. Different groups will receive distinct patterns of bias, and many of those will be mixed: positive along with negative stereotypes, ambivalent emotions, and facilitative as well as harmful behavior. This mixed bias will be harder to recognize, and people can deny their negative biases because they can express their positive responses.

Future Directions

Some students in my lab. are concentrating on neural indicators of emotional responses to certain outgroups, as measures of immediate affect. So far, we have found that the lowest of the low outgroups, homeless people and drug addicts, elicit responses consistent with disgust (insula activation). What's more, they fail to elicit the reliable response to social stimuli that normally appears in the medial prefrontal cortex (mPFC), as if people are dehumanizing them (Harris & Fiske, 2006). This dehumanizing response fits cases in which people torture and kill other people because they do not see them as people (Fiske, Harris, & Cuddy, 2004).

Being social psychologists, we believe these neural responses depend on social context (Fiske et al., 2004). Normally, the social-cognitive mPFC activations occur when people think about the other person's mind, for example, when making dispositional attributions (Harris, Todorov, & Fiske, 2005). We drew on this finding to predict that people would "re-humanize" the extreme outgroups, if they only had to think about what was in their minds. For example, a soup-kitchen volunteer might have to think about how to feed a homeless person. Indeed, when participants had to decide what vegetable the person might eat, areas of the mPFC activate even to the homeless people (Harris & Fiske, 2007).

In the future, we hope to examine responses to pitied and envied groups, based on findings related to social neuroscience of emotion. For now, we come back to racial prejudice, Tom Pettigrew's focus of insight for so many decades. We join other researchers in finding that white Americans react to simple yearbook photographs of unfamiliar black Americans with neural activations characteristic of emotional vigilance, namely in the amygdala (Hart et al., 2000; Phelps et al., 2000; Wheeler & Fiske, 2005). Our twist was applying the same principle of asking participants to infer the other person's vegetable preferences, which we find also eliminates the amygdala response in this case. When people think about other people's minds, they can cross intergroup boundaries.

Another project takes seriously this idea in the context of global inter-group boundaries. Moving back to the more macro level of analysis, and building on cross-cultural extensions of ambivalent sexism and of the SCM, our lab is also examining cultural expectations about friendship and close relationships. Because friendship is the main means for constructive intergroup contact interventions, we see a connection to Pettigrew here as well. If people can better understand each other's expectations about friendships, perhaps the fruits of intergroup contact will be even more constructive. For example, casual friendships are far more common in the United States than in Japan, so friendship has distinct cultural meanings (Lee et al. 2007).

Pettigrew and Policy Implications

Tom Pettigrew's example emboldened our work in two additional ways, besides those already mentioned. First, he empowered us to operate at dramatically different levels of analysis, from cultural comparisons, to random sample surveys, to laboratory experiments, to (in our case) brain-imaging studies. The Harvard Social Relations program was still active during Pettigrew's and my overlapping nine years in the 1970s. One hallmark of the program was this interplay across levels of analysis. Other graduates of the program in that era also work at a wide range of levels, for example, Eliot Smith.

Pettigrew's other empowering example was in the implications for policy, even beyond the expert witnessing noted earlier. Universities, public school districts, and governments have frequently drawn on his expertise. In my case, the policy consultation has been limited to my own universities and my child's schools. Nevertheless, the implications of current work of prejudice are several.

As a result of Pettigrew's pioneering work and his heirs' work, we now know that bias is more automatic, more ambivalent, and more ambiguous than ordinary people think. This means, for example, that we cannot count on prejudice being blatant, despite its blatant effects on housing, education, health, and employment. People can stereotype and prejudge without awareness, intent, antipathy, or uniformity. First, policymakers need to know this, rather than relying on their lay theories of how discrimination operates (for a legal example, see Krieger & Fiske, 2006). Second, we need to build structures to check people's unexamined biases. Monitoring the outcomes of under-represented groups, affirmative action, and constructive intergroup contact are structural counterweights to people's unexamined biases.

Thanks to Lewin, Allport, Pettigrew, and their heirs, we now know how inevitably human nature brings us to stereotype, prejudge, and discriminate, but we also know how other aspects of human nature can ameliorate these all-too-human failings. We can apply a few modern practical theories to improve intergroup relations.

References

Allport, G. W. (1954). *The nature of prejudice*. Reading, MA: Addison-Wesley.

Borgida, E., & Fiske, S. T. (Eds.) (1995). Gender stereotyping, sexual harassment, and the law. *Journal of Social Issues, 51*.

Borgida, E., & Fiske, S. T. (Eds.) (2008). *Psychological science in the courtroom: Beyond common knowledge*. Oxford: Blackwell.

Caprariello, P. A., Cuddy, J. C., & Fiske, S. T. (2007). *Beliefs about social structure cause variations in stereotypes, prejudice, and discrimination: A test of the stereotype-content model*. Manuscript submitted for publication.

Clausell, E., & Fiske, S. T. (2005). When do the parts add up to the whole? Ambivalent stereotype content for gay male subgroups. *Social Cognition, 23*, 157–176.

Cuddy, A. J. C., Fiske, S. T., & Glick, P. (2007). The BIAS map: Behaviors from intergroup affect and stereotypes. *Journal of Personality and Social Psychology, 92*, 631–648.

Cuddy, A. J. C., Fiske, S. T., Kwan, V. S. Y., Glick, P., Demoulin, S., Leyens, J.-Ph., et al. (in press). Is the stereotype content model culture-bound?

A cross-cultural comparison reveals systematic similarities and differences. *British Journal of Social Psychology.*

Cuddy, A. J. C., Norton, M. I., & Fiske, S. T. (2005). This old stereotype: The pervasiveness and persistence of the elderly stereotype. *Journal of Social Issues, 61,* 265–283.

Dépret, E. F., & Fiske, S. T. (1999). Perceiving the powerful: Intriguing individuals versus threatening groups. *Journal of Experimental Social Psychology, 35,* 461–480.

Erber, R., & Fiske, S. T. (1984). Outcome dependency and attention to inconsistent information. *Journal of Personality and Social Psychology, 47,* 709–726.

Fiske, S. T. (1980). Attention and weight in person perception: The impact of negative and extreme behavior. *Journal of Personality and Social Psychology, 38,* 889–906.

Fiske, S. T. (1993). Controlling other people: The impact of power on stereotyping. *American Psychologist, 48,* 621–628.

Fiske, S. T. (1995). From the still small voice of discontent to the Supreme Court: How I learned to stop worrying and love social cognition. In G. G. Branigan & M. R. Merrens (Eds.), *The social psychologists: Research adventures* (pp. 19–34). New York: McGraw-Hill.

Fiske, S. T. (1998). Stereotyping, prejudice, and discrimination. In D. T. Gilbert, S. T. Fiske, & G. Lindzey (Eds.), *Handbook of social psychology: Vol. 2* (4th ed.) (pp. 357–411). New York: McGraw-Hill.

Fiske, S. T. (2000). Interdependence reduces prejudice and stereotyping. In S. Oskamp (Ed.), *Reducing prejudice and discrimination* (pp. 115–135). Mahwah, NJ: Erlbaum.

Fiske, S. T., & Berdahl, J. (2007). Social power. In A. Kruglanski & E. T. Higgins (Eds.), *Social psychology: A handbook of basic principles* (2nd ed., pp. 678–692). New York: Guilford.

Fiske, S. T., Bersoff, D. N., Borgida, E., Deaux, K., & Heilman, M. E. (1991). Social science research on trial: The use of sex stereotyping research in "Price Waterhouse v. Hopkins." *American Psychologist, 46,* 1049–1060.

Fiske, S. T., & Borgida, E. (1999). Social framework analysis as expert testimony in sexual harassment suits. In S. Estreicher (Ed.), *Sexual harassment in the workplace* (pp. 575–583). New York: New York University Press.

Fiske, S. T., Cuddy, A. J. C., & Glick, P. (2007). Universal dimensions of social perception: Warmth, then competence. *Trends in Cognitive Science, 11,* 77–83.

Fiske, S. T., Cuddy, A. J., Glick, P., & Xu, J. (2002). A model of (often mixed) stereotype content: Competence and warmth respectively follow from perceived status and competition. *Journal of Personality and Social Psychology, 82,* 878–902.

Fiske, S. T., Harris, L. T., & Cuddy, A. J. C. (2004). Policy Forum: Why ordinary people torture enemy prisoners. *Science, 306,* 1482–1483.

Fiske, S. T., Kenny, D. A., & Taylor, S. E. (1982). Structural models for the mediation of salience effects on attribution. *Journal of Experimental Social Psychology*, *18*, 105–127.

Fiske, S. T., & Neuberg, S. L. (1990). A continuum model of impression formation, from category-based to individuating processes: Influence of information and motivation on attention and interpretation. In M. P. Zanna (Ed.), *Advances in experimental social psychology: Vol. 23* (pp. 1–74). New York: Academic Press, New York.

Fiske, S. T., Neuberg, S. L., Beattie, A. E., & Milberg, S. J. (1987). Category-based and attribute-based reactions to others: Some informational conditions of stereotyping and individuating processes. *Journal of Experimental Social Psychology*, *23*, 399–427.

Fiske, S. T., & Taylor, S. E. (1984). *Social cognition*. New York: Random House.

Fiske, S. T., Xu, J., Cuddy, A. C., & Glick, P. (1999). (Dis)respecting versus (dis)liking: Status and interdependence predict ambivalent stereotypes of competence and warmth. *Journal of Social Issues*, *55*, 473–491.

Glick, P., & Fiske, S. T. (1996). The Ambivalent Sexism Inventory: Differentiating hostile and benevolent sexism. *Journal of Personality and Social Psychology*, *70*, 491–512.

Glick, P., & Fiske, S. T. (1999). The Ambivalence toward Men Inventory: Differentiating hostile and benevolent beliefs about men. *Psychology of Women Quarterly*, *231*, 519–536.

Glick, P., Fiske, S. T., Mladinic, A., Saiz, J. L., Abrams, D., Masser, B., et al. (2000). Beyond prejudice as simple antipathy: Hostile and benevolent sexism across cultures. *Journal of Personality and Social Psychology*, *79*, 763–775.

Glick, P., Lameriras, M., Fiske, S. T., Eckes, T., Masser, B., Volpato, C., et al. (2004). Bad but bold: Ambivalent attitudes toward men predict gender inequality in 16 nations. *Journal of Personality and Social Psychology*, *86*, 713–728.

Glick, P., Wilk, K., & Perreault, M. (1995). Images of occupations: Components of gender and status in occupational stereotypes. *Sex Roles*, *32*, 565–582.

Glick, P., Zion, C., & Nelson, C. (1988). What mediates sex discrimination in hiring decisions? *Journal of Personality and Social Psychology*, *55*, 178–186.

Goodwin, S. A., Gubin, A., Fiske, S. T., & Yzerbyt, V. (2000). Power can bias impression formation: Stereotyping subordinates by default and by design. *Group Processes and Intergroup Relations*, *3*, 227–256.

Harris, L. T., & Fiske, S. T. (2006). Dehumanizing the lowest of the low: Neuro-imaging responses to extreme outgroups. *Psychological Science*, *17*, 847–853.

Harris, L. T., & Fiske, S. T. (2007). Social groups that elicit disgust are differentially processed in mPFC. *Social Cognitive and Affective Neuroscience*, *2*, 45–51.

Harris, L. T., Todorov, A., & Fiske, S. T. (2005). Attributions on the brain: Neuro-imaging dispositional inferences, beyond theory of mind. *NeuroImage, 28,* 763–769.

Hart, A. J., Whalen, P. J., Shin, L. M., McInerney, S. C., Fischer, H., & Rauch, S. L. (2000). Differential response in the human amygdala to racial outgroup vs. ingroup face stimuli. *Neuroreport: For Rapid Communication of Neuroscience Research, 11,* 2351–2355.

Keltner, D., Gruenfeld, D. H., & Anderson, C. (2003). Power, approach, and inhibition. *Psychological Review, 110,* 265–284.

Krieger, L. H., & Fiske, S. T. (2006). Behavioral realism in employment discrimination law: Implicit bias and disparate treatment. *California Law Review, 94,* 997–1062.

Langer, E. J., Taylor, S. E., Fiske, S. T., & Chanowitz, B. (1976). Stigma, staring, and discomfort: A novel stimulus hypothesis. *Journal of Experimental Social Psychology, 12,* 451–463.

Lee, T. L., & Fiske, S. T. (2006). Not an outgroup, but not yet an ingroup: Immigrants in the stereotype content model. *International Journal of Intercultural Relations, 30,* 751–768.

Lee, T. L., Fiske, S. T., & Glick, P. (2007). *Sexism in close relationships.* Unpublished manuscript, Princeton University.

Lee, T. L., Fiske, S. T., & Miyamoto, S. (2007). *Relationship expectations: A comparative analysis.* Unpublished manuscript, Princeton University.

Lin, M. H., Kwan, V. S. Y., Cheung, A., & Fiske, S. T. (2005). Stereotype content model explains prejudice for an envied outgroup: Scale of Anti-Asian American Stereotypes. *Personality and Social Psychology Bulletin, 31,* 34–47.

Neuberg, S. L., & Fiske, S. T. (1987). Motivational influences on impression formation: Outcome dependency, accuracy-driven attention, and individuating processes. *Journal of Personality and Social Psychology, 53,* 431–444.

Pettigrew, T. F. (1979). The ultimate attribution error: Extending Allport's cognitive analysis of prejudice. *Personality and Social Psychology Bulletin, 5,* 461–476.

Pettigrew, T. F., & Tropp, L. R. (2006). A meta-analytic test of intergroup contact theory. *Journal of Personality and Social Psychology, 90,* 751–783.

Phelps, E. A., O'Connor, K. J., Cunningham, W. A., Funayama, E. S., Gatenby, J. C., Gore, J. C., et al. (2000). Performance on indirect measures of race evaluation predicts amygdala activation. *Journal of Cognitive Neuroscience, 12,* 729–738.

Rojahn, K., & Pettigrew, T. F. (1992). Memory for schema-relevant information: A meta-analytic resolution. *British Journal of Social Psychology, 31,* 81–109.

Ruscher, J. B., & Fiske, S. T. (1990). Interpersonal competition can cause individuating processes. *Journal of Personality and Social Psychology, 58,* 832–843.

Russell, A. M., & Fiske, S. T. (2007). *You are how you relate: Applying the stereotype content model to individual interactions.* Poster presented at the meetings of the Society for Personality and Social Psychology, Memphis, TN.

Spence, J. T., & Helmreich, R. (1972). Who likes competent women? Competence, sex role congruence of interests, and subjects' attitudes toward women as determinants of interpersonal attraction. *Journal of Applied Social Psychology, 2,* 197–213.

Stangor, C., & McMillan, D. (1992). Memory for expectancy-congruent and expectancy-incongruent social information: A meta-analytic review of the social psychological and social developmental literatures. *Psychological Bulletin, 111,* 42–61.

Stevens, L. E., & Fiske, S. T. (2000). Motivated impressions of a power-holder: Accuracy under task dependency and misperception under evaluative dependency. *Personality and Social Psychology Bulletin, 26,* 907–922.

Swim, J. K., Aikin, K. J., Hall, W. S., & Hunter, B. A. (1995). Sexism and racism: Old-fashioned and modern prejudices. *Journal of Personality and Social Psychology, 68,* 199–214.

Talaska, C. A., Fiske, S. T., & Chaiken, S. (in press). Legitimating racial discrimination: A meta-analysis of the racial attitude-behavior literature shows that emotions, not beliefs, best predict discrimination. *Social Justice Research.*

Taylor, S. E., Crocker, J., Fiske, S. T., Sprinzen, M., & Winkler, J. D. (1979). The generalizability of salience effects. *Journal of Personality and Social Psychology, 37,* 357–368.

Taylor, S. E., & Fiske, S. T. (1975). Point of view and perceptions of causality. *Journal of Personality and Social Psychology, 32,* 439–445.

Taylor, S. E., & Fiske, S. T. (1978). Salience, attention, and attribution: Top-of-the-head phenomena. In L. Berkowitz (Ed.), *Advances in Experimental Social Psychology: Vol. 11.* New York: Academic Press.

Taylor, S. E., Fiske, S. T., Etcoff, N. L., & Ruderman, A. J. (1978). Categorical and contextual bases of person memory and stereotyping. *Journal of Personality and Social Psychology, 36,* 778–793.

Tougas, F., Brown, R., Beaton, A. M., & Joly, S. (1995). Neosexism: Plus ça change, plus c'est pareil. *Personality and Social Psychology Bulletin, 21,* 842–849.

Tropp, L. R., & Pettigrew, T. F. (2005). Differential relationships between intergroup contact and affective and cognitive dimensions of prejudice. *Personality and Social Psychology Bulletin, 31,* 1145–1158. Erratum. *Personality and Social Psychology Bulletin, 31,* 1456.

Wheeler, M. E., & Fiske, S. T. (2005). Controlling racial prejudice and stereotyping: Social cognitive goals affect amygdala and stereotype activation. *Psychological Science, 16,* 56–63.

4

Rediscovering the Emotional Aspects of Prejudice and Intergroup Behavior

Eliot R. Smith

Through my career, my research interests and approaches have ranged widely, but in many ways they have continued to reflect the influence and inspiration of Thomas F. Pettigrew. He was my major advisor in my Ph.D. program at Harvard in the 1970s, and I am equally proud that (through him), Gordon Allport was my academic grandfather. I think of Thomas Pettigrew's influences on me as falling into three categories. First, from him I learned to be comfortable with a wide range of research methods, and especially to value the strengths of sample surveys as well as controlled laboratory experiments. Second, Pettigrew exemplified for me an Allportian approach to multilevel thinking, analyzing any issue (such as prejudice) not from one standpoint or level of analysis but from many—as in his seminal work (1958) showing that prejudice was a function of social conformity more than of disordered personality. Of course, Allport's magisterial *The Nature of Prejudice* (1954) was a model of multilevel thinking. And finally, Pettigrew taught me to identify research problems in a way that is shaped by practical and political concerns, as well as by the theoretical leverage they offer.

My earliest large-scale research project reflected all these influences from Pettigrew. In collaboration with sociologist James R. Kluegel, I obtained funding to conduct a large-scale survey of a representative sample of the U.S. population, to investigate Americans' beliefs about economic opportunity, racial inequality, and related issues. The survey data were collected in 1980, and our subsequent analyses resulted in insights into a number of topics. We investigated how self-interest, prejudice against racial minority groups, and general beliefs about the structure of inequality contributed to people's views on the topic (polically charged, then as now) of affirmative action (Kluegel & Smith, 1983). We analyzed popular beliefs about economic opportunity for blacks and for women, uncovering intriguing similarities and differences between the two (Smith & Kluegel, 1984). These and other findings were summarized in a monograph (Kluegel & Smith, 1986). This work involved applying basic principles of social psychology— principles such as the interactions of cognitive beliefs and affective reactions to social groups—to understanding the ways people think about social and economic inequality, the place of different groups in the hierarchical system, and their preferences for candidates, political parties, and governmental policies.

Role of Emotions in Prejudice and Intergroup Behavior

Although I have done much research in other areas, especially in social cognition (e.g., Smith, 1998; Smith & DeCoster, 2000), my recent work that most directly reflects the influences of Thomas F. Pettigrew has been the investigation (in collaboration with Diane Mackie) of the role of emotions in prejudice and intergroup behavior.

Historical Background

Surprising as it may seem, this topic was neglected for about a generation. At midcentury the *Authoritarian Personality* researchers (Adorno, Frenkel-Brunswik, Levinson, & Sanford, 1950) took a psychodynamic approach to the study of prejudice. In their model, prejudice reflected deep-seated inner personality conflicts within prejudiced individuals, which predisposed them to follow strong leaders and to reject and mistreat outgroups and deviants. Prejudice was seen as strongly affectively driven. However, the overall approach, based in Freudian theory, received severe criticism and declined in popularity through the 1950s.

The views of prejudice and intergroup behavior that sprang up in the 1960s and 1970s, in contrast, emphasized cognitive factors. Social cognition researchers focused on negative beliefs about outgroups (stereotypes), studying how they were learned and changed and the ways in which they drove prejudice and discriminatory behavior. Social identity researchers traced prejudice and discrimination to the desire to see one's own group as superior to others (Tajfel, 1978). Although early formulations of social identity theory referred to the ingroup as having affective significance for group members, research (especially in the influential self-categorization theory tradition; Turner, Hogg, Oakes, Reicher, & Wetherell, 1987) rarely pursued this insight. The cognitive rather than affective emphasis in both of these traditions was consistent with the general spirit of the times (the "cognitive revolution" within psychology), and these approaches have continued to be extraordinarily fruitful and generally dominant to the present day.

However, in the past couple of decades research has examined the possibility that intergroup relations and especially intergroup conflict might involve emotional responses. This work first emerged around the middle of the 1980s (Dijker, 1987; Gaertner & Dovidio, 1986; Stephan & Stephan, 1985). The focus was on the negative emotions experienced when people encounter individual members of outgroups, triggered by cultural differences (e.g., an outgroup member may violate ingroup norms) or by an anxious desire to make the interaction go smoothly and not to give offense. We now know that these emotional reactions of irritation and anxiety can occur, and can motivate avoidance of outgroup members.

Still other types of negative emotions can arise in intergroup interaction, including self-directed emotions like guilt. For example, recognition of one's own stereotypic or prejudiced thoughts can trigger guilt feelings in people who wish to be unprejudiced (Devine & Monteith, 1993). These in turn can motivate people to try to suppress stereotypic thoughts or to exert control over their behavior, with the goal of appearing unprejudiced to others as well as to themselves.

Also in the 1970s and 1980s, relative deprivation attracted considerable attention as a potential cause of both political attitudes and behaviors and extra-political acts such as rioting. Although relative deprivation has been conceptualized and measured in a variety of ways, Walker and Pettigrew (1984) made two important points. First, accumulated evidence supported the distinction between comparing oneself with other individuals and comparing one's ingroup with other groups, a distinction that has been labeled egoistic versus fraternal relative deprivation (Runciman, 1966). Much research (e.g., Vanneman & Pettigrew, 1972) establishes that group-based fraternal relative deprivation has more potent consequences for political attitudes and behavior. Second, the affective rather than cognitive aspects of relative deprivation are what give it a real behavioral "kick": people are moved to act not just when they perceive that "we are not doing as well as they are" but when that perception leads to emotions of anger, frustration, and resentment.

Intergroup Emotions Theory

Thus, by the late 1980s there were scattered indications that the previous neglect of the role of emotions was being reversed, and in the 1990s this became a major trend (Pettigrew, 1997). The theoretical perspective with which I have worked (Mackie, Devos, & Smith, 2000; Mackie, Maitner, & Smith, in press) takes as its conceptual starting point the idea (from social identity and self-categorization theory) that when people identify with a social group, the group becomes part of the psychological self. As a result, objects (such as outgroups) or events (such as intergroup conflict) that affect the group become emotionally relevant—*even if they have no direct effect on the individual perceiver* (Smith, 1993). When objects or situations are appraised or interpreted as helping or harming the group, therefore, they will trigger emotions, just as self-relevant events generally do, in the process described by appraisal theories of emotion (e.g., Scherer, 1984). Thus, just as people can experience emotions when events impinge on their individual selves, they also can experience emotions when events impinge on a group, if they think of themselves as members of that group.

As an example, consider the situation of a female employee who sees another female promoted into the all-male ranks of upper management—a promotion that she herself also desired. If the perceiver is reacting as an individual, she may experience emotions such as disappointment, resentment, or even envy. In contrast, if she thinks of herself as a woman and strongly identifies with that group membership, she may appraise the event positively, responding with happiness or pride because of its positive implications for her group (cf. Brewer & Weber, 1994). The distinction between appraising an event as an individual versus as a group member is parallel to that between egoistic and fraternal relative deprivation (Runciman, 1966), mentioned earlier.

Intergroup Emotions Theory makes several additional assumptions. First, it is not simply membership in a group, but identification with it, that makes a group part of the self. Hence group identification is assumed to be a key condition for experiencing intergroup emotions. Second, emotions directed at threatening outgroups may be of several distinct types, depending on the nature of the group and the particular circumstances. An outgroup may be viewed with fear, anger, disgust, or perhaps additional emotions, and each of these will have its own particular associated behavioral tendency (e.g., to attack or to avoid the outgroup; Cottrell & Neuberg, 2005). Third, just as individual-level emotions are part of a functional self-regulatory system, group-based emotions are functional in regulating people's attitudes and behaviors toward their own and other groups. Group-based emotions should motivate acts such as affiliating with the ingroup, avoiding or attacking an outgroup, supporting governmental programs that help or harm groups, etc.

Evidence

My colleagues and I, as well as others, have conducted research that supports many of the assumptions and hypotheses of Intergroup Emotions Theory. One fundamental assumption is that people can experience emotions on behalf of a group or fellow group members even when the perceivers are not personally affected (Mackie, Silver, & Smith, 2004). Supporting this point, people report feeling unhappy and angry when they learn of an event that harms other members of an ingroup that is situationally salient, even though the event has no conceivable implications for the perceivers as individuals (Yzerbyt, Dumont, Wigboldus, & Gordijn, 2003).

In a more direct examination of several theoretical hypotheses, Smith, Seger, and Mackie (in press) asked students to report the extent to which they generally felt a number of distinct emotions, as individuals and as members of several different ingroups (e.g., university and political party groups). People were asked both "as an individual, to what extent do you feel . . ." anger, pride, and other emotions, and "as a Democrat, to what extent do you feel . . ." the same list of emotions. As might be expected, reports of the same emotion experienced as an individual and as a group member correlate at approximately .30, such that people who generally feel more angry as individuals also tend to report feeling more angry as group members. Notwithstanding this correlation, profiles of group emotions and individual emotions were meaningfully distinct. For example, people might be more proud as individuals than as Americans, and more angry as Americans than as individuals.

Smith et al. (in press) also found that people's group-level emotions are socially shared, and shared more strongly by people who identify more with the group. That is, each social group (Democrats, university students, etc.) has a specific profile of group-level emotions (such as high happiness, low anger, moderate guilt). When reporting their emotions for that particular group, members tend to converge toward the group profile. For example, suppose someone reports an individual level of anger of "3" on a 1–7 scale, while the average level of anger as an American is "5." How much anger will this individual experience as an American? Our findings show that on average, he or she will report over 4.5 on the scale—moving more than 75% of the way from his or her individual emotion level (a kind of baseline) toward the group-typical level of the emotion. Moreover, people who identify more strongly with the group converge more, demonstrating that the effect has to do with the person's degree of psychological attachment to the group (rather than some less interesting factor like a generally known association of particular groups with particular emotions). We have replicated this finding of emotion convergence within a group with more than a half-dozen specific groups (e.g., Americans, Indiana University students, Democrats, Republicans, men, women).

Smith et al. (in press) also found that group emotions predicted action tendencies directed at both the ingroup and the outgroup, such as ingroup support and solidarity, outgroup confrontation, and outgroup avoidance. The results suggested that anger at the outgroup and positive emotions (pride, happiness, satisfaction) about the ingroup were the most powerful predictors across all categories of action tendencies. These findings are consistent with the idea that group emotions motivate and regulate behavior toward social groups. Yet another aspect of behavioral regulation by intergroup emotions is that if intergroup emotions are functional, successfully carrying out an emotion-linked behavioral tendency should allow the emotional feelings to dissipate, whereas impeding the behavioral tendency should intensify the emotion. Maitner, Mackie, & Smith (2006) investigated these hypotheses by examining the emotional consequences of satisfying or thwarting behavioral intentions related to intergroup emotions. Their studies showed that if an attack on the ingroup produced anger, retaliation increased satisfaction, but if an attack produced fear, retaliation increased fear and guilt. Outgroup-directed anger instigated by an insult to the ingroup dissipated when the ingroup successfully responded, but was increased by an unsuccessful response. Responding in an emotionally appropriate way was satisfying, but ingroup failure to respond elicited anger directed at the ingroup. A final study showed that ingroup guilt following aggression was diminished when the ingroup made reparations, but was exacerbated when the ingroup aggressed again. These findings demonstrate that intergroup emotions regulate and motivate behavioral intentions associated with the emotion.

The theme that intergroup emotions regulate and direct people's attitudes and behaviors toward an outgroup has specific implications for understanding prejudice, which has been central to Thomas Pettigrew's interests. Pettigrew (1998) suggested that intergroup contact has its effects on reducing prejudice especially through emotional mediators (e.g., the creation of a friendship, the reduction of intergroup anxiety) rather than through cognitive mediators such as debunking stereotypes. Miller, Smith, and Mackie (2004) examined the role of intergroup emotions directed at a specific outgroup (African Americans) in predicting Whites' prejudice against that group. The studies replicated large bodies of research showing that intergroup contact reduces prejudice, and that Social Dominance Orientation (SDO), a personality-like individual difference reflecting desires to maintain hierarchies of group inequality, increases prejudice. The studies also demonstrated that intergroup emotions experienced when encountering or thinking about African Americans played a major role in mediating both of those effects. Specifically, the effect of past intergroup contact was mediated by positive intergroup emotions, and there was more tentative evidence suggesting mediation by negative emotions. The effect of SDO was mediated by both positive and negative intergroup emotions. People high in SDO tended to perceive certain outgroups as threatening, leading to negative emotions such as fear, anger, or resentment, which in turn increased prejudiced attitudes. Thus, intergroup emotions play a key role in mediating the known, powerful effects of both intergroup contact and SDO on prejudice. The Miller et al. studies also examined stereotypes of the outgroup as an alternative potential mediator, permitting a comparison of their role with that of intergroup emotions. Stereotypes had no significant role in mediating the effects of past intergroup contact, and mediated part of the effect of SDO in one of the two studies. These results fit with other empirical and conceptual evidence for the priority of affective (emotional) over cognitive (stereotype beliefs) mediators of effects on prejudice (Tropp & Pettigrew, 2005).

Future Directions

An approach that understands group-based emotions as a major component of prejudice, going beyond the past emphasis on stereotypes and intergroup differentiation, offers new theoretical insights and novel possibilities for intervention and remediation, at both an individual and societal level.

First, much research has focused on the conditions under which people's prejudiced views of social groups might be changed, especially by seeking to change stereotypes. Intergroup Emotions Theory suggests that thinking about ways to change *emotional* reactions to groups might offer a completely new portfolio of approaches to prejudice reduction. For example, two emotion-regulation strategies have been extensively studied (Gross, 1998). Reappraisal strategies involve thinking about an event in such a way that no emotions are felt, for example looking at an upsetting image of a mutilated body while trying to focus on color and shape. Suppression strategies involve trying to minimize behavioral expressions of an emotion such as facial expressions—trying to act such that an observer would not know that the person was experiencing an emotion. Research suggests that reappraisal is both more effective and less cognitively costly than suppression. Research can and should be conducted applying these and other strategies of emotion regulation to negative emotional reactions to social groups, to assess their effectiveness in reducing prejudice. Can people be trained to reappraise situations of intergroup interaction to reduce their feelings of threat, resentment, or anxiety? If the research on emotion regulation generalizes to this domain, such reappraisal strategies should be more effective than simply trying to suppress or cover up emotional responses.

Second, thinking about emotions as an important component of people's reactions to outgroups also leads to new insights regarding time. Traditional stereotypes and prejudiced attitudes toward an outgroup are regarded as highly stable (in fact, their resistance to change has been a core issue motivating much research). In contrast, emotions are self-evidently changeable, varying over seconds, minutes, and hours (Smith & Mackie, 2006). New research questions result, concerning effects of transitory emotional states on people's thoughts, attitudes, and behaviors toward an outgroup. Research has begun to examine these issues, finding for example that when people are feeling angry for extraneous reasons they also have more negative reactions to outgroups (DeSteno, Dasgupta, Bartlett, & Cajdric, 2004).

Third, as described above, for 50 years intergroup contact has been the prejudice reduction mechanism best-researched by social psychologists (Allport, 1954). Contact effects are important not only for theoretical but for practical reasons, for intergroup contact can be effectively influenced by governmental policies (e.g., by desegregation of schools or other major social institutions). A recent meta-analysis (Pettigrew & Tropp, 2006) confirms that contact decreases prejudice almost across the board, although certain conditions strengthen and facilitate the effect. In Pettigrew's interpretation (1998), what these factors have in common is that they promote the formation of friendships, rather than mere acquaintanceships. However, formation of a long-term friendship is not necessary for prejudice reduction. As Wright, Aron, McLaughlin-Volpe, & Ropp (1997) have shown, prejudice can be reduced by the procedure of Aron, Melinat, Aron, and Vallone (1997), which uses programmed mutual compliments and self-disclosures, which generates feelings of closeness in a relatively brief time (around a half hour). Galinsky and Moskowitz (2000) used a cognitive "perspective taking" manipulation which asked participants to take a few minutes and think about seeing the world through the eyes of an outgroup member, and showed that it effectively reduced prejudice.

Our recent research suggests that an even more minimal intervention, interpersonal touch, can have similar effects. A. P. Fiske (2004) describes touch (along with physical proximity and behavioral synchrony) as an embodied cue of "communal sharing" or close relationships. Supporting this theoretical principle, interpersonal touch causes people to act in more helpful and generous ways toward the person who touches them (e.g., Cruscoe & Wetzel, 1984).

But can touch, like an actual friendship, produce not only positive feelings about the individual toucher, but also reduced prejudice toward his or her group? The answer is yes, according to our recent study (Seibt, Schubert, Strack, Hall, Seger, & Smith, 2006). A female African American experimenter briefly and casually touched some participants (randomly assigned) while leaning over them to press a computer key to start the experiment, while not touching others. The experimenter then departed while all dependent variables were collected by computer. A touch lasting a second or two significantly reduced participants' implicit prejudice against African Americans, as measured by an evaluative priming task. In contrast to the older literature on interpersonal touch, our study demonstrates an effect that goes beyond participants' reactions to the toucher as an individual, to influence their evaluation of the toucher's group. This study opens the fascinating prospect that, as Fiske's (2004) model would predict, brief and relatively minimal manipulations of embodied cues such as touch, or interpersonal behavioral synchrony or mimicry, might have real effects on prejudice and intergroup behavior.

Finally, a direction my collaborators and I are taking in some of our most recent work is to attempt to understand social attitudes and behaviors (including prejudice) as an aspect of "situated cognition" (Smith & Semin, 2004), emerging from the interaction of the individual and the social context instead of reflecting only inner mental representations and processes. Mason, Conrey, and Smith (in press) have recently outlined a framework for investigating social influence processes as an aspect of situated cognition—similar to Pettigrew's (1958) emphasis that prejudice owes much to social conformity rather than purely individual personality or cognitive structures. Most theoretical approaches to conformity consider either conformity to the mainstream views of the culture as a whole (reflected, for example, in the media or in majority public opinion), or conformity to the norms of a specific ingroup (Turner et al., 1987). In reality, people's social environments are probably best characterized as *social networks.* People have links of acquaintanceship, friendship, etc. to particular other people, which interconnect them in a complex web. Social influence can flow along social network links, as one person conforms to the opinions he or she hears from a friend. Equally, however, people can change their network links, forming new friendships and losing others, a process that is probably based to some extent on similarity, agreement, and liking.

The social-psychological study of the effects of such networks on attitudes, opinions, and social behavior is in its infancy (Mason et al., in press). But already there are intriguing demonstrations that social networks systematically shape information that is transmitted along network links, with stereotype- and prejudice-consistent information often tending to have an advantage (Lyons & Kashima, 2003; Thompson, Judd, & Park, 2000). Studies by Wright et al. (1997) even show that prejudice is reduced by knowing that a friend of a friend— a person who is *two* network links away—is a member of an outgroup. Findings like these strongly suggest that the study of social networks could play a major role in the formulation of effective strategies for reducing prejudice. For example, one could seek to identify individuals at key structural positions in a network, and target them for interventions (such as the creation of a cross-group friendship) in such a way as to maximize the influence of this intervention by the flow of social influence throughout the whole network. This represents a direction for future research that will hark back in important ways to Pettigrew's pioneering (1958) work showing that prejudice is grounded in social as well as cognitive processes.

Acknowledgment

Preparation of this chapter was facilitated by NIMH grant R01 MH-63762 and NSF grant BCS-0527249.

References

Adorno, T. W., Frenkel-Brunswik, E., Levinson, D. J., & Sanford, R. N. (1950). *The authoritarian personality.* New York: Harper.

Allport, G. W. (1954). *The nature of prejudice.* Reading, MA: Addison-Wesley.

Aron, A., Melinat, E., Aron, E. N., & Vallone, R. D. (1997). The experimental generation of interpersonal closeness: A procedure and some preliminary findings. *Personality and Social Psychology Bulletin, 23,* 363–377.

Brewer, M. B., & Weber, J. G. (1994). Self-evaluation effects of interpersonal versus intergroup social comparison. *Journal of Personality and Social Psychology, 66,* 268–275.

Cottrell, C. A., & Neuberg, S. L. (2005). Different emotional reactions to different groups: A sociofunctional threat-based approach to "prejudice." *Journal of Personality and Social Psychology, 88,* 770–789.

Cruscoe, A. H., & Wetzel, C. G. (1984). The Midas Touch: The effects of interpersonal touch on restaurant tipping. *Personality and Social Psychology Bulletin, 10,* 512–517.

DeSteno, D., Dasgupta, N., Bartlett, M. Y., & Cajdric, A. (2004). Prejudice from thin air: The effect of emotion on automatic intergroup attitudes. *Psychological Science, 15,* 319–324.

Devine, P. G., & Monteith, M. J. (1993). The role of discrepancy-associated affect in prejudice reduction. In D. M. Mackie & D. L. Hamilton (Eds.), *Affect, cognition, and stereotyping* (pp. 317–344). San Diego: Academic Press.

Dijker, A. J. (1987). Emotional reactions to ethnic minorities. *European Journal of Social Psychology, 17,* 305–325.

Fiske, A. P. (2004). Four modes of constituting relationships: Consubstantial assimilation; space, magnitude, time, and force; concrete procedures; abstract symbolism. In N. Haslam (Ed.), *Relational Models Theory: A contemporary overview* (pp. 61–146). Mahwah, NJ: Lawrence Erlbaum Associates.

Gaertner, S. L., & Dovidio, J. F. (1986). The aversive form of racism. In J. F. Dovidio & S. L. Gaertner (Eds.), *Prejudice, discrimination, and racism* (pp. 61–90). Orlando, FL: Academic Press.

Galinsky, A. D., & Moskowitz, G. B. (2000). Perspective-taking: Decreasing stereotype expression, stereotype accessibility, and in-group favoritism. *Journal of Personality and Social Psychology, 78,* 708–724.

Gross, J. J. (1998). Antecedent- and response-focused emotion regulation: Divergent consequences for experience, expression, and physiology. *Journal of Personality and Social Psychology, 74,* 224–237.

Kluegel, J. R., & Smith, E. R. (1983). Affirmative action attitudes: Effects of self-interest, racial affect, and stratification beliefs on whites' views. *Social Forces, 61,* 797–824.

Kluegel, J. R., & Smith, E. R. (1986). *Beliefs about inequality: Americans' views of what is and what ought to be.* Hawthorne, NY: Aldine de Gruyter.

Lyons, A., & Kashima, Y. (2003). How are stereotypes maintained through communication? The influence of stereotype sharedness. *Journal of Personality and Social Psychology, 85*, 989–1005.

Mackie, D. M., Devos, T., & Smith, E. R. (2000). Intergroup emotions: Explaining offensive action tendencies in an intergroup context. *Journal of Personality and Social Psychology, 79*, 602–616.

Mackie, D. M., Maitner, A., & Smith, E. R. (in press). Intergroup emotions theory. In T. D. Nelson (Ed.), *Handbook of prejudice, stereotyping, and discrimination*. Mahwah, NJ: Lawrence Erlbaum Associates.

Mackie, D. M., Silver, L., & Smith, E. R. (2004). Intergroup emotions: Emotion as an intergroup phenomenon. In: L. Z. Tiedens & C. W. Leach (Eds.), *The social life of emotions* (pp. 227–245). Cambridge, UK: Cambridge University Press.

Maitner, A. T., Mackie, D. M., & Smith, E. R. (2006). Evidence for the regulatory function of intergroup emotion: Emotional consequences of implemented or impeded intergroup action tendencies. *Journal of Experimental Social Psychology, 42*, 720–726.

Mason, W. A., Conrey, F. R., & Smith, E. R. (in press). Situating social influence processes: Dynamic, multidirectional flows of influence within social networks. *Personality and Social Psychology Review*.

Miller, D. A., Smith, E. R., & Mackie, D. M. (2004). Effects of intergroup contact and political predispositions on prejudice: Role of intergroup emotions. *Group Processes and Intergroup Relations, 7*, 221–237.

Pettigrew, T. F. (1958). Personality and sociocultural factors in intergroup attitudes: A cross-national comparison. *Journal of Conflict Resolution, 2*, 29–42.

Pettigrew, T. F. (1997). The affective component of prejudice: Empirical support for the new view. In S. A. Tuch & J. K. Martin (Eds.), *Racial attitudes in the 1990s: Continuity and change* (pp. 76–90). Westport, CT: Praeger.

Pettigrew, T. F. (1998). Intergroup contact theory. *Annual Review of Psychology, 49*, 65–85.

Pettigrew, T. F., & Tropp, L. R. (2006). A meta-analytic test of intergroup contact theory. *Journal of Personality and Social Psychology, 90*, 751–783.

Runciman, W. G. (1966). *Relative deprivation and social justice*. Berkeley, CA: University of California Press.

Scherer, K. R. (1984). Emotion as a multicomponent process: A model and some cross-cultural data. *Review of Personality and Social Psychology, 5*, 37–63.

Seibt, B., Schubert, T. W., Strack, F., Hall, E. P., Seger, C. R., & Smith, E. R. (2006). *Embodied contact: Being touched affects social identification and prejudice*. Manuscript submitted for publication.

Smith, E. R. (1993). Social identity and social emotions: Toward new conceptualizations of prejudice. In D. M. Mackie & D. L. Hamilton (Eds.), *Affect, cognition, and stereotyping: Interactive processes in group perception* (pp. 297–315). San Diego: Academic Press.

Smith, E. R. (1998). Mental representation and memory. In D. Gilbert, S. Fiske, & G. Lindzey (Eds.), *Handbook of social psychology* (pp. 391–445). (4th ed.). New York: McGraw-Hill.

Smith, E. R., & DeCoster, J. (2000). Dual process models in social and cognitive psychology: Conceptual integration and links to underlying memory systems. *Personality and Social Psychology Review, 4*, 108–131.

Smith, E. R., & Kluegel, J. R. (1984). Beliefs and attitudes about women's opportunity: Comparisons with beliefs about blacks and a general perspective. *Social Psychology Quarterly, 47*, 81–95.

Smith, E. R., & Mackie, D. M. (2006). It's about time: Intergroup emotions as time dependent phenomena. In R. Brown & D. Capozza (Eds.), *Social identities: Motivational, emotional, cultural influences* (pp. 173–187). New York: Psychology Press.

Smith, E. R., Seger, C., & Mackie, D. M. (in press). Can emotions be truly group-level? Evidence regarding four conceptual criteria. *Journal of Personality and Social Psychology*.

Smith, E. R., & Semin, G. R. (2004). Socially situated cognition: Cognition in its social context. *Advances in Experimental Social Psychology, 36*, 53–117.

Stephan, W. G., & Stephan, C. W. (1985). Intergroup anxiety. *Journal of Social Issues, 41*, 157–175.

Tajfel, H. (1978). *Differentiation between social groups: Studies in the social psychology of intergroup relations*. London: Academic Press.

Thompson, M. S., Judd, C. M., & Park, B. (2000). The consequences of communicating social stereotypes. *Journal of Experimental Social Psychology, 36*, 567–599.

Tropp, L. R., & Pettigrew, T. F. (2005). Differential relationships between intergroup contact and affective and cognitive dimensions of prejudice. *Personality and Social Psychology Bulletin, 31*, 1145–1158.

Turner, J. C., Hogg, M. A., Oakes, P. J., Reicher, S. D., & Wetherell, M. S. (1987). *Rediscovering the social group: A self-categorization theory*. Oxford: Blackwell.

Vanneman, R. D., & Pettigrew, T. F. (1972). Race and relative deprivation in the urban United States. *Race, 13*, 461–486.

Walker, I., & Pettigrew, T. F. (1984). Relative deprivation theory: An overview and conceptual critique. *British Journal of Social Psychology, 23*, 301–310.

Wright, S. C., Aron, A., McLaughlin-Volpe, T., & Ropp, S. A. (1997). The extended contact effect: Knowledge of cross-group friendships and prejudice. *Journal of Personality and Social Psychology, 73*, 73–90.

Yzerbyt, V. Y., Dumont, M., Wigboldus, D., & Gordijn, E. (2003). I feel for us: The impact of categorization and identification on emotions and action tendencies. *British Journal of Social Psychology, 42*, 533–549.

5

The Role of Threat in Intergroup Relations

Walter G. Stephan, C. Lausanne Renfro, and Mark D. Davis

Intergroup relations researchers have learned a great deal about the causes and consequences of prejudice in the past century. Despite these wide-ranging accomplishments, it is surprising that only in the past decade or so have social scientists begun to take a systematic approach to what now appears to be a major cause of prejudice and other negative aspects of intergroup relations. The major cause to which we refer consists of perceptions of threat. Perhaps threat was over-looked because so much attention in early theorizing about preju-dice focused on personality traits, such as authoritarianism, and more cognitive phenomena, such as stereotyping. An exception to this trend was the work of LeVine and Campbell (1972) on ethnocen-trism. In their book, they discussed threat in the context of relations between nations. It was some time before the relevance of threat to relations between groups within the same nation was recognized. Now, in our rapidly changing world, threats both between and within nations are widely acknowledged—threats from terrorism, threats from immigration, threats arising from social policies favoring one group over others, threats arising from religious, ethnic and cultural differences, and threats due to the clash of civilizations (Brewer & Alexander, 2002; Devos, Silver, Mackie, & Smith, 2002; Greenberg et al., 1990; Neuberg & Cottrell, 2002).

In this chapter we will discuss the relationship between contact theory and threat theory. We follow this discussion with a description of the evolution of our own research program on threat, integrating the work of others where it is relevant. We begin that description with a brief background concerning the constructs of our original threat theory and then present an overview of research on this theory. This is followed by an outline of our revised theory, which broadens the domains of antecedents and consequences of threats that are included and reconceptualizes the threats themselves. Then we will summarize some of the research we have done employing the revised threat theory and make some concluding comments.

Contact Theory and Intergroup Threat Theory Compared

The essence of intergroup threat, as conceptualized in the integrated threat theory, is the expectation that future intergroup relations will be harmful in some way to the ingroup. Intergroup threat theory is closely related to intergroup contact theory in a least two important ways, one concerning structure and the other concerning content.

First, the structure of the two theories is quite similar. In each theory, a central concept (contact, threat) occupies a mediating role between a set of antecedent factors and a set of consequences. In traditional contact theory, it was argued that the outcomes of intergroup contact would be positive under specified conditions. In Allport's (1954) original formulation of the contact hypothesis he argued that, "Prejudice . . . may be reduced by equal status contact between majority and minority groups in pursuit of common goals. The effect is greatly enhanced if this contact is sanctioned by institutional supports . . . and is of the sort that leads to the perception of common interests and common humanity" (p. 267). In his work on contact theory, Pettigrew (Pettigrew, 1960; 1971; 1986; 1998; Pettigrew & Tropp, 2000; 2006) greatly expanded the purview of Allport's contact hypothesis by specifying a number of relevant antecedent factors as well as adding a variety of other potential consequences of contact, particularly affective and behavioral outcomes. In his early work, he was primarily concerned with the roles that societal and situational factors play in determining the effects of contact (Pettigrew, 1960; 1971). Among the societal factors he mentioned were the institutional contexts in which contact occurs, culturally sanctioned levels of prejudice toward minority groups, socialization practices, prior conflict between groups, and racial and ethnic group ratios. In addition to the situational factors specified by Allport (1954), Pettigrew mentioned reference group norms and the similarity of the participants. Moreover, he noted a number of personality factors, such as authoritarianism and the need to conform to social norms. Later, Pettigrew extended contact theory to include negative as well as positive contact and added a temporal dimension because contact unfolds over time (Pettigrew, 1998; Pettigrew & Tropp, 2000). Thus, in Pettigrew's hands, contact theory has focused on the conditions that foster intergroup contact and lead to changes in intergroup relations.

Similarly, in the integrated threat theory it is postulated that a set of antecedent conditions closely related to those specified by Pettigrew lead to perceptions of threat, which in turn have an impact on attitudes, affect, and behavior. The structural parallel between the theories is no accident. In the work that one of us (WGS) carried out with Pettigrew, the interrelationships between the psychological and sociological branches of social psychology were examined (Stephan, Stephan, & Pettigrew, 1991). The importance of taking both approaches to social psychology into account is reflected in contact and threat theory. In particular, the societal context in which contact and perceptions of threat occur occupies a prominent position in both theories.

The second way in which the two theories are related concerns the interrelationships of the two central constructs. In intergroup threat theory, intergroup contact serves as both an antecedent of threat and an outcome of threat. Negative prior contact between members of two groups is one of the antecedent variables that causes people to feel threatened by the outgroup. But it is also the case that feeling threatened can have an impact on future contact between the two groups. Most often threat leads to avoidance of the outgroup, but sometimes it leads to hostile contact (e.g., aggression), and more rarely it leads to positive contact (e.g., conflict resolution, reconciliation). Threat can also have an impact on affect (e.g., fear). Likewise, in contact theory, intergroup threat can be conceptualized as both an antecedent and a consequence of contact. Perceived threat may lead to avoidance or negative contact or it may complicate attempts to create positive contact. As an outcome variable, perceptions of threat are likely to be created by negative contact and lessened by positive contact. Thus, understanding the role of threat in intergroup relations has important implications for contact theory—and vice versa.

The Constructs of Integrated Threat Theory

Next, we consider the basic constructs of the integrated threat theory. There are four types of threat that were included in the original version of the theory: Realistic threats, symbolic threats, intergroup anxiety, and negative stereotypes. The original theory also specified some of the antecedents of these threats. It included only one outcome of threat—prejudice. Prejudice was defined as negative evaluations of outgroups (Stephan, 1985).

Types of Threat

Realistic threats consist of threats to the ingroup's political power, economic power, or physical well-being. *Symbolic threats* are threats to the ingroup's values, beliefs, or worldview. People experience *intergroup anxiety* when they anticipate negative outcomes during inter-group interaction (Stephan & Stephan, 1985). In such interactions, people are often concerned about being exploited, physically harmed, or being met with disapproval from either outgroup or ingroup members. Stereotypes simplify a complex social world by providing guidelines for social interactions and furnishing explanations for the behavior of outgroups. They are also used to justify the behavior of the ingroup and enhance group-based self-esteem. *Negative stereotypes* lead people to expect outgroup members to behave in ways that may be harmful to the ingroup and for this reason negative stereotypes are considered to be threats to the ingroup.

Antecedents of Threat

The original integrated threat theory also included four antecedents of threat. First, *strong identification* with the ingroup can create perceptions of threat because people who are strongly attached to the ingroup have more to lose if their ingroup is harmed. Second, *negative personal contact* with outgroup members can lead to threat because people may infer that future contacts might also have negative outcomes. Third, a *history of conflict* between the groups may lead to the perception of threat. Fourth, substantial *disparities in the status* between the two groups may lead members of both the dominant and the subordinate group to experience a heightened sense of threat. The dominant group might feel threatened by the potential loss of its power and privileges, whereas the subordinate group may feel threatened because it anticipates being exploited.

Support for the Original Theory

The integrated threat theory has now been examined using a wide range of target groups. In general, these studies provide strong support for the model. For instance, one of the first studies on the theory examined the threats posed by Mexican, Asian, and Cuban immigrants to the United States (Stephan, Ybarra, & Bachman, 1999). All four threats were significant predictors of prejudice for each of the three types of immigrant groups. The four predictors accounted for an average of 60% of the variance in attitudes toward these immigrant groups.

Across the various studies in which they have been included, all four antecedents have been found to be related to threats. For instance, one study examined the attitudes of Whites and Blacks in the United States (Stephan et al., 2002). For Whites, it was found that realistic threat, symbolic threat, and intergroup anxiety mediated the effects of negative personal contact, ingroup identification, and perceived intergroup conflict on their attitudes toward Blacks. Symbolic threats and intergroup anxiety mediated the effects of status differences on attitudes. Taken together with the other studies on the antecedents of threat, it appears that: (1) negative contact is a very strong predictor of threat (Corenblum & Stephan, 2001; Stephan, Stephan, Demitrakis, Yamada, & Clason, 2000; Stephan et al., 2002); (2) strength of ingroup identity is often a significant predictor of threat (Corenblum & Stephan, 2001; Stephan et al., 2002; Renfro, Duran, Stephan, & Clayson, 2006); and (3) a history of conflict and perceived disparities in status are less frequently significant predictors of threat (Stephan et al., 2002).

The literature on the integrated threat theory and related threat studies has been recently subjected to meta-analysis by Riek, Mania, and Gaertner (2006). The target outgroups included Blacks and Whites, men and women, Mexicans and Americans, Native Canadians and Anglo Canadians, immigrants to the United States, Canada, Israel, and Europe, AIDS victims, victims of terminal cancer, obese people, gays, religious and political outgroups, and the beneficiaries of affirmative action. Riek et al. (2006) found that across 95 samples representing 37,000 participants, all four threats were solid predictors of intergroup attitudes. They also found that identification with the ingroup was a consistent predictor of the threat variables. The status of the ingroup was a consistent moderator of the relationship between the threats and prejudice: Groups that were higher in social status displayed a stronger relationship between the threats and prejudice than did groups that were lower in social status.

In addition to these correlational studies, a number of experimental laboratory studies have manipulated threats and assessed their effects on prejudice (Branscombe & Wann, 1994; Esses, Jackson, &

Armstrong, 1998; Esses Jackson, Nolan, & Armstrong et al., 1999; Maio, Esses, & Bell, 1994; Stephan, Renfro, Esses, Stephan, & Martin, 2005). These studies have helped to establish the role that threats play in causing prejudice. For example, one set of experimental studies manipulated realistic threats, symbolic threats, intergroup anxiety, and negative stereotypes and found that all four types of threats cause prejudice toward immigrant groups (Stephan et al., 2005).

Revised Threat Theory

Although the original version of the theory was well supported in the studies conducted on it, over time these studies revealed some short-comings of the theory. There were problems in conceptualizing the types of threat, while the number of antecedents and consequences was too limited. These concerns led to a revision of the original threat theory (Stephan & Renfro, 2002). The goals of the revised theory were to expand the range of the theory and bring greater conceptual clarity to the concepts included in it.

Types of Threat

In the revised theory, the basic distinction between realistic and symbolic threats was retained (see Figure 5.1). The revised theory, however, made a distinction between threats to the ingroup as a whole and threats to individual members of the ingroup. *Realistic group threats* are threats to the group's power, resources, and general welfare. *Symbolic group threats* are threats to the group's religion, cultural

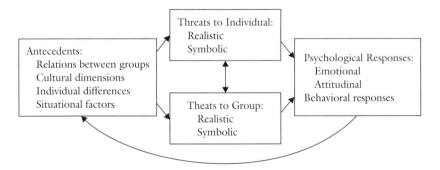

Figure 5.1   Revised model of the integrated threat theory.

values, belief systems, ideology, philosophy, morality, or worldview. *Realistic individual threats* concern actual physical or material harm to the individual such as pain, torture, or death as well as economic loss, deprivation of valued resources, and threats to health or personal security. *Symbolic individual threats* concern loss of face or honor and undermining self-identity or self-esteem.

In the original theory, negative stereotypes could refer to either individual or group threats (e.g., the outgroup's "aggressiveness" could be directed at me or my group). Thus, if stereotypes were to be included when using the revised theory, it would be necessary to specify whether the threats were experienced at the individual or group level. Similarly, if intergroup anxiety were to be included, it would be necessary to indicate whether the threats are experienced at the symbolic or realistic level. That is, is the person anxious because their values are being challenged or because their welfare is in jeopardy?

Antecedents of Threat

The revised theory expands the domains of antecedent variables that can influence the perception of threats from outgroups. The four domains now included are: Relations between groups, individual difference variables, dimensions of cultural (or group) difference, and situational factors:

- *Relations between groups*: The original theory included intergroup conflict and status inequalities as intergroup relations variables. The revised theory adds the size of the outgroup relative to the ingroup in a given society (Cornielle, Yzerbyt, Rogier, & Buidin, 2001).
- *Individual difference variables*: The original theory included strength of ingroup identity and negative personal contact as individual difference variables. The revised theory adds social dominance orientation (Esses et al., 1998; Sidanius & Pratto, 1999) and self-esteem (Luhtanen & Crocker, 1992).
- *Cultural dimensions*: The revised theory also includes a new domain of antecedents: cultural variables that can influence perceived threats. Among the cultural variables included in the revised theory are individualism/collectivism (Triandis, 1995), power distance (Hofstede, 1980) and uncertainty avoidance (Gudykunst, 1995; Hofstede, 1980; 1991).
- *Situational factors*: A second domain of new variables consists of situational factors that affect perceptions of threat. In the revised

theory, the threats are thought to be highly dynamic, changing across situations and over time. Contact theory suggests a number of situational variables that may influence perceived threats (Pettigrew, 1998; Pettigrew & Tropp, 2000; 2006), including the setting in which the intergroup interaction occurs, the degree to which the interaction is structured, the extent to which norms exist for intergroup relations, the ratio of ingroup and outgroup members in the particular context, the goals of the interaction, the status of ingroup and outgroup members in the context, the degree of support for the interaction from relevant authority figures, and the cooperative or competitive nature of the interaction.

Consequences of Threat

In addition to prejudice, the revised theory posits a number of other potential outcomes. The consequences may be either psychological or behavioral in nature (Leung & Stephan, 1998). Psychological reactions are largely internal and may consist of both cognitive and affective reactions. Cognitive responses could include changes in outgroup stereotypes, perceived homogeneity, or opposition to policies favoring the outgroup. Emotional reactions could include fear, anger, resentment, or helplessness. Behavioral responses could include withdrawal, submission, negotiation, aggression, retaliation, protests, strikes, class action lawsuits, warfare, or other forms of open intergroup conflict.

The revised model is circular. That is, psychological and behavioral consequences of threat have an impact on future relations between groups by influencing the variables considered to be "antecedents" of threat. For instance, if people respond to threats by acting aggressively toward the outgroup, their actions will become a component of their subsequent perceptions of "prior intergroup conflict" and have an impact on perceptions of threat and the outcomes of these threats and so on.

Research on the Revised Model

The terrorist attacks on the World Trade Towers in New York on September 11, 2001 provided an opportunity to examine the distinction made in the revised theory between group and individual threats. In the context of the terrorist attacks, group threats concern threats to the American economy and system of government, as well as threats to the American way of life. Individual threats concern the worries people had about their own safety as well as the challenges posed to their values and beliefs by Muslim fundamentalism.

The study of the 9/11 attacks focused primarily on the emotional, attitudinal, and behavioral consequences of threat (Renfro & Stephan, 2002). It was anticipated that people who perceived high levels of threat would respond with negative emotions and negative attitudes which would lead them to advocate harsh retaliatory measures against the attackers. It was expected that individual threats would cause people to be concerned about their own welfare leading them to turn their attention inward, whereas group threats would turn people's attention outward toward a concern for their ingroup as a whole. Thus, it was hypothesized that individual threats would be related to inwardly directed emotions, such as helplessness or fear, while group threats would be related to outwardly directed emotions, such as anger and resentment. It was also expected that people who had the most negative attitudes toward militant Muslim fundamentalists and exhibited more outwardly directed emotions would advocate that strong retaliatory actions be taken against the terrorists. The retaliatory actions measured in the study included such responses as attacking terrorist base camps, undermining governments that harbored terrorists, and expelling militant Muslim fundamentalists from the United States.

A structural equation model was used to test these ideas. The variables in this model accounted for 27% of the variance in the harshness of the actions advocated against militant Muslims fundamentalists. The results showed that feelings of helplessness partially mediated the relationship between perceived individual threats and advocating strong retaliatory actions (see Figure 5.2). The greater the individual threat, the greater the feelings of helplessness. Stronger feelings of helplessness were associated with advocating *less* harsh retaliatory actions, perhaps because people who were feeling helpless were concerned that harsh retaliatory actions would not prevent further attacks. To a lesser degree, anger and negative attitudes toward militant Muslim fundamentalists also mediated the relationship between perceived individual threats and retaliatory actions. As perceived threats increased, so too did anger and negative attitudes, which in turn were related to the harshness of the retaliatory actions advocated. In addition, individual threats were directly related to the harshness of the retaliatory actions advocated. The effects of group threats on retaliatory actions were mediated only by negative attitudes. In this case, the greater the perceived threats, the more negative the attitudes. Negative attitudes were then associated with advocating harsher retaliatory actions.

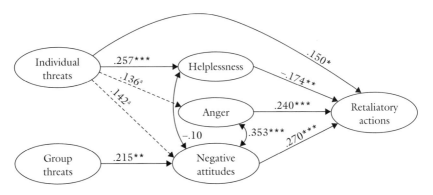

Figure 5.2   Structural equation model of responses to 9/11.
Note: a = p < .10, * = p < .05, ** = p < .01, *** = p < .001.

The results of this study provided considerable support for the construct validity of the distinction between individual and group threats. Specifically, each type of threat had a separate effect on attitudes, while only individual threats were related to emotions.

Laboratory Study of Threats and Emotions

The next study was conducted to replicate the finding that individual threats are associated with inwardly directed emotions and to try again to find evidence that group threats are associated with outwardly directed emotions (Davis & Stephan, 2005). This study employed videotaped footage of the terrorist attacks of 9/11 to examine American students' emotional responses to threat. The video was three minutes in duration. It was broken into six segments that alternated between actual footage of the attacks and non-action footage of news coverage of the events. Participants in the study were asked to view videotapes of the attacks under one of two instructional sets. One set of instructions was designed to invoke group threats by leading the participants to identify with how Americans felt about these events, while the other was designed to invoke individual threats by leading them to process these events in terms of their own individual reactions to these events.

Emotional reactions were assessed by facial electromyography (EMG) which measures the reactivity of muscles in the face. EMG is an effective technique to assess the emotions people initially register in response to a stimulus (Tassinary & Cacioppo, 2000). In this study, the facial muscles associated with fear (frontalis) and anger

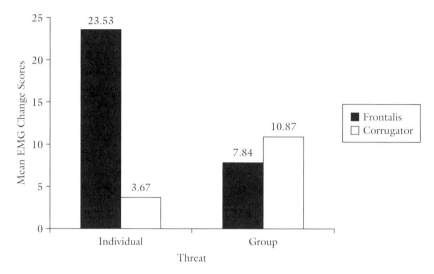

Figure 5.3 Electromyographic analyses of responses to 9/11 videos.

(corrugator) were examined. It was expected that people would display more anger than fear in the group threat condition, whereas they would display more fear than anger in the individual threat condition. The results supported these predictions (see Figure 5.3). One explanation for this difference in emotional responses to group vs. individual threats is the adaptiveness of these responses. The chances of responding successfully to a hostile outgroup are greater for a group than they would be for an individual ingroup member acting alone. When an individual is feeling threatened by an outgroup (even vicariously, as in this study) it may be more adaptive to respond with fear because fear is likely to lead to avoidance. On the other hand, when the entire ingroup has been threatened, anger may be a more adaptive response because it can lead to mobilizing the ingroup to respond to the threat. The results of this study also validate the distinction between individual and group threats since the two types of threat displayed different patterns of effects on emotions.

Attitudes Toward Women

A subsequent test of the revised threat theory examined the four threats as predictors of men's attitudes toward women as well as the roles that hostile and benevolent sexism may play as mediators between the perceived threats posed by women and men's attitudes toward women (Renfro & Stephan, 2005). Attitudes between the sexes are an atypical case of intergroup relations because individual men and women have intimate relations with one another at the same time that relations between these groups are characterized by status inequalities and a long history of gender discrimination. The ambivalent feelings between the sexes (hostility on the one hand and benevolence on the other) have been the subject of a considerable number of recent investigations in the United States and elsewhere around the world (Glick, 2006). It was expected that the four threats would be positively related to hostile components of sexism. The relationships of the threats to benevolent sexism were expected to be inconsistent because benevolent sexism contains both positive feelings toward women (cherishing them) and condescending and paternalistic feelings toward women. We also expected to find, as did Glick and Fiske (1996), that hostile sexism was more closely related to negative attitudes toward women than benevolent sexism.

To examine the relationships among the variables, structural equation modeling was employed. Our model examined the two dimensions of ambivalent sexism (hostile and benevolent) as mediators of the relationship between the four threat variables (realistic-individual threats, symbolic-individual threats, realistic-group threats, symbolic-group threats) and attitudes toward women (see Figure 5.4).

The variables in this model accounted for 45% of the variance in a sample of college males' attitudes toward women. The values for the comparative fit index (.99) and the goodness of fit index (.99)

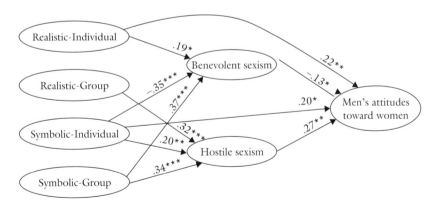

Figure 5.4 Structural equation model of men's attitudes toward women. *Note:* * = p < .05, ** = p < .01, *** = p < .001.

suggest a good fit between the data and the model. The effects of three of the four threat variables on attitudes toward women were mediated by hostile sexism: Realistic-group threats, symbolic-group threats, and symbolic-individual threats. In each case, the greater the perceived threat the higher the participants scored on hostile sexism. Higher levels of hostile sexism were associated with more negative attitudes toward women. The results also indicated that both of the individual threat variables (realistic-individual threats and symbolic-individual threats) had a direct effect on negative attitudes toward women.

Benevolent sexism also mediated the relationship between three of the threats (symbolic-individual, symbolic-group and realistic-individual) and negative attitudes toward women, but as anticipated, these relationships were complex. The greater the perceived symbolic-individual threat, the less benevolent the men's perceptions of women were. Low levels of benevolent sexism were associated with more negative attitudes toward women. Symbolic-individual threats were also directly related to negative attitudes toward women. In essence, these results suggest that men whose masculinity is threatened by women have less paternalistic, but more negative, attitudes toward them. For symbolic-group and realistic-individual threats, the greater the perceived threat, the *more* benevolent their perceptions of women were— suggesting that these types of threat make men feel condescending and paternalistic toward women which leads them to hold less negative attitudes toward them. The complex relationships between the threats and benevolent sexism help to understand the sometimes extreme positive and negative behaviors men display toward women—from adoration on the one hand to violence on the other. As Katz, Wackenhut, and Hass (1986) have argued, ambivalence leads to amplified responses to outgroups—both negative and positive ones.

The results of this study suggest that the four types of threat in the revised model have distinct relationships to attitudes toward women and thus they provide additional evidence for the construct validity of the threats. Specifically, the two individual threats were directly related to men's attitudes toward women, while the group threats were not. In addition, both hostile and benevolent sexism mediated the effects of three types of threat on men's attitudes toward women.

Concluding Comments

There is one other important contribution that contact theory can make to threat theory. Contact theory can contribute to understanding the circumstances under which intergroup threats can be reduced. The conditions specified in Allport's contact hypothesis and those revealed in Pettigrew's research and theorizing on contact would seem to be ideally suited to reducing perceived intergroup threats. In particular, the idea of experiencing a sense of shared humanity and pursuing common interests should undercut all four types of threat. Similarly, the opportunity to become acquainted with outgroup members on an individual basis should reduce individual symbolic and realistic threats. All three of these conditions are present in cooperative learning groups as they are implemented in classrooms in a wide variety of countries (see Stephan & Stephan, 2001 for a review of this and other techniques of improving intergroup relations). This intervention technique typically involves students working together on standard curriculum materials that have been adapted for use by small mixed groups of students working cooperatively to prepare for examinations. Cooperative learning groups may not be as effective in reducing group-based realistic threats, except perhaps by reducing stereotypes of outgroups. This type of threat may be addressed more effectively by another type of intervention program—dialogue groups. This technique is most often used with mixed groups of students who are somewhat older than the students involved in cooperative learning groups. These groups involve students talking directly to members of outgroups about intergroup relations issues and conflicts, under the supervision of trained facilitators and following a set of guidelines for interaction. Consistent with contact theory, in both cooperative learning groups and intergroup dialogues, attempts are made to equalize the status of the participants, attention is paid to maintaining equal ratios of participants across groups, and strong institutional support is provided for intergroup contact. In addition, the interactions among the participants are somewhat structured, but not formal. Norms favoring respectful intergroup interactions are also emphasized and the facilitators work to create a safe, non-threatening environment. Unfortunately, to our knowledge no research has been conducted examining the effects of cooperative learning groups, dialogue groups, or other related techniques (e.g., intercultural relations training, multicultural education, conflict resolution training) on intergroup threat and its consequences.

In addition to a need for research on techniques of reducing threat, more research is needed to understand the complex relations between various categories of antecedents and their effects. For instance, how do structural factors interact with situational factors to increase or decrease threat? Are people from some types of cultural backgrounds or with certain types of personality characteristics more likely to perceive that they are threatened by outgroups? Similarly, do different antecedent factors work through different mediating variables (i.e. types of threat) to affect different types of outcomes of threat (affective, cognitive, or behavioral)? For example, do people from collectivistic cultures who are placed in cooperative learning groups experience less individual realistic threat and consequently less fear than people from individualistic cultures who participate in such groups? Ultimately, it would be desirable to know what types of people from which types of cultures or groups benefit most from which types of interventions—and why.

And finally, to end on a more personal note, we applaud Tom Pettigrew for his role in helping to create a discipline. When Pettigrew started writing, there were a very small handful of specialists in race relations in sociology and a few psychologists who wrote about prejudice and stereotyping. But Pettigrew and others with similar interests created the field of intergroup relations. And it was not simply his insights into intergroup contact and its causes and consequences that helped to create this discipline, but also his steadfast adherence to the importance of structural issues in intergroup relations, his championing of school desegregation, and his basic research into intergroup phenomena.

Pettigrew has been a gadfly in two disciplines—a sort of multi-disciplinary scourge. He has chastised Southerners for their prejudices, presidents for their policies, sociologists for the refusal to acknowledge the importance of psychological factors, and psychologists for their refusal to acknowledge the importance of sociological factors. He loves to point out the error of our ways. He even named one of his basic research findings the ultimate attribution error (Pettigrew, 1979). But he has done this all in good spirits, with unflagging enthusiasm, and a work ethic that would not quit. In fact, he has not even been able to allow himself to retire, which has been to all our benefit.

References

Allport, G. W. (1954). *The nature of prejudice*. Reading, MA: Addison-Wesley.

Branscombe, N. R., & Wann, D. L. (1994). Collective self-esteem consequences of outgroup derogation when a valued social identity is on trial. *European Journal of Social Psychology, 24*, 641–657.

Brewer, M. B., & Alexander, M. G. (2002). Intergroup emotions and images. In D. M. Mackie & E. R. Smith (Eds.), *From prejudice to intergroup emotions* (pp. 209–225). New York: Psychology Press.

Corenblum, B., & Stephan, W. G. (2001). White fears and native apprehensions: An integrated threat theory approach to intergroup attitudes. *Canadian Journal of Behavioral Science*, *33*, 251–268.

Cornielle, O., Yzerbyt, V. Y., Rogier, A., & Buidin, G. (2001). Threat and the group attribution error: When threat elicits judgments of extremity and homogeneity. *Personality and Social Psychology Bulletin*, *27*, 437–446.

Davis, M., & Stephan, W. G. (2005). *Electromyographic analyses of responses to intergroup threat.* Poster presented at Association for Psychological Science meeting, Los Angeles.

Devos, T., Silver, L. A., Mackie, D. M., & Smith, E. R. (2002). Experiencing emotions. In D. M. Mackie & E. R. Smith (Eds.), *From prejudice to intergroup emotions* (pp. 111–134). New York: Psychology Press.

Esses, V. M., Jackson, L. M., & Armstrong, T. L. (1998). Intergroup competition and attitudes toward immigrants and immigration: An instrumental model of group conflict. *Journal of Social Issues*, *54*, 699–724.

Esses, V. M., Jackson, L. M., Nolan, J. M., & Armstrong, T. L. (1999). Emotional threat and attitudes toward immigrants. In L. Halli and L. Drieger (Eds.), *Immigrant Canada: Demographic, economic, and social challenges* (pp. 202–229). Toronto: University of Toronto Press.

Glick, P. (2006). Ambivalent sexism, power distance, and gender inequality across cultures. In S. Guimond (Ed.), *Social comparison and social psychology: Understanding cognition, intergroup relations, and culture* (pp. 283–302). New York: Cambridge University Press.

Glick, P., & Fiske, S. T. (1996). The ambivalent sexism inventory: Differentiating hostile and benevolent sexism. *Journal of Personality and Social Psychology*, *70*, 491–512.

Greenberg, J., Pyszczynski, T., Solomon, S., Rosenblatt, A., Veeder, M., Kirkland, S., et al. (1990). Evidence for terror management theory II: The effects of mortality salience on reactions to those who threaten or bolster the cultural worldview. *Journal of Personality and Social Psychology*, *58*, 308–318.

Gudykunst, W. B. (1995). Anxiety/uncertainty management (AUM) theory: Development and current status. In R. L. Wiseman (Ed.), *Intercultural communication theory* (pp. 8–51). Thousand Oaks, CA: Sage.

Hofstede, G. (1980). *Cultures consequences.* Beverly Hills: Sage.

Hofstede, G. (1991). *Cultures and organizations.* London: McGraw-Hill.

Katz, I., Wackenhut, J., & Hass, R. G. (1986). *Racial ambivalence, value duality, and behavior.* In J. F. Dovidio & S. L. Gaertner (Eds.), *Prejudice, discrimination, and racism* (pp. 61–90). San Diego, CA: Academic Press.

Leung, K., & Stephan, W. G. (1998). Perceptions of injustice in intercultural relations. *Applied and Preventive Psychology*, *7*, 195–205.

LeVine, R. A., & Campbell, D. T. (1972). *Ethnocentrism: Theories of conflict, ethnic attitudes, and group behavior.* New York: Wiley.

Luhtanen, R., & Crocker, J. (1992). A collective self-esteem scale: Self-evaluation of one's own identity. *Personality and Social Psychology Bulletin*, *18*, 302–318.

Maio, G. R., Esses, V. M., & Bell, D. W. (1994). The formation of attitudes toward new immigrant groups. *Journal of Applied Social Psychology, 24,* 1762–1776.

Neuberg, S. L., & Cottrell, C. A. (2002). Intergroup emotions: A bicultural approach. In D. M. Mackie & E. R. Smith (Eds.), *From prejudice to intergroup emotions* (pp. 265–283). New York: Psychology Press.

Pettigrew, T. F. (1960). Social distance attitudes of South African students. *Social Forces, 38,* 246–253.

Pettigrew, T. F. (1971). *Racially separate or together?* New York: McGraw-Hill.

Pettigrew, T. F. (1979). The ultimate attribution error: Extending Allport's cognitive analysis of prejudice. *Personality and Social Psychology Bulletin, 5,* 461–476.

Pettigrew, T. F. (1986). The contact hypothesis revisited. In M. Hewstone & R. Brown (Eds.), *Contact and conflict in intergroup encounters* (pp. 169–195). Oxford: Blackwell.

Pettigrew, T. F. (1998). Intergroup contact theory. *Annual Review of Psychology, 49,* 65–85.

Pettigrew, T. F., & Tropp, L. (2000). Does intergroup contact reduce prejudice? Recent meta-analytic findings. In S. Oskamp (Ed.), *Reducing prejudice and discrimination: Social psychological perspectives* (pp. 93–114). Mahwah, NJ: Erlbaum.

Pettigrew, T. F., & Tropp, L. (2006). A meta-analytic test of intergroup contact theory. *Journal of Personality and Social Psychology, 90,* 1–33.

Renfro, C. L., Duran, A., Stephan, W. G., & Clason, D. L. (2006). The role of threat in attitudes toward affirmative action and its beneficiaries. *Journal of Applied Social Psychology, 36,* 41–74.

Renfro, C. L., & Stephan, W. G. (2002, June). *Psychological reactions to the threats posed by the terrorist attacks of 9/11.* Paper presented at the convention of the Society for the Psychological Study of Social Issues.

Renfro, C. L., & Stephan, W. G. (2005). *The role of threats in men's attitudes toward women.* Unpublished manuscript, New Mexico State University.

Riek, B. M., Mania, E. W., & Gaertner, S. L. (2006). Intergroup threat and outgroup attitudes: A meta-analytic review. *Personality and Social Psychology Review, 10,* 336–353.

Sidanius, J., & Pratto, F. (1999). *Social dominance: An intergroup theory of social hierarchy and oppression.* Cambridge: Cambridge University Press.

Stephan, W. G. (1985). Intergroup relations. In G. Lindzey & E. Aronson (Eds.), *Handbook of social psychology. Vol. 3* (pp. 599–658). New York: Addison-Wesley.

Stephan, W. G., Boniecki, K. A., Ybarra, O., Bettencourt, A., Ervin, K. S., Jackson, L. A., et al. (2002). Racial attitudes of Blacks and Whites: An integrated threat theory analysis. *Personality and Social Psychology Bulletin, 28,* 1242–1254.

Stephan, W. G., Renfro, C. L., Esses, V. M., Stephan, C. W., & Martin, T. (2005). The effects of feeling threatened on attitudes toward immigrants. *International Journal of Intercultural Relations, 29*, 1–19.

Stephan, W. G., & Stephan, C. W. (1985). Intergroup anxiety. *Journal of Social Issues, 41*, 157–175.

Stephan, W. G., & Renfro, C. L. (2002). The role of threat in intergroup relations. In D. M. Mackie & E. R. Smith (Eds.), *From prejudice to intergroup emotions: Differentiated reactions to social groups* (pp. 191–207). New York, NY: Psychology Press.

Stephan, W. G., & Stephan, C. W. (2001). *Improving intergroup relations.* Thousand Oaks, CA: Sage.

Stephan, C. W., Stephan, W. G., Demitrakis, K., Yamada, A. M., & Clason, D. (2000). Women's attitudes toward men: An integrated threat theory analysis. *Psychology of Women Quarterly, 24*, 63–73.

Stephan, C. W., Stephan, W. G., & Pettigrew, T. F. (Eds.) (1991). *The future of social psychology: Defining the relationships between sociology and psychology.* New York: Springer-Verlag.

Stephan, W. G., Ybarra, O., & Bachman, G. (1999). Prejudice toward immigrants: An integrated threat theory. *Journal of Applied Social Psychology, 29*, 2221–2237.

Tassinary, L. G., & Cacioppo, J. T. (2000). The skeletomotor system: Surface electromyography. In J. T. Cacioppo, L. G. Tassinary, & G. G. Berntson (Eds.), *Handbook of psychophysiology*, 2nd ed. (pp. 163–199), New York: Cambridge University Press.

Triandis, H. C. (1995). *Individualism and collectivism.* Boulder, CO: Westview.

Part II

Functions of Intergroup Contact in Improving Intergroup Relations

6

From When to Why

Understanding How Contact Reduces Bias

John F. Dovidio, Samuel L. Gaertner,
Tamar Saguy, and Samer Halabi

For the past 50 years, intergroup contact theory (Allport, 1954) has represented one of psychology's most effective strategies for improving intergroup relations. This framework proposes that it is possible to structure intergroup contact in specifiable ways to ameliorate intergroup prejudice and conflict. In the present chapter, we examine the critical ideas that have shaped intergroup contact theory, including the seminal conceptual and empirical contributions made by Thomas Pettigrew.

In his presentation of the "contact hypothesis," Allport (1954) integrated and refined a range of ideas and evidence from different disciplines to identify when intergroup contact can most effectively reduce intergroup bias. Allport's reformulation of intergroup contact theory included four prerequisite features for contact to be successful at reducing intergroup conflict and achieving intergroup harmony. These four features are: (1) equal status within the contact situation; (2) intergroup cooperation; (3) common goals; and (4) support of authorities, law, or custom.

Since Allport's (1954) formulation, contact theory has received extensive empirical attention. In fact, interest appears to be escalating (see Dovidio, Gaertner, & Kawakami, 2003), probably in part from the recognition of the robustness of the benefits of intergroup contact on attitudes between groups. Pettigrew and Tropp (2006) have provided an extensive meta-analysis of 515 studies involving 713 independent samples, conducted in a variety of intergroup contexts, testing the effects of intergroup contact on attitudes. Their findings demonstrated that intergroup contact indeed reduces intergroup prejudice (mean $r = -.215$). Furthermore, Pettigrew and Tropp found that the beneficial effect of contact was greater when Allport's optimal conditions were present in the contact situation than when they were not (mean $r = -.287$ vs. mean $r = -.204$).

Building on the widely recognized formulation of the "contact hypothesis" by his mentor, Gordon Allport, Pettigrew has significantly extended research on contact theory not only by extensively documenting the effectiveness of contact for reducing intergroup bias but also by considering how contact functions to reduce intergroup bias. The current chapter first considers potential mediating mechanisms and illustrates how the psychological processes that underlie the effects of contact have far-reaching theoretical and practical implications. After that, we consider moderating factors and demonstrate evidence suggesting new directions in intergroup contact research. We draw on Pettigrew's uniquely valuable insights and evidence within and across these sections. We conclude by identifying promising directions for future work.

Psychological Processes Underlying the Effects of Contact

Recent approaches have considered the role of basic group processes, such as social categorization, for understanding the nature of intergroup biases and ways to reduce them. From a social categorization perspective, one universal facet of human perception essential for efficient functioning is the ability to sort people, spontaneously and with minimum effort or awareness, into a smaller number of meaningful categories (Brewer, 1988; see also Fiske, Lin, & Neuberg, 1999). Social categorization further involves a basic distinction between the group containing the self, the ingroup, and other groups, the outgroups— between the "wes" and the "theys" (see Social Identity Theory, Tajfel & Turner, 1979; Self-Categorization Theory, Turner, Hogg, Oakes, Reicher, & Wetherell, 1987).

When social identity is salient, the distinction between ingroup and outgroup members has a profound influence on social perception, affect, cognition, and behavior (see Gaertner & Dovidio, 2000 for a review). Perceptually, when people or objects are categorized into groups, differences between the groups become magnified, and members of the other group are seen as more similar to one another. Emotionally, people react spontaneously more positively to other members of the ingroup than to members of the outgroup. Cognitively, people retain more information, particularly positive information, about ingroup members than about outgroup members. And behaviorally, people are more prosocially oriented toward ingroup members than toward outgroup members. Thus, although the functional nature of the relations between groups can further influence the degree to which discrimination is manifested, the process of social categorization itself provides the basis for social biases to develop and to be maintained.

Social categorization is a dynamic process, however, and people possess many different group identities and are capable of focusing on different social categories. By modifying a perceiver's goals, motives, perceptions of past experiences, and expectations, there is opportunity to alter the level of category inclusiveness that will be primary or most influential in a given situation. This malleability of the level at which impressions are formed is important because of its implications for altering the way people think about members of ingroups and outgroups, and consequently about the nature of intergroup relations. Attempts to combat these biases can, therefore, be directed at altering the nature of social categorization.

Two such approaches are decategorization and recategorization. Decategorization refers to influencing whether people identify themselves primarily as group members or as distinct individuals (Brewer & Miller, 1984; Wilder, 1981). Recategorization, in contrast, is not designed to reduce or eliminate categorization, but rather to restructure or redefine the nature of group categorization to reduce intergroup bias (Allport, 1954; see Gaertner & Dovidio, 2000).

In each case, reducing the salience of the original group boundaries is expected to decrease intergroup bias. With decategorization, group boundaries are degraded, inducing members of different groups to conceive of themselves and others as separate individuals (Wilder, 1981) and encouraging more personalized interactions. In personalized interactions, people focus on the unique qualities of the individual rather than on their membership in a particular group, thereby further reducing category-based biases (Brewer & Miller, 1984; see also Miller, 2002).

With recategorization, as proposed by the Common Ingroup Identity Model (Gaertner & Dovidio, 2000), the goal is to alter systematically the perception of intergroup boundaries, redefining who is conceived of as an ingroup member, to reduce bias. If members of different groups are induced to conceive of themselves as part of a single more inclusive, superordinate group, rather than just as two completely separate groups, attitudes toward former outgroup members would be expected to become more positive through processes involving proingroup bias, thereby reducing intergroup bias. That is, the processes that lead to favoritism toward ingroup members would now be directed toward former outgroup members (see Gaertner & Dovidio, 2000). Perceptions of common ingroup identity can be achieved by increasing the salience of existing common superordinate memberships (e.g., a school, a company, a nation) or by making salient new elements that redefine group relations (e.g., common goals or shared fate).

We have examined the different ways that decategorization and recategorization strategies can reduce bias. In one experiment (Gaertner, Mann, Murrell, & Dovidio, 1989), members of two separate laboratory-formed groups were induced through various structural interventions (e.g., seating arrangement) either to decategorize themselves (i.e., conceive of themselves as separate individuals) or to recategorize themselves as one superordinate group. Supporting the proposed value of altering the level of category inclusiveness, both of these changes in the perceptions of intergroup boundaries reduced intergroup bias—but they did so in different ways. Decategorizing members of the two groups reduced bias by decreasing the attractiveness of former ingroup members. In contrast, recategorizing ingroup and outgroup members as members of a more inclusive group reduced bias by increasing the attractiveness of the former outgroup members. Across a number of studies, involving both laboratory groups and more enduring groups, we have found consistent evidence that many of the key features specified by contact theory (e.g., cooperative interdependence, equal status) operate, at least in part, through the mechanism of transforming people's representations of others from "us" versus "them" to a more inclusive "we" (see Gaertner & Dovidio, 2000).

Yet, because membership in particular groups satisfies many psychological and material needs, people may often resist interventions designed to make superordinate group identity primarily salient. Pre-existing socialstructural relations between groups may also create strong barriers to changes in category boundaries. Even in the absence of overt conflict, asymmetries between social groups in size, power, or status create additional sources of resistance.

These challenges to processes of decategorization/recategorization led Hewstone and Brown (1986) to recommend an alternative approach to intergroup contact wherein cooperative interactions between groups are introduced without degrading the original ingroup–outgroup categorization (see also Brown & Hewstone, 2005). More specifically, this approach, Mutual Intergroup Differentiation, involves encouraging groups working together to perceive complementarity by recognizing and valuing mutual assets and weaknesses within the context of an interdependent cooperative task or common, super-ordinate goals. In this way, both groups can maintain positive distinctiveness within a cooperative framework.

Recognizing the potential for threat to subgroup identities, we have noted that recategorization can take two forms. First, two distinct social entities can be combined to form a single superordinate category, that is, one inclusive group. Alternatively, members can recategorize people within a "dual identity," in which they maintain recognition of initial subgroup identities within the context of a superordinate category (Gaertner & Dovidio, 2000; Gaertner et al., 1989). Whereas a dual identity within the Common Ingroup Identity Model (Gaertner & Dovidio, 2000) involves the simultaneous activation of subgroup and superordinate group representations, the Mutual Intergroup Differentiation Model focuses on the activation of subgroup identities in the context of a positive functional relationship, cooper-ative interdependence.

Rather then viewing decategorization, recategorization, and mutual intergroup differentiation as competing approaches, they may be seen as complementary perspectives. Thus, it may be particularly useful, theoretically and practically, to move beyond arguments about which process is stronger or more influential to consider *when* each strategy is most effective.

Pettigrew (1998; see also Hewstone, 1996) emphasized the importance of considering the effects of these different processes longitudinally, examining how these different processes can operate in complementary ways sequentially. He posited that intergroup interaction under the conditions proposed in intergroup contact theory might initially produce decategorized representations of the participating members, which results in a lessening of anxiety, reduced perceptions of threat, greater liking, and enhanced oppor-tunities for personalized exchanges. Then, because of the greater resources involved in maintaining individuated rather than group rep-resentations (Brewer, 1988; Fiske et al., 1999), along with other salient cues in the environment, salient categorization may be reinstated but now in the context of positive interdependence. With salient group representations, the benefits of contact are likely to generalize beyond those involved in the contact setting, because the outgroup members present are now directly associated with the outgroup as a whole (Brown & Hewstone, 2005). Furthermore, when members of one group recognize the heterogeneity of members of another group and develop more positive attitudes toward them, intergroup boundaries may become more permeable and flexible, thereby facilitating recategorization of both groups within a common superordinate identity.

Other possible sequences may also be effective (see Gaertner & Dovidio, 2005). Success in cooperative activities in which groups maintain their separate identities (mutual intergroup differentiation) may facilitate the groups' subsequent acceptance of a common superordinate identity. The development of a common ingroup identity, in turn, may not only produce more positive attitudes toward people formerly perceived only as outgroup members but also may lead to more individuated perceptions of them and encourage more self-disclosing interactions. Even though the salience of a common ingroup identity may be relatively unstable because of contextual pressures or historical relations between the original groups (Hewstone, 1996), these personalized interactions may then create more enduring positive attitudes, orientations, and social networks between members of the groups, as well as the recognition and development of cross-cutting group identities.

Pettigrew's (1998) insights about the sequential and potentially reinforcing effects of decategorization, recategorization, and mutual intergroup differentiation reveal the importance of exploring the causal bidirectionality of these processes. For example, in separate studies we examined the relationship between common ingroup identity and the exchange of personalized information. Supportive of Pettigrew's perspective, one study showed that creating a common group identity facilitates self-disclosure (Dovidio, Gaertner, Validzic, Matoka, Johnson, & Frazier, 1997); the other further demonstrated that self-disclosure enhances the development of a common ingroup identity (Gaertner, Rust, & Dovidio, 1997).

In summary, whereas much of the traditional research on contact theory summarized by Pettigrew and Tropp (2006) investigated the different elements of situations that are necessary or important for contact to reduce intergroup bias, recent research has moved from the question of when contact reduces bias to how and why contact ameliorates bias and improves intergroup attitudes. Pettigrew's (1998) reformulation of intergroup contact theory drew further attention to the relationships among different hypothesized mediating mechanisms. He asserted that future research needs to address how the "contact processes of change are activated and become important at each stage" (p. 77). We agree, and our data suggest the promise of this valuable insight.

In addition to focusing more on the mediating mechanisms, Tropp and Pettigrew (2005) have noted the importance of appreciating a particular moderating factor in the effectiveness of intergroup contact for reducing bias—the status, or relative position, of the groups. In the next section of the chapter, we consider the role of majority and minority group status on the effectiveness of intergroup contact for reducing bias.

Intergroup Contact and the Perspective of Majority and Minority Group Members

Although equal status contact has continued to be a key element of intergroup contact theory, Pettigrew (1998) also emphasized that it is important to consider the broader social context in which intergroup contact occurs. That is, even though groups may be functionally equivalent in status within the constraints of the contact situation, majority and minority group members bring different resources, perspectives, expectations, and motivations to their interactions.

Tropp and Pettigrew (2005) found that the different experiences and orientations that majority and minority group members bring with them to contact situations have direct implications for the success of intergroup contact for reducing intergroup bias. Their meta-analysis, which involved the same database as the one used by Pettigrew and Tropp (2006), revealed that, overall, intergroup contact was significantly more effective at reducing intergroup bias for majority group members (mean $r = -.23$) than it was for minority group members (mean $r = -.18$). Moreover, whereas the optimal conditions specified by intergroup contact theory moderated the effect of contact for majority group members, these conditions had no significant effect for minority group members. In this section of the chapter, we expand on those insights to understand how the different perspectives of majority and minority group members moderate the nature and outcome of intergroup contact.

One fundamental difference between majority and minority group members involves their motivations in the contact situation. Several different theoretical perspectives, such as Social Identity Theory (Tajfel & Turner, 1979), Social Dominance Theory (Sidanius & Pratto, 1999), and the Group Position perspective (Bobo, 1999) converge to posit that whereas members of majority groups are likely to desire the stability of the social system that benefits them, members of minority groups are typically more motivated toward social change. As a consequence, majority and minority group members are likely to have different objectives for the nature and consequences of their contact.

Within the contact situation as well as beyond it, one way that minority groups can promote social change to improve their group position is to maneuver the nature of discourse to bring injustice and inequality into people's conscious awareness. In contrast, majority groups may wish to promote ideological messages that obscure and draw attention *away from* group-based inequality (Maoz, 2005) in order to maintain the *status quo* (Jackman, 1994; Ruscher, 2001; Sidanius & Pratto, 1999). Within the intergroup context, this can be achieved by emphasizing commonalities between the groups. That is, focusing on a common category (e.g., all Americans as opposed to Whites and Blacks), can serve to deflect attention from group-based hierarchy and thus maintain existing inequalities.

We sought to examine whether these group-based orientations would influence the way group members approach situations of inter-group contact. We anticipated that majority and minority group members would attempt to direct the content of their interaction in strategic ways. Whereas members of minority groups may wish to highlight separate group identities and associated inequities, majority group members may desire to focus on commonalities between the groups. We note, however, that minority group members may not want to avoid addressing commonalities altogether when interacting with majority group members. In fact, to the extent that promoting social change *within a society* is the objective, minority group members are likely to emphasize both common social connections and group differences within that shared social identity. This dual emphasis may serve the desire to maintain positive connections with those in higher status and control in the social system while maintaining the potential for social change by not masking group-based disadvantage.

We have found converging evidence for these hypotheses across both laboratory and field settings (Saguy, Dovidio, & Pratto, 2008). One study directly manipulated the status of laboratory groups by giving one group, the majority group, control over the resources (labor-atory credits) available to members of both groups. The other study compared the responses of members of high and low status ethnic groups in Israel (Ashkenazim vs. Mizrahim). Across both studies, minor-ity, compared to majority, group members expressed a strong desire to talk about power differences between the groups in an anticipated intergroup interaction. Though members of both groups wanted to address commonalities in the contact situation, among majority group members this desire was significantly stronger than their desire to address group differences and power disparities. Both studies also revealed that motivations for changing the *status quo* explained the group-based desires to address power. Thus, as expected, perspectives that are driven from group membership influenced the content of contact that group members desired for their intergroup interaction.

Another implication of this perspective is that the types of group representations that are most critical for reducing intergroup bias may differ for majority and minority group members. As we noted earlier, within the context of the Common Ingroup Identity Model recategorization can take two forms. One form involves the recategorization of two groups within a single, superordinate identity. A second form is a *dual identity*, in which the superordinate identity is salient but in conjunction with a salient subgroup identity (a "different groups working together on the same team" representation). These representations correspond to different models of acculturation (Berry, 1997). Whereas a common ingroup identity reflects an assimilationist perspective, a dual identity represents a pluralistic or integration orientation (Dovidio, Gaertner, & Kafati, 2000).

Majority and minority group members differ in their preference for these acculturation approaches (van Oudenhoven, Prins, & Buunk, 1998; see also Plaut, 2007) and group representations (Dovidio et al., 2000). Majority group members generally prefer assimilation and one-group representations, whereas minority group members desire integration and dual identities. We therefore investigated the hypotheses that majority and minority groups, in general, and Whites and racial/ethnic minorities, in particular, have different preferences for one-group and dual-identity representations, and that these representations mediate the beneficial effects of favorable intergroup contact on bias in different ways (Dovidio et al., 2000).

We reasoned that because Whites typically hold assimilationist cultural values and racial/ethnic minorities possess pluralistic values, one-group and dual-identity representations would probably operate differently as mediators of the effect of intergroup contact on intergroup attitudes for members of these two groups. Supportive of this hypothesis, we found that perceptions of favorable intergroup contact predicted more positive intergroup attitudes for both White and minority college students, but they did so in different ways (Dovidio et al., 2000). For White students, more favorable perceptions of intergroup contact predicted stronger one-group representations, which, in turn, mediated more positive attitudes towards minorities. For minority students, it was the strength of the dual identity, not the one-group representation that mediated the relationship between favorable conditions of contact and positive attitudes toward Whites.

Complementing these findings for White students and students of color, we have also found that, within a sample of predominantly White students, status moderates the relationship between a dual identity and bias (Johnson, Gaertner, & Dovidio, 2001). Status was based on whether students, who were expected to perform the same tasks within a superordinate workgroup, were admitted directly into the university (lower status) or into the prestigious Honors Program (higher status). For high status participants (Honors students), the more the workgroup felt like one group, the more favorable were their attitudes toward low status participants (regular students) in the session; the more the high status Honors students reported that the workgroup felt like two subgroups within a group (a dual identity), the greater their bias against the regularly admitted students. In contrast, among the lower status, regularly admitted students, stronger perceptions of a dual identity significantly predicted less bias toward the high status Honors students in their session. Taken together, these findings suggest that understanding the extent to which intergroup contact will be more or less successful requires attention to differences in status and power that the groups bring to the contact situation.

These different orientations of majority and minority group members are further reflected in helping relationships between the groups. To the extent that majority group members are motivated to maintain their advantaged status over minority group members, they are particularly likely to offer assistance that reinforces the dependency of the minority group and de-emphasizes group differences in identity and disparity. We (Halabi, Dovidio, & Nadler, 2007) found in a laboratory study that Israeli Jews were more likely to offer Arabs assistance that reinforced the Arabs' dependency (giving them answers on a test) than on helping in a way that promoted the Arabs' autonomy (showing them how to solve the problems). Providing answers directly also enabled Israeli Jews to limit and control the nature of intergroup contact. This difference in helping was greater among Jews higher in social dominance orientation (Sidanius & Pratto, 1999), which reflects a desire to maintain group hierarchy, and when participants perceived greater threat to the *status quo*. The reactions of Arabs to assistance from Israeli Jews, however, was more negative to dependency-oriented than to autonomy-oriented help. Negative responses to dependency-oriented help were particularly strong among Arabs who identified more strongly with their ethnic group (Nadler & Halabi, 2006).

Overall, consistent with the important insights of Pettigrew (1998; see also Tropp & Pettigrew, 2005), our results demonstrate that even though group statuses may be equivalent in the narrowly defined roles of the contact situation, it is valuable to appreciate more broadly the importance of the groups' relations within the societal context. The psychological perspectives, experiences, and realities that majority and minority group members bring to the situation are shaped substantially by their statuses outside the limited circumstances of contact. Importantly, as our research reveals, the types of interventions and activities within the contact situation that are most beneficial for majority group members may be much less beneficial for minority group members, and often may arouse resistance and antagonism. Efforts that make one group respond more positively, if not carefully considered, can stimulate the other group to respond more negatively.

Nevertheless, understanding the existence and effects of different group perspectives based on group power and status differences can help inform interventions that can be effective for both majority and minority group members. For example, even though majority group members may generally tend to try to ignore group differences, interventions that increase the salience of group differences in ways that do not threaten a superordinate identity (e.g., as Black and White *Americans*) can lead them to increase their support for policies (e.g., affirmative action) that directly benefit the minority group (Smith & Tyler, 1996). Also, emphasizing superordinate group connection while respecting subgroup memberships increases minority group members' level of intergroup trust and cooperation with majority group members (Huo, Smith, Tyler, & Lind, 1996).

Alternatively, although self- and group-serving biases may lead majority group members to attribute their superior status to internal factors (e.g., merit and effort), and system-justifying ideologies can mask the role of historical and contemporary discrimination (Sidanius & Pratto, 1999), people are fundamentally motivated by principles of fairness, justice, and legitimacy. Thus, raising awareness of the illegitimacy of social inequality can motivate majority group members, as well as minority group members, toward social change. For instance, we have found that emphasizing that majority group members' advantaged status was unfairly achieved because of past discrimination toward the minority group increased majority groups members' motivation for social change and, consequently, their willingness to talk about disparities and group differences in intergroup contact situations in ways consonant with those of minority group members (Saguy et al., 2008). Understanding the processes by which contact operates to reduce bias can, therefore, contribute to more effective ways of reducing bias and eliminating inequities between groups.

Future Directions

Allport's (1954) book, *The Nature of Prejudice*, became a classic in part because his formulation of the contact hypothesis in it reflected ideas that not only integrated previous decades of research but also guided subsequent generations of scholars. Now, over 50 years later, Thomas Pettigrew's legacy in this area of intergroup relations will be similar in substance and magnitude. His exhaustive meta-analytic reviews of the literature with Linda Tropp (Pettigrew & Tropp, 2006; Tropp & Pettigrew, 2005) summarize an extensive body of literature spanning six decades and more than 250,000 participants from 38 countries. The general message is clear: Intergroup contact, particularly under specifiable conditions, significantly improves intergroup attitudes. Furthermore, the insights he provides about different mediating mechanisms that can operate in complementary ways over time and the value of recognizing the impact of group power differences outside the contact situation will influence research in this area for decades to come.

Building on these foundational insights, we identify three promising directions for future research. Each builds on Pettigrew's ideas. One direction, directly derivative of Pettigrew's (1998) recommendation, is to discover how and when the different underlying processes—specifically decategorization, recategorization, and mutual intergroup differentiation—operate in a complementary fashion. It is likely that the ways in which these different processes relate are moderated by the ongoing nature of the intergroup relationship. When relations are highly antagonistic, attempts to form a common ingroup identity through recategorization are likely to be futile and may further increase bias because of identity threat. Under those conditions, as Pettigrew suggests, decategorization may represent the most productive initial step. Thus, future research may incorporate these basic principles and processes into a range of different contact situations and explore how the effectiveness of different *sequences* may be determined by the nature of the existing intergroup relations.

A second promising direction for future research on intergroup contact theory can focus more directly on intergroup interactions.

Despite the impressive literature on intergroup contact reviewed by Pettigrew and Tropp (2006) and Tropp and Pettigrew (2005), very little of that literature directly studied such interactions. Of these studies, 72% involve only the responses of majority group members and 20% include only the reactions of minority group members; just 8% examined the responses of majority and minority group members within the same situation. To understand how contact influences intergroup *relations*, studying intergroup interactions is critical. As our research (e.g., Halabi et al., 2007; Saguy et al., 2008) revealed, the perspectives and motivations of majority and minority group members could lead them to influence the nature of their interaction in systematic but not necessarily in compatible or ultimately productive ways. These efforts to shape the interactions can create further intergroup misunderstandings that can exacerbate, rather than alleviate, bias and conflict even under the circumstances identified as "optimal" for intergroup contact. Future research, therefore, needs to go beyond the focus on the structure of the contact situation to a close examination of the forces shaping the content of the interaction and its consequences.

A third valuable direction for future research relates to Pettigrew's emphasis on the importance of social structures on intergroup relations (Pettigrew, 1998). In particular, the vast preponderance of research on intergroup contact uses intergroup attitudes as the ultimate measure of interest. Intergroup attitudes often do not translate into intergroup actions or orientations, however (Brown, Brown, Jackson, Sellers, & Manuel, 2003; Jackman & Crane, 1986; Struch & Schwartz, 1989). Jackman and Crane (1986) found that whereas intergroup contact predicted improved attitudes, it did not affect support for policies that would ameliorate social inequality. Thus it would be particularly valuable for future research to expand the current focus on contact and intergroup attitudes to examine more centrally the effect of contact (and consequent attitudes) on the type of beliefs, emotions and actions that will alter the structure of society and intergroup relations in more direct, profound, and enduring ways.

In conclusion, our discipline's knowledge about the effects of intergroup contact for reducing intergroup bias and conflict has evolved substantially within the past 50 years. Thanks largely to the work of Thomas Pettigrew, we now have a more definitive understanding of the effects of contact, the psychological processes engaged by positive contact experiences, how contact can be structured to be even more effective, and how these effects are moderated by majority and minority group membership. Pettigrew's legacy identifies what is known about the effects of intergroup contact and, perhaps just as importantly, what is not known, thereby offering critical guidance and inspiration to future generations of researchers.

Acknowledgment

Preparation of this chapter was supported by NSF Grant BCS-0613218 awarded to the first two authors.

References

Allport, G. W. (1954). *The nature of prejudice.* Cambridge, MA: Addison-Wesley.

Berry, J. W. (1997). Immigration, acculturation, and adaptation. *Applied Psychology: An International Review, 46,* 5–34.

Bobo, L. D. (1999). Prejudice as group position: Microfoundations of a sociological approach to racism and race relations. *Journal of Social Issues, 55,* 445–472.

Brewer, M. B. (1988). A dual process model of impression formation. In T. S. Srull & R. S. Wyer (Eds.), *Advances in social cognition* (Vol. 1) (pp. 1–36). Hillsdale, NJ: Erlbaum.

Brewer, M. B., & Miller, N. (1984). Beyond the contact hypothesis: Theoretical perspectives on desegregation. In N. Miller & M. B. Brewer (Eds.), *Groups in contact: The psychology of desegregation* (pp. 281–302). Orlando, FL: Academic Press.

Brown, K. T., Brown, T. N., Jackson, J. S., Sellers, R. M., & Manuel, W. J. (2003). Teammates on and off the field? White student athletes. *Journal of Applied Social Psychology, 33,* 1379–1403.

Brown, R., & Hewstone, M. (2005). An integrative theory of intergroup contact. In M. P. Zanna (Ed.), *Advances in experimental social psychology* (Vol. 37) (pp. 255–343). San Diego, CA: Academic Press.

Dovidio, J. F, Gaertner, S. L., & Kafati, G. (2000). Group identity and intergroup relations: The Common In-Group Identity Model. In S. R. Thye, E. J. Lawler, M. W. Macy, & H. A. Walker (Eds.), *Advances in group processes* (Vol. 17) (pp. 1–34). Stamford, CT: JAI Press.

Dovidio, J. F., Gaertner, S. L., & Kawakami, K. (2003). Intergroup contact: Past, present, and the future. *Group Processes and Interpersonal Relations, 6,* 5–21.

Dovidio, J. F., Gaertner, S. L., Validzic, A., Matoka, K., Johnson, B., & Frazier, S. (1997). Extending the benefits of re-categorization: Evaluations, self-disclosure and helping. *Journal of Experimental Social Psychology, 33,* 401–420.

Fiske, S. T., Lin, M., & Neuberg, S. L. (1999). The continuum model: Ten years later. In S. Chaiken & Y. Trope (Eds.), *Dual process theories in social psychology* (pp. 231–254). New York: Guilford.

Gaertner, S. L., Mann, J. A., Murrell, A. J., & Dovidio, J. F. (1989). Reduction of intergroup bias: The benefits of recategorization. *Journal of Personality and Social Psychology, 57*, 239–249.

Gaertner, S. L., & Dovidio, J. F. (2000). *Reducing intergroup bias: The Common Ingroup Identity Model.* Philadelphia, PA: The Psychology Press.

Gaertner, S. L., & Dovidio, J. F. (2005). Categorization, recategorization, and intergroup bias. In J. F. Dovidio, P. Glick, & L. A. Rudman (Eds.), *On the nature of prejudice: Fifty years after Allport* (pp. 71–88). Malden, MA: Blackwell.

Gaertner, S. L., Rust, M. C., & Dovidio, J. F. (1997). [The value of a superordinate identity for reducing intergroup bias.] Unpublished raw data. Department of Psychology, University of Delaware.

Halabi, S., Dovidio, J. F., & Nadler, A. (2007). *Offering help to the outgroup: The relationship of Social Dominance Orientation and status threat on amount and type of assistance.* Manuscript submitted for publication.

Hewstone, M. (1996). Contact and categorization: Social psychological interventions to change intergroup relations. In C. N. Macrae, C. Stangor, & M. Hewstone (Eds.), *Stereotypes and stereotyping* (pp. 323–368). New York: Guilford.

Hewstone, M., & Brown, R. J. (1986). Contact is not enough: An intergroup perspective on the "Contact Hypothesis." In M. Hewstone & R. Brown (Eds), *Contact and conflict in intergroup encounters* (pp. 1–44). Oxford: Basil Blackwell.

Huo, Y. J., Smith, H. H., Tyler, T. R., & Lind, A. E. (1996). Superordinate identification, subgroup identification, and justice concerns: Is separatism the problem. Is assimilation the answer? *Psychological Science, 7*, 40–45.

Jackman, M. R. (1994). *The velvet glove.* Berkeley, CA: University of California Press.

Jackman, M. R., & Crane, M. (1986). 'Some of my best friends are Black . . .': Interracial friendship and Whites' racial attitudes. *Public Opinion Quarterly, 50*, 459–486.

Johnson, K. M., Gaertner, S. L., & Dovidio, J. F. (2001). [The effect of equality of job assignment on ingroup identity and bias for low and high status groups]. Unpublished raw data. Department of Psychology, University of Delaware.

Maoz, I. (2005). Evaluating the communication between groups in dispute: Equality in contact interventions between Jews and Arabs in Israel. *Negotiation Journal, 21*, 131–146.

Miller, N. (2002). Personalization and the promise of Contact Theory. *Journal of Social Issues, 58*, 387–410.

Nadler, A., & Halabi, S. (2006). Intergroup helping as status relations: Effects of status stability in-group identification and type of help on receptivity to help from high status group. *Journal of Personality and Social Psychology*, *91*, 97–110.

Pettigrew, T. F. (1998). Intergroup contact theory. *Annual Review of Psychology*, *49*, 65–85.

Pettigrew, T. F., & Tropp, L. (2006). A meta-analytic test of intergroup contact theory. *Journal of Personality and Social Psychology*, *90*, 751–783.

Plaut, V. C. (2007). *Attitudes toward diversity: What do race and status buy you?* Paper presented at the 8th Annual Conference of the Society for Personality and Social Psychology, Memphis, TN.

Ruscher, J. B. (2001). *Prejudiced communication: A social psychological perspective*. New York: Guilford Press.

Saguy, T., Dovidio, J. F., & Pratto, F. (2008). Beyond contact: Intergroup contact in the context of power relations. *Journal of Personality and Social Psychology Bulletin*.

Sidanius, J., & Pratto, F. (1999). *Social dominance: An intergroup theory of social hierarchy and oppression*. New York: Cambridge University Press.

Smith, H. J., & Tyler, T. R. (1996). Justice and power: When will justice concerns encourage the advantaged to support policies which redistribute economic resources and the disadvantaged to willingly obey the law? *European Journal of Social Psychology*, *26*, 171–200.

Struch, N., & Schwartz, S. H. (1989). Intergroup aggression: Its predictors and distinctness from in-group bias. *Journal of Personality and Social Psychology*, *56*, 364–373.

Tajfel, H., & Turner, J. C. (1979). An integrative theory of intergroup conflict. In W. G. Austin & S. Worchel (Eds.), *The social psychology of intergroup relations* (pp. 33–48). Monterey, CA: Brooks/Cole.

Tropp, L. R., & Pettigrew, T. F. (2005). Relationship between intergroup contact and prejudice among minority and majority status groups. *Psychological Science*, *16*, 951–957.

Turner, J. C., Hogg, M. A., Oakes, P. J., Reicher, S. D., & Wetherell, M. S. (1987). *Rediscovering the social group: A self-categorization theory*. Oxford: Basil Blackwell.

van Oudenhoven, J. P., Prins, K. S., & Buunk, B. (1998). Attitudes of minority and majority members towards adaptation of immigrants. *European Journal of Social Psychology*, *28*, 995–1013.

Wilder, D. A. (1981). Perceiving persons as a group: Categorization and intergroup relations. In D. L. Hamilton (Ed.), *Cognitive processes in stereotyping and intergroup behavior* (pp. 213–257). Hillsdale, NJ: Erlbaum.

7

The Role of Trust in Intergroup Contact

Its Significance and Implications for Improving Relations between Groups

Linda R. Tropp

To date, the most influential statements on intergroup contact theory have placed a special emphasis on conditions of the contact situation, stressing that certain optimal conditions are necessary to reduce prejudice and promote positive intergroup relations (Allport, 1954; Williams, 1947; see also Pettigrew, 1998; Pettigrew & Tropp, 2005). This emphasis grew largely from the view that intergroup relations are characterized by open hostility, conflict, and segregation (see Brameld, 1946; Myrdal, 1944). Hence, to set the stage for positive relations between groups, optimal conditions such as cooperation, equal status, common goals, and authority sanction must be established firmly and explicitly within the contact situation.

However, research on intergroup contact has experienced a renaissance in recent years, with a virtual explosion of studies being conducted from a range of research directions (see Brown & Hewstone, 2005 for a recent review). Recent theorizing suggests that it may not be sufficient to focus simply on conditions imposed within the contact situation in order to improve intergroup relations (Pettigrew & Tropp, 2006). Rather, emerging perspectives have emphasized our need to understand how conditions of the contact situation translate into the development of meaningful relationships across group boundaries.

At the forefront of this work, Thomas Pettigrew (1997a; 1997b; 1998) has encouraged us to return to a focus on affective processes, both in terms of the kinds of contact that are most likely to improve intergroup attitudes, and the kinds of positive outcomes we can expect from such contact (see also Pettigrew & Tropp, 2006; in press; Tropp & Pettigrew, 2005a). In a seminal paper, Pettigrew (1997a) presented compelling evidence that the affective ties generated by close, cross-group friendships can be especially effective in promoting positive intergroup attitudes. With survey responses from seven European samples, Pettigrew (1997a) found that intergroup contact in the form of cross-group friendships was consistently and negatively associated with a range of prejudice measures. Moreover, the positive effects of cross-group friendships were particularly strong for prejudice measures based on affective responses, such as feelings of sympathy and admiration for the outgroup. By contrast, less intimate contact with outgroup members, such as with coworkers or neighbors, yielded considerably smaller effects.

Such findings have fueled a great deal of interest in the role of cross-group friendships as a means of improving intergroup relations (see also Vonofakou et al., this volume). Many recent studies have found that having friendships with outgroup members relates to significantly lower levels of intergroup prejudice (Levin, van Laar, & Sidanius, 2003; Page-Gould, Mendoza-Denton, & Tropp, 2007; Paolini, Hewstone, Cairns, & Voci, 2004; Wright, Aron, McLaughlin-Volpe, & Ropp, 1997). Complementing Pettigrew's (1997a) findings, cross-group friendships have also been shown to relate more strongly to reduced prejudice than more distant forms of contact (Herek & Capitanio, 1996), and particularly when affective dimensions of prejudice such as feelings and emotions toward outgroup members are involved (Tropp & Pettigrew, 2005a).

Although theorists have long acknowledged the general importance of closeness between groups (Amir, 1976; Cook & Sellitz, 1955; Williams, 1947), few have attempted to integrate the significance of this factor with more traditional views regarding optimal conditions of the contact situation. Pettigrew (1998) takes important steps in this direction by proposing the condition of *friendship potential*, which he defines as the ability of the contact situation to provide participants with opportunities to become friends. Friendship potential typically involves extensive and repeated contact across a range of social contexts, which over time would encourage greater degrees of shared experience, self-disclosure, and other friendship-building processes (Pettigrew, 1997; see also Miller, 2002).

At the same time, Pettigrew and others note that in addition to focusing on positive features of the contact situation, greater attention must be granted to negative forces that are likely to undermine contact's effects (Pettigrew & Tropp, 2006). Contact with outgroup members can provoke substantial anxiety (Stephan & Stephan, 1985), as people are unsure of how they will be perceived and evaluated by outgroup members (Devine & Vasquez, 1998; Vorauer, Main, & O'Connell, 1998). In turn, anxieties about cross-group interactions can make intergroup contact less likely to occur (Plant & Devine, 2003; Stephan & Stephan, 1985), thereby precluding the potential for positive, generalizable outcomes to emerge from contact (Dovidio, Gaertner, Kawakami, & Hodson, 2002). Nonetheless, other recent work suggests that close contact can reduce intergroup anxiety (Levin et al., 2003; Tropp, 2003), and anxiety mediates the relationships between intergroup contact and prejudice, such that greater reductions in prejudice are achieved to the extent that anxiety is reduced through contact (Paolini et al., 2004; Pettigrew & Tropp, in press).

Taking these perspectives into account, we must pay close attention to how we conceptualize optimal conditions for intergroup contact. Indeed, beyond focusing on *situational* conditions that are conducive to developing close intergroup relationships, these patterns of findings compel us to consider *psychological* conditions that may be necessary for people to willingly develop and nurture meaningful relationships across group boundaries. It appears that much of this willingness hinges on the concept of *trust*, and the extent to which contact can affect people's general readiness to trust members of other groups. While optimal conditions of the situation typically facilitate positive contact experiences (Pettigrew & Tropp, 2006), we must consider the special kinds of contact experiences that will be most likely to encourage feelings of trust to develop between members of different groups.

Defining Trust in Intergroup Relationships

The concept of trust has long been recognized as a crucial component of psychological functioning and a primary motivation that people have as they navigate their social relationships (see Fiske, 2003). Growing from one's life experiences, trust may be defined as a social bond that is characterized by feelings of security and confidence in others' good intentions and goodwill. As such, trust implies an absence of perceived threat (Stephan & Stephan, 2000), in that one feels that others genuinely care about one's welfare and have one's best interests at heart (Tyler, 2001).

Unfortunately, intergroup relationships are often characterized by distrust, corresponding with feelings of suspicion and a lack of confidence in others' good intentions (see Dovidio et al., 2002; Insko & Schopler, 1998; Kramer & Messick, 1998). People generally have negative expectations regarding how they will be viewed by outgroup members (Krueger, 1996; Vorauer et al., 1998), which can hinder the potential for intergroup contact to promote positive relations between groups (Frey & Tropp, 2006). Moreover, distrust can easily grow from histories of social experiences and violations of trust (Lindskold, 1986), which is especially likely when intergroup relationships involve differences in power or status (Kramer & Messick, 1998). As such, understanding the role of distrust may be particularly crucial in examining intergroup relationships from the perspective of minority status groups, whose contact experiences are often marked by prejudice, devaluation, and discrimination (Tropp, 2006).

Distrust in Minority–Majority Relations

Indeed, a growing body of work suggests that, due to the devaluation they face, members of racial minority groups are particularly likely to experience racial distrust in intergroup contexts (Cohen & Steele, 2002; Tropp, 2006). This lack of trust can have a significant impact on racial minority group members' attitudes and behaviors in a range of intergroup contexts (Whaley, 2001), such as having lower occupational aspirations (Terrell, Terrell, & Miller, 1993), more negative views of White counselors in clinical settings (Watkins & Terrell, 1988), less positive expectations for academic experiences with White mentors (Grant-Thompson & Atkinson, 1997), and less confidence in the ability of diversity programs to improve intergroup relations (Ervin, 2001).

Viewing intergroup relations through the lens of trust may help us to understand why intergroup contact effects typically vary for members of minority and majority status groups (see Tropp & Pettigrew, 2005b). Minority and majority group members often have markedly different perceptions of their intergroup relationships (Dovidio et al., 2002; Sigelman & Welch, 1993) and how much progress has been made toward racial equality (Eibach & Ehrlinger, 2006). For example, Black Americans perceive significantly more racial discrimination against their group relative to White Americans (National Conference for Community and Justice, 2000) at the same time as most White Americans believe Blacks in their communities are treated as well as Whites (Gallup Organization, 2001). Black Americans also tend to see racial tensions as a bigger problem in our society relative to Whites, and they tend to be more pessimistic about the potential for American race relations to improve in the future (Gallup Organization, 2001; National Conference for Community and Justice, 2000). In turn, members of racial minority and majority groups often perceive the same contact situations in different ways (Cohen, 1982; Robinson & Preston, 1976); in particular, members of racial minority groups may view the majority with vigilance and suspicion until they feel confident that majority group members are worthy of their trust (see Brown & Dobbins, 2004; Cohen & Steele, 2002).

Perhaps not surprisingly, then, the positive effects of intergroup contact tend to be weaker among members of racial minority groups than among members of the racial majority (Sigelman & Welch, 1993; Tropp, 2007; Tropp & Pettigrew, 2005b) In some of our recent work, we used data from our meta-analytic study of intergroup contact effects (Pettigrew & Tropp, 2006) to examine patterns of contact–prejudice relationships among members of racial minority and majority groups. Overall, the mean relationship between contact and prejudice was significantly weaker in our racial minority samples (mean $r = -.18$) than in our racial majority samples (mean $r = -.24$), $Q_B(1) = 9.15$, $p < .01$. Regression analysis also showed that this effect emerged even after controlling for variables associated with research design, the type and quality of measures used to assess contact and prejudice, sample size, and whether participants were able to choose to engage in the contact. Moreover, these effects were consistent even for those samples where optimal conditions had been implemented within the contact situation (Tropp & Pettigrew, 2005b).

Further research has considered how positive contact effects may be inhibited among members of racial and ethnic minority groups, due to their experiences with prejudice and devaluation. In a separate study (Tropp, 2007), intergroup contact effects were examined using survey responses from nationally representative samples of Black and White Americans. To assess contact and prejudice, respondents indicated whether they do or do not currently have contact with the racial outgroup, along with reporting their feelings toward outgroup members in general. Replicating Tropp and Pettigrew (2005b), results showed that relationship between contact and prejudice tends to be weaker among Black respondents ($r = .078$) than among White respondents ($r = .223$), and these patterns persist even after controlling for a range of demographic indicators (age, gender, region, level of education, family income, political ideology, and religiosity). Additionally, analyses revealed that perceptions of racial discrimination moderated these effects of contact in different ways for members of these groups. Among both Black and White respondents who perceived little discrimination against their racial group, interracial contact predicted significantly more positive feelings toward the other racial group. However, among those who perceived a great deal of racial discrimination, contact still predicted more positive interracial attitudes among White respondents, yet contact no longer predicted more positive interracial attitudes among Black respondents. It is also important to note that over half of the Black respondents in this sample reported a great deal of racial discrimination, indicating its significance in terms of how racial minority group members are likely to view and interpret relations with members of the racial majority group.

Additionally, experimental evidence reveals that expressions of prejudice from a member of the racial outgroup can affect how racial minority group members feel about intergroup contact (Tropp, 2003). In one study, racial minority participants (Asian Americans and Latinos) learned that they were randomly assigned to interact with a White participant, ostensibly as part of a study on communication styles. Participants then overheard one of two scripted dialogues between a confederate participant and the experimenter, in which this confederate did or did not make a prejudiced comment in relation to the participant's racial group. Following these procedures, participants completed questionnaires including measures of hostility and anxiety, as well as feelings about interacting with the White partner and with Whites in general. Results from this study revealed that participants exposed to prejudice reported significantly greater levels of hostility and anxiety, and tended to have less positive feelings about interacting with both their partner and with Whites in general, as compared to those who were not exposed to a prejudiced comment. Furthermore, correlational analyses revealed that chronic perceptions of discrimination predicted stronger feelings of hostility and anxiety, and less positive feelings about interacting with their White partner, even after controlling for exposure to prejudice within the experimental setting. Together, these findings indicate that exposure to even a single instance of prejudice from the racial outgroup can have profound, negative effects on racial minority group members' feelings about intergroup contact, which may be exacerbated further by ongoing perceptions of racial prejudice and discrimination. Thus, with good reason, minority group members' responses to contact with the racial majority are likely to be tainted by prior histories of prejudice and discrimination, thereby plaguing the intergroup relationship with continued suspicion and distrust.

Intergroup Contact and the Promotion of Intergroup Trust

Such issues involving distrust need to be taken into account as we consider different strategies to encourage positive relations between groups. In line with more traditional perspectives on intergroup contact, many have stressed that conditions of equal status and institutional support must, therefore, include substantial representations of both groups, and authorities who explicitly value diversity (Jones, Lynch, Tenglund, & Gaertner, 2000; Khmelkov & Hallinan, 1999; Schofield & Eurich-Fulcer, 2001), as their absence can perpetuate distrust (Brewer, von Hippel, & Gooden, 1999; Kramer & Messick, 1998; Purdie-Vaughns, Steele, Davies, & Randall-Crosby, 2007).

Though select situational features can surely help to reduce suspicion and distrust within a given intergroup context, we must work to create broader shifts in how people view and interpret their intergroup relationships (Frey & Tropp, 2006), in order to promote the kinds of psychological conditions that allow for trust to develop across group boundaries. Here is where Pettigrew's (1997a; 1998) focus on close cross-group friendships appears to be most critical. Optimal situational conditions can help to establish norms regarding how groups should interact with each other, which can in turn facilitate the development of meaningful, trusting relationships between individual members of different groups. However, it is the intimacy of those forged relationships that serves as the cornerstone for promoting a broader willingness to trust across group boundaries and more fundamental shifts in how people view relations between their groups.

Complementing this view, recent work has emphasized that close cross-group relationships can be highly effective in reducing intergroup prejudice and changing the nature of the intergroup relationship (Levin et al., 2003; Paolini et al., 2004; Pettigrew, 1997a; van Laar et al., this volume; Wright et al., 1997). New theoretical perspectives suggest that close cross-group relationships will be effective in reducing prejudice to the extent that they encourage us to empathize with outgroup members (Finlay & Stephan, 2000; Hewstone, Cairns,

Voci, Hamberger, & Niens, 2006; Pettigrew & Tropp, in press) and propel us to include outgroup members in our selves (see Aron et al., 2004 for a recent review). According to these perspectives, close cross-group relationships compel us to become more generous in interpreting outgroup members' intentions and behaviors, such that we begin to grant them the same kinds of positive associations that we typically reserve for members of our own groups (Aron et al., 2004; Wright, Aron, & Tropp, 2002). More broadly, close relationships with individual outgroup members also promote changes in perceived relations between groups, as the psychological connectedness between ingroup and outgroup members contributes to dissolving intergroup boundaries (Aron & McLaughlin-Volpe, 2001).

As such, the benefits of close, cross-group friendships are likely to extend far beyond the initial context of intergroup contact. Through the development of cross-group friendships, people may become more inclined to trust not only the individual outgroup members they know, but to demonstrate a broader willingness to trust outgroup members as their views of relations between the groups begin to shift. Indeed, research suggests that close cross-group relationships correspond with a stronger motivation to improve intergroup relations (Sigelman & Welch, 1993), and a greater tendency to have diverse social networks later in life (Ellison & Powers, 1994). Research has also shown that, among Black Americans, those who have close White friends are more likely to see the motivations of Whites in a positive light as they grow older (Powers & Ellison, 1995).

This final result is particularly striking as it suggests that, even in the face of negative intergroup experiences and histories of conflict between groups, cross-group friendships may still help to cultivate a certain willingness to trust. In line with this view, Hewstone et al., (2006) have shown among Catholics and Protestants in Northern Ireland that contact with outgroup friends corresponds with a greater willingness to forgive and trust the outgroup, even among those who had personally suffered due to the conflict.

Similar patterns of findings are observed in research with members of racial minority groups who have been subjected to prejudice and discrimination by the racial majority. Extending the analyses of Tropp (2003), supplementary correlations revealed that cross-group friendships corresponded with more positive feelings toward future intergroup contact among Asian and Latino participants, and even among those who had been exposed to an experimental manipulation of prejudice. Further analysis of the national survey data (Tropp, 2007) also reveals that cross-group friendships may counteract some of the negative effects of discrimination when predicting feelings of intergroup closeness among Black Americans. In this study, those respondents who reported having contact also indicated whether they have contact with an outgroup member "as a good friend." Among Black respondents, having a White friend predicted greater feelings of closeness to Whites in general, even after controlling for the demographic indicators, $\beta = .11$, $F_{change} (1, 610) = 7.63$, $p < .01$. Moreover, although perceived discrimination predicted less intergroup closeness among Black respondents who reported no White friends, $\beta = -.26$, $p < .01$, perceived discrimination did not significantly predict less intergroup closeness among those who reported having a White friend, $\beta = -.06$, $p = .22$.

Taken together, these findings suggest that while prejudice and discrimination typically define relations between racial minority and majority groups (see Feagin, 1991; Tropp, 2006), such factors may play less prominent roles in predicting general feelings toward the racial majority when minority group members have interracial friendships. These cross-group friendships may offer alternate, positive sources of information that inform minority group members' feelings toward the racial majority, thereby diminishing the extent to which their attitudes would necessarily be formed in relation to prejudice and discrimination against their groups (see Alexander, Brewer, & Livingston, 2005; Monteith & Spicer, 2000). As such, rather than automatically approaching intergroup relations from a position of distrust, cross-group friendships may encourage minority group members to envision the potential of achieving positive relations between the groups.

Such far-reaching, positive effects of cross-group friendships have even been observed among people who are most concerned about being rejected due to their racial group membership. In a recent study by Page-Gould et al. (2007), Latino and White students interacted with either a same- or cross-race friendship partner three times over a period of three weeks, during which self-report and physiological indicators of stress and anxiety were assessed. Among participants assigned to a cross-race partner, those high in race-based rejection sensitivity initially experienced high levels of anxiety during the first cross-race meeting. However, their anxious responses were attenuated in subsequent cross-race meetings, such that they were comparable to those observed among participants initially low in race-based rejection sensitivity. Thus, even among those group members who are most apprehensive about becoming targets of prejudice and discrimination, cross-group friendships hold the potential to minimize discomfort in intergroup contact and foster more positive intergroup relationships.

Contact, Trust, and Improving Intergroup Relations: A Call for Cautious Optimism

Although the research presented in this chapter emphasizes the many benefits to be gained from cross-group friendships, we must be careful to acknowledge potential limitations regarding the positive effects we hope to achieve through such relationships (see Hewstone, 2003 for a related view). Encouraging people to trust outgroup members unconditionally would probably be both unrealistic and maladaptive in contexts where histories of relations have been rife with tension and conflict (see Kramer & Messick, 1998) or where outgroup members fail to demonstrate that they are worthy of trust (see Cohen & Steele, 2002). Moreover, strategies designed to enhance intimacy and trust between groups without addressing structural inequalities can inadvertently sustain the dominant group's privileged status and undermine efforts toward social change (Hopkins & Kahani-Hopkins, 2006; Jackman & Crane, 1986; Wright & Lubensky, 2006). Thus, seeking the development of cross-group friendships may be seen in terms of promoting a willingness to trust outgroup members, rather than allowing a dismissal of the possibility that trusting relationships could develop across group boundaries.

Additionally, even when cross-group friendships are forged, group members may still maintain a degree of healthy skepticism in relations with unfamiliar members of the other group (see Cohen & Steele, 2002; Ervin, 2001; Tropp, 2006). For example, Tropp and Bianchi (2006) examined predictors of interest in intergroup contact among members of racial minority and majority groups. In one study, Black participants completed surveys concerning their interest in intergroup contact, in which they reported on their cross-race friendships, perceptions of racial discrimination, the extent to which they value diversity, and the extent to which they believe Whites generally value diversity. Preliminary results showed that Black participants' interest in contact was significantly associated with greater numbers of White friends, $r(67) = .59$, $p < .001$, weaker perceptions of racial discrimination, $r(67) = -.29$, $p < .05$, and stronger beliefs that Whites generally value diversity, $r(66) = .34$, $p < .01$. However, even after controlling for cross-group friendships and perceived discrimination, Black participants' interest in contact was further predicted by the extent to which they believed Whites generally value diversity, $\beta = .28$, $t = 3.12$, $p < .01$. Thus, while cross-group friendships can predict some interest in intergroup contact, minority group members may still be attuned to the perceived values and intentions of members of the racial majority group.

An additional study yielded virtually identical patterns of findings, while also examining whether broader social norms in support of diversity would further predict minority group members' feelings about contact with the racial majority. Once again, perceiving that Whites value diversity predicted greater interest in contact among racial minority participants, even after controlling for cross-group friendships and perceived discrimination, $\beta = .40$, $t = 3.71$, $p < .01$; however, perceiving broader norms in support of diversity did not contribute further to predicting their interest in contact, $\beta = -.18$, $t = -1.72$, $p = .09$. Extending findings from the previous study, these results suggest that broad social norms may not necessarily contribute to reducing suspicion between groups; rather, group members' histories of prior intergroup experiences, and their beliefs about the values and intentions of outgroup members, may be the most central predictors of their interest in contact with members of other groups.

Conclusions

Beyond contact theory's traditional focus on implementing conditions within the contact situation, we must enhance our understanding of psychological conditions that may be necessary for close relationships and a willingness to trust to emerge across group boundaries. Recognition of this shift in emphasis raises a number of issues for us to consider as we attempt to design effective strategies to improve relations between groups. Strategies should seek to enhance an underlying sense of trust in intergroup relationships, such that members of each group can truly feel confident in the goodwill and good intentions of the other. At the same time, we must recognize that these feelings of trust must be earned, as group members are understandably cautious when histories of relations between groups have been marked by tension and conflict. As such, building trust across group boundaries may involve an incremental process, whereby the accrual of positive intergroup experiences, such as through cross-group friendships, can encourage us to consider alternate interpretations and attributions as we reflect more broadly on our relations with outgroup members. Close cross-group relationships may also help us to maintain a modicum of trust even as we face negative experiences with certain outgroup members, rather than allowing potential steps toward positive intergroup relations to unravel completely. Thus, as we look toward future work on intergroup contact, we must attend to both strengths and obstacles involved in group members' attempts to develop close, trusting relationships across group boundaries, as these kinds of relationships hold the potential for effecting broader changes in the nature and structure of relations between groups.

References

Alexander, M., Brewer, M. B., and Livingston, R. (2005). Putting stereotype content in context: Image theory and interethnic stereotypes. *Personality and Social Psychology Bulletin, 31*, 781–794.

Allport, G. W. (1954). *The nature of prejudice.* Reading, MA: Addison-Wesley.

Amir, Y. (1976). The role of intergroup contact in change of prejudice and ethnic relations. In P. A. Katz (Ed.), *Toward the elimination of racism* (pp. 245–308). Elmsford, NY: Pergamon Press.

Aron, A., & McLaughlin-Volpe, T. (2001). Including others in the self: Extensions to own and partner's group memberships. In C. Sedikides & M. B. Brewer (Eds.), *Individual self, relational self, collective self* (pp. 89–108). Philadelphia: Psychology Press.

Aron, A., McLaughlin-Volpe, T., Mashek, D., Lewandowski, G., Wright, S. C., & Aron, E. N. (2004). Including others in the self. In W. Stroebe & M. Hewstone (Eds.), *European Review of Social Psychology, 15,* 101–132.

Brameld, T. (1946). *Minority problems in the public schools.* New York: Harper.

Brewer, M. B., von Hippel, W., & Gooden, M. P. (1999). Diversity and organizational identity: The problem of entrée after entry. In D. A. Prentice and D. T. Miller (Eds.), *Cultural divides: Understanding and overcoming group conflict* (pp. 337–363). New York: Russell Sage.

Brown, L. M., & Dobbins, H. (2004). Students' of color and European American students' stigma-relevant perceptions of university instructors. *Journal of Social Issues, 60,* 157–174.

Brown, R., & Hewstone, M. (2005). An integrative theory of intergroup contact. In M. P. Zanna (Ed.), *Advances in Experimental Social Psychology* (pp. 255–343). San Diego, CA: Academic Press.

Cohen, E. G. (1982). Expectation states and interracial interaction in school settings. *Annual Review of Sociology, 8,* 209–235.

Cohen, G. L., & Steele, C. M. (2002). A barrier of mistrust: How negative stereotypes affect cross-race mentoring. In J. Aronson (Ed.), *Improving academic achievement: Impact of psychological factors on education* (pp. 303–327). San Diego, CA: Academic Press.

Cook, S. W., & Sellitz, C. (1955). Some factors which influence the attitudinal outcomes of personal contact. *International Social Science Bulletin, 7,* 51–58.

Devine, P. G., & Vasquez, K. A. (1998). The rocky road to positive inter-group relations. In J. L. Eberhardt, & S. T. Fiske (Eds.), *Confronting racism: The problem and the response* (pp. 234–262).Thousand Oaks, CA: Sage.

Dovidio, J. F., Gaertner, S. L., Kawakami, K., & Hodson, G. (2002). Why can't we just get along? Interpersonal biases and interracial distrust. *Cultural Diversity and Ethnic Minority Psychology, 8*, 88–102.

Eibach, R. P., & Ehrlinger, J. (2006). "Keep your eyes on the prize": Reference points and racial differences in assessing progress toward equality. *Personality and Social Psychology Bulletin, 32*, 66–77.

Ellison, C. G., & Powers, D. A. (1994). The contact hypothesis and racial attitudes among Black Americans. *Social Science Quarterly, 75*, 385–400.

Ervin, K. S. (2001). Multiculturalism, diversity, and African American college students: Receptive, yet skeptical? *Journal of Black Studies, 31*, 764–776.

Feagin, J., (1991). The continuing significance of race: Anti-Black discrim-ination in public places. *American Sociological Review, 56*, 101–116.

Finlay, K., & Stephan, W. G. (2000). Reducing prejudice: The effects of empathy on intergroup attitudes. *Journal of Applied Social Psychology, 30*, 1720–1737.

Fiske, S. T. (2003). Five core social motives, plus or minus five. In S. J. Spencer, S. Fein, M. P. Zanna, & J. M. Olson (Eds.), *Motivated social cognition: The Ontario symposium* (Vol. 9) (pp. 233–246). Mahwah, NJ: Erlbaum.

Frey, F. E., & Tropp, L. R. (2006). Being seen as individuals versus as group members: Extending research on metaperception to intergroup contexts. *Personality and Social Psychology Review, 10*, 265–280.

Gallup Organization (2001). *Black-White relations in the United States: 2001 update.* Washington, DC: The Gallup Organization.

Grant-Thompson, S. K., & Atkinson, D. R. (1997). Cross-cultural mentor effectiveness and African American male students. *Journal of Black Psychology, 23*, 120–134.

Herek, G. M., & Capitanio, J. P. (1996). "Some of my best friends": Intergroup contact, concealable stigma, and heterosexuals' attitudes toward gay men and lesbians. *Personality and Social Psychology Bulletin, 22*, 412–424.

Hewstone, M. (2003). Intergroup contact: Panacea for prejudice? *The Psychologist, 16*, 352–355.

Hewstone, M., Cairns, E., Voci, A., Hamberger, J., & Niens, U. (2006). Intergroup contact, forgiveness, and experience of "The Troubles" in Northern Ireland. *Journal of Social Issues, 62*, 99–120.

Hopkins, N., & Kahani-Hopkins, V. (2006). Minority group members' theories of intergroup contact: A case study of British Muslims' concep-tualizations of Islamaphobia and social change. *British Journal of Social Psychology, 45*, 245–264.

Insko, C. A., & Schopler, J. (1998). Differential distrust of groups and individuals. In C. Sedikides & J. Schopler (Eds.), *Intergroup cognition and intergroup behavior* (pp. 75–107). Mahwah, NJ: Erlbaum.

Jackman, M. R., & Crane, M. (1986). "Some of my best friends are Black . . .": Interracial friendship and Whites' racial attitudes. *Public Opinion Quarterly*, *50*, 459–486.

Jones, J. M., Lynch, P. D., Tenglund, A., & Gaertner, S. L. (2000). Toward a diversity hypothesis: Multidimensional effects of intergroup contact. *Applied and Preventative Psychology*, *9*, 53–62.

Khmelkov, V. T., & Hallinan, M. T. (1999). Organizational effects on race relations in schools. *Journal of Social Issues*, *55*, 627–645.

Kramer, R. M., & Messick, D. M. (1998). Getting by with a little help from our enemies: Collective paranoia and its role in intergroup relations. In C. Sedikides & J. Schopler (Eds.), *Intergroup cognition and intergroup behavior* (pp. 233–255). Mahwah, NJ: Erlbaum.

Krueger, J. (1996). Personal beliefs and cultural stereotypes about racial characteristics. *Journal of Personality and Social Psychology*, *71*, 536–548.

Levin, S., van Laar, C., & Sidanius, J. (2003). The effects of ingroup and outgroup friendship on ethnic attitudes in college: A longitudinal study. *Group Processes and Intergroup Relations*, *6*, 76–92.

Lindskold, S. (1986). Reducing distrust through carefully introduced conciliation. In S. Worchel & W. G. Austin (Eds.), *Psychology of intergroup relations* (pp. 137–154). Chicago, IL: Nelson Hall.

Miller, N. (2002). Personalization and the promise of contact theory. *Journal of Social Issues*, *58*, 387–410.

Monteith, M. and Spicer, C. V. (2000). Contents and Correlates of Whites' and Blacks' Racial Attitudes. *Journal of Experimental Social Psychology*, *36*, 125–154.

Myrdal, G. (1944). *An American dilemma: The Negro problem and modern democracy*. New York: Harper & Brothers.

National Conference for Community and Justice (2000). *Taking America's pulse: NCCJ's survey of intergroup relations in the United States*. New York: NCCJ.

Page-Gould, E., Mendoza-Denton, R., & Tropp, L. R. (2007). *With a little help from my cross-group friend: Reducing anxiety in intergroup contexts through cross-group friendship*. Manuscript submitted for publication.

Paolini, S., Hewstone, M., Cairns, E., & Voci, A. (2004). Effects of direct and indirect cross-group friendships on judgments of Catholics and Protestants in Northern Ireland. The mediating role of an anxiety-reduction mechanism. *Personality and Social Psychology Bulletin*, *30*, 770–786.

Pettigrew, T. F. (1997a). Generalized intergroup contact effects on prejudice. *Personality and Social Psychology Bulletin*, *23*, 173–185.

Pettigrew, T. F. (1997b). The affective component of prejudice: Empirical support of the new view. In S. A. Tuch & J. K. Martin (Eds.), *Racial attitudes in the 1990s: Continuity and change* (pp. 76–90). Westport, CT: Praeger.

Pettigrew, T. F. (1998). Intergroup contact theory. *Annual Review of Psychology*, *49*, 65–85.

Pettigrew, T. F., & Tropp, L. R. (2005). Allport's intergroup contact hypothesis: Its history and influence. In J. F. Dovidio, P. Glick, & L. Rudman (Eds.), *On the nature of prejudice: Fifty years after Allport* (pp. 262–277). Malden, MA: Blackwell.

Pettigrew, T. F., & Tropp, L. R. (2006). A meta-analytic test of intergroup contact theory. *Journal of Personality and Social Psychology, 90,* 751–783.

Pettigrew, T. F., & Tropp, L. R. (in press). How does intergroup contact reduce prejudice? Meta-analytic tests of three mediators. *European Journal of Social Psychology.*

Plant, E. A., & Devine, P. G. (2003). The antecedents and implications of interracial anxiety. *Personality and Social Psychology Bulletin, 29,* 790–801.

Powers, D. A., & Ellison, C. G. (1995). Interracial contact and Black racial attitudes: The contact hypothesis and selectivity bias. *Social Forces, 74,* 205–226.

Purdie-Vaughns, V. J., Steele, C., Davies, P., & Randall-Crosby (2007). *Social identity contingencies: How diversity cues signal threat or safety for African-Americans in mainstream institutions.* Manuscript submitted for publication.

Robinson, J. W., & Preston, J. D. (1976). Equal status contact and modification of racial prejudice: A reexamination of the contact hypothesis. *Social Forces, 54,* 911–924.

Schofield, J. W., & Eurich-Fulcer, R. (2001). When and how school desegregation improves intergroup relations. In R. Brown & S. L. Gaertner (Eds.), *Blackwell handbook of social psychology: Intergroup processes* (pp. 475–494). Oxford: Blackwell.

Sigelman, L., & Welch, S. (1993). The contact hypothesis revisited: Black–White interaction and positive racial attitudes. *Social Forces, 71,* 781–795.

Stephan, W. G., & Stephan, C. W. (1985). Intergroup anxiety. *Journal of Social Issues, 41,* 157–175.

Stephan, W. G., & Stephan, C. W. (2000). An integrated threat theory of prejudice. In S. Oskamp (Ed.), *Reducing prejudice and discrimination* (pp. 23–45). Mahwah, NJ: Erlbaum.

Terrell, F., Terrell., S. L., & Miller, F. (1993). Level of cultural mistrust as a function of educational and occupational expectations among Black students. *Adolescence, 28,* 573–578.

Tropp, L. R. (2003). The psychological impact of prejudice: Implications for intergroup contact. *Group Processes and Intergroup Relations, 6,* 131–149.

Tropp, L. R. (2006). Stigma and intergroup contact among members of minority and majority status groups. In S. Levin & C. van Laar (Eds.), *Stigma and group inequality: Social psychological perspectives* (pp. 171–191). Mahwah, NJ: Erlbaum.

Tropp, L. R. (2007). Perceived discrimination and interracial contact: Predicting interracial closeness among Black and White Americans. *Social Psychology Quarterly, 70,* 70–81.

Tropp, L. R., & Bianchi, R. A. (2006). Valuing diversity and intergroup contact *Journal of Social Issues, 62,* 533–551.

Tropp, L. R., & Pettigrew, T. F. (2005a). Differential relationships between intergroup contact and affective and cognitive indicators of prejudice. *Personality and Social Psychology Bulletin, 31,* 1145–1158.

Tropp, L. R., & Pettigrew, T. F. (2005b). Relationships between intergroup contact and prejudice among minority and majority status groups. *Psychological Science, 16,* 951–957.

Tyler, T. R. (2001). Why do people rely on others? Social identity and the social aspects of trust. In K. S. Cook (Ed.), *Trust in society* (pp. 285–306). New York: Russell Sage.

Vorauer, J. D., Main, K. J., & O'Connell, G. B. (1998). How do individuals expect to be viewed by members of lower status groups? Content and implications of meta-stereotypes. *Journal of Personality and Social Psychology, 75,* 917–937.

Watkins, C. E., & Terrell, F. (1988). Mistrust level and its effects on counseling expectations in Black client–White counselor relationships. *Journal of Counseling Psychology, 35,* 194–197.

Whaley, A. L. (2001). Cultural mistrust and mental health services for African-Americans: A review and meta-analysis. *The Counseling Psychologist, 29,* 513–531.

Williams, R. M., Jr. (1947). *The reduction of intergroup tensions.* New York: Social Science Research Council.

Wright, S. C., Aron, A., McLaughlin-Volpe, T., & Ropp, S. A. (1997). The extended contact effect: Knowledge of cross-group friendships and prejudice. *Journal of Personality and Social Psychology, 73,* 73–90.

Wright, S. C., Aron, A., & Tropp, L. R. (2002). Including others (and groups) in the self: Self-expansion and intergroup relations. In J. P. Forgas & K. D. Williams (Eds.), *The social self: Cognitive, interpersonal, and intergroup perspectives* (pp. 343–363). New York: Psychology Press.

Wright, S. C., & Lubensky, M. (2006). *Prejudice reduction or collective action: Does reducing prejudice undermine protest?* Paper presented at the 2006 biennial meeting of the Society for the Psychological Study of Social Issues, Long Beach, CA.

8

The Impact of Direct and Extended Cross-Group Friendships on Improving Intergroup Relations

Christiana Vonofakou, Miles Hewstone, Alberto Voci, Stefania Paolini, Rhiannon N. Turner, Nicole T. Tausch, Tania Tam, Jake Harwood, and Ed Cairns

This chapter deals with two of the major recent developments in theory and research on intergroup contact: the focus on direct cross-group friendships, as the most effective form of prejudice-reducing contact, and the impact of extended cross-group friendships (mere knowledge that other in-group members have outgroup friends). Thomas Pettigrew (1997, 1998) is largely responsible for the focus on cross-group friends, and he has suggested that contact in general, and friendship contact in particular, would most likely have its effects via affective processes. We review the impact of these two developments, with special focus on results of our own extensive research program. Our research has provided, first, a systematic analysis of the impact of four affective processes in direct contact with friends: reduced intergroup anxiety, reciprocal self-disclosure, and the promotion of empathy and perspective taking. Our research has also identified mediators of extended contact. We conclude by: (1) emphasizing the importance and complementarity of both forms of contact, direct and extended; (2) pointing to the many applications of this work, such as planned interventions; and (3) referring to some of our current and planned research. Throughout the chapter, as is appropriate in this volume tracing the legacy of Thomas Pettigrew, we highlight his crucial role in the development of these ideas.[1]

Direct Cross-Group Friendship

The contact hypothesis suggests that contact between members of different groups, under appropriate conditions, lessens intergroup prejudice (Allport, 1954; Pettigrew, 1971). Allport proposed that intergroup contact would lead to reduced intergroup prejudice if the contact situation meets four conditions: *equal status between the groups in the situations, common goals, no competition between groups*, and *authority sanction for the contact* (Allport, 1954). Pettigrew (1998) stressed that Allport's four conditions are key facilitating conditions. However, he also added a fifth condition, *friendship potential*, that he regarded as crucial for demonstrating effects of intergroup contact, and which is now also accepted as a facilitating condition (see Dovidio, Gaertner, & Kawakami, 2003). In fact, Pettigrew stressed that Allport's conditions can be considered important partly because they make intergroup friendship possible. Allport (1954) and Amir (1969) had already stressed this point by favoring intimate, rather than trivial, contact, while Cook (1962) referred to it as *acquaintance potential*. However, the importance of cross-group friendship had not been explicitly stated before Pettigrew's (1998) article.

Cross-group friendship implies three of Allport's key conditions (authority sanction is the exception), signifying high-quality contact (e.g., Pettigrew, 1998), and implying long-term contact over a variety of settings. Pettigrew (1998) proposed that contact, especially close contact via cross-group friendships, can reduce prejudice by generating affective ties with the outgroup. Recent research has indeed shown that affective ties with outgroup members, such as feelings of intergroup comfort and liking, develop through close, cross-group friendships (see also Herek & Capitanio, 1996).

Pettigrew (1997) himself undertook the most extensive research on intergroup friendship to date (see also Hamberger & Hewstone, 1997). Over 3,800 majority group respondents in seven probability samples across Europe were asked about their attitudes towards numerically large minority groups in their country, and whether they had friends of another nationality, race, culture, religion or social class. In all samples, Europeans with cross-group friends scored significantly lower on five prejudice measures. The largest effect occurred for a measure of affective prejudice, whereby participants reported how often they had felt sympathy and admiration for the outgroup. The effect of neighbor and coworker contact on prejudice was considerably weaker. Moreover, friendship was related to reduced prejudice towards nine different minority groups, showing that the positive effects of friendship with a member of one group can generalize even to groups not directly involved in the contact.

Pettigrew's (1997, 1998) recommendation that intergroup contact research should focus on cross-group friendship has recently generated several studies on this specific form of intergroup contact. Wagner, Van Dick, Pettigrew, & Christ (2003) investigated the effect of opportunity for contact and cross-group friendship with foreigners in former East and West Germany. They found that respondents from East versus West Germany had less opportunity for contact and fewer cross-group friends. Cross-group friendship subsequently led to more positive outgroup attitudes towards minority groups.

Our own research in Northern Ireland also attests to the importance of opportunity for contact if cross-group friendships are to develop. In a comparison of segregated and mixed areas of Belfast, Tausch, Hewstone, Cairns, & Hughes, (2006) found that, even after relevant sociodemographic variables were partialed out, respondents from mixed areas showed significantly less ingroup bias, felt less anxious when interacting with outgroup members, and felt less threatened by the outgroup, compared to respondents from segregated areas. Respondents from mixed areas also had significantly more contact with cross-group friends than did respondents from segregated areas. Most interestingly, the effects of area on indices of anxiety, threat, and prejudice were mediated by cross-group friendship, indicating that these between-area differences are, in part, due to differences in contact with friends (on average, quantity of contact accounted for 22% of the variance relating to differences between types of neighborhood). Thus, it is not simply a matter of "living together." Geographic proximity does not necessarily predict increased contact (see Grannis, 1998). This opportunity for contact must be taken up, and actual contact must occur. Moreover, in a survey of Hindus and Muslims in India, Tausch, Hewstone, Singh, Ghosh, & Biswas (2006) conducted multiple regressions revealing that contact with friends was significantly associated with reduced social distance, more positive emotions towards the outgroup, and greater support for policies in favor of the outgroup, even when other relevant variables such as conflict experience, perceived status differences between the groups, and ingroup identification were controlled for.

Levin, van Laar, & Sidanius (2003) conducted a relatively rare longitudinal study examining the effect of cross-group friendship on subsequent ingroup bias among a large sample of U.S. college students of White, Asian American, Latino and African American origin. They examined the effects of students' level of ingroup bias at the end of their first year of college on cross-group friendships formed during their second and third year of college. Then, controlling for respondents' initial level of friendship and bias, as well as the influence of a number of background variables, Levin et al. (2003) assessed the effects of these friendships on levels of ingroup bias at the end of the students' fourth year of college. They found that students who had more outgroup friends in their second and third years were less biased in favor of their ethnic group at the end of their fourth year in college. The relation between cross-group friendship and prejudice was, however, reciprocal; students' ingroup bias at the end of their first year of college was associated with fewer outgroup friends in their second and third years of college.

Extended Cross-Group Friendship

In contrast to direct cross-group friendships, extended contact (Wright, Aron, McLaughlin-Volpe, & Ropp, 1997) is based on the idea that the benefits associated with cross-group friendship might also stem from "vicarious" experiences of friendship. That is, knowledge that an ingroup member has a close relationship with an outgroup member can also lead to more positive outgroup attitudes (Wright et al., 1997). Wright and colleagues demonstrated the beneficial effects of extended contact in two cross-sectional studies (Studies 1 and 2), as well as experimentally (Studies 3 and 4). In Studies 1 and 2, for example, White respondents who knew at least one ingroup member with an outgroup friend (Asian American, African American or Latina/Latino) reported weaker outgroup prejudice towards that target group than did those who had no extended outgroup friends; moreover, the more extended outgroup friends a participant had, the weaker the prejudice became (see also Cameron & Rutland, 2006; Liebkind & McAlister, 1999).

Wright et al. (1997) proposed four specific mechanisms that might explain the relationship between extended contact and prejudice. The first mechanism is reduced intergroup anxiety. Intergroup anxiety generally refers to the arousal that occurs as a result of individuals' negative expectations of rejection or discrimination during cross-group interactions, or fears that the interaction partner, or they themselves, may behave in an incompetent or offensive manner (Stephan & Stephan, 1985), but it can also refer to fear of sanctions from ingroup members for fraternizing with the outgroup. Wright and colleagues argued that extended contact should reduce such anxiety, as it involves observing a cross-group friendship that has gone unpunished by other ingroup members or has positive outcomes for the ingroup member involved in the contact. As a result, fear of sanctions, which might otherwise help to maintain negative ingroup norms about the outgroup, might be reduced. Moreover, because extended contact does not involve any actual interaction for the observers, they can observe intergroup contact without the anxiety inherent in face-to-face intergroup encounters (Stephan & Stephan, 1985).

A second potential mediator of extended contact is the perception of positive ingroup norms about the outgroup. Extended contact involves observing the behavior of another ingroup member as they interact with an outgroup member. Observing an ingroup member apparently holding positive attitudes towards the outgroup should lead to the perception that there are positive ingroup norms regarding the outgroup (Haslam, McGarty, & Turner, 1996). A third potential mediator of extended contact is the perception of positive outgroup norms about the ingroup. Watching an outgroup member behaving in a pleasant manner towards the ingroup provides information about the attitudes and norms of the outgroup, showing the observer that the outgroup is interested in positive intergroup relations.

Finally, extended contact should reduce prejudice by increasing the extent to which the outgroup is included in the self. Including others in the self has been shown to be an important aspect of close relationships in the interpersonal literature (Aron, Aron, & Smollan, 1992). We spontaneously incorporate close others in the self, including ingroup members (Smith & Henry, 1996). Thus, when people observe an ingroup member in a close relationship with an outgroup member, they will perceive there to be a considerable overlap between the two. Consequently, they come to see the outgroup member, and eventually the outgroup, as part of the self as well.

Now that we can clearly see the benefits of direct and extended cross-group friendship, it is vital that we obtain a deeper understanding of how and why direct and extended cross-group friendships reduce prejudice. Below we outline our research findings, which have focused specifically on elucidating the mediating mechanisms involved in the effects of direct and extended cross-group friendships.

Mediating Processes in the Effects of Direct and Extended Cross-Group Friendship

Negative Affect—Intergroup Anxiety

Since Pettigrew (1998) argued that cross-group friendship can reduce prejudice via affective processes, particularly reduced intergroup anxiety, we investigated *intergroup anxiety* as a potential mediating variable between direct and extended cross-group friendships and outgroup judgments. We conducted two surveys of cross-community relationships in Northern Ireland (Paolini, Hewstone, Cairns, & Voci, 2004) and found that both direct and extended cross-group friendships between Catholics and Protestants were associated with reduced prejudice towards the religious outgroup and increased perceptions of outgroup variability. In both cases, the effects involved an anxiety-reduction mechanism: intergroup anxiety *completely* mediated the relationship between direct friendship and perceived outgroup variability, and between extended friendship and prejudice, and *partially* mediated the direct friendship–prejudice and extended friendship–variability links.

In addition, we examined the mediating effects of intergroup anxiety between direct cross-group friendship and attitude strength properties (Vonofakou, Hewstone, & Voci, 2007). Attitude strength is generally used to describe attitudes that are more stable over time, more resistant to change, more likely to influence information processing and judgments, and more likely to guide behavior (see Petty & Krosnick, 1995). Bassili (1996) categorized measures of attitude strength by dividing them into meta-attitudinal and operative measures. By meta-attitudinal, Bassili referred to measures that are based on the person's own assessment of his/her attitude, while operative measures are "linked to the judgment processes responsible for attitude responses" (1996, p. 638). Such attitude strength properties have been shown to be related similarly to all four aspects of strength: persistence, resistance, impact on cognition, and impact on behavior (e.g., see Petty & Krosnick, 1995). Thus, we argue that it is not enough to know that prejudicial attitudes can be changed by intergroup contact. One has to show too that the newly changed attitudes are themselves sufficiently strong to prove consequential. Hence, we explored the effects of cross-group friendship on specific attitude strength properties, complementing the assessment of explicit attitudes.

Two studies examined the effects of direct cross-group friendship on heterosexuals' attitudes towards gay men. We tested the effects of cross-group friendships with gay men on outgroup attitudes, meta-attitudinal strength, and a reaction-time measure of attitude accessibility, while simultaneously exploring the mediating effects of intergroup anxiety. Since many researchers have averaged together meta-attitudinal strength properties (see Visser, Bizer, & Krosnick, 2006 for a review), we similarly assessed meta-attitudinal strength via questions concerning attitude certainty, importance, and frequency of thought and discussion. A computer task assessed attitude accessibility based on previous measures of response latencies to attitudinal enquiries (e.g., Houston & Fazio, 1989).

In Study 1, path analysis showed that cross-group friendships were associated with meta-attitudinally stronger and more accessible outgroup attitudes, and the effects on all three criterion variables were fully mediated by intergroup anxiety. In Study 2, structural equation modeling (SEM) showed that cross-group friendships were associated with meta-attitudinally stronger and more accessible outgroup attitudes; friendships had indirect effects on all three criterion variables, via closeness of friendship and intergroup anxiety. Hence, the mediating effects of intergroup anxiety between direct cross-group friendship and attitude strength properties further attested to the broad influence of intergroup anxiety on outgroup judgments. The results also showed that cross-group friendship was associated not only with more positive outgroup attitudes, but also with meta-attitudinally stronger and more accessible outgroup attitudes.

Negative and *Positive Affect*

Our empirical investigations of affective processes in intergroup contact have not been restricted to studies of negative affect, such as intergroup anxiety. In a study of the effects of direct and extended cross-group friendship among White and South Asian[2] high school students on outgroup judgments (Turner, Hewstone, & Voci, 2007), we also investigated self-disclosure as a potential mediating variable, in addition to intergroup anxiety. Self-disclosure is the voluntary presentation of significant aspects of oneself, or information that is of an intimate or personal nature, to another person (Miller, 2002). Self-disclosure is considered to be an important aspect of interpersonal relationships and features prominently in theories of friendship development (e.g., Reis & Shaver, 1988). Specifically, Pettigrew (1998) himself argued that cross-group friendships are especially effective in reducing prejudice, because friendships are more likely to generate self-disclosure.

We conducted four cross-sectional studies (Turner et al., 2007). Studies 1 and 4 specifically investigated the effects of direct cross-group friendship, while Studies 2 and 3 examined both the effects of direct and extended cross-group friendship. In Study 1, direct cross-group friendship among White elementary school children predicted more positive explicit outgroup attitudes, mediated by intergroup anxiety *and* self-disclosure; more specifically, Study 4 showed that reciprocal self-disclosure improved outgroup attitudes via empathy, importance of contact, and intergroup trust. In Study 2, direct and extended cross-group friendship among White and South Asian high school students positively predicted explicit outgroup attitudes, mediated by intergroup anxiety *and* self-disclosure; while Study 3 replicated these findings in a larger independent sample. Reciprocal self-disclosure was assessed by asking participants to report how often they disclosed information of a personal nature to members of the outgroup, and how often individual outgroup members disclosed information of a personal nature to them.

It should also be noted that we assessed implicit attitudes via the Implicit Association Test (IAT, Greenwald, McGhee, & Schwartz, 1998) in Studies 1, 2, and 3. Study 1 found that cross-group friendship had a direct impact on implicit attitudes, while in Studies 2 and 3 opportunity for contact (which had not been measured in Study 1) had a direct impact on implicit attitudes (whereas cross-group friendship did not). Thus, while cross-group friendships had an effect on explicit attitudes via deliberative mediating processes, opportunity for contact seemed to bypass those processes to influence implicit attitudes directly.

Building on the previous findings showing that cross-group friendships do not merely exert their effects by reducing negative affect (intergroup anxiety), but also by promoting positive affect (e.g., self-disclosure, empathy), we investigated the effects of direct and extended cross-group friendships among high school students attending religiously segregated or integrated schools in Northern Ireland. We examined the interplay between self-disclosure, peer outgroup attitudes, and empathy as possible mediating variables (Tam, Hewstone, Cairns, & Geddes, 2006). Results showed that both forms of contact had somewhat different underlying mechanisms. While direct cross-group friendship increased self-disclosure between group members, extended cross-group friendship improved the perceptions of peer attitudes toward the outgroup (see also discussion of the study by

Turner, Hewstone, Voci, & Vonofakou, in press, below). However, both the increase in self-disclosure and the improvement in perceived peer attitudes toward the outgroup then led to increased empathy toward the outgroup. It was this empathy that was extremely important to prejudice reduction—it was, in fact, the key mediating variable in our model. This result is in line with our previous finding regarding direct cross-group friendships, showing that self-disclosure improves outgroup attitudes via empathy (Turner et al., 2007, Study 4).

We conducted two further cross-sectional studies examining positive and negative intergroup emotions, in addition to empathy, as potential mediating variables of direct cross-group friendships in two studies of undergraduate students at universities in Northern Ireland (Tam, Hewstone, Kenworthy, et al., 2006). These students are especially interesting to study, as their time at a mixed university provides for many the first significant experience of mixing across the religious divide. Mackie and Smith (1998) have argued that emotions are particularly important for predicting behavior, as compared to attitudes. Tam, Hewstone, Kenworthy et al. (2006, Study 1) showed that positive emotions and empathy were strong mediators of the effects of direct cross-group friendship on behavioral tendencies toward the outgroup; this effect held over and above the mediating effect of negative emotions, even when controlling for outgroup attitudes. In particular, Study 1 provided evidence of the strong mediating effect of empathy between direct cross-group friendship and positive and negative behavioral tendencies toward the outgroup, respectively. As an extension, Tam, Hewstone, Kenworthy, et al. (2006, Study 2) incorporated two types of empathy—*affective empathy* ("empathic emotion") and *cognitive empathy* ("perspective-taking"). The results showed that both types of empathy mediated the impact of direct cross-group friendship on behavioral tendencies (positive and negative) toward the outgroup. Thus, these studies again demonstrate the importance of not only reducing negative emotions, but also of encouraging positive emotions.

Focusing on extended cross-group friendships, we investigated intergroup trust in Northern Ireland as a potential mediating variable between extended cross-group friendships and behavioral tendencies (Tam, Hewstone, Kenworthy, & Cairns, 2006). Intergroup trust entails a variety of perceptions, including the belief that the other group will attempt to cooperate and is open-minded and prepared to engage in earnest, cooperative problem-solving (Kramer & Carnevale, 2001). Structural equation modeling revealed that intergroup trust (but neither attitude nor inter*personal* trust) mediated the effects of extended cross-group friendship on outgroup behavioral tendencies. This fits with the notion of trust as a more demanding criterion of intergroup relations than attitudes, because trusting an outgroup or its members involves a potential risk to the self or the ingroup that holding a positive outgroup attitude does not. Trust implies an interdependence between the groups that is not required for the development of attitudes toward them.

Finally, we tested the specific mechanisms underlying extended cross-group friendship, as proposed by Wright et al. (1997; Turner et al., in press). As mentioned earlier, Wright et al. proposed four processes that might explain the relationship between extended contact and reduced prejudice: reduced intergroup anxiety, positive ingroup norms, positive outgroup norms, and the inclusion of the outgroup in the self. Our research provided the first comprehensive test of the mediators of extended contact across two independent samples, in the context of White British experiences with, and attitudes towards, South Asians[2] in the United Kingdom. We conducted two studies, one among undergraduate students and another among teenagers attending British high schools. Supporting the extended contact hypothesis, we found all four proposed mechanisms to mediate the relationship between extended contact and outgroup attitudes, controlling for the effect of direct contact. A number of alternative models were ruled out, indicating that the four mediators operate at the same level rather than predicting one another.

Discussion: Implications and Future Directions

The above review of research on direct and extended cross-group friendships demonstrates the importance and complementarity of both forms of contact. Direct cross-group friendships are highly effective in bringing about positive outgroup judgments. By showing that direct cross-group friendship plays a key part in determining meta-attitudinal strength, as well as the accessibility of outgroup attitudes, our research has also come one step closer to demonstrating *why* close direct experience is so very important for designing maximally effective contact interventions that will change outgroup attitudes. However, a prerequisite for the formation of direct cross-group friendships is opportunity for contact. In cases where there is limited opportunity for contact (e.g., where there is extensive residential, or educational, segregation) the importance of extended contact cannot be over-emphasized.

In addition, where cross-group friendships arise, they may provide access to friendship networks; by meeting other outgroup members through each existing outgroup friend, more cross-group friendships may develop. That is, access gained to friendship networks can be a major source of increasing cross-group friendships (Miller & Harrington, 1990; Slavin, 1985). Such social relations have also been shown to affect minority students' academic achievement, while access to desegregated networks can help them to obtain better employment (Braddock & McPartland, 1987; Pettigrew, 1967; Schofield, 1991). As Pratto, Sidanius, and Levin (2007) noted, recommending friends for jobs favors members of the dominant group in society (and maintains the social hierarchy) when unemployment rates differ by group, and friendship patterns are segregated.

Despite the difficulties of instigating cross-group friendships in segregated settings, the impact of extended cross-group friendship increases optimism about our ability to improve intergroup relations. One person who has cross-group friends has the potential to affect the attitudes of many individuals who do not. Extended contact, because it is associated with lower intergroup anxiety and higher category salience, could also prove a potent means of *preparing* participants for intergroup contact. Thus, exposing people to extended contact prior to direct contact might be a particularly powerful prescription for challenging pernicious prejudice. We also believe that experience of extended contact may moderate between opportunities for contact and actual contact, thus explaining why some individuals "take up" opportunities for contact provided by mixed environments, while others do not.

Furthermore, the above review yielded ample support for Pettigrew's (1998) emphasis on affective (positive and negative) mediating processes between cross-group friendships and outgroup judgments (Brown & Hewstone, 2005). We also obtained support for the proposed mediating processes involved in extended cross-group friendship (Wright et al., 1997). Consequently, the findings discussed point to several practical implications to be considered when designing contact interventions. For example, given the impact of both direct and extended cross-group friendships on outgroup attitudes through the mechanism of self-disclosure, contact schemes might include school exchanges, community activities and youth clubs aimed at linking White and South Asian communities in the UK (see Raw, 2005–6). In fact, any form of integration that encourages friendship should be encouraged. This will generate empathy and trust in the outgroup which, in turn, should result in more positive intergroup relations. Interventions should also emphasize the benefits of outgroup self-disclosure for achieving personal goals, for example learning more about other cultures and developing interpersonal skills (we have discussed the policy implications of our work in Northern Ireland, specifically, in Hewstone et al., 2005).

Future Research Directions

We acknowledge that "to be a friend" has different meanings in different languages and cultures, and that individuals vary widely in how they label another person as a close friend, a friend, or just an acquaintance (Triandis, Bontempo, Villareal, & Asai, 1988). Van Dick et al. (2004) noted that perceived importance appears to be less prone to such differences. Van Dick et al. demonstrated that the perceived importance of intergroup contact mediates much of the effect of intergroup contact (e.g., cross-group acquaintances and friends) on prejudice. They argued that the simple fact that an individual has outgroup friends is not the key in reducing prejudice itself but, rather, it is the subjective appraisal of a valuable interpersonal relationship. Thus, future research may expand the work presented in this chapter by employing more "sensitive" indices of cross-group friendships. Research should also explore a wider range of social relationships as forms of intergroup contact. For example, we have shown that relationships with grandparents predicted attitudes towards older adults, as one would expect from the literature on cross-group friends. Grandparent contact was most effective when it took place with the grandparent one felt closest to, and contact was mediated and moderated by the same processes identified in research on cross-group friends (Harwood, Hewstone, Paolini, & Voci, 2005).

The research presented in this chapter has focused primarily on the effects of cross-group friendships for majority group members. However, it should be noted that recent meta-analytic reviews by Pettigrew and Tropp (2000, 2006; Tropp & Pettigrew, 2005) showed that while intergroup contact had a reliable impact on outgroup judgments, this effect was much more apparent for majorities. Hopkins and Kahani-Hopkins (2006) have also argued that intergroup situations may be perceived and interpreted in distinct ways for majority and minority members, and may, thus, have different intergroup effects. Pettigrew and Tropp's work showed that even when intergroup contact was optimally arranged to maximize beneficial intergroup effects, minorities displayed less change than majorities. In particular, for majority group samples, Allport's contact conditions yielded the strongest relationships between contact and reduced prejudice, whereas for minority group samples there was no such effect (Tropp & Pettigrew, 2005). Thus, future research should investigate how to optimize the beneficial effects of cross-group friendships for the minority party.

Finally, we do not claim to have exhausted the set of important mediating variables involved. For example, it has been proposed that contact may function to reduce prejudice because familiarity fosters liking (e.g., Pettigrew & Tropp, 2006). However, Buttny and Williams' (2000) interview data with African-Americans showed that the value given to receiving respect, irrespective of being liked, often shapes their contact experiences. Shelton, Richeson, and Vorauer (2007), in their work on interracial encounters, place especially high emphasis on respondents' perceptions that they are being rejected on the basis of their race ("race-based rejection sensitivity"); they report that Blacks with strong rejection sensitivity have fewer White friends.

Conclusion

The study of intergroup contact has come a very long way since the pioneering work of Gordon Allport (1954), over 50 years ago. It is fitting that the most recent developments, and improvements, owe so much to the work of Thomas Pettigrew, himself a graduate student of Allport's at Harvard University. In this chapter we have sought to show the importance, and impact, of theory and research on direct and indirect friendships, two concepts which we believe are central to the demonstrable success of contact and its huge potential as a social intervention for reducing prejudice. Using a variety of analyses focusing on the identification of mediating variables (analyses which have only been developed since Allport's work), we believe we have extended Allport's and Pettigrew's insights, and strengthened their view that intergroup contact has massive policy potential.

Acknowledgment

The preparation and writing of this chapter was funded, in part, by grants from the Economic and Social Research Council, the Russell Sage Foundation, and the Community Relations Unit, Northern Ireland.

Notes

1　We also take this opportunity to thank Tom for the inspiration he has provided, and the many forms of support—intellectual, social, and moral—he has provided to our research endeavors. He is the perfect embodiment of scholarly endeavor applied, with rigor, to activist social science committed to improving our society.
2　The term "South Asians" refers to Indian, Pakistani, and Bangladeshi people who are living in the UK.

References

Allport, G. W. (1954). *The nature of prejudice.* Oxford, UK: Addison-Wesley.

Amir, Y. (1969). Contact hypothesis in ethnic relations. *Psychological Bulletin, 71,* 319–342.

Aron, A., Aron, E. N., & Smollan, D. (1992). Inclusion of other in the self scale and the structure of interpersonal closeness. *Journal of Personality and Social Psychology, 63,* 596–612.

Bassili, J. N. (1996). Meta-judgmental versus operative indexes of psychological attributes: The case of measures of attitude strength. *Journal of Personality and Social Psychology, 71,* 637–653.

Braddock, J. H. II., & McPartland, J. (1987). How minorities continue to be excluded from equal employment opportunities: Research on labor market and institutional barriers. *Journal of Social Issues, 43,* 5–39.

Brown, R., & Hewstone, H. (2005). An interactive theory of intergroup contact. In M. Zanna (Ed.), *Advances in experimental social psychology* (Vol. 37) (pp. 255–343). San Diego, CA: Academic Press.

Buttny, R., & Williams, P. L. (2000). Demanding respect: The uses of reported speech in discursive constructions of interracial contact. *Discourse and Society, 11,* 109–133.

Cameron, L., & Rutland, A. (2006). Extended contact through story reading in school: Reducing children's prejudice towards the disabled. *Journal of Social Issues, 62,* 489–510.

Cook, S. W. (1962). The systematic analysis of socially significant events: A strategy for social research. *Journal of Social Issues, 18,* 66–84.

Dovidio, J. F., Gaertner, S. L., & Kawakami, K. (2003). Intergroup contact: The past, present, and the future. *Group Processes and Intergroup Relations, 6,* 5–20.

Grannis, R. (1998). The importance of trivial streets: Residential streets and residential segregation. *American Journal of Sociology, 103,* 1530–1564.

Greenwald, A. G., McGhee, D. E., & Schwartz, J. L. K. (1998). Measuring individual differences in implicit cognition: The implicit association test. *Journal of Personality and Social Psychology, 74,* 1464–1480.

Hamberger, J., & Hewstone, M. (1997). Inter-ethnic contact as a predictor of prejudice: Tests of a model in four West European nations. *British Journal of Social Psychology, 36*, 173–190.

Harwood, J., Hewstone, M., Paolini, S., & Voci, A. (2005). Grandparent–grandchild contact and attitudes towards older adults: Moderator and mediator effects. *Personality and Social Psychology Bulletin, 31*, 393–406.

Haslam, S. A., McGarty, C., & Turner, J. C. (1996). Salient group membership and persuasion: The role of social identity in the validation of beliefs. In J. L. Nye & A. M. Brown (Eds.), *What is social about social cognition? Research on socially shared cognition in small groups* (pp. 29–56). Thousand Oaks, CA: Sage.

Herek, G. M., & Capitanio, J. P. (1996). "Some of my best friends": Intergroup contact, concealable stigma, and heterosexuals' attitudes toward gay men and lesbians. *Personality and Social Psychology Bulletin, 22*, 412–424.

Hewstone, M., Cairns, E., Voci, A., Paolini, S., McLernon, F., Crisp, R., et al. (2005). Intergroup contact in a divided society: Challenging segregation in Northern Ireland. In D. Abrams, J. M. Marques, & M. A. Hogg (Eds.), *The social psychology of inclusion and exclusion* (pp. 265–292). Philadelphia: Psychology Press.

Hopkins, N., & Kahani-Hopkins, V. (2006). Minority group members' theories of intergroup contact: A case study of British Muslims' conceptualizations of "Islamophobia" and social change. *British Journal of Social Psychology, 45*, 245–264.

Houston, D. A., & Fazio, R. H. (1989). Biased processing as a function of attitude accessibility: Making objective judgments subjectively. *Social Cognition, 7*, 51–66.

Kramer, R. M., & Carnevale, P. J. (2001). Trust and intergroup negotiation. In R. Brown & S. Gaertner (Eds.), *Blackwell handbook of social psychology: Intergroup processes* (pp. 431–450). Malden, MA: Blackwell Publishing.

Levin, S., van Laar, C., & Sidanius, J. (2003). The effects of ingroup and outgroup friendship on ethnic attitudes in college: A longitudinal study. *Group Processes and Intergroup Relations, 6*, 76–92.

Liebkind, K., & McAlister, A. L. (1999). Extended contact through peer modelling to promote tolerance in Finland. *European Journal of Social Psychology, 29*, 765–780.

Mackie, D. M., & Smith, E. R. (1998). Intergroup relations: Insights from a theoretically integrative approach. *Psychological Review, 105*, 499–529.

Miller, N. (2002). Personalization and the promise of contact theory. *Journal of Social Issues, 58*, 387–410.

Miller, N., & Harrington, H. J. (1990). A model of social category salience for intergroup relations: Empirical tests of relevant variables. In P. Drenth, J. Sergeant, & R. Takens (Eds.), *European perspectives in psychology* (Vol. 3) (pp. 205–220). Chichester, UK: Wiley.

Paolini, S., Hewstone, M., Cairns, E., & Voci, A. (2004). Effects of direct and indirect cross-group friendships on judgments of Catholics and Protestants in Northern Ireland: The mediating role of an anxiety-reduction mechanism. *Personality and Social Psychology Bulletin, 30,* 770–786.

Pettigrew, T. (1967). Social evaluation theory: Convergences and applications. In D. Levine (Ed.), *Nebraska symposium on motivation* (Vol. 15) (pp. 241–311). Lincoln, NE: University of Nebraska Press.

Pettigrew, T. F. (1971). *Racially separate or together?* New York: McGraw-Hill.

Pettigrew, T. F. (1997). Generalized intergroup contact effects on prejudice. *Personality and Social Psychology Bulletin, 23,* 173–185.

Pettigrew, T. F. (1998). Intergroup contact theory. *Annual Review of Psychology, 49,* 65–85.

Pettigrew, T. F., & Tropp, L. R. (2000). Does intergroup contact reduce prejudice? Recent meta-analytic findings. In S. Oskamp (Ed.), *Reducing prejudice and discrimination* (pp. 93–114). Mahwah, NJ: Erlbaum.

Pettigrew, T. F., & Tropp, L. (2006). A meta-analytic test of intergroup contact theory. *Journal of Personality and Social Psychology, 90,* 751–783.

Petty, R. E., & Krosnick, J. A. (Eds.) (1995). *Attitude strength: Antecedents and consequences.* Mahwah, NJ: Erlbaum.

Pratto, F., Sidanius, J., & Levin, S. (2007). Social dominance theory and the dynamics of intergroup relations: Taking stock and looking forward. In W. Stroebe & M. Hewstone (Eds.), *European Review of Social Psychology* (Vol. 17) (pp. 271–320). Hove, UK: Psychology Press.

Raw, A. (2005–6). *Schools linking project 2005–06: Final evaluation report.* Unpublished report.

Reis, H. T., & Shaver, P. (1988). Intimacy as an interpersonal process. In S. Duck (Ed.), *Handbook of personal relationships* (pp. 367–389). Chichester: Wiley.

Schofield, J. W. (1991). School desegregation and intergroup relations: A review of the literature. In G. Grant (Ed.), *Review of research in education* (Vol. 17) (pp. 335–409). Washington, DC: American Educational Research Association.

Shelton, J. N., Richeson, J. A., & Vorauer, J. D. (2007). Threatened identities and interethnic interactions. In W. Stroebe & M. Hewstone (Eds.), *European Review of Social Psychology* (Vol. 17) (pp. 321–58). Hove, UK: Psychology Press.

Slavin, R. E. (1985). Cooperative learning: Applying contact theory in desegregated schools. *Journal of Social Issues, 41,* 45–62.

Smith, E. R., & Henry, S. (1996). An in-group becomes part of the self: Response-time evaluation. *Personality and Social Psychological Bulletin, 22,* 635–642.

Stephan, W. G., & Stephan, C. W. (1985). Intergroup anxiety. *Journal of Social Issues, 41,* 157–175.

Tam, T., Hewstone, M., Cairns, E., & Geddes, L. (2006). *The effects of segregation and integration in the Northern Irish educational system.* Unpublished manuscript.

Tam, T., Hewstone, M., Kenworthy, J., Cairns, E., Voci, A., & van Dick, R. (2006). *Intergroup emotions and empathy in contact between Catholics and Protestants in Northern Ireland*. Unpublished manuscript.

Tam, T., Hewstone, M., Kenworthy, J., & Cairns, E. (2006) *Intergroup trust in Northern Ireland*. Unpublished manuscript.

Tausch, N., Hewstone, M., Cairns, E., & Hughes, J. (2006). *A comparison of segregated and mixed areas of Belfast*. Manuscript in preparation.

Tausch, N., Hewstone, M., Singh, P., Ghosh, E.S.K., & Biswas, U.N. (2006). *Friendship between Hindus and Muslims in India as a predictor of outgroup attitude, policy support, and intergroup emotions*. Manuscript in preparation.

Triandis, H. C., Bontempo, R., Villareal, M. J., & Asai, M. (1988). Individualism and collectivism: Cross-cultural perspectives on self–ingroup relationships. *Journal of Personality and Social Psychology*, *54*, 323–338.

Tropp, L. R., & Pettigrew, T. F. (2005). Differential relationships between intergroup contact and affective and cognitive dimensions of prejudice. *Personality and Social Psychology Bulletin*, *31*, 1145–1158.

Turner, R. N., Hewstone, M., & Voci, A. (2007). Reducing explicit and implicit outgroup prejudice via direct and extended contact: The mediating role of self-disclosure and intergroup anxiety. *Journal of Personality and Social Psychology*, *93*, 369–388.

Turner, R. N., Hewstone, M., Voci, A., & Vonofakou, C. (in press). A test of the extended intergroup contact hypothesis: The mediating role of intergroup anxiety, perceived ingroup and outgroup norms, intergroup anxiety and inclusion of the outgroup in the self. *Journal of Personality and Social Psychology*.

Van Dick, R., Wagner, U., Pettigrew, T. F., Christ, O., Wolf, C., Petzel, T., et al. (2004). The role of perceived importance in intergroup contact. *Journal of Personality and Social Psychology*, *87*, 211–227.

Visser, P. S., Bizer, G. Y., & Krosnick, J. A. (2006). Exploring the latent structure of strength-related attitude attributes. In M. Zanna (Ed.), *Advances in Experimental Social Psychology* (pp. 1–68). Orlando, FL: Academic Press.

Vonofakou, C., Hewstone, M., & Voci, A. (2007). Contact with outgroup friends as a predictor of meta-attitudinal strength and accessibility of attitudes towards gay men. *Journal of Personality and Social Psychology*, *92*, 804–820.

Wagner, U., Van Dick, R., Pettigrew, T. F., & Christ, O. (2003). Ethnic prejudice in East and West Germany: The explanatory power of intergroup contact. *Group Processes and Intergroup Relations*, *6*, 22–36.

Wright, S. C., Aron, A., McLaughlin-Volpe, T., & Ropp, S. A. (1997). The extended contact effect: Knowledge of cross-group friendships and prejudice. *Journal of Personality and Social Psychology*, *73*, 73–90.

Part III

Intergroup Relations and Reflections on One's Own Group Membership

9

Ingroup and Outgroup Contact

A Longitudinal Study of the Effects of Cross-Ethnic Friendships, Dates, Roommate Relationships and Participation in Segregated Organizations

Colette van Laar, Shana Levin, and Jim Sidanius

All three of us have been profoundly influenced by Thomas Pettigrew's work: by his continuing emphasis on the role of social structure as crucial to understanding relations between groups (Pettigrew, 1988; 1996; 1998a; 2006); by his focus on cutting-edge methodologies, including his call to investigate intergroup relations in their most real form—longitudinally, in long-term complex relations between groups (Pettigrew, 1998b; Pettigrew & Tropp, 2006); and, most crucially, by his synthesis and integration of the state of knowledge with regard to contact processes between groups (Pettigrew, 1998b; 2002; Pettigrew & Tropp, 2005; 2006). His recent meta-analysis with Linda Tropp answers the central question of the literature, namely, does contact actually affect prejudice, or is it the other way around? There are very few researchers in social psychology who can be said to have definitively settled a theoretical question. Pettigrew is one of them. At the same time, this work has identified where more research is needed, in particular on the effects of long-term intergroup contact, on factors in the ingroup contact situation that may negatively affect intergroup relations, and on relations between multiple groups and how the contact effects may differ across these groups (Pettigrew & Tropp, 2000; 2006). These are the questions that we have pursued in our own research.

In this chapter, we summarize the results of our longitudinal work on contact at a large multiethnic university in the United States (Levin, Taylor, & Caudle, 2007; Levin, Van Laar, & Foote, 2006; Levin, Van Laar, & Sidanius, 2003; Sidanius, Van Laar, Levin, & Sinclair, 2004; Van Laar, Levin, Sinclair, & Sidanius, 2005). Specifically, we examine how being friends with, having romantic relationships with, and being roommates with members of different ethnic groups on a large university campus affect intergroup attitudes and behaviors. As students are living, socializing, and taking classes with individuals with different ethnicities, the college experience provides, in principle, many opportunities for cross-group relationships to develop. Also, contact with ethnically diverse friends, romantic partners, and roommates meets many of the conditions thought to facilitate prejudice reduction: equal status, cooperative interaction, common goals, acquaintance potential, and support of relevant authorities for interethnic contact (Allport, 1954; Amir, 1969; Pettigrew, 1998b). As such, the ethnically diverse campus environment provides an ideal setting for testing the contact hypothesis. At the same time, however, there were ethnic tensions on the campus we studied. In such an environment, positive contact processes could be especially meaningful in improving intergroup relations.

A Longitudinal Study of Intergroup Contact

The study followed a representative cohort of 2,132 students from the time they entered the University of California, Los Angeles (UCLA) in 1996 through the next five years (see Sidanius, Levin, Van Laar, & Sears, 2007). Each year, students completed telephone surveys regarding their academic, social, and psychological experiences during college, and indicated their attitudes toward and contact with members of the four main ethnic groups on campus: Whites, Asians, Latinos, and African Americans. UCLA is quite typical of large multiethnic universities in the United States. It has high levels of ethnic diversity: At the time of the study, 34% of students were White, 39% Asian, 17% Latino, and 6% African American. At this time, there were also conflicts on campus over university and societal resources, with recent anti-immigrant propositions on the California election ballots, civil unrest in Los Angeles following the acquittal of four White police officers charged with the (videotaped) beating of a Black motorist,

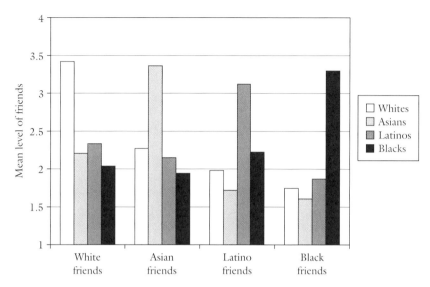

Figure 9.1 Ethnicity of friends during the second and third years of college combined, by ethnic group.
Note: Means range from 1–5 (1 = none, 2 = few, 3 = many, 4 = most, 5 = all).

Rodney King, and strong challenges to affirmative action programs targeting African American and Latino students on campuses across the United States. The UCLA campus is also somewhat ethnically segregated, with students tending to be friends with, live with, and have romantic relationships with members of their own ethnic group (see Figures 9.1, 9.2, and 9.3). There are also many ethnic organizations serving students of particular ethnic groups, such as the African student union, and various Latino social groups. As a result of the history shaping American ethnic relations, African American and Latino students perceive more ethnic discrimination on campus against themselves and their ethnic groups than do White and Asian American students. Despite a potentially very positive ethnic environment, then, integration of students of different ethnicities is actually far from complete at UCLA, and many inequalities exist between students of the different ethnic groups.

Research Questions and Analytic Strategy

Using this multiethnic campus environment as our intergroup setting, and the contact hypothesis (Allport, 1954; Amir, 1969; Pettigrew,

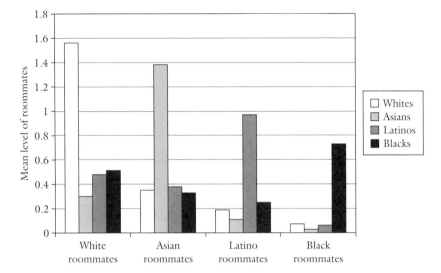

Figure 9.2   Ethnicity of roommates during the second and third years of college combined, by ethnic group.

Note: Bars indicate mean number of roommates from each group.

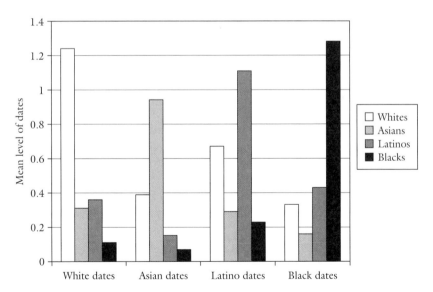

Figure 9.3   Ethnicity of dates during the second and third years of college combined, by ethnic group.

Note: Means range from 0–2 (0 = did not have any dates of that ethnicity, 1 = dated someone of that ethnicity in either second or third year, 2 = dated someone of that ethnicity in both second and third year).

1998b) and the social identity perspective (Tajfel & Turner, 1979; 1986; Turner, Hogg, Oakes, Reicher, & Wetherell, 1987) as our theoretical frameworks, we examined whether more positive ethnic attitudes and behaviors developed at the end of college as a result of the contact students had with ethnically diverse friends, romantic partners, and roommates during college. Due to the longitudinal design, we were able to examine how students' ethnic attitudes at the beginning of college affected their contact choices during college, and—controlling for these selection effects—examine the effects of this contact during college on intergroup attitudes and behaviors at the end of college. Also, as students were randomly assigned to their roommates in the first year of college, the study included a natural experiment on the effects of contact with ethnically diverse roommates (Van Laar et al., 2005).

We were able to examine contact between several groups at once. Previous research has tended to restrict its focus to contact between two groups. Such a simplification can restrict the external validity of contact effects, as contact in the real world often involves contact between multiple groups. Examination of contact between multiple groups raises at least three research questions worthy of further investigation. First, do the characteristics of the various groups engaged in contact influence the outcome of this contact? The limited research available on this question suggests that individuals' group memberships and the group memberships of the people they come into contact with may influence the extent to which contact reduces prejudice. Second, an examination of multiple group contact allows us to examine whether the beneficial effects of contact with members of one outgroup generalize to other outgroups (Brown, Vivian, & Hewstone, 1999; Dovidio, Gaertner, & Kawakami, 2003; Gonzalez & Brown, 2003; Pettigrew, 1997; Pettigrew & Tropp, 2006). Third, an examination of contact between multiple groups—including members of one's own group—allows us to examine whether contact with ingroup members increases prejudice. In ethnically heterogeneous contexts, extensive contact with ingroup members may decrease opportunities for interaction with outgroup members and reinforce biased ingroup norms (Blanchard, Lilly, & Vaughn, 1991; Turner, 1991).

A focus on ingroup contacts also allows us to examine the effects of ethnically segregated environments. Although efforts to diversify college campuses have led to the increased representation of minorities in the student body, in many institutions students from different ethnic groups remain largely segregated by ethnicity. Some fear that such ethnic segregation leads to increased ethnocentrism and racial intolerance (D'Souza, 1991); others argue that segregation is a barrier to racial integration because it undermines efforts to establish firm institutional norms of intergroup acceptance (Pettigrew, 1998c). Still others argue that segregation is beneficial and should not be discouraged among minority individuals in predominantly White institutions, because for these individuals same-race peer groups provide the resources necessary to overcome barriers erected by a hostile racial climate (Hurtado, Milem, Clayton-Pedersen, & Allen, 1998; 1999; Loo & Rolison, 1986).

A particular case of segregation that we were able to examine comes in the form of ethnically oriented student organizations on campus, such as the African Student Union and the Latin American Student Association. Most prior research has examined the effects of membership in minority ethnic organizations on minority students and has found significant effects of such ingroup contact on intergroup attitudes and behaviors (e.g., see Trevino, 1992). Going beyond this research, we argue that membership in mostly-White fraternities and sororities is likely to affect White students in a similar fashion. Primary among such predominantly White organizations are the fraternities and sororities belonging to the "Greek system," referring to the Greek letters that serve as names of these organizations.

The history of American fraternities and sororities makes it clear that such organizations have served as exclusive enclaves of racial and socioeconomic privilege for most of American history. Although these fraternities and sororities were always exclusionist in both racial and socioeconomic terms, explicitly discriminatory entrance requirements did not become widespread until the beginning of the twentieth century. By 1928, more than half of the national fraternities and sororities had written rules and constitutions explicitly excluding applicants on the basis of religious affiliation and "race." These explicitly discriminatory practices were not seriously challenged until the end of World War II. Thus, when exploring the effects of ethnically oriented student organizations, we argue that one should not restrict attention to organizations directed towards students from minority groups, but should also extend one's focus to include predominantly White Greek organizations.

We examined the effects of membership in minority and Greek organizations and contact with ingroup and outgroup friends, dates, and roommates on three different dimensions of prejudice: affective, cognitive, and behavioral. Meta-analytic findings indicate that affective measures are more likely to show the benefits of contact than cognitive measures (Tropp & Pettigrew, 2005). The two affective indicators of prejudice that we used were negative feelings toward members of other ethnic groups and intergroup anxiety (feelings of unease and lack of competence when interacting with members of other ethnic groups; Stephan & Stephan, 2000). The cognitive indicators of prejudice were symbolic racism (Sears & Henry, 2005), social dominance orientation (Sidanius & Pratto, 1999) and antimiscegenation attitudes. Finally, the behavioral indicators of prejudice were the ethnic heterogeneity of one's friends and romantic partners. The analytic strategy we used was to examine the impact of college contact experiences on these measures of prejudice, controlling for various self-selection variables—including precollege attitudes and behaviors, precollege contact experiences, and various demographic factors—using hierarchical regression techniques (see Levin et al., 2003; 2006; 2007; Sidanius et al., 2004; Van Laar et al., 2005 for details). As such, we removed much of the variance in prejudice associated with individual variability, including preexisting differences in attitudes and behaviors, demographic factors, and previous contact experiences that may have predisposed individuals to engage in intergroup contact in college.

Self-Selection Effects on Contact

Examining the results, we first found clear effects of self-selection: students who came into college with more positive intergroup attitudes, and those who had more contact experiences with members of other ethnic groups prior to college entry were more likely to have contact with members of ethnic outgroups in college. Controlling for these self-selection effects, the results also showed both beneficial and harmful effects of interethnic and ingroup contact.

Effects of Contact on Affective, Cognitive and Behavioral Indicators of Prejudice

The most reassuring findings were that interethnic roommate, romantic and friendship relationships during college had positive effects on later ethnic attitudes and behaviors (Levin et al., 2003; 2007; Van Laar et al., 2005). Specifically, longitudinal analyses indicated that, controlling for precollege attitudes and contacts and a number of background variables, students who had more friends and romantic partners of other ethnicities during college became less biased in favor of their ethnic group (contact with outgroup friends $\beta = -.11$,

$p < .001$; contact with outgroup romantic partners $\beta = -.12$, $p < .01$) and felt less anxious interacting with members of other ethnic groups at the end of college (contact with outgroup friends $\beta = -.14$, $p < .001$; contact with outgroup romantic partners $\beta = -.08$, $p < .05$). Similarly, the ethnic heterogeneity of one's roommates during college was associated with increased interethnic competence ($\beta = .08$, $p < .05$), lower intergroup unease ($\beta = -.08$, $p < .05$), decreased symbolic racism ($\beta = -.07$, $p < .05$), decreased social dominance orientation ($\beta = -.08$, $p < .01$), and increased outgroup dating at the end of college ($\beta = .10$, $p < .05$).

Beyond these general effects of roommate heterogeneity, contact with roommates of specific ethnic groups during college also made independent contributions to intergroup attitudes at the end of college (Van Laar et al., 2005). Specifically, with the exception of contact with Asian American roommates ($\beta = -.03$ p), these analyses showed that interethnic roommate contact was consistently associated with more positive feelings directed toward the ethnic group that one's roommate belonged to (contact with Whites $\beta = .10$, $p < .01$; contact with Latinos $\beta = .08$, $p < .05$, contact with African Americans $\beta = .07$, $p < .05$). When living with Asian American students, White students actually showed increased intergroup unease ($\beta = .11$, $p < .01$), and increased symbolic racism ($\beta = .05$, $p < .10$) and social dominance orientation ($\beta = .06$, $p < .10$). These exceptional effects of contact with Asian American students may have occurred because relative to other groups, Asian American students showed relatively high initial levels of prejudice (see Van Laar et al., 2005); students who roomed with them could have adopted these higher levels of prejudice through peer socialization processes (e.g., conformity to the perceived norm of greater prejudice among their Asian American roommates).

These conclusions were bolstered by field experimental findings showing that contact with randomly assigned outgroup roommates during students' first year of college had positive effects on later interethnic attitudes and behavioral intentions (see Van Laar et al., 2005). Specifically, the greater the ethnic heterogeneity of students' randomly assigned roommates in the student dormitories during their first year, the more positive feelings these students exhibited toward ethnic outgroups (toward Whites $\beta = .06$, $p < .10$; toward Asian Americans $\beta = .08$, $p < .05$; toward Latinos $\beta = .12$, $p < .001$; toward African Americans $\beta = .09$, $p < .01$), the more competent they felt interacting with members of different groups ($\beta = .07$, $p < .05$), the less opposition they exhibited toward interethnic dating and marriage ($\beta = -.08$, $p < .01$), and the lower their symbolic racism tended to be at the end of their first year ($\beta = -.06$, $p < .10$). Again, exposure to roommates from specific ethnic groups made independent contributions to prejudice reduction, especially in terms of generating more positive feelings toward the ethnic group that one's roommate belonged to (contact with Asian Americans $\beta = .07$, $p < .05$; contact with African Americans $\beta = .08$, $p < .01$).

Of particular note were findings of cross-over effects between exposure to Black and Latino roommates and feelings toward the other group (see Van Laar et al., 2005). That is, in both the experimental and longitudinal correlational analyses, contact with Latino roommates tended to improve feelings toward African Americans (experimental $\beta = .07$, $p < .05$; longitudinal correlational $\beta = .08$, $p < .05$) and contact with African American roommates tended to improve feelings toward Latinos (experimental $\beta = .06$, $p < .10$; longitudinal correlational $\beta = .06$, $p < .05$). Such cross-over effects may have been found for these two groups as they have similarly low status in the American ethnic hierarchy (see Sidanius and Pratto, 1999). Insights and observations stimulated by contact with one low-status group may thus have influenced feelings toward the other low-status group (see also Pettigrew, 1997). Friendship patterns among Latinos and African Americans may also be able to explain this effect. Relative to White and Asian American students, Black students were more likely to have Latino friends and vice-versa. Furthermore, according to research on the "extended contact effect," simply knowing that a close other has a friend of a particular ethnicity may improve one's attitudes toward that ethnic group (Wright, Aron, McLaughlin Volpe, & Ropp, 1997).

Effects of Ingroup Contact

The results with regard to contact with members of one's own group (ingroup contact) showed some positive, but mostly negative effects. On the one hand, findings from the experimental data indicated that increased exposure to roommates of one's own ethnicity actually decreased rather than increased prejudice (e.g., lower symbolic racism the more Black participants were exposed to Black roommates, $\beta = -.41$, $p < .01$; increased outgroup dating the more Asian American participants were exposed to Asian American roommates, $\beta = .23$, $p = .03$; lower intergroup unease the more White participants were exposed to White roommates, $\beta = -.12$, $p < .10$; Van Laar et al., 2005). Similarly, the longitudinal analyses of roommate contact showed little support for the notion that contact with ingroup roommates increases prejudice (e.g., lower SDO and more positive feelings towards Latinos, Asian Americans and Blacks the more Latino participants were exposed to Latino roommates, $\beta = -.22$, $p < .05$; $\beta = .26$, $p < .01$; $\beta = .22$, $p < .05$; and $\beta = .28$, $p < .01$; respectively). However, negative effects of ingroup contact were found for contact with ingroup friends and ingroup organizations (Levin et al., 2003; 2006; Sidanius et al., 2004). This suggests that the negative effects of ingroup contact may be more likely when ingroup contact is oriented toward social activities, emphasizes self-disclosure, and/or consumes a great deal of individuals' discretionary time. Specifically, the results showed that having more ingroup friends increased ingroup bias ($\beta = .07$, $p < .05$) and intergroup anxiety ($\beta = .12$, $p < .001$). In addition, having more ingroup friends increased perceptions of discrimination on campus ($\beta = .10$, $p < .001$), especially for Black students ($B = .52$, $p < .01$), and the reverse causal relationship was also found: greater perceptions of discrimination on campus lead Black students in particular to have more ingroup friends ($B = .17$, $p < .01$).[1] These findings give more insight into the interplay between these factors and fit with previous research suggesting that Black students who face a negative racial climate may seek out ingroup others for support in an effort to protect their psychological well-being (e.g., Branscombe, Schmitt, & Harvey, 1999). Consistent with this line of reasoning, we found positive effects of ingroup friendships on the academic adjustment of Black students: such contact increased the importance that Black students place on getting a high GPA ($B = .33$, $p < .05$) and increased their commitment to stay in college ($B = .30$, $p < .10$; Levin et al., 2006). Therefore, such tendencies to form ingroup friendships, although potentially harmful for feelings of ingroup bias and intergroup anxiety, may be particularly adaptive for protecting the psychological well-being and academic motivation and commitment of Black students.

However, we do not find such buffering effects of ingroup friendships for Latino students, who tend to show lower feelings of belonging and academic performance in college the more friends they have of their own ethnicity (belonging $B = -.28$, $p < .001$; academic performance $B = -.17$, $p < .01$). These results are consistent with previous work by Steward, Germain, & Jackson (1992) showing that for Latino students, the experience of alienation on campus could be decreased through the development of intimate relationships with White students. Oliver, Rodriguez, & Mickelson (1985) also found that alienation from general campus life was a significant predictor of poor academic performance among Latino students, but not among

Black students. It appears that Latino students, who more closely resemble the prototypical White group, may be able to pass more smoothly into the larger campus community—and feel and perform better academically to the degree that they do. African American students, meanwhile—who are less accepted and more strongly stereotyped—show the benefits of engaging in campus life from a strong base of ingroup support (see Levin et al., 2006).

The longitudinal correlational results for ingroup contacts through ethnic organizations also show that such contacts tended to increase focus on the ingroup (see Sidanius et al., 2004). Among minority students, controlling for precollege attitudes, membership in ethnically oriented organizations during college was associated with higher levels of ethnic identification ($\beta = .13$, $p < .01$) and ethnic activism at the end of college ($\beta = .10$, $p < .01$). These findings suggest that ethnic organizations increased a sense of collective identity among minority students. Among White students, the data provided consistent evidence of the "ethnic" nature of ostensibly ethnically neutral fraternities and sororities. First, White students were found to be significantly overrepresented in these organizations (standardized residual = 7.4, $p < .01$).[2] Second, among White students, the probability of joining a Greek organization during college showed a significant relationship with precollege White ethnic identity (odds ratio = 1.22, $p < .01$).[3] Moreover, and in contrast to the findings among minorities, among White students the decision to join a Greek organization showed a net association with precollege negative attitudes towards outgroups; specifically, with precollege ingroup bias (odds ratio = 1.39, $p < .01$) and opposition towards affirmative action (odds ratio = 1.19, $p < .01$). Controlling for these precollege attitudes, membership in Greek organizations during college in turn had broad effects on the ethnic attitudes of White students at the end of college. While such membership increased White students' attachment to the university ($\beta = .13$, $p < .05$), it also increased their opposition to an ethnically diverse campus ($\beta = .14$, $p < .05$), their belief that ethnic organizations promote separatism ($\beta = .19$, $p < .01$), opposition to interracial marriage and dating ($\beta = .15$, $p < .01$), symbolic racism ($\beta = .17$, $p < .01$), and their sense of ethnic victimization ($\beta = .18$, $p < .01$). Among Whites, then, membership in fraternities and sororities produced even more ethnocentric, conflict-inducing and exclusionary effects than membership in ethnic organizations produced among minority students. Furthermore, at least a portion of these conflict-inducing effects among White students was mediated by White ethnic identity: membership in Greek organizations increased

Whites' ethnic identity, which in turn affected a host of intergroup attitudes (see Sidanius et al., 2004). The effects of ingroup contact through fraternities and sororities may be especially negative (e.g., compared to ingroup contact with White friends) because social norms allowing the expression of hostile intergroup attitudes are likely to be stronger in organizations than in interpersonal contacts.

Discussion and Conclusions

In conclusion, the results of this large longitudinal study on a multi-ethnic university campus provide substantial support for the contact hypothesis, with both the field experimental and longitudinal tests providing converging evidence. Contacts with members of ethnic outgroups had broad and pervasive positive effects on intergroup attitudes and behaviors over a 4-year period. Moreover, the sizes of these effects of contact were similar in magnitude to those found by Pettigrew and Tropp (2006), which were based on mostly cross-sectional data. Also, consistent with Pettigrew and Tropp, we found the strongest effects of contact on the affective indicators of prejudice, and the strongest effects of contact through the friendships students made as opposed to other forms of contact. Moreover, we were able to observe these effects even though contact was a subtle predictor variable examined over a period of several years in which students were exposed to many other influences, and despite the fact that intergroup attitudes tend to be highly stable. Such positive changes in intergroup attitudes can have profound influences on the kinds of behavioral choices individuals make beyond college in their private and professional lives, in turn affecting intergroup relations within a wider context.

The results also highlight the dangers of ingroup contact. Ingroup contact tended to increase both a focus on the ingroup and negative attitudes towards outgroups. The results emphasize, however, the need to consider the consequences of ingroup contact separately for members of different ethnic groups. While ingroup contact generally has negative effects for White students, it fulfills important psychological needs for social support among minority individuals, especially in a negative racial climate.

In the short term, then, the results suggest that the best way to foster more positive intergroup attitudes and social and academic adjustment may be to promote intergroup contacts that address the negative effects of segregation among White students, and at the same time encourage minority students to find understanding and social support in the company of members of their own ethnic group. Increased attention to the positive benefits of diversifying the curriculum, and promoting activities and programs that stimulate positive contacts between White and minority students would address the potential dangers of segregation among White students. Allowing room for minority students to develop ingroup organizations would meanwhile address the needs of minority students to find social support among others with similar experiences. However, in the long term, policy makers should focus on improving the racial climate in order to eliminate the need for minority individuals to have more ingroup contacts in the first place. This would involve identifying whether procedures used by the educational institution are sensitive to diversity issues, identifying where current conflicts between ethnic groups exist, and working with all groups involved to identify ways to reduce conflict. Various examples of such successful programs exist, such as the WISE program instituted by the University of Michigan to address both campus climate issues and the academic success of minority students (e.g. Steele, 1992). If institutions can maximize the positive conditions of contact by establishing clear institutional norms of intergroup acceptance, such efforts should be beneficial both in terms of ethnic attitudes and in terms of social and academic adjustment.

Acknowledgments

This research was supported by grants from the Russell Sage Foundation, the UCLA Office of the Chancellor, and the National Science Foundation (Award BCS-9808686). Special thanks are due to David Sears, Stacey Sinclair, Pamela Taylor, and Marilynn Brewer for their collaboration on this joint research project, and Michael Greenwell for his efforts in data collection.

Notes

1   Note that in discussing regression coefficients we use the standard procedure of presenting standardized regression coefficients when presenting coefficients for the whole population, while when discussing coefficients for particular groups B's are used (following centering of the variables for the population as a whole) to allow comparisons of coefficients across ethnic groups.
2   Standardized residuals are essentially z-scores that show whether an observed frequency in a cell is above or below what might be expected by chance.

3   The odds-ratio indicates the factor by which a White student's odds of joining a fraternity or sorority increases for every unit increase in the predictor (in this case ethnic identity).

References

Allport, G. W. (1954). *The nature of prejudice*. Reading, MA: Addison-Wesley.

Amir, Y. (1969) Contact hypothesis in ethnic relations. *Psychological Bulletin*, *7*, 319–342.

Blanchard, F. A., Lilly, T., & Vaughn, L. A. (1991). Reducing the expression of racial prejudice. *Psychological Science*, *2*, 101–105.

Branscombe, N. R., Schmitt, M. T., & Harvey, R. D. (1999). Perceiving pervasive discrimination among African Americans: Implications for group identification and well-being. *Journal of Personality and Social Psychology*, *77*, 135–149.

Brown, R., Vivian, J., & Hewstone, M. (1999). Changing attitudes through intergroup contact: The effects of group membership salience. *European Journal of Social Psychology*, *29*, 741–764.

Dovidio, J. F., Gaertner, S. L., & Kawakami, K. (2003). Intergroup contact: The past, present, and the future. *Group Processes and Intergroup Relations*, *6*, 5–20.

D'Souza, D. (1991). *Illiberal education: The politics of race and sex on campus*. New York: Free Press.

Gonzalez, R., & Brown, R. (2003). Generalization of positive attitude as a function of subgroup and superordinate group identifications in intergroup contact. *European Journal of Social Psychology*, *33*, 195–214.

Hurtado, S., Milem, J. F., Clayton-Pedersen, A. R., & Allen, W. R. (1998). Enhancing campus climates for racial/ethnic diversity: Educational policy and practice. *Review of Higher Education*, *21*, 279–302.

Hurtado, S., Milem, J. F., Clayton-Pedersen, A. R., & Allen, W. R. (1999). *Enacting diverse learning environments: Improving the climate for racial/ ethnic diversity in higher education*: ASHE-ERIC Higher Education Report.

Levin, S., Taylor, P. L., & Caudle, E. (2007). Interethnic and interracial dating in college: A longitudinal study. *Journal of Social and Personal Relationships*, *24*, 323–341.

Levin, S., Van Laar, C., & Foote, W. (2006). Ethnic segregation and perceived discrimination in college: Mutual influences and effects on social and academic life. *Journal of Applied Social Psychology*, *36*, 1471–1501.

Levin, S., Van Laar, C., & Sidanius, J. (2003). The effects of ingroup and outgroup friendship on ethnic attitudes in college: A longitudinal study. *Group Processes and Intergroup Relations*, *6*, 76–92.

Loo, C. M., & Rolison, G. (1986). Alienation of ethnic minority students at a predominantly White university. *Journal of Higher Education*, *57*, 58–77.

Oliver, M. L., Rodriguez, C. J., & Mickelson, R. A. (1985). Brown and Black in White: The social adjustment and academic performance of Chicano and Black students in a predominantly White university. *Urban Review*, *17*, 3–23.

Pettigrew, T. F. (1988). Influencing policy with social psychology. *Journal of Social Issues*, *44*, 205–219.

Pettigrew, T. F. (1996). *How to think like a social scientist*. New York: HarperCollins.

Pettigrew, T. F. (1997). Generalized intergroup contact effects on prejudice. *Personality and Social Psychology Bulletin*, *23*, 173–185.

Pettigrew, T. F. (1998a). Applying social psychology to international social issues. *Journal of Social Issues*, *54*, 663–675.

Pettigrew, T. F. (1998b). Intergroup contact theory. *Annual Review of Psychology*, *49*, 65–85.

Pettigrew, T. F. (1998c). Prejudice and discrimination on the college campus. In J. L. Eberhardt & S. T. Fiske (Eds.), *Confronting racism: The problem and the response* (pp. 263–279). Thousand Oaks, CA: Sage.

Pettigrew, T. F. (2002). Summing up: Relative deprivation as a key social psychological concept. In I. Walker & H. J. Smith (Eds.), *Relative deprivation: Specification, development, and integration* (pp. 351–373). New York: Cambridge University Press.

Pettigrew, T. F. (2006). The advantages of multilevel approaches. *Journal of Social Issues*, *62*, 615–620.

Pettigrew, T. F., & Tropp, L. R. (2000). Does intergroup contact reduce prejudice: Recent meta-analytic findings. In S. Oskamp (Ed.), *Reducing prejudice and discrimination. "The Claremont Symposium on Applied Social Psychology"* (pp. 93–114). Mahwah, NJ: Lawrence Erlbaum.

Pettigrew, T. F., & Tropp, L. R. (2005). Allport's intergroup contact hypothesis: Its history and influence. In J. F. Dovidio, P. Glick, & L. A. Rudman (Eds.), *On the nature of prejudice: Fifty years after Allport* (pp. 262–277). Malden, MA: Blackwell.

Pettigrew, T. F., & Tropp, L. R. (2006). A meta-analytic test of intergroup contact theory. *Journal of Personality and Social Psychology*, *90*, 751–783.

Sears, D. O., & Henry, P. J. (2005). Over thirty years later: A contemporary look at symbolic racism. In M. P. Zanna (Ed.), *Advances in experimental social psychology* (Vol. 37) (pp. 95–150). San Diego, CA: Elsevier Academic Press.

Sidanius, J., Levin, S., Van Laar, C., & Sears, D. O. (2007). *The dynamics of social identity and intergroup relations on campus: Continuity and change across the college years.* Manuscript submitted for publication.

Sidanius, J., & Pratto, F. (1999). *Social dominance: An intergroup theory of social hierarchy and oppression.* New York: Cambridge University Press.

Sidanius, J., Van Laar, C., Levin, S., & Sinclair, S. (2004). Ethnic enclaves and the dynamics of social identity on the college campus: The good, the bad and the ugly. *Journal of Personality and Social Psychology*, *87*, 96–110.

Steele, C. M. (1992). Race and the schooling of black Americans. *The Atlantic Monthly, 269,* 68–78.

Stephan, W. G., & Stephan, C. W. (2000). An integrated threat theory of prejudice. In S. Oskamp (Ed.), *Reducing prejudice and discrimination* (pp. 23–45). Mahwah, NJ: Lawrence Erlbaum.

Steward, R. J., Germain, S., & Jackson, J. D. (1992). Alienation and interactional style: A study of successful Anglo, Asian, and Hispanic university students. *Journal of College Student Development, 33,* 149–156.

Tajfel, H., & Turner, J. C. (1979). An integrative theory of intergroup conflict. In W. G. Austin & S. Worchel (Eds.), *The social psychology of intergroup relations.* Monterey, CA: Brooks/Cole Publishing Company.

Tajfel, H., & Turner, J. C. (1986). The social identity theory of intergroup behavior. In S. W. Worchel & W. G. Austin (Eds.), *The psychology of intergroup relations* (pp. 7–24). Chicago, IL: Nelson-Hall.

Trevino, J. G. (1992). *Participation in ethnic/racial student organizations.* Unpublished Doctoral thesis, University of California–Los Angeles.

Tropp, L. R., & Pettigrew, T. F. (2005). Differential relationships between intergroup contact and affective and cognitive indicators of prejudice. *Personality and Social Psychology Bulletin, 31,* 1145–1158.

Turner, J. C. (1991). *Social influence.* Pacific Grove, CA: Brooks/Cole.

Turner, J. C., Hogg, M. A., Oakes, P. J., Reicher, S. D., & Wetherell, M. S. (1987). *Rediscovering the social group: A self-categorization theory.* New York: Basil Blackwell.

Van Laar, C., Levin, S., Sinclair, S., & Sidanius, J. (2005). The effect of university roommate contact on ethnic attitudes and behavior. *Journal of Experimental Social Psychology, 41,* 329–345.

Wright, S. C., Aron, A., McLaughlin Volpe, T., & Ropp, S. A. (1997). The extended contact effect: Knowledge of cross-group friendships and prejudice. *Journal of Personality and Social Psychology, 73,* 73–90.

10

Extended Contact and Including Others in the Self

Building on the Allport/Pettigrew Legacy

Stephen C. Wright, Arthur Aron, and Salena M. Brody

In the early 1950s when Thomas Pettigrew began graduate school at Harvard, Gordon Allport was completing what would become a classic contribution to social psychology and to the study of intergroup relations—*The Nature of Prejudice* (1954). Among the contributions in this volume was a detailed formulation of the Intergroup Contact Hypothesis. This hypothesis—that interactions between members of different groups, under specific conditions, can lead to reductions in prejudice—would become one of the most enduring and influential themes in the social psychology of intergroup relations. Ensuring this endurance and centrality is a critical component of Pettigrew's academic legacy. For more than half a century, he has been a central figure in the development and testing of Allport's hypothesis.

At a meeting of the Society of Experimental Social Psychology (SESP) in Lake Tahoe, CA in 1994, Thomas Pettigrew presented initial findings from what would become his highly influential publication of a multination study of intergroup attitudes in Europe (Pettigrew, 1997). He provided compelling evidence that friendship was the form of contact most likely to produce positive attitude change. It was Pettigrew's focus on friendship that inspired Art Aron to seek out Steve Wright and propose the rather radical idea that theory and research in close relationships might have something to offer our understanding of intergroup contact. The outcome of this meeting and many more that would follow was the *extended contact hypothesis*, and what is now a 12-year collaborative effort connecting ideas from Aron and Aron's (1986) self-expansion model to work on intergroup contact. A couple of years later when the first seeds of this work were starting to bear fruit, Pettigrew served as a Discussant (and thus legitimizer) at a standing-room-only SESP symposium bringing together in the same room for the first time relationship and intergroup researchers. Thus, Pettigrew was instrumental not only for articulating some of the ideas that inspired the work presented here, but also for helping to get the field of social psychology to pay attention.

Allport's (1954) original statement of the contact hypothesis recognized that societal, situational, and personal variables can undermine or enhance the positive effects of contact. He proposed four critical conditions needed for contact to reduce prejudice. In the past decade, however, theoretical work has focused more on *how* contact changes attitudes than on identifying conditions that undermine or promote attitude change. One promising direction, highlighted by Pettigrew's work in the 1990s, is the special role of friendship as opposed to other kinds of contact (see also, Aron et al., 2005; Brown & Hewstone, 2005; Pettigrew, Christ, Wagner, & Stellmacher, 2007; Wright, Brody, & Aron, 2005). Using an international European sample, Pettigrew (1997) found that having an outgroup friend (vs. coworker or neighbor) predicted lower levels of subtle and blatant prejudice, and more support for pro-outgroup policies. In a review, Pettigrew (1998) proposed that opportunity for friendship development be added to Allport's four conditions, making friendship the fifth essential condition for positive contact.

We (Wright et al., 2005) have subsequently taken this notion even further. A review of the friendship literature (e.g., Fehr, 1996) shows that many of the necessary or facilitating conditions for successful contact enumerated by Allport and others are also described in the friendship literature as conditions that facilitate friendship formation. For example, cooperation to achieve shared goals, support for the relationship from authorities and peers, feelings of equality and interdependence (equal status), and frequent interaction over time, are all found in lists of facilitating conditions of both intergroup contact and friendship formation. Thus, we claim that the optimal conditions for contact can be more parsimoniously described as conditions that make friendship more likely, and it is feelings of friendship that mediate the contact/prejudice relationship.

A second central theme for contact theorists is the question of generalization—how contact with a single individual generalizes to attitudes about the outgroup as a whole. Emerging from social identity approaches (e.g., Turner, Hogg, Oakes, Reicher, & Wetherell, 1987), which emphasize the distinction between interpersonal and intergroup interactions, came the argument that contact between individuals interacting only as individuals (i.e., personalized contact) should have little impact on attitudes towards the group as a whole (Hewstone & Brown, 1986). If only personal identities are salient, positive feelings should be experienced exclusively towards the individual. This idea is also consistent with work on subtyping (e.g., Richards & Hewstone, 2001), where individuals who disconfirm our view of the outgroup are "fenced off" from the group, leaving our view of the group unaffected. Focusing on a partner's unique personal character should enhance subtyping. Thus, at some point, group identities must be salient for positive interpersonal interactions to affect intergroup attitudes.

Jointly, these two themes suggest that contact is most effective when it involves interpersonal closeness and when participants are seen as representatives of their group. However, when group memberships are highly salient cross-group interactions can be fraught with threat and anxiety (e.g., Blascovitch, Mendes, Hunter, Lickel, & Kowai-Bell, 2001; Islam & Hewstone, 1993; Vorauer, 2006); feelings unlikely to promote interpersonal closeness. Though there are probably others, we have proposed that extended contact provides one means by which cross-group closeness and group salience can be simultaneously high, while interaction anxiety remains low.

The Extended Intergroup Contact Hypothesis

The extended contact hypothesis holds that knowing that an ingroup member has a close relationship with an outgroup member can lead to a more positive attitude toward that outgroup. In cross-group friendships, the friendship partners themselves may attend primarily to the individuating features of their partner and specifics of their interpersonal relationship. However, an observer is likely to be less attentive to personalizing information. Rather, the friends' differing group memberships are likely to be maximally salient. Thus, for the observer, recognition of cross-group intimacy and high group salience occur simultaneously. Further, observing cross-group interactions involving others should not generate feelings of threat or anxiety often felt by actual participants.

In introducing the concept of extended contact, (Wright, Aron, McLaughlin-Volpe, & Ropp, 1997) we presented evidence from four studies using three research paradigms. Two studies utilized a within-subjects-comparison survey approach to measure the impact of extended contact among White, Latino(a), and African American students. Participants reported their attitudes toward several ethnic outgroups and their knowledge of ingroup members with friends in each outgroup. Their own cross-group friendships were also measured to control for direct contact when assessing extended contact effects. The results clearly and strongly supported the extended contact hypothesis. In both studies, less prejudice towards a particular outgroup was predicted by: (1) more ingroup members known to have friends in that outgroup; and (2) greater perceived closeness in the closest cross-group friendship. Importantly, these associations remained significant (with about the same effect size) even after partialing out parallel measures of direct outgroup friendships.

The third study introduced a paradigm inspired by Sherif, Harvey, White, Hood, & Sherif's (1961) Robbers Cave studies. We tested the impact of introducing extended contact into an existing competitive intergroup context both experimentally and longitudinally. Participants were randomly assigned to one of two 7-person groups and participated in a day-long (9-hour) experiment. The experiment involved five phases. In Phase 1 (*ingroup solidarity phase*), participants were told that their assignment to a "Blue" or "Green" group was based on the similarity of their responses on pretest personality questionnaires (actually random). The groups were separated, given green or blue "team T-shirts," engaged in "ice-breaker" games and cooperative problem-solving tasks, and designed a team logo and name; all intended to promote familiarity, ingroup solidarity, and liking.

During Phases 2 and 3, (*intergroup rivalry phases*), the groups engaged in a series of intergroup competitive activities. In Phase 2, teams competed on analytical and creative tasks. Following each task, opposing teams critically evaluated their opponent's work. These critiques were surreptitiously edited to leave only negative statements before being given to the target group. Phase 3 involved physical problem solving games, after which "winners" (randomly determined) were announced and prizes given. After each phase, participants completed measures of intergroup attitudes in individual cubicles. It was clear from observing the interactions (they were videotaped), from participants' comments at debriefing, as well as from formal measures of intergroup attitudes that these procedures created high levels of intergroup rivalry.

During Phase 4, two *cross-group friendships* were formed. While the other group members completed individual personality question-naires, two people from each group were randomly selected to "help another experimenter." These four participants were put into two cross-group pairs. Each pair completed a "closeness-generating procedure" consisting of a series of self-disclosure and relationship-building tasks, a procedure shown in other research to create high levels of felt closeness (Aron, Melinat, Aron, Vallone, & Bator, 1997). After completing this procedure, participants returned to their original groups and were encouraged to describe what they had been doing, "in order to bring everyone up to date."

In Phase 5, *intergroup competition* was re-established with another competitive task and participants completed a final measure of intergroup attitudes. The extended contact hypothesis predicted that among those participants *not* involved in a cross-group friendship, there would be a decrease in negative intergroup attitudes after they became aware of the cross-group friendships. Results clearly and strongly supported this hypothesis. The change on all three measures of intergroup attitudes from the end of Phases 2 and 3 (before the intervention) to Phase 5 (after the intervention) were positive, large and, despite small degrees of freedom, statistically significant. Crucially, these analyses were based only on data from participants who did *not* participate in the cross-group friendships.

The fourth study used an adapted "minimal group" procedure (Tajfel, Billig, Bundy, & Flament, 1971). Participants were led to believe they had been divided into groups based on their performance on an object-estimation task. They then observed an ingroup and an outgroup member (actually confederates) interacting on a puzzle task through a one-way mirror. The confederates' behavior was scripted to suggest that their pre-existing relationship was that of warm friends, unacquainted strangers, or disliked acquaintances. For ex-ample, in the friendly condition, upon meeting, they expressed delight at seeing an old friend, and hugged; in the neutral condition they showed no sign of previous acquaintance; and in the hostile condi-tion they showed surprise and displeasure at being paired with this person, implying a long-standing hostile relationship. (Manipulation checks showed appropriate large, significant differences across condi-tions.) Again, results clearly supported the extended contact hypo-thesis. Participants who observed a friendly cross-group interaction provided significantly more positive evaluations of the outgroup, and showed less ingroup bias in a resource allocation task than those observing the neutral or hostile interaction.

Subsequent studies have also supported the extended contact hypothesis. Liebkind and McAlister (1999) showed that telling stories about cross-group friendships to Finnish adolescents led to more positive attitudes towards immigrants. Similarly, Cameron and Rutland (2006) demonstrated the power of stories about cross-group friendships in improving the attitudes of non-disabled children towards children with disabilities. Paolini, Hewstone, Cairns, & Voci (2004), using survey data, showed the positive effects of extended contact on intergroup attitudes among Catholics and Protestants in Northern Ireland. Pettigrew et al. (2007) found that extended contact was associated with lower prejudice towards "foreigners" and Muslims in a German sample, and that extended contact had about the same effect on prejudice as a direct friendship with a member of these outgroups. In a laboratory experiment, Shelton and Richeson (2005) found that when college students in the United States were asked to imagine that a friend knew one individual among a group of outgroup members in a dining hall, they were more likely to say they would join the group than if they were not told of this cross-group friendship.

This very recent wave of research provides growing support for the idea that extended contact may provide an alternative to direct interpersonal contact as a means of improving intergroup attitudes. This is a particularly optimistic claim as it implies that intergroup attitudes may be meaningfully improved without everyone having to have their own cross-group friend. A single cross-group friendship may have the power to improve the attitudes of many group members.

Mechanism

In our initial presentation of extended contact (Wright et al., 1997), we proposed several mechanisms that might account for its effectiveness. These mechanisms fall under three primary processes: anxiety reduction, changing perceived norms, and transitory inclusion in the self. There is evidence that the relationship between direct contact and prejudice reduction is partially mediated by reductions in anxiety. Consistent with this, we proposed that extended contact may "reduce fears and negative expectation in the observer, leading to a more positive impression of the outgroup and perhaps even to actual positive interactions with the outgroup that would permit direct contact effects to operate" (p. 75). While our initial research did not provide a direct test of this effect, Paolini et al. (2004) found that a measure of intergroup anxiety was a significant mediator of the relationship between extended contact and reduced prejudice. Relatedly, Pettigrew et al. (2007) have found that reductions in perceived collective threat partially mediated the relationship between extended contact and lower prejudice.

Regarding changes in the observer's perception of group norms, we proposed that the friendly behavior of the ingroup member may lead observers to infer that ingroup norms support positive attitudes and actions toward the outgroup. Thus, extended contact may be effective because it leads observers to follow what they believe are norms prescribing a positive orientation toward the outgroup. Similarly, the actions of the outgroup friendship partner may lead the observer to infer that outgroup norms prescribe positive attitudes and actions towards the ingroup. Thus, extended contact may alter the perceived norms of both groups in ways that make positive intergroup attitudes seem appropriate and mutual.

However, the most striking and unusual mechanism we proposed emerged from research and theorizing in close relationships. This was the idea that extended contact sets in motion a "transitive inclusion process" in which the outgroup becomes part of the observer's self-concept. As part of their Self-Expansion Model, Aron and Aron (1986) proposed that as people form close relationships, they "include the other in the self," that is, they come to experience themselves as to some extent possessing their partner's resources, perspectives and identities. In numerous studies, Aron and colleagues (e.g., Aron, Aron, Tudor, & Nelson, 1991; Mashek, Aron, & Boncimino, 2005) have demonstrated that close others (and not non-close others) function cognitively like self in tasks including money allocations, attributions, memory for imaged words, source memory, and a self–other Stroop-type reaction time task. Aron and Fraley (1999) showed that measures of including the other in the self can also distinguish *degree* of felt closeness. In addition, Aron and colleagues (e.g., Mashek et al., 2003) have demonstrated that the inclusion of the other in self-effect is distinguishable from mere similarity or familiarity effects. These various results suggest that cognitive structures of self and of close others are richly interconnected so that accessing features of self spontaneously accesses features of close others. Importantly, as the partner is increasingly included in the self, the partner is treated increasingly like the self, including "self-serving" biases in attribution, feeling pain at their troubles, taking pride in their successes, generously sharing resources, and so on.

In related work, Aron, Aron, & Smollan (1992) presented participants with seven pairs of circles representing self and other as overlapping to varying degrees (the Inclusion of Other in the Self, or IOS, Scale) and asked them to indicate which pair of circles best described their relationship with a particular person. The extent of overlap selected was strongly associated with, and generally performed as well or better than, other, much longer measures of interpersonal closeness, suggesting that the metaphor of overlapped selves may reflect fairly directly how relationships are cognitively represented.

Extending this idea, Smith and Henry (1996) adapted Aron et al.'s (1991) reaction-time procedure and showed that individuals spontaneously include ingroup members (but not outgroup members) in the self. Tropp and Wright (2001) demonstrate the reliability and validity of a version of the IOS Scale that assesses overlap of self and ingroup, demonstrating that groups, as entities, can also be included in the self, and explicitly describing this inclusion of the ingroup in the self as the essence of ingroup identification. McLaughlin-Volpe (2004) found that the "inclusion in the self" mechanism provides a potential explanation for direct contact effects by showing that: (1) people include outgroup friends in the self; (2) the extent to which they do so predicts how much they include the outgroup as a whole in the self; and (3) the extent to which they include the outgroup in the self predicts less stereotyping of that outgroup. The positive orientation towards the outgroup is thought to reflect the fact that the outgroup is now treated more like one treats the self. Thus, lower prejudice results from the positive orientation towards the self being extended to the outgroup because of its psychological connection to the self.

In order to widen this model to produce the "transitive inclusion process" that can explain extended contact, one additional element is needed. Fortunately, this final piece is provided in a finding described by Sedikides, Olsen, & Reis (1993). They found that observers treat partners in a close relationship as a single cognitive unit (e.g., spontaneously clustering them together in recall) in a manner that Sedikides et al. (1993) explicitly associate with inclusion of others in the self. Thus, the logic of the transitive inclusion mechanism is as follows. When I observe a cross-group friendship, the ingroup member is to some degree, part of myself because of our shared membership in the ingroup. The outgroup member is perceived as part of that ingroup member's self as a result of their interpersonal relationship. Thus, through the ingroup member, the outgroup member is to some extent part of myself. As long as group memberships

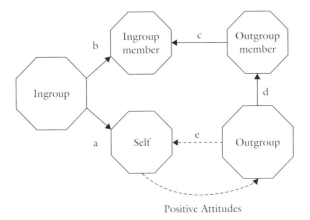

Figure 10.1 The transitive inclusion process.
Note: The arrows between circles (marked a through d) represent the inclusion of one entity in another. The strength of these inclusions moderate the extended contact effect. The dotted arrow (e) represents the inclusion of the outgroup in the self that is responsible for the more positive intergroup attitudes (the dashed arrow).

are salient, the outgroup member is seen to be connected to the outgroup, allowing the outgroup to be part of what I include in myself. Thus, the observed cross-group friendships provide a conduit by which the outgroup itself can be included in the self, and because it is now to some degree part of the self, the outgroup receives some of the positive regard and supportive actions usually reserved for the self. This transitive inclusion process is represented visually in Figure 10.1.

The logic of this transitive process is closely related to Heider's (1958) balance theory. If there are unit relations between self and ingroup, between ingroup member and the ingroup, between ingroup member and outgroup friend, and between outgroup member and outgroup, then balance theory prescribes a unit relationship between self and outgroup. However, the present logic goes beyond balance theory, positing a more specific process of how a unit relationship operates. In addition, this transitive inclusion mechanism bears more generally on ideas put forward by social psychologists from Cooley (1902) to Andersen and Chen (2002), that not only are we shaped by the characteristics of those with whom we are close, but we may also be shaped by the characteristics of those who are close to those to whom we are close.

Recent Research

Thus, we see the extended contact effect as controlled by three mechanisms: intergroup anxiety reduction, changing perceived social norms, and the inclusion of the outgroup in the self. As mentioned earlier, studies have shown the importance of intergroup anxiety as a mediator of extended contact effects (e.g., Paolini et al., 2004). In a recent survey of heterosexuals' attitudes towards gays and lesbians, we (Wright, Davies, & Sanders, 2007) also found evidence for the ingroup norm mechanism. Compared to those knowing of few cross-group friendships, heterosexuals who knew more ingroup members with gay friends believed that heterosexuals were generally more positive towards gay men and that most heterosexuals supported cross-group friendships. This perception of more positive ingroup norms partially accounted for the positive effect of extended contact on attitudes towards gay men.

However, our current research has focused primarily on testing elements of the transitive inclusion process. We have completed two experiments modeled on the minimal group paradigm used in Study 4 of our original article (Wright et al., 1997). The first (Kiu, Wright, & Teows, 2007) tested the importance of three of the proposed links in the transitive inclusion model: the inclusion of the ingroup in the self (connection *a* in Figure 10.1), the inclusion of the ingroup member in the ingroup (connection *b* in Figure 10.1), and the inclusion of the outgroup in the outgroup member (connection *d* in Figure 10.1). Tropp and Wright (2001) described the inclusion of the ingroup in the self as conceptually equivalent to ingroup identification (see also Wright, Aron, & Tropp, 2001). The overlap between the ingroup member and the ingroup, and between the out-group member and the outgroup was operationalized in terms of how prototypical each was in terms of group defining characteristics.

In individual cubicles, participants completed a "Teamwork Profile Survey," which they were led to believe showed that they clearly fit the "Promoters" profile (i.e., that they were highly prototypical members of the Promoter group). They were given a blue t-shirt to represent this group membership. Through a one-way mirror, they saw a larger room where they would soon be involved in an interaction with another participant, but first they were to watch and evaluate a recorded interaction from the previous session. The recorded interaction between a Promoter (ingroup member, also wearing a blue t-shirt) and a Performer (wearing a red t-shirt) actually involved confederates and was scripted to demonstrate a close friendship. Upon entering the room, the confederates expressed surprise and delight, embraced and exchanged pleasant remarks. During the task, they looked at each other frequently, smiled and laughed, and touched the other's arm.

The degree of overlap between the actors and their relevant ingroups was manipulated by providing participants with information about each actor's performance on the "Teamwork Profile Survey." Their score on the survey was displayed on the screen above each actor. It clearly indicated that the actor fit her ingroup profile either very well or quite poorly. In addition to these manipulations of the prototypicality of the ingroup and outgroup members, participants completed a measure of identification with their Promoter ingroup. The dependent measures included: the inclusion of the outgroup in the self; anxiety about a subsequent interaction with an outgroup member; and general evaluations of the outgroup.

Although attempts were made to heighten ingroup identification, several measures showed that a meaningful subset of participants felt little identification with their ingroup. As predicted by the transitive inclusion mechanism, these low identifiers showed little inclusion of the outgroup in the self and less positive feelings towards the outgroup compared to high identifiers. However, for those who identified with the ingroup, observing a friendly cross-group interaction between a prototypical ingroup member and a prototypical outgroup member resulted in more positive intergroup attitudes compared to observing the same friendly cross-group interactions between atypical ingroup and/or atypical outgroup members. Thus, for those who are identified with their ingroup, observing cross-group friendship can improve intergroup attitudes and reduce intergroup anxiety when there is thought to be strong overlap between the ingroup member and the ingroup as well as between the outgroup member and the outgroup. The typicality of the outgroup member was particularly critical in determining participants' inclusion of the outgroup in the self (the effect for typicality of the ingroup member was in the expected direction but was not statistically significant for this measure).

In Experiment 2, participants performed an object-estimation task, which they believed resulted in them being assigned to the "underestimator" group. They were given a red t-shirt to represent this group membership. They then observed, through a one-way mirror, another underestimator (also wearing a red shirt) interacting with an overestimator (wearing a blue shirt). Replicating our original 1997 experiment, the interaction was scripted so as to represent one of three relationships. The "close friends" condition presented an interaction similar to the one used in Experiment 1, with partners expressing surprise and delight, embracing, and exchanging pleasant remarks. In the "stranger acquaintance" condition, confederates showed no signs of knowing each other, exchanging polite introductions, and were appropriately pleasant but reserved during the task. In the "hostile" condition, they demonstrated surprise and dissatisfaction at seeing each other, made dismissive initial statements, sat further apart with crossed arms, and were uncooperative and critical during the task.

This study also tested a modification of the transitive inclusion process that proposes a more direct connection between the ingroup member and the self. As shown in Experiment 1, shared membership in the ingroup can be enough for an ingroup member's friendship with an outgroup member to improve one's intergroup attitudes. However, this was likely only for those who were identified with the ingroup and when the ingroup member was perceived to be highly prototypical. If these two links in the transitive inclusion process were not strong, extended contact had little impact. However, there is an alternative, more direct, route by which the ingroup member can be included in the self—through a close personal relationship. If the ingroup member is a personal friend, direct overlap of self and the ingroup member could replace the connection mediated by shared ingroup membership and thus positive extended contact effect may result even when ingroup identification is low. This alternative process could be described as "the friend of a friend" mechanism (see Figure 10.2).

In Study 2, we included a manipulation of personal closeness between the participant and the ingroup member whom they observed in the cross-group interaction (connection *f* in Figure 10.2). Pairs of friends were recruited and came to the laboratory together, but were immediately separated in individual cubicles. In the "Ingroup Friend" condition, one of the friends was randomly selected and approached by a staff confederate to enact either a friendly, neutral, or hostile interaction. While their friend was completing the estimation task, the newly recruited confederate was trained to enact the appropriate relationship with the staff confederate. In the "Ingroup Stranger" condition, both participants observed ingroup and outgroup members they did not know. After watching the interaction through a one-way mirror, participants completed outgroup evaluation measures.

Thus, we had a 2 × 3 design, with manipulations of level of inclusion of the ingroup member in the self (ingroup member is one's friend or a stranger) and type of cross-group relationship (friendly, neutral, hostile). The results clearly supported the importance of both variables. Attitudes towards the outgroup were *most* positive following

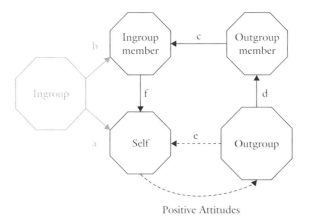

Figure 10.2 The "friend of a friend" inclusion process.
Note: Arrows between circles represent the inclusion of one entity in another. These moderate the extended contact effect. The dotted arrow (e) represents the inclusion of the outgroup in the self that is responsible for the positive intergroup attitudes (the solid arrow). Here, the direct connection between self and the ingroup member (arrow f) replaces the shared ingroup membership in the original process.

the observation of a friendly cross-group interaction when the ingroup member was a friend. Attitudes towards the outgroup were less positive when the ingroup friend was involved in a neutral cross-group interaction, and attitudes were *least* positive when the ingroup friend was involved in a hostile cross-group interaction. When the ingroup member was a stranger, attitudes towards the outgroup were less influenced by the type of cross-group interaction. As the transitive inclusion process would predict, cross-group friendships involving an ingroup member who is included in the observer's self are more likely to lead to a more positive perception of the outgroup. Not surprisingly perhaps, our data also show that observing a negative cross-group relationship will have a more detrimental impact on outgroup attitudes when the ingroup member is included in the self, compared to when the ingroup member is a stranger.

Together the two experiments test all of the proposed links in the transitive inclusion process and show that the strength of each connection influences that impact of observing cross-group friendships on intergroup attitudes. Positive extended contact effects are more pronounced: (1) when the interaction between the ingroup and outgroup members clearly demonstrates inclusion of the other in the self (they are friends); (2) when the outgroup member is clearly connected to the outgroup (is a prototypical member); and (3) when the ingroup member is clearly connected to the self, either directly through self/other inclusion (is a personal friend), or indirectly when the ingroup is included in the self (ingroup identification is high) and the ingroup member is clearly connect to the ingroup (is a prototypical member).

Implications and New Developments

Uncovering the mechanisms that underpin extended contact effects is crucial not only for advancing theory and scientific understanding of the phenomenon. It also has clear and important implications for the application. For example, the transitive inclusion mechanism makes clear the importance of representing participants in terms of their collective identities. If extended contact is to be effective, both the ingroup and the outgroup member must be clearly recognized as strongly connected to their relevant groups. For example, in a classroom context, if the teacher wishes to enhance the likelihood that a single cross-group friendship will influence the attitudes of students who do not have their own cross-group friendships, it would be unwise to discourage recognition of the friendship partners' collective identities. The seemingly widespread view that positive intergroup relations will be enhanced by reducing the salience of group memberships (perhaps an offshoot of the common "color-blind" orientation) is inconsistent with our model and the supporting findings.

In addition, the more general idea—that contact (direct or extended) works to improve intergroup attitudes by facilitating the inclusion of the outgroup in the self—represents a significant departure from traditional thinking about prejudice reduction. From our perspective, improved attitudes result indirectly from changes in the nature and content of the self. More positive attitudes and actions towards the outgroup are, from this perspective, a by-product of changes in the self. If we take this perspective seriously, we might want to reevaluate much of the prejudice reduction enterprise, focusing less on strategies that teach people to think differently about the outgroup and its members, and instead focus on things that will enhance changes to their understanding of themselves.

Finally, just as there are conditions that limit the positive effects of direct contact, there should also be limiting conditions to extended contact. Understanding the mechanisms underlying extended contact can also provide insights into these limiting conditions. For example, observing an ingroup member befriending a member of a strongly disliked outgroup could very well lead to rejection and vilification of the ingroup member rather than improved attitudes toward the outgroup (see Neuberg, Smith, Hoffman, & Russell, 1994). However, this becomes less likely to the degree that the ingroup member is included in the self. That is, when ingroup members are close others, it is more difficult to reject or vilify them. Similarly, if ingroup members are highly prototypical and respected group members, and one is highly identified with the group, it is more difficult to reject them. In both cases the likelihood of reevaluation of the disliked outgroup increases. Thus, the mechanisms that determine extended contact may also point out the parameters of the effect and illuminate situations where it will be less effective or even fail entirely.

References

Allport, G. W. (1954). *The nature of prejudice*. Don Mills, ON: Addison-Wesley.

Anderson, S. M., & Chen, S. (2002). The relational self: An interpersonal social-cognitive theory. *Psychological Review, 109*, 619–645.

Aron, A., & Aron, E. N. (1986). *Love and the expansion of self: Understanding attraction and satisfaction*. Washington, DC: Hemisphere Publishing.

Aron, A., Aron, E. N., & Smollan, D. (1992). Inclusion of other in the self scale and the structure of interpersonal closeness. *Journal of Personality and Social Psychology, 63*, 596–612.

Aron, A., Aron, E. N., Tudor, M., & Nelson, G. (1991). Close relationships as including other in the self. *Journal of Personality and Social Psychology, 60*, 241–253.

Aron, A., & Fraley, B. (1999). Relationship closeness as including other in the self: Cognitive underpinnings and measures. *Social Cognition, 17*, 140–160.

Aron, A., McLaughlin-Volpe, T., Mashek, D., Lewandowski, G., Wright, S. C., & Aron, E. (2005). Including others in the self. *European Review of Social Psychology, 14*, 101–132.

Aron, A., Melinat, E., Aron, E. N., Vallone, R., & Bator, R. (1997). The experimental generation of interpersonal closeness: A procedure and some preliminary findings. *Personality and Social Psychology Bulletin, 23*, 363–377.

Blascovich, J., Mendes, W. B., Hunter, S. B., Lickel, B., & Kowai-Bell, N. (2001). Perceiver threat in social interactions with stigmatized others. *Journal of Personality and Social Psychology, 80*, 253–267.

Brown, R., & Hewstone, H. (2005). An integrative theory of intergroup contact. In M. Zanna (Ed.), *Advances in experimental social psychology* (Vol. 37) (pp. 255–343). San Diego, CA: Academic Press.

Cameron, L., & Rutland, A. (2006). Extended contact through story reading in school: Reducing children's prejudice toward the disabled. *Journal of Social Issues, 62*, 469–488.

Cooley, C. H. (1902). *Human nature and the social order.* New York: Scribner.

Fehr, B. (1996). *Friendship processes.* Thousand Oaks, CA: Sage.

Heider, F. (1958). *The psychology of interpersonal relations.* New York: Wiley.

Hewstone, M., & Brown, R. (1986). Contact is not enough: An intergroup perspective on the "Contact Hypothesis." In M. Hewstone & R. Brown (Eds.), *Contact and conflict in intergroup encounters* (pp. 1–44). Oxford: Blackwell.

Islam, M. R., & Hewstone, M. (1993). Dimensions of contact as predictors of intergroup anxiety, perceived out-group variability, and out-group attitude: An integrative model. *Personality and Social Psychology Bulletin, 19*, 700–710.

Kiu, L., Wright, S. C., & Teows, M. (2007). *The extended contact effect: The influence of group typicality on intergroup attitudes.* Paper presented at the Society for Personality and Social Psychology, Memphis, TN.

Liebkind, K., & McAlister, A. L. (1999). Extended contact through peer modelling to promote tolerance in Finland. *European Journal of Social Psychology, 29*, 765–780.

Mashek, D., Aron, A., & Boncimino, M. (2003). Confusions of self with close others. *Personality and Social Psychology Bulletin, 29*, 382–392.

McLaughlin-Volpe, T. (2004). *The intergroup contact effect as including an outgroup other in the self.* Unpublished doctoral dissertation, State University of New York at Stony Brook.

Neuberg, S. L., Smith, D. M., Hoffman, J. C., & Russell, F. J. (1994). When we observe stigmatized and "normal" individuals interacting: Stigma by association. *Personality and Social Psychology Bulletin, 20*, 196–209.

Paolini, S., Hewstone, M., Cairns, E., & Voci, A. (2004). Effects of direct and indirect cross-group friendships on judgments of Catholics and Protestants in Northern Ireland: The mediating role of an anxiety-reduction mechanism. *Personality and Social Psychology Bulletin, 30*, 770–786.

Pettigrew, T. F. (1997). Generalized intergroup contact effects on prejudice. *Personality and Social Psychology Bulletin, 23*, 173–185.

Pettigrew, T. F. (1998). Intergroup contact theory. *Annual Review of Psychology, 49*, 65–85.

Pettigrew, T. F., Christ, O., Wagner, U., & Stellmacher, J. (2007). Direct and indirect intergroup contact effects on prejudice: A normative interpretation. *International Journal of Intercultural Relations, 31*, 411–425.

Richards, Z., & Hewstone, M. (2001). Subtyping and subgrouping: Processes for the prevention and promotion of stereotype change. *Personality and Social Psychology Review, 5*, 52–73

Sedikides, C., Olsen, N., & Reis, H. T. (1993). Relationships as natural categories. *Journal of Personality and Social Psychology, 54*, 13–20.

Shelton, J. N., & Richeson, J. A. (2005). Intergroup contact and pluralistic ignorance. *Journal of Personality and Social Psychology*, *88*, 91–107.

Sherif, M., Harvey, O. J., White, B. J., Hood, W. R., & Sherif, C. W. (1961). *Intergroup conflict and cooperation: The Robbers Cave experiment.* Norman, OK: University of Oklahoma Book Exchange.

Smith, E. R., & Henry, S. (1996). An in-group becomes part of the self: Response time evidence. *Personality & Social Psychology Bulletin*, *22*, 635–642.

Tajfel, H., Billig, M. G., Bundy, R. P., & Flament, C. (1971). Social categorization and intergroup behaviour. *European Journal of Social Psychology*, *1*, 149–178.

Tropp, L. R., & Wright, S. C. (2001). Ingroup identification as the inclusion of ingroup in the self. *Personality and Social Psychology Bulletin*, *27*, 585–600.

Turner, J. C., Hogg, M. A., Oakes, P. J., Reicher, S. D., & Wetherell, M. S. (1987). *Rediscovering the social group: A self-categorization theory.* Oxford: Blackwell.

Vorauer, J. (2006). An information search model of evaluative concerns in intergroup interaction. *Psychological Review*, *113*, 862–886.

Wright, S. C., Aron, A., McLaughlin-Volpe, T., & Ropp, S. A. (1997). The extended contact effect: Knowledge of cross-group friendships and prejudice. *Journal of Personality and Social Psychology*, *73*, 73–90.

Wright, S. C., Aron, A., & Tropp, L. R. (2001). Including others (and groups) in the self: Self-expansion and intergroup relations. In J. P. Forgas & K. D. Williams (Eds.), *The social self: Cognitive, interpersonal and inter-group perspectives* (pp. 343–363). Philadelphia, PA: Psychology Press.

Wright, S. C., Brody, S. M., & Aron, A. (2005). Intergroup contact: Still our best hope for improving intergroup relations. In C. Crandall & M. Schaller (Eds.), *The social psychology of prejudice: Historical perspectives* (pp. 115–142). Seattle, WA: Lewinian Press.

Wright, S. C., Davies, K., & Sanders, L. (2007). *Direct and extended contact effects on attitudes towards lesbians and gay men: Testing mechanisms.* Unpublished manuscript, Simon Fraser University.

11

Deprovincialization
Social Identity Complexity and Outgroup Acceptance

Marilynn B. Brewer

In a large field study of the effects of intergroup friendship on prejudice toward minority immigrant groups in Western Europe, Tom Pettigrew (1997) noted a particularly intriguing finding. Not only did intergroup friendship (with members of national, cultural, or religious outgroups) generalize to attitudes toward specific ethnic minority groups as a whole, it was also associated with reduced prejudice (more positive affect) toward a wide range of national and ethnic outgroups, for which the respondents had had no direct personal contact. For example, British participants who reported having friendships with West Indian immigrants in the UK were significantly less prejudiced toward Turks (an outgroup that most British respondents were not likely to have had contact with) than those without such outgroup friendships. Further, the results of nonrecursive structural equation modeling suggested that the path from intergroup friendship to generalized attitudes toward outgroups is larger than the reverse causal path from prejudice to friendship, indicating that the finding is not simply the result of generally nonprejudiced people having more intergroup friendships.

Although a large body of research supports the conclusion that personalized contact with members of an ethnic outgroup generalizes to attitudes and feelings toward the outgroup as a whole (Pettigrew & Tropp, 2006), this European study is one of very few that have investigated the broader question of generalization to other outgroups. But the evidence for such generalized effects was quite compelling in the data from the European survey and suggested that we might need to look for some new mechanisms through which personalized contact with individual members of an ethnic outgroup generalizes to intergroup attitudes quite broadly. As one possible explanation for the generalized contact effect, Pettigrew (1997) introduced the concept of "deprovincialization," the idea that extensive intergroup contact not only instigates reappraisal of the outgroup as a whole, it may often involve a reappraisal of the individual's *ingroup*. As Pettigrew (1997, p. 174) puts it, for individuals with extensive personal contact with members of an outgroup:

> In-group norms, customs, and lifestyles turn out not to be the only ways to manage the social world. The new perspective not only individualizes and "humanizes" out-group members but serves to distance you from your in-group . . . Those with out-group friends gain distance from their own group and form a less provincial perspective on other groups in general.

So the unique insight suggested by generalized contact effects is the idea that changes in attitudes toward outgroups may derive, at least in part, from changes in the way an individual conceptualizes his or her own ingroups. This chapter explores further this concept of "deprovincialization" by linking it to another concept related to how individuals think about their ingroups—the concept of *social identity complexity* (Roccas & Brewer, 2002).

Social Identity Complexity

The logic of deprovincialization is similar to the logic underlying crossed-categorization effects in intergroup relations (cf. Crisp & Hewstone, 2006). Crossed categorization refers to the fact that individuals belong to more than one ingroup across different domains of social life—groups that overlap only partially in terms of membership. As a consequence, another individual who is a fellow ingroup member according to one basis of categorization may turn out to be an outgroup member when a different basis of social categorization is considered (e.g., someone who shares my religious identity may well be a member of a different occupational ingroup).

Cross-cutting categorizations (and associated multiple identities) may diffuse or prevent the more invidious consequences of ingroup–outgroup differentiation and intergroup comparison. This insight that complex, cross-cutting patterns of social differentiation increase social stability and tolerance has been independently generated by anthropologists (e.g., Gluckman, 1955; Murphy, 1957), sociologists (e.g., Blau, 1977; Coser, 1956; Flap, 1988), and political scientists (e.g., Almond & Verba, 1963; Lipset, 1959). Coser (1956, pp. 153–154) hypothesized, for instance:

> In flexible social structures, multiple conflicts crisscross each other and thereby prevent basic cleavages along one axis. The multiple group affiliations of individuals makes them participate in various group conflicts so that their total personalities are not involved in any single one of them. Thus segmental participation in a multiplicity of conflicts constitutes a balancing mechanism within the structure . . .

In other words, membership in cross-cutting group memberships may lead to distancing from any one ingroup in much the same way that Tom Pettigrew hypothesized in describing deprovincialization as one possible outcome of personalized intergroup contact.

Objective Versus Subjective Complexity

In a complex society with cross-cutting dimensions of social differentiation, the different groups that a particular individual belongs to across different domains of social life (for example, ethnicity, religious affiliation, occupational category) are likely to overlap only partially when assessed objectively. However, mere membership in objectively cross-cutting categories may not be sufficient to produce deprovincialization. Roccas and Brewer (2002) have suggested that individuals differ in whether they *perceive* their various membership groups as cross-cutting (partially overlapping) or as convergent (substantially overlapping). They refer to this variation in how individuals mentally integrate their multiple social group identities as social identity complexity. Social identity complexity refers to the extent to which individuals represent their multiple group memberships such that different identities are both differentiated and integrated in an individual's subjective cognitive representation of those combined group memberships.

Put another way, an individual may perceive his or her ingroups as having highly overlapping sets of members, such that a set of group memberships may even form a single, exclusive compound category (e.g., White Catholic Republican doctors). This would be described as a *simple* identity structure. The opposite end of the continuum would be characterized by an individual who recognizes that his or her ingroup memberships are composed of distinct but overlapping member sets. This would be described as a *complex* identity structure (e.g., Whites *and* Catholics *and* Republicans *and* doctors). In this conceptualization, a simple subjective representation of multiple converging social categories produces a very *exclusive* ingroup identity. By contrast, the additive combination of multiple ingroup members produces a complex and *inclusive* representation of the ingroup.

In the limited research on social identity complexity conducted up to this point (Brewer & Pierce, 2005; Miller & Brewer, 2006; Roccas & Brewer, 2002), social identity complexity has been operationalized using a self-report measure that directly asks individuals about the extent to which they perceive the memberships and characteristics of their social groups to be overlapping. In this methodology, the first step is to elicit from each participant the names of three or four important group memberships (e.g., religious affiliation, political organizations, occupational group, etc.). Then, for each pair of their own ingroups, they are asked to rate (on a 10-point scale) how likely it is that members of Group A are also members of Group B. The extent of the perceived overlap among an individual's various ingroup memberships is then averaged to generate a membership overlap score that is theorized to reflect an individual's social identity complexity. According to Roccas and Brewer (2002), individuals who perceive a greater overlap among their identities (i.e., high scorers) have simpler identities, while those who perceive less overlap (i.e., low scorers) have more complex identities. Therefore, an individual's score on such an overlap measure is inversely related to his or her social identity complexity.

Social Identity Complexity and tolerance

Roccas and Brewer (2002) hypothesized that social identity complexity should be associated with tolerance toward outgroups, for both cognitive and motivational reasons. They note that individuals with high levels of social identity complexity are more likely to be cognitively aware that other persons who are outgroup members on some group dimension might be ingroup members when considered on some different dimension. Also, the motivation to favor one's ingroup may be diminished when one recognizes the partially overlapping nature of ingroup memberships, which reduces both the importance of the ingroup in intergroup comparisons as well as the significance of any particular social identification for an individual's self-definition and collective self-esteem.

Results of initial exploratory research supported the hypothesized relationship between individual differences in social identity complexity and tolerance-related variables. Roccas and Brewer (2002) presented initial data indicating that higher social identity complexity was associated with higher endorsement of openness, lower power orientation, and higher universalism values on the Schwartz Value Inventory (Schwartz, 1992). In a second exploratory study, greater social identity complexity was associated with less social distance to an outgroup (Russian immigrants) among Israeli participants.

More recently, Brewer and Pierce (2005) assessed the relationship between social identity complexity and tolerance in a large-sample mail and phone survey of adults from Ohio. In this study, a mail survey was used to identify potential participants for a phone survey and to obtain a listing of group memberships from each respondent. These group memberships were then used to construct a personalized phone interview for each respondent contacted. Specifically, three of the participant's own identified ingroup memberships across different domains, along with the ingroup "American," were used when asking each respondent about the extent of the overlap between each of these groups. The phone interview also elicited responses to items measuring attitudes toward affirmative action and multiculturalism, as well as emotional distance from outgroups as measured by "feeling thermometer" questions. These variables were then tested for a relationship to the overlap measure of social identity complexity.

The results confirmed that social identity complexity was associated with both tolerance-related policy preferences and affect toward outgroups. Among the white men and women respondents, the mean overlap score across four ingroups was significantly correlated with attitudes toward affirmative action, multiculturalism, and affect toward outgroups after controlling for age, education, and ideology. Individuals with higher social identity complexity (low perceived overlap among their four ingroups) were more likely to endorse affirmative action and multiculturalism and to show less affective distance toward ethnic minorities than were individuals with low social identity complexity (high overlap scores). In a follow-up study, Miller and Brewer (2006) replicated these findings with a college student sample, using a computerized technique for eliciting ingroup memberships and constructing a social identity complexity score. Again, the overlap measure of complexity proved to be significantly correlated with racial policy issues and with affect toward ethnic outgroups on both explicit and implicit measures.

In summary, across several studies, holding the number and diversity of ingroups constant, individual differences in the subjective representation of these multiple group memberships proved to be a significant predictor of intergroup attitudes. This finding seems particularly compelling when it is noted that the overlap scores computed in these studies did not include the participants' racial and ethnic group memberships, but were based on categories such as religious affiliation, occupational category, and sports fanships. The subjective representation of these non-ethnic groups was nonetheless related to tolerance of ethnic outgroups in the manner predicted by Roccas and Brewer (2002).

Antecedents of Social Identity Complexity

Given the consistent evidence that social identity complexity (as measured by perceived overlap among one's ingroup memberships) is related to attitudes toward ethnic outgroups, it behooves us to learn more about the nature of social identity complexity as an individual difference variable and its correlated characteristics. In their original theoretical framework, Roccas and Brewer (2002) posited that ideology (personal values) and cognitive needs might be sources of individual differences in social identity complexity. Ideology has been investigated as a correlate of social identity complexity in several studies. Membership overlap scores have been found to be correlated (in the predicted direction) with universalistic values (Roccas & Brewer, 2002) and with self-rated liberalism-conservatism (Brewer & Pierce, 2005; Miller & Brewer, 2006). In a subsequent study exploring various measures of cognitive style, social identity complexity (again, as measured by overlap scores) was most consistently correlated with a measure of need for cognition (Cacioppo, Petty, & Kao, 1984). In general, individuals who scored high on need for cognition were also higher in social identity complexity (low overlap scores), suggesting that social identity complexity is associated with the motivation to think carefully and elaboratively about one's social world.

Importantly, the direct relationship between membership overlap and intergroup attitudes remains significant when controlling for both political ideology and need for cognition. In fact, once social identity complexity is entered into a regression predicting affect toward ethnic outgroups, neither ideology nor need for cognition have any significant effect (Miller & Brewer, 2006). This suggests that social identity complexity has a more proximal relationship with intergroup attitudes, consistent with an account wherein need for cognition and ideological orientation are potential antecedents of social identity complexity, but not themselves direct determinants of intergroup affect.

Although two important individual difference variables (ideology and cognitive style) have been investigated as likely antecedents of social identity complexity, we know relatively little about the *experiential* antecedents of social identity complexity. The most obvious factor that may affect social identity complexity is the actual complexity of the experienced social environment. Social contexts in which different bases for ingroup-outgroup distinctions are both salient and cross-cutting rather than convergent confront the individual with knowledge about the differences in meaning and composition of their various social categorizations. So the question is, to what extent do subjective representations of one's own multiple ingroup memberships reflect personal exposure to a complex social environment?

Even in a complex society, much of the time, individuals are surrounded by others who are similar to themselves on multiple dimensions (Kelley & Evans, 1995). We are first exposed to our family members, who naturally belong to the same race, religion, socio-economic status as ourselves. Youngsters go to school with children who live in the same neighborhood, and consequently homogeneity of the immediate social environment is maintained, albeit to a lesser degree. The immediate social environment within which most people are socialized is objectively less complex than the society as a whole. Thus, the local social structure may encourage the perception of relatively high similarity and overlap between ingroups, leading to a relatively simple social identity. To develop a complex social identity, special conditions are necessary—conditions that enhance the simultaneous awareness of more than one ingroup and the awareness that these ingroups overlap only partially.

Living in a multicultural society, for instance, may enhance awareness that social categorization based on ethnic heritage and social categorization based on national citizenship do not completely overlap and hence raise social identity complexity. Note however, that living in a diverse, multicultural society may not always be sufficient to provide the conditions for complex identity formation. The impact of a multicultural environment may be experienced differently for different participants, depending on their actual exposure to diversity. In addition, the effects of a multicultural society on development of social identity complexity is likely to be moderated by societal norms concerning multiculturalism. When people of many cultural backgrounds live together, the cultural groups they form are often not equal in power. Accordingly, some groups are dominant, and their ideology may have extensive influence both on the actual diversity and on the perception of diversity of the whole society. Some dominant groups are explicitly assimilationist, and hold an ideology that promotes a single culture in the nation, while others are integrationist and explicitly encourage the maintenance of the cultural heritage of non-dominant groups (Berry, 1997). It is likely that an integrationist ideology enhances the social identity complexity of members of the dominant group, because it encourages the various ethnocultural groups to express their diversity, and raise its salience. Thus, when integrationist norms prevail, members of the dominant group are more likely to be aware of nonoverlap between their ethnic or racial group and the other groups to which they belong.

Social Identity Complexity and Intergroup Contact

The relationship between interethnic contact experience and social identity complexity was explored in the survey study conducted by Brewer and Pierce (2005). To assess the role of intergroup contact in those data, a contact index was constructed from respondents' answers to a set of questions about racial composition of their neighborhood, friends, workplace, and chosen ingroups. This contact measure proved not to be related to overlap complexity scores (r = .03). However, this study did not provide for a very strong test of the potential effect of intergroup contact on social identity complexity. The interview respondents in the Ohio survey had, on average, very little interracial contact experience overall. On a scale from 1–6 (where 6 = little or no racial diversity or personal contact), the mean contact for this sample of white respondents was 5.27, with very low variability (s.d. = .64). In a population with a greater range of contact experience, it is very likely that intergroup contact would prove to be a significant predictor of social identity complexity, particularly in contexts where multicultural ideals are promulgated. Nonetheless, the results from the Ohio survey indicate that perceiving one's multiple ingroups as cross-cutting categories is associated with more positive attitudes toward ethnic outgroups and more tolerant political views *even in the absence of direct interethnic contact experience*. This raises interesting questions of why and how complexity of representations of nonethnic ingroups influences attitudes towards ethnic outgroups specifically.

Possible Paths from Multiple Identities to Outgroup Acceptance

Social identity complexity is essentially a cognitive construct. Given that individuals acknowledge their membership in multiple distinct social groups or categories, identity complexity refers to how these multiple memberships are subjectively represented by the individual. High social identity complexity means that the individual recognizes that his or her different group memberships overlap only partially, so that the total of the shared memberships is additive and larger than any single ingroup alone. Individuals with low social identity complexity, on the other hand, see their various ingroups as highly overlapping and redundant. Hence the total shared membership (as perceived) is no larger than that of a single ingroup.

Roccas and Brewer (2002) speculated that this aspect of the cognitive representation of one's own ingroups would be related to the degree of tolerance and acceptance of outgroups in general, and ethnic outgroups in particular. Subsequent research has supported this speculation, but the exact mechanisms whereby subjective perceptions of one's ingroups leads to acceptance of specific outgroups have yet to be fully explored. In this section, I will discuss three possible mechanisms for the observed relationship between social identity complexity and interethnic attitudes.

Extended "Extended Contact"

In a seminal paper in the intergroup contact literature, Wright, Aron, McLaughlin-Volpe, & Ropp (1997) introduced the concept of "extended contact" effects. Extended contact is, basically, a form of *indirect* contact with outgroup members through knowing or observing ingroup members who have friendships with members of ethnic outgroups. In a series of field and experimental studies, Wright et al. (1997) demonstrated that such indirect contact had effects similar to those of positive direct intergroup contact. Mere knowledge of cross-group friendships led to less negative attitudes toward the outgroup as a whole. Wright and his colleagues speculated that extended contact might even have some benefits over direct intergroup contact experience in that group membership remains salient but without arousing intergroup anxiety. Under such circumstances, seeing the outgroup member as a positive exemplar would be more likely to generalize to the outgroup as a whole. In addition, observing cross-group friendships might lead to "the inclusion of the outgroup member's group membership in the self" (Wright et al., 1997, p. 73). Subsequent research among Finnish teenagers (Liebkind & McAlister, 1999) and among Catholics and Protestants in Northern Ireland (Paolini, Hewstone, Cairns, & Voci, 2004) has also supported the idea that extended contact can benefit intergroup relations.

The implication of extended contact research is that *vicarious* contact experiences might have at least some of the benefits associated with cross-group friendship. This has led some researchers to suggest that merely *imagining* being involved in an intergroup interaction may have similar benefits (Turner, Crisp, & Lambert, 2007). This is idea is supported by research demonstrating that extended contact through story reading to school children was effective in reducing children's prejudice toward the disabled (Cameron & Rutland, 2006). More directly, Turner et al. (2007) conducted three experiments in which participants were asked to imagine themselves talking to a member of an outgroup. Young participants who imagined talking to an elderly person subsequently showed lower levels of intergroup age bias than participants who simply "thought about" elderly people, and heterosexual men who imagined talking to a homosexual man subsequently evaluated gay men more positively, compared to a control group. These experiments on vicarious or imagined intergroup contact might be thought of as the "extended extended contact" effect.

Vicarious contact might also provide one explanation for why social identity complexity is associated with more positive attitudes toward ethnic minorities, even in the absence of direct intergroup contact. In effect, persons who are high in social identity complexity recognize that some people who are outgroup members on one dimension (e.g., a member of an ethnic outgroup) might at the same time be members of their ingroup on some other dimension (e.g., a member of the same profession). Thus, they represent their ingroups as diverse (i.e., not everyone in this group is like me in every dimension). As a consequence, when they think of a particular ingroup (e.g., members of my profession), they may readily imagine that some of their fellow ingroupers are from a different ethnic group than themselves. Even without knowing such individuals personally, merely being aware that some ethnic outgroup members are part of one's own ingroup may create a positive affect that is generalized to the ethnic outgroup as a whole. Sharing ingroup membership with *some* ethnic outgroupers may create the conditions for inclusion of the outgroup member's group membership in the self, as suggested by Wright et al. (1997).

Superordinate Identity: The Recategorization Mechanism

Another mechanism of attitude change that is associated with cooperative intergroup contact is the creation of a common ingroup identity (Gaertner & Dovidio, 2000). Across a series of laboratory experiments and field studies, Gaertner, Dovidio, and their colleagues have demonstrated that positive effects of intergroup contact are mediated (at least in part) by *perceptions* that members of the ingroup and the outgroup are united in a single superordinate group identity that encompasses both—a process that they refer to as *recategorization*. When ingroup and outgroup are recategorized in a more inclusive common ingroup, the benefits of shared ingroup membership are extended to the former outgroup members, with a consequent reduction of intergroup bias.

Social identity complexity may be associated with the creation of superordinate category identities that encompass members of ethnic ingroups and outgroups. As mentioned earlier, individuals with high social identity complexity see their various ingroups as additive (Roccas & Brewer, 2002). That is, the total membership of the multiple ingroups combined is much more inclusive than the membership of any single ingroup. In order to incorporate all these collectives into their social identity, these individuals may self-categorize a high level of superordinate category identity—a superordinate group that encompasses their own diverse group memberships. So, for example, a complex individual who is a member of the American Lutheran Church, a Euro-American, an American dentist, and an avid fan of the New York Yankees may see all of these groups as cross-cutting (partially overlapping) subgroups of a broader American identity. His or her primary social identity may be vested in this more inclusive superordinate level of categorization. So even though only *some* members of an ethnic outgroup (such as African-Americans) share a specific ingroup membership (e.g., fellow Yankee fans), *all* members of that ethnic group are included in the shared superordinate, American. There is experimental evidence that evaluations of crossed category targets are more positive and inclusive in the context of a common (superordinate) ingroup, particularly when identification with the superordinate is more important than that of any of the subordinate ingroups (Crisp, Walsh, & Hewstone, 2006).

Importantly, my reasoning assumes that social identity complexity not only leads to a more inclusive level of social identity, but that the superordinate category is, itself, represented as a complex group. That is, the superordinate encompasses the complexity and diversity of the individual's own multiple ingroups. This complexity of representation of the superordinate group is critical to acceptance of subgroups different from one's own (cf. Mummendey & Wenzel, 1999; Waldzus, Mummendey, Wenzel, & Weber, 2003). Individuals who are strongly identified with a superordinate category but have a simple, prototypic representation of the superordinate group (e.g., American = White, Protestant, Midwesterner) will view subgroups that deviate from that prototype as unacceptable ingroup members, thus perpetuating (or exacerbating) intergroup bias and discrimination (Mummendey & Wenzel, 1999). Thus, recategorization at the superordinate level must entail both inclusiveness and complexity in order to account for acceptance of ethnic outgroups.

As a preliminary test of the idea that social identity complexity is associated with complex representation of a superordinate identity, we reanalyzed some data from the Brewer and Pierce (2005) survey dataset. We first recalculated each respondent's social identity complexity score by averaging the perceived overlap among pairs of their *three* ingroup memberships, excluding the group "Americans." We then computed a new measure based on mean ratings of perceived similarity between each of their three ingroups and "Americans." The logic of this latter measure is that high perceived similarity indicates ethnocentric projection of the characteristics of their own ingroups to the superordinate national prototype (Mummendey & Wenzel, 1999). As predicted, the correlation between ingroup membership overlap scores and perceived similarity between own groups and Americans was significant (r = .52). Thus, those with high overlap scores (low social identity complexity) showed high ethnocentric projection to the prototype of American, whereas those with higher social identity complexity perceived less similarity between their various ingroups and American as a whole, suggesting a less projective and more complex representation of the nation as a superordinate category.

Cognitive Consequences of Crossed Categorization: The Decategorization Mechanism

When an individual embraces an inclusive superordinate social group identity, differentiation and intergroup bias among subgroups are reduced or eliminated. However, for those very reasons, individuals are often resistant to recategorization at a superordinate level, particularly if it implies losing valued and distinctive ingroup identities (Crisp, Stone, & Hall, 2006; Hornsey & Hogg, 2000). When motivation to preserve distinctive social identities is high, efforts to reduce intergroup differentiation through common ingroup identity can actually exacerbate intergroup bias rather than reduce it (Crisp et al., 2006; Crisp & Hewstone, 2007).

In many ways, creating shared identities with outgroups through cross-cutting category distinctions may be less threatening to ingroup identity than an all-inclusive superordinate categorization might be (Marcus-Newhall, Miller, Holtz, & Brewer, 1993). With multiple cross-cutting categorizations, ingroup and outgroup overlap only partially in terms of crossed category membership. Hence, the common identity does not supersede or replace the separate component categories. Nonetheless, in the classic analysis of the bias-reducing effects of crossed categorization, it was assumed that cross-cutting categories weaken category differentiation and that this blurring of category differences is responsible for the reduction of intergroup discrimination (Crisp, Hewstone, & Rubin, 2001; Deschamps & Doise, 1978; Vanbeselaere, 1987; 1991). From that perspective, the mechanisms underlying the effects of recategorization and crossed-categorization are essentially the same. In either case, bias is eliminated through loss of ingroup-outgroup category distinctiveness and differentiation.

More recently, Crisp and Hewstone (2007) have argued that the effects of common ingroup identity and of crossed-categorization represent qualitatively different processes. Instead of focusing on *inter*category differentiation, they point out that multiple cross-cutting categories increase *intra*category differentiation. When individuals are aware that various ingroup-outgroup distinctions are uncorrelated (so that ingroups and outgroups overlap across dimensions), one consequence is a more cognitively complex representation of each ingroup considered singly. (That is, each ingroup contains some members who are part of outgroups on a different dimension.) Particularly when multiple social categorizations are simultaneously salient (i.e., more than two cross-cutting categories), Crisp and Hewstone suggest that perceivers are likely to shift to an *individuated* mode of processing of social information—a shift that Brewer & Miller (1984) referred to as "decategorization." Decategorization in this sense is qualitatively different from loss of category distinctions or boundaries. Rather, it refers to the loss of *importance* of category information in forming judgments or impressions of other persons or in social interaction. As Crisp and Hewstone (2007, p. 221) put it:

> considering multiple criteria for social categorization could produce a decategorization effect by virtue of the implied decrease in usefulness of any one dimension of social comparison for forming an impression

. . . In effect, it becomes less likely that any one category dimension will be used as a basis for discrimination . . .

Social identity complexity is the subjective representation of one's ingroups as parts of cross-cutting categories. By recognizing that shared group membership varies across different dimensions and that each ingroup contains members with diverse characteristics and multiple group identities, individuals with high social identity complexity are less likely to regard any one category distinction as highly meaningful or important. Distinctions, differences, and diversity are recognized, but category distinctions are not evaluatively significant, at least not across contexts. To bring us back full circle, the decategorization process associated with social identity complexity and multiple cross-cutting social categories sounds a lot like "deprovincialization," as described by Tom Pettigrew in his 1997 article.

Implications for Social Policy in Pluralistic Societies

Like intergroup contact, social identity complexity is a joint function of social-structural and individual characteristics and processes. Structural desegregation provides the *opportunity* for intergroup contact and exchange, but whether the opportunity is realized in the formation of intergroup friendships and extensive cross-group social interaction depends on individual motivation and affect, interpersonal orientations, and understandings of social norms. Similarly, a complex social structure in which various socially meaningful cleavages are cross-cutting rather than convergent is a necessary condition for individuals to have multiple cross-cutting social group memberships. But a complex social structure is not necessarily represented subjectively as social identity complexity at the individual level. The translation of societal complexity to social identity complexity requires that individuals *experience* cross-cutting ties in their own social relationships and have the cognitive ability and motivation to acknowledge and integrate multiple social categorizations in their self-definitions and interactions with others.

Pluralistic societies provide the context for multiple social identities and the development of social identity complexity. At the institutional level, we need to take care that the potential for cross-cutting social categories is fully realized. Organizations, for instance, should regularly take stock to be sure that demographic characteristics and organizational roles are not highly correlated, so that the advantages of diversity can be realized without creating "faultlines" within the organization (Brewer, 1995; Lau & Murnighan, 1998). Diversity training should focus more on cross-cutting ties, rather than simple messages of assimilation ("we're all alike") or exclusive emphasis on cultural difference. There is evidence that multiple categorization skills can be trained, with subsequent reduction in social stereotyping (Bigler & Liben, 1992) and intergroup bias (Hall & Crisp, 2005). Educational interventions can be designed to enhance multiple social categorization beginning at the elementary school level. Ultimately, the conditions that promote successful intergroup contact will also promote social identity complexity, and vice versa. If societal complexity is reflected in individual social identities, difference and diversity will not only be tolerated but actively valued and embraced.

Acknowledgment

The research cited in this chapter was funded by a grant from the National Science Foundation [BCS-1412328].

References

Almond, G. A., & Verba, S. (1963). *The civic culture: Political attitudes in five nations*. Princeton, NJ: Princeton University Press.

Berry, J. W. (1997). Immigration, acculturation, and adaptation. *Applied Psychology: An International Review, 46,* 5–68.

Bigler, R. S., & Liben, L. S. (1992). Cognitive mechanism in children's gender stereotyping: Theoretical and educational implications of a cognitive-based intervention. *Child Development, 63,* 1351–1363.

Blau, P. M. (1977). *Inequality and heterogeneity: A primitive theory of social structure.* New York: Free Press.

Brewer, M. B. (1995). Managing diversity: The role of social identities. In S. Jackson & M. Ruderman (Eds.), *Diversity in work teams* (pp. 47–68). Washington DC: American Psychological Association.

Brewer, M. B., & Miller, N. (1984). Beyond the contact hypothesis: Theoretical perspectives on desegregation. In N. Miller & M. Brewer (Eds.), *Groups in contact: The psychology of desegregation* (pp. 281–302). San Diego: Academic Press.

Brewer, M. B., & Pierce, K. P. (2005). Social identity complexity and outgroup tolerance. *Personality and Social Psychology Bulletin, 31,* 428–437.

Cacioppo, J. T., Petty, R. E., & Kao, C. F. (1984). The efficient assessment of "need for cognition." *Journal of Personality Assessment, 48,* 306–307.

Cameron, L., & Rutland, A. (2006). Extended contact through story reading in school: Reducing children's prejudice toward the disabled. *Journal of Social Issues*, *62*, 469–488.

Coser, L. A. (1956). *The functions of social conflict*. New York: Free Press.

Crisp, R. J., & Hewstone, M. (Eds.) (2006). *Multiple social categorization*. Hove, UK: Psychology Press.

Crisp, R. J., & Hewstone, M. (2007). Multiple social categorization. In M. Zanna (Ed.), *Advances in experimental social psychology* (Vol. 39) (pp. 163–254). San Diego: Academic Press.

Crisp, R. J., Hewstone, M., & Rubin, M. (2001). Does multiple categorization reduce intergroup bias? *Personality and Social Psychology Bulletin*, *27*, 76–89.

Crisp, R. J., Stone, C. H., & Hall, N. R. (2006). Recategorization and subgroup identification: Predicting and preventing threats from common ingroups. *Personality and Social Psychology Bulletin*, *32*, 230–243.

Crisp, R. J., Walsh, J., & Hewstone, M. (2006). Crossed categorization in common ingroup contexts. *Personality and Social Psychology Bulletin*, *32*, 1204–1218.

Deschamps, J.-C., & Doise, W. (1978). Crossed category memberships in intergroup relations. In H. Tajfel (Ed.), *Differentiation between social groups* (pp. 141–158). Cambridge, Cambridge University Press.

Flap, H. D. (1988). *Conflict, loyalty and violence: The effects of social networks on behaviour*. Frankfurt am Main: Lang.

Gaertner, S. L., & Dovidio, J. F. (2000). *Reducing intergroup bias: The common ingroup identity model*. Philadelphia: Psychology Press.

Gluckman, M. (1955). *Customs and conflict in Africa*. Oxford: Blackwell.

Hall, N. R., & Crisp, R. J. (2005). Considering multiple criteria for social categorization can reduce intergroup bias. *Personality and Social Psychology Bulletin*, *31*, 1435–1444.

Hornsey, M. J., & Hogg, M. A. (2000). Subgroup relations: A comparison of mutual intergroup differentiation and common ingroup identity models of prejudice reduction. *Personality and Social Psychology Bulletin*, *26*, 242–256.

Kelley, J., & Evans, M. D. (1995). Class and class conflict in six western nations. *American Sociological Review*, *60*, 157–178.

Lau, D. C., & Murnighan, J. K. (1998). Demographic diversity and fault lines: The compositional dynamics of organizational groups. *Academy of Management Review*, *23*, 325–340.

Liebkind, K., & McAlister, A. L. (1999). Extended contact through peer modeling to promote tolerance in Finland. *European Journal of Social Psychology*, *29*, 765–780.

Lipset, S. M. (1959). Some social requisites of democracy: Economic development and political legitimacy. *American Political Science Review*, *53*, 69–105.

Marcus-Newhall, A., Miller, N., Holtz, R., & Brewer, M. B. (1993). Cross-cutting category membership with role assignment: A means of reducing intergroup bias. *British Journal of Social Psychology*, *32*, 125–146.

Miller, K. P., & Brewer, M. B. (2006). *Social identity complexity, cognitive style, and interracial attitudes.* Unpublished manuscript, Ohio State University.

Mummendey, A., & Wenzel, M. (1999). Social discrimination and tolerance in intergroup relations: Reactions to intergroup difference. *Personality and Social Psychology Review*, *3*, 158–174.

Murphy, R. F. (1957). Intergroup hostility and social cohesion. *American Anthropologist*, *59*, 1018–1035.

Paolini, S., Hewstone, M., Cairns, E., & Voci, A. (2004). Effects of direct and indirect cross-group friendships on judgments of Catholic and Protestants in Northern Ireland: The mediating role of an anxiety-reduction mechanism. *Personality and Social Psychology Bulletin*, *30*, 770–786.

Pettigrew, T. F. (1997). Generalized intergroup contact effects on prejudice. *Personality and Social Psychology Bulletin*, *23*, 173–185.

Pettigrew, T. F., & Tropp, L. R. (2006). A meta-analytic test of intergroup contact theory. *Journal of Personality and Social Psychology*, *90*, 751–783.

Roccas, S., & Brewer, M. B. (2002). Social identity complexity. *Personality and Social Psychology Review*, *6*, 88–106.

Schwartz, S. H. (1992). Universals in the content and structure of values: Theoretical advances and empirical tests in 20 countries. In M. Zanna (Ed.), *Advances in experimental social psychology* (Vol. 25) (pp 1–65). San Diego, CA: Academic Press.

Turner, R. N., Crisp, R. J., & Lambert, E. (2007). Imagining intergroup contact can improve intergroup attitudes. *Group Processes and Intergroup Relations*, *10*, 427–441.

Vanbeselaere, N. (1987). The effect of dichotomous and crossed social categorizations upon intergroup discrimination. *European Journal of Social Psychology*, *17*, 143–156.

Vanbeselaere, N. (1991). The different effects of simple and crossed categorizations: A result of the category differentiation process or of differential category salience? *European Review of Social Psychology*, *2*, 247–278.

Waldzus, S., Mummendey, A., Wenzel, M., & Weber, U. (2003). Towards tolerance: Representations of superordinate categories and perceived ingroup prototypicality. *Journal of Experimental Social Psychology*, *39*, 31–47.

Wright, S. C., Aron, A., McLaughlin-Volpe, T., & Ropp, S. A. (1997). The extended contact effect: Knowledge of cross-group friendships and prejudice. *Journal of Personality and Social Psychology*, *73*, 73–90.

Part IV

Focusing on Social Context in Improving Intergroup Relations

12

Intergroup Contact, Social Context and Racial Ecology in South Africa

Gillian Finchilescu and Colin Tredoux

> In 1956, South African race relations were like what race relations must have been in my native South about a decade before my birth. Indeed, there is a 20- to 30-year lag in much of South African history compared with that of the American South.
>
> *(Pettigrew, 1993, p. 163)*

In 1956, Thomas Pettigrew visited the Union of South Africa with his supervisor and mentor, Gordon Allport. He spent six months working at the Institute for Social Research at the University of Natal in Durban, continuing his research on racism, intrigued by the parallels between South Africa and his native American South.

Pettigrew's work in this period addressed individual and societal racism, and the corresponding political issues of segregation and desegregation. The prevailing theories of prejudice were individualistic, the Authoritarian Personality taking centre stage (Adorno, Frenkel-Brunswik, Levinson, & Sanford, 1950; Duckitt, 1992). While in South Africa, Pettigrew conducted a series of projects investigating race attitudes and race perception, social distance, authoritarianism, and conformity (Pettigrew, 1958; 1960). Of most significance was the 1958 comparative study on the relationship between authoritarianism and racist attitudes in South Africa and the American South. This study showed that while the level of racism in both places was manifestly higher than in most other regions, the level of authoritarianism and the correlation between race attitudes and authoritarianism did not differ. These findings led Pettigrew to reassess the role of personality factors in racial prejudice in favor of a sociocultural explanation linking the heightened levels of prejudice to conformity to the politics, norms, and supremacist ideology of the South African and American Southern societies. This argument was influential then, and the paper is still considered seminal (Hogg & Abrams, 2001).

Pettigrew's work offers a rich legacy for social psychological research, as this volume attests. A key principle in this heritage is that research is not merely an intellectual activity; it ought to be actively political and committed to social justice. This is exemplified in Pettigrew's research and advocacy on intergroup contact, which is widely regarded as an important mechanism for improving intergroup relations. In this chapter we interrogate the role of interracial contact in race relations in South Africa. We begin with an overview of the small body of research conducted during Apartheid, and then discuss research conducted after the instatement of universal franchise in South Africa. A particular focus will be our own work in this area.[1]

Intergroup Contact: The Apartheid Years

Race segregation and discrimination did not begin with Apartheid. From the arrival of the Dutch settlers in 1652, the history of South Africa was marked by intergroup conflict. Expansionist wars over land and resources were fought at various times and in various combinations between the Dutch (or Boer) settlers, the Khoisan, Xhosa, Zulu, Sotho, and Ndebele, and the British. The ultimate victors (usually the Boers or the British) imposed racialized privilege on the vanquished (when they were Black), including seizure of their land, restriction of residence and movement, and invariably disenfranchisement.

This period of South African history follows a similar pattern to other European colonies. What is different is the period after 1900, and particularly after 1948, when the vision of a totally segregated South Africa was given legislative and political force. While the rest of the world was moving towards the elimination of legislative and sanctioned race discrimination, the South African government was elaborating and enforcing the extensive segregationist and racist program of "Apartheid."[2] This program made White South Africa globally infamous for nearly half a century. People were assigned to one of four race groups at birth (Whites and the three Black groups— Africans, Coloreds and Indians/Asians), which were rigidly separated in all aspects of life, including education, residence, and leisure, reserving the best for the White group. Entire countries within the national borders were invented for Black people, and they were forcibly removed to them, causing immense hardship. A vast repressive political and military apparatus was created in order to oversee this phantasmagoric scheme. (For a more extensive introduction to the history of Apartheid in South Africa, see Worden, 2000).

The segregationist policies of Apartheid South Africa led to its characterization as a "non-contact society" (Foster & Finchilescu, 1986). However, this did not imply that there was absolutely no contact between race groups. Interracial contact existed, but was largely hierarchical (e.g., boss–servant) or bureaucratic (state agent–supplicant), and was frequently oppressive and violent. Occasional exceptions resulted from "loopholes" in Apartheid legislation, allowing a small number of Black students to enroll at "White" universities and attend private or church schools. This near exclusion of positive interracial contact undoubtedly discouraged research on the effects of intergroup contact, but the sociopolitical context was also important. Apartheid ideology was deeply internalized by the White population. In addition, the government controlled and censored radio, television, newspapers, and school curricula, limiting the potential for intellectual resistance. Only a small number of activist academics produced research and writings antagonistic to Apartheid, placing themselves at considerable risk (Savage, 1981). Many were placed under house-arrest or assassinated (e.g., Rick Turner, David Webster), and their writing was often banned or restricted (e.g., Govan Mbeki, Ruth First). In this climate, it is perhaps no surprise that few researchers (most of whom were White) questioned the desirability of segregation or actively promoted the reduction of prejudice. However, it cannot be gauged whether the limited research in this area stems from the lack of contact opportunities or the political pressures.

South African research on intergroup contact dates mostly from the 1950s and early 1960s, before the Nationalist government had consolidated its power, or from the 1980s when the regime was losing its grip under extreme pressure from resistance forces both within and outside the country. The main sites for research on interracial contact were neighborhoods or educational institutions.

It is unclear what predictions should have been made for the effects of intergroup contact at that time. The contact hypothesis suggested that interracial contact, under specific conditions, would diminish prejudice. However, the extreme prohibition against interracial mixing coming from authoritative institutions in South Africa violates the most basic of Allport's optimal conditions. Pettigrew and Tropp

(2006) have argued that Allport's conditions are facilitative rather than necessary. Their findings demonstrate that contact can have a positive effect without the optimal conditions being present. However, other research has shown that contact that is perceived as threatening or anxiety-provoking can exacerbate prejudice instead of diminishing it (Paolini, Hewstone, Cairns, & Voci, 2004; Stephan & Stephan, 1985).

Of the small body of research, only one study was quasi-experimental and could make any claim of establishing a causal relationship. Luiz and Krige (1981) instituted a contact intervention among White and Colored school girls. They measured the race attitudes of the White girls before and after the contact, and compared these with a group that did not have contact. This study provided clear evidence of the positive effect of contact on intergroup attitudes, an effect that was still evident a year later (Luiz & Krige, 1985).

In another rare study of schoolchildren in this period, Mynhardt (1982) considered the attitudes of White English-speaking girls from ten private secondary schools who had mixed classes containing some Black children. Significantly more negative attitudes were found in the respondents who had contact with Black children than those who had no contact (reported in Mynhardt & du Toit, 1991). A sociometric study by Melamed (1969) of a racially mixed class consisting of African, Indian and Colored university students also found strong ethnocentrism and reluctance to mix.

The only pre-democracy study on residential contact was conducted by Russell (1961). She interviewed members of a mixed Durban neighborhood, and found a range of different attitudes, some people refusing to interact with neighbors of a different race, and others developing friendships. In support of the contact hypothesis, she found a correspondence between lower degrees of prejudice and greater degrees of residential proximity.

A number of studies used contact in the work situation as the site of research. Spangenberg and Nel (1983) compared White lecturers working at a Colored university (with Colored colleagues and students) with a group of White lecturers in an almost all-White university. The contact group was found to have more positive attitudes to Coloreds than the non-contact group. However, this difference was not as strong when only Afrikaans-speaking respondents were considered. This study also found that cross-race friendships were associated with more positive race attitudes. Finchilescu (1988) investigated the effect of interracial contact among nurses training at private hospitals. One hospital trained White and Indian nurses, another trained African and Indian nurses, and the two non-contact hospitals trained White and African nurses respectively. Interracial contact had a positive effect on attitudes (toward Indians), but only for the White respondents. Indian and African respondents exhibited strong ethnocentric attitudes. Van Dyk (1988, cited in Mynhardt & du Toit, 1991) considered the relationship between White housewives and their Black domestic servants, which was a site of extensive interracial contact during the apartheid years. She found that the housewives were generally positive towards their domestic servants, but these attitudes did not extend to the Black group in general.

A study in 1986 investigated the effect of a number of contact variables (amount of social contact, general contact, and experience of contact) as well as a number of demographic variables and group identification on the attitudes of Afrikaans-speaking Whites and Coloreds to each other in the Western Cape (Bornman & Mynhardt, 1991). Attitudes were generally negative, influenced by gender and group identification. However contact, particularly social contact, was found to be associated with more positive attitudes among White Afrikaners, but not for the Colored sample. The exception was the working Colored subsample, where experience of contact was associated with more positive attitudes to White Afrikaners. This asymmetric result reflects a frequent finding in the literature—the relation between contact and prejudice is weaker, and often qualitatively different, for subordinate groups relative to dominant groups (Tropp & Pettigrew, 2005).

These studies do not provide much support for the notion that contact improved intergroup relations in South Africa during Apartheid. With the exception of the Luiz and Krige (1981) study, the studies were correlational in nature, lacked longitudinal measures and generally involved anomalous situations. Thus, the positive results cannot be causally attributed to the effect of intergroup contact. However, neither do the studies indicate that contact leads to deterioration of race relations, one of the central justifications of the Apartheid regime. The obvious point is that the political and ideological context was overwhelming, and it would have been foolhardy in the Apartheid years to expect that anything but radical and fundamental political change could improve intergroup relations.

The Post-Apartheid Years

The Apartheid edifice began to disintegrate in the late 1980s, leading to the unbanning of the African National Congress (ANC) and the

1990 release of Nelson Mandela, in what has been called a bloodless revolution. In 1994 the first democratic elections took place, and the ANC came to power. Apartheid laws were scrapped and desegregation commenced. However, sites of contact remain limited, and there is still polarization of wealth and resources along race lines. This, together with cultural and linguistic differences, has retarded racial transformation. Neighborhoods were slow to change and by 2001 were barely more integrated than under Apartheid (Christopher, 2005). The desegregation of schools was accomplished under resistance, with frequent eruptions of intergroup violence among pupils (Vally & Dalamba, 1999). The high levels of crime, which had previously afflicted mainly the Black communities, spread to the White suburbs. The fear of crime, often seen as racially based by Whites, further deters intergroup contact. Thus, the main sites of naturally occurring racial contact in South Africa are educational institutions and the workplace. The university context arguably provides the best instance of an interracial contact situation in which the groups meet on a relatively equal status basis.

The number of studies testing the effect of contact on race relations, post 1990, is still small. A number of surveys have been conducted, giving largely positive results. Gibson's 2000/2001 survey questioned a representative sample of 3,700 South Africans and found strong relationships between reported level of interracial contact and an index of positive attitudes toward race reconciliation —Africans: $r = 0.24$; Whites: $r = 0.45$; Coloreds: $r = 0.38$; Indians $r = 0.40$ (Gibson, 2004a). Finchilescu, Tredoux, Muianga, Mynhardt, and Pillay (2006) surveyed 2,559 African and White students from four universities, measuring the amount of interracial contact and prejudice using both an affective prejudice scale and a social distance measure. They found strong inverse relationships (i.e., the greater the amount of contact, the lower the affective prejudice) for all groups in these universities, ranging in magnitude from $r = -0.23$ to $r = -0.56$. Somewhat lower correlations were found on the social distance measure, particularly in the case of the Black students. Cross-race friendships and experience of contact were also important predictors of improved intergroup relations. Dixon, Durrheim, and Tredoux (2007) report a nationally representative survey of 1,917 Black and White South Africans, in which self-reported contact was correlated with support for policies and practices aimed at rectifying the injustices of Apartheid. They found that among Whites, greater contact was associated with greater support for such measures, but that the reverse pattern held true for Blacks—greater contact led to greater opposition to such measures. This pattern may be difficult to interpret, but it does resonate with the frequently reported asymmetric contact effect for minorities or subordinate groups.

A number of recent studies have considered the effect of contact in school and university settings. Holtman, Louw, Tredoux, and Carney's (2005) study involved 1,119 learners in 18 schools consisting of African, Colored, White English-speaking and White Afrikaans-speaking adolescents. A number of measures assessed contact (i.e., in the school, outside the school premises, quality of contact), and attitudes of each group toward others. Contact, and particularly contact outside of school, emerged as a strong predictor of positive intergroup attitudes in all subsamples, and after taking additional potentially important variables into account (e.g., strength of ingroup identity). Additionally, MohololA and Finchilescu (2006) compared the attitudes toward Whites of Black learners who attended a multiracial school with those attending an all-Black school. Black students' attitudes were significantly more positive in the multiracial school; furthermore, the amount of contact with Whites they reported was significantly related to less-prejudiced attitudes.

An array of small group programs aimed at improving interracial relations have been developed and tried in South Africa. Central to all these programs is that they bring together people from different races to discuss or work on mutual tasks. Most of these programs report a decrease in prejudicial attitudes (Druker, 1996; Louw-Potgieter, Kamfer, & Boy, 1991; Naidoo, 1990; Nott, 2000; Wilhelm, 1994). Many of these studies are unpublished theses, often using qualitative measures. An exception is the study by McCool, du Toit, Petty, & McCauley (2006), reporting a program of prejudice-reduction seminars. The seminars failed to produce changes in scores on measures of intergroup attitudes.

Given the small number of interracial studies conducted in the dozen or so years of democracy, it could be argued that these results present an optimistic picture of the prejudice reducing effect of intergroup contact in South Africa. However, the causal sequence problem (Pettigrew, 1998) remains an issue—we cannot be sure that it was the contact that resulted in improved race attitudes. It could equally be argued that the participants who agreed to work or take part in these interracial contact situations may already have been less prejudiced. The strongest effects of intergroup contact occur where it is possible to control extraneous variables, and to ensure the (facilitating) conditions identified by Allport (Pettigrew & Tropp, 2006). This leads to more confidence that the effects are causal, but it also raises concerns about the ecological validity of the contact hypothesis.

In order for intergroup contact to have a positive effect on intergroup relations in naturalistic settings, groups must come into contact with each other as a regular part of their lives.

The question, therefore, goes to the frequency and nature of inter-racial contact. Of central concern is the extent of "natural" intergroup contact in society; how this manifests; and how it is perceived by the protagonists. Are opportunities for contact under favorable conditions available, or are they actively avoided? In the remaining part of the chapter we will discuss recent attempts to address these questions in South Africa. Specifically, we will consider investigations that estimate the incidence of interracial contact and friendship, as well as studies that investigate interracial contact *in situ*.

The Ecology of Interracial Contact

A strong theme in social psychological research in post-Apartheid South Africa, and in our own work, is the study of what could be called "the ecology of interracial contact" (Dixon & Durrheim, 2003, p. 4). This research investigates the interactions between race groups in a variety of contexts, using a variety of methods from surveys to observational methods.

Self-Reported Interracial Contact

Several nationally representative social surveys have been conducted in South Africa in the period 2001–2006, and they have gathered data that allow us to estimate the amount and quality of intergroup contact. Gibson (2004b) reports a representative nationwide survey (N = 3,727), conducted in cooperation with the Institute for Justice and Reconciliation (IJR); and Durrheim and colleagues have recently conducted a representative cellular telephone survey on a sample of 2,091 South Africans (Dixon et al., 2007). We will report the data for only African and White South Africans here (which together constitute over 90% of the South African population).

Each of these surveys posed specific questions about the amount and kinds of contact respondents experienced with members of other groups, in a variety of formal and informal settings. Though posed in slightly different ways, the results are very similar: They reveal a racially skewed picture. A near majority (> 40%) of Africans have very little contact of any kind with Whites, inside or outside of work settings, whereas most Whites report some degree of daily or weekly contact.

When questioned about social contact (e.g., contact in one's own home), more than 60% of Africans (as opposed to 25% of Whites) report no contact (Gibson, 2004b). The survey by Durrheim and colleagues also found that most African respondents reporting interracial interactions with Whites indicated that the White people they interacted with were of higher social status, whereas most White respondents reported interactions with Africans of equal social status. The majority of both African and White respondents reported that such contact as did occur was cooperative.

Interracial Friendship

Pettigrew's (1998) restatement of contact theory stresses the centrality of cross-race friendship. But if interracial contact is to have significant positive effects in real intergroup settings, then cross-race friendships need to arise in the ordinary course of group interaction. To what extent is this happening?

In Gibson's (2004b) survey, prevalence of interracial friendship in South Africa was estimated using a rating scale. He found that the majority of Black South Africans have no White friends at all, while only a small number of Whites (6.6%) report having "quite a number of African friends" (p. 163). It should of course be remembered that Africans make up approximately 80% of the South African population. It is thus unsurprising that most friendships that Africans have are with other African people. What is more pertinent is the rate at which cross-race friendship occurs when the opportunity arises.

University campuses may provide such opportunities. Prior to 1990, South African universities were highly segregated along race lines by law, but have changed dramatically since that time. For instance, the percentage of White students enrolled at the University of the Witwatersrand changed from 91.2% in 1980 to 36% in 2005. Many universities make provision for accommodating students on campus, and residences that house students usually have considerable numbers of both Black and White students. Since students share common facilities, such as dining and television/leisure rooms, a considerable amount of face-to-face interracial contact in these settings seems inevitable.

In a recent longitudinal study conducted over a six month period, Schrieff (2005) examined the formation of friendships among first-year university students in mixed race residences located in a university with a strong liberal reputation (University of Cape Town). Few students knew any other students on entrance. By the end of the study, 285 friendships had been formed of which only 51 were cross-race. Friendships developed mostly along race lines. This pattern of friendship choices was matched by starkly segregated seating patterns in the residence dining rooms. Schrieff measured these using the dissimilarity (D) and interaction indices (xPy), treating individual tables as areal units with scores varying between 0 and 1, in opposite directions. She found average values of .9 and .04, respectively, indicating nearly complete segregation. Unfortunately, Schrieff has not yet reported cross-lagged or other analyses that could shed light on longitudinal change in this sample.

Observational Studies of Interracial Contact

Observational studies of interracial contact situations in South Africa have been conducted using beaches (e.g., Dixon & Durrheim, 2003), student refectories (Schrieff, Tredoux, Dixon, & Finchilescu, 2005), open outdoor spaces (Tredoux, Dixon, Underwood, Nunez, & Finchilescu, 2005) and nightclubs (Tredoux & Dixon, 2007) as research sites. This approach is rooted in the contention that research has tended to divorce intergroup dynamics from their societal contexts, failing to attend to the lived experience of intergroup interactions (Dixon & Durrheim, 2003). Observation and description, therefore, serve the function of contextualizing intergroup contact situations, of telling us something about the role of contact in the total intergroup repertoire. This question has a direct political purpose—if contact between races is to improve the state of race relations in South Africa, can we expect it to occur as a consequence of encounter?

The answer from a study of beaches on the South Coast of Kwa-Zulu Natal is "no" (Dixon & Durrheim, 2003). That study set out to investigate patterns of racial interaction, but the researchers discovered that interaction rarely occurred, and more importantly, that it was effectively precluded by the way people positioned themselves on the beaches spatially and temporally. Whites tended to arrive well before Blacks, early in the day, and usually left the beach before Blacks arrived in sizeable numbers. When Blacks and Whites were on the beach simultaneously, they occupied separate spaces. Indeed, time animations show a movement of Whites away from "Black spaces" as these become occupied, and an analysis of "umbrella spaces" (the base "areal unit" declared by the researchers) shows that 99.9% of these were racially homogeneous (N = 2,654). In short, race groups structured their encounters with each other to achieve segregation, and by inference to avoid contact with members of other race groups. Face-to-face research interviews with several dozen people on the beach reinforced this inference, Whites declaring that they felt "pushed out" of the space, and Blacks declaring that Whites appeared to be "running away from them."

Several observational studies of student residences at South African universities point to similar patterns of self-segregation and apparent avoidance of contact. Schrieff et al. (2005) demonstrated that Black and White students in two (male and female) residences self-segregated in a shared dining room at multiple levels; Alexander (2003) found the same pattern in the same residence one year later. Segregation on campus and the disinclination to form cross-race friendships are experienced by Black students as a system of exclusion. Woods (2001) reports a study of Black South African university students, who revealed that under the apparent "segregated but harmonious co-living" of race groups on campus, relations were in fact tense. Intergroup relations on campus were understood by respondents as ordered by "unspoken rules" to remain apart. While some reported agreeable relationships with White students, the vast majority experienced their White peers as racist. Aware that race groups on campus congregated in separate areas, Whites were perceived by Black students as making a concerted effort to maintain racial distance through consistently preferring separate social spaces.

Segregated seating patterns within a university residence dining room may simply reflect cross-race friendship choices: students sitting with friends and not making a conscious decision to avoid other races. However, an observational study found that segregation occurred in a particularly "fluid" informal space on one university campus (Tredoux et al., 2005). The space in question is a set of steps leading up to the central auditorium, which is used by students as an informal gathering area, typically over lunch. Spatio-temporal analysis of seating patterns over 5 days showed self-segregation of race groups in this space, and also showed the consistency of this segregation, Black and White students typically occupying the same areas on a daily basis. Data collected in a similar 5-day period two years later showed the long-term replication of this normative spatial racialization, despite the replacement of most students on campus through graduation and new enrolment.

The reproduction of "racial territories" as an apparent function of racial encounter is also shown in a set of studies conducted in the nightclub area of Cape Town (Tredoux & Dixon, 2007). Eight nightclubs that were reputed to have a good degree of racial mixing were selected for study. These were sampled at various times over two years. Distribution of race groups over these clubs supported the general impression of racial integration. However, as the granularity of analysis was made finer, it became clear that the distribution of race groups was uneven. Whites and Blacks consistently occupied separate sub-sections of the clubs, and rarely sat at the same tables. They also rarely interacted—more than 80% of interactions involving White people were monoracial in character, for instance (but note the somewhat different figure of 57% for Black people).

Conclusion

What Does the Ecology of Racial Interaction in South Africa Tell Us?

An essential condition for interracial contact to improve intergroup relations is that race groups do come into face-to-face contact a significant amount of the time, and that they allow their interaction to unfold in a manner that promotes intimate acquaintance. It stands to reason that an important adjunct to contact theory is the study of race groups in interaction, in natural settings—what Dixon and Durrheim (2003) refer to as a "racial ecology." This requires that we should attempt to establish the dominant behavioral forms that emerge when race groups are spatially and temporally copresent.

We have described a number of studies in South Africa that attempt this. The picture they reveal is one of continuing and profound racial isolation. There is, in particular, little contact of an intimate kind, and few cross-race friendships or marriages are formed. This is not explicable as a function of differences in spatial demography, as South African university students fail to make cross-race friends in significant numbers even when the opportunities are extremely good. Observational studies of interracial contact situations suggest that race groups in interaction self-segregate, actively avoiding contact.

This research does not say that intergroup contact does not "work." It says instead that contact is not occurring, at least in South Africa at present. South Africa has only had universal franchise for a dozen or so years, and there is a bitter legacy of political and legal oppression, as well as pervasive social and economic inequality. This racial ecology may be specific to the South African situation. However, the intransigence of racial segregation and inequality in the United States (Anderson & Massey, 2001), despite considerable public investment in desegregation, suggests there are similarities.

One potentially fruitful line of future research concerns the determinants of contact avoidance. Prejudice itself is an obvious factor, as are socialization and conformity to social norms. Another obstacle to interracial contact is individuals' anxiety about how they will be received by members of the other group in a contact situation. A form of metaperception termed metastereotypes is a useful concept here. Metastereotypes refer to the stereotypes that members of a group believe that members of an outgroup hold of them (Vorauer, Main, & O'Connell, 1998). Some of our recent research has shown that metastereotypes are a significant predictor of intergroup attitudes and desire for contact. A number of experimental studies involving simulated interracial contact suggest that metastereotypes are more important than prejudice in accounting for the anxiety felt by individuals in an intergroup contact situation (Finchilescu, 2006). Metastereotypes also emerged as significant factors in understanding prejudicial attitudes in the survey by Finchilescu et al. (2006) and the study by Moholola and Finchilescu (2006).

In this chapter we have shown that even in the worst days of Apartheid there were indications that intergroup contact may improve intergroup relations, particularly in laboratory and quasi-experimental studies. But, the numerous studies highlighting the persistence of informal segregation points to the necessity for research to address this issue. Understanding and combating resistance to interracial contact and mixing is an important step in improving intergroup relations.

Notes

1 This research was supported by Grant 02/21 from the South Africa Netherlands Research Programme on Alternatives in Development (SANPAD).
2 Beinart and Dubow (1995) argue that the various laws in existence in South Africa before the Apartheid era were more extreme than the "Jim Crow" laws in the United States.

References

Adorno, T. W., Frenkel-Brunswik, E., Levinson, D. J., & Sanford, R. N. (1950/1982). *The authoritarian personality.* New York: W. W. Norton & Company.
Alexander, L. (2003). *Invading pure space: Disrupting segregated spaces amongst Black & White students.* Unpublished thesis, University of Cape Town.

Anderson, E. E., & Massey, D. S. (Eds.) (2001). *Problem of the century: Racial stratification in the United States.* New York: Russell Sage Foundation.

Beinart, W., & Dubow, S. (1995). Introduction: The historiography of segregation and apartheid. In W. Beinart, & S. Dubow (Eds.), *Segregation and* apartheid *in Twentieth-Century South Africa* (pp. 1–24). London: Routledge.

Bornman, E., & Mynhardt, J. C. (1991). Social identity and intergroup contact in South Africa with specific reference to the work situation. *Genetic, Social, & General Psychology Monographs, 117,* 437–462.

Christopher, A. J. (2005). The slow pace of desegregation in South African cities, 1996–2001. *Urban Studies, 42,* 2305–2320.

Dixon, J. A., & Durrheim, K. (2003). Contact and the ecology of racial division: Some varieties of informal segregation. *British Journal of Social Psychology, 42,* 1–23.

Dixon, J. A., Durrheim, K., & Tredoux, C. G. (2007). Intergroup contact and attitudes towards the principle and practice of racial equality *Psychological Science, 18,* 867–872.

Druker, B. (1996). *Adolescent experience of intergroup contact in South Africa and its impact on identity development: A qualitative study.* Unpublished master's thesis, University of Cape Town.

Duckitt, J. H. (1992). Psychology and prejudice: A historical analysis and integrative framework. *American Psychologist, 47,* 1182–1193.

Finchilescu, G. (1988). Interracial contact in South Africa within the nursing context. *Journal of Applied Social Psychology, 18,* 1207–1221.

Finchilescu, G. (2006, July). *Anxiety in a simulated situation of inter-racial interaction: The role of metastereotypes and prejudice.* Paper presented at the conference, "Contact and Intergroup Relations: 50 Years On," Ithala Game Lodge, South Africa.

Finchilescu, G., Tredoux, C., Muianga, L., Mynhardt, J., & Pillay, J. (2006, July). *Testing contact theory in South African: A study of four universities.* Paper presented at the conference, "Contact and Intergroup Relations: 50 Years On," Ithala Game Lodge, South Africa.

Foster, D., & Finchilescu, G. (1986). Contact in a non-contact society: The case of South Africa. In M. Hewstone & R. Brown (Eds.), *Contact and conflict in intergroup encounters* (pp. 119–136). Oxford: Basil Blackwell.

Gibson, J. L. (2004a). Does truth lead to reconciliation? Testing the causal assumptions of the South African truth and reconciliation process. *American Journal of Political Science, 48,* 201–217.

Gibson, J. L. (2004b). *Overcoming Apartheid: Can truth reconcile a divided nation?* Cape Town: HSRC Press.

Hogg, M. A., & Abrams, D. (Eds.) (2001). *Intergroup relations.* Philadelphia, PA: Psychology Press.

Holtman, Z., Louw, J., Tredoux, C., & Carney, T. (2005). Prejudice and social contact in South Africa: A study of integrated schools ten years after apartheid. *South African Journal of Psychology, 35,* 473–493.

Louw-Potgieter, J., Kamfer, L., & Boy, R. G. (1991). Stereotype reduction workshop. *South African Journal of Psychology, 21*, 219–224.

Luiz, D., & Krige, P. (1981). The effect of social contact between South African white and coloured adolescent girls. *The Journal of Social Psychology, 113*, 153–158.

Luiz, D., & Krige, P. (1985). The effect of social contact between South African white and coloured adolescent girls: A follow-up study. *The Journal of Social Psychology, 125*, 407–408.

McCool, A., du Toit, F., Petty, C. R., & McCauley, C. (2006). The impact of a program of prejudice-reduction seminars in South Africa. *Journal of Applied Social Psychology, 36*, 586–613.

Melamed, L. (1969). Friendship in a multi-racial South African classroom. *Journal of Behavioural Science, 1*, 26–32.

Moholola, F., & Finchilescu, G. (2006, July). *Intergroup attitudes of Black South African students attending multiracial and single race schools.* Paper presented at the conference, "Contact and Intergroup Relations: 50 Years On," Ithala Game Lodge, South Africa.

Mynhardt, J., & du Toit, A. (1991). Contact and change. In D. Foster & J. Louw-Potgieter (Eds.), *Social psychology in South Africa* (pp. 271–314). Johannesburg, South Africa: Lexicon.

Naidoo, L. R. (1990). *An experimental study of the effectiveness of group therapeutic techniques in improving Black–White relations among university students.* Unpublished doctoral thesis, University of Natal.

Nott, B. (2000). *The impact of a social skills training programme on interracial contact at an integrated secondary school.* Unpublished master's thesis, Potchefstroom University.

Paolini, S., Hewstone, M., Cairns, E., & Voci, A. (2004). Effects of direct and indirect cross-group friendships on judgments of Catholics and Protestants in Northern Ireland: The mediating role of an anxiety-reduction mechanism. *Personality and Social Psychology Bulletin, 30*, 770–786.

Pettigrew, T. F. (1958). Personality and sociocultural factors in intergroup attitudes: a cross-national comparison. *Journal of Conflict Resolution, 2*, 29–42.

Pettigrew, T. F. (1960). Social distance attitudes of South African students. *Social Forces, 38*, 246–253.

Pettigrew, T. F. (1993). How events shape theoretical frames. A personal statement. In J. H. Stanfield II (Ed.), *A history of race relations research: First generation recollections* (pp. 159–178). Beverly Hills, CA: Sage.

Pettigrew, T. F. (1998). Intergroup contact theory. *Annual Review of Psychology, 49*, 68–85.

Pettigrew, T. F., & Tropp, L. (2006). A meta-analytic test of intergroup contact theory. *Journal of Personality and Social Psychology, 90*, 751–783.

Russell, M. (1961). *A study of a South African interracial neighbourhood.* Unpublished master's thesis, University of Natal, Durban, South Africa.

Savage, M. (1981). Constraints on, and functions of, research in sociology and psychology in contemporary South Africa. In J. Rex (Ed.), *Apartheid and social research* (pp. 45–65). Paris: UNESCO.

Schrieff, L. (2005). *Understanding the seating patterns in a university residence dining hall: A longitudinal study of intergroup contact and friendship.* Unpublished master's dissertation, University of Cape Town.

Schrieff, L., Tredoux, C. G., Dixon, J. A., & Finchilescu, G. (2005). Patterns of racial segregation in residence dining halls. *South African Journal of Psychology, 35*, 433–443.

Spangenberg, J., & Nel, E. M. (1983). The effect of equal-status contact on ethnic attitudes. *Journal of Social Psychology, 121*, 173–180.

Stephan, W. G., & Stephan, C. W. (1985). Intergroup anxiety. *Journal of Social Issues, 41*, 157–175.

Tredoux, C. G., & Dixon, J. A. (2007). *Mapping the multiple contexts of racial isolation: Some reflections on the concept of scale in segregation research.* Manuscript submitted for publication.

Tredoux, C. G., Dixon, J. A., Underwood, S., Nunez, D., & Finchilescu, G. (2005). Preserving spatial and temporal dimensions in observational data of segregation. *South African Journal of Psychology, 35*, 412–432.

Tropp, L. R., & Pettigrew, T. F. (2005). Relationships between intergroup contact and prejudice among minority and majority status groups. *Psychological Science, 16*, 951–957.

Vally, S., & Dalamba, Y. (1999). *Racism, "racial integration" and desegregation in South African public secondary schools.* A report by the South African Human Rights Commission (SAHRC).

Vorauer, J. D., Main, K. J., & O'Connell, G. B. (1998). How do individuals expect to be viewed by members of low status groups? Content and implications of metastereotypes. *Journal of Personality and Social Psychology, 75*, 917–937.

Wilhelm, M. (1994). *Interracial contact and racial perceptions among Black and White adolescents.* Unpublished master's dissertation, University of the Witwatersrand, Johannesburg.

Woods, R. L. (2001). "Oh sorry, I'm a racist": Black student experiences at the University of Witwatersrand. In R. O. Mabokela & K. L. King (Eds.), *Apartheid no more. Case studies of South African universities in the process of transformation* (pp. 91–110). Connecticut: Bergin & Garvey.

Worden, N. (2000). *The making of modern South Africa.* Oxford: Blackwell.

13

Social and Political Context Effects on Intergroup Contact and Intergroup Attitudes

Ulrich Wagner, Oliver Christ, Hinna Wolf, Rolf van Dick, Jost Stellmacher, Elmar Schlüter, and Andreas Zick

In this chapter, we focus on the influence of the social context on intergroup relations. More specifically, we discuss the effects of ethnic minority proportion in geographical areas on the majority–minority relation. We extend this sociological perspective with a social psychological view by focusing on two important psychological mediators between the proportions of ethnic minorities on the majority's perception of minorities: intergroup contact and intergroup threat. We thus aim to meet the demand for a "contextual social psychology." When Thomas Pettigrew introduced this term in 1991, he addressed a variety of related scientific and methodological criteria: One is the simultaneous consideration of psychological and sociostructural variables in explaining social phenomena. Another involves the simultaneous inclusion of different levels of analysis. According to the latter, social psychological phenomena, such as intergroup discrimination, can only be understood as a result of both social interactions (e.g., interactions between ethnic groups and their members) *and* influences of the broader social and societal context (e.g., racist ideologies and institutional discrimination in a specific society at a specific time). This approach also implies a focus on relevant psychological mechanisms that help to explain relationships between different levels of analysis (see also Kelman, this volume). Pettigrew (1996) also pointed out the importance of maintaining precision by "keeping levels straight" and thus avoiding certain fallacies. The question then becomes: what are the psychological processes that explain how societies influence their members to accept a specific view of the world? As we show below, the relationship between ethnic minority proportion in a geographical unit on the one hand and the indigenous population's attitudes toward ethnic minority groups in that area on the other, varies substantially—depending on the size of the geographical area analyzed. This approach requires that we have to develop hypotheses bridging different levels of analysis in order to understand cross-level interactions.

From the very beginning of his career, Pettigrew's work was prototypical for such a "contextual social psychology" approach. In 1958, he published a now classic paper on the interplay of personality and sociocultural factors on intergroup attitudes in the *Journal of Conflict Resolution*. Using data from South Africa and the Southern United States, he convincingly demonstrated the combined influence of personality and sociocultural variables on intergroup attitudes. By focusing on just one level (i.e., personality characteristics at the microlevel *or* sociocultural variables at the macrolevel), which was and still is being done in the social sciences, differences in intergroup attitudes would hardly be detected and explained (see also Pettigrew, 1959).

In a more recent paper based on the Eurobarometer 30 data, Pettigrew et al. (1998) compared the influence of different social psychological variables on intergroup attitudes in four different European countries (France, Germany, The Netherlands, UK). In accordance with the universality hypothesis, the analyses confirmed the assumption that relevant social psychological concepts, such as intergroup contact or relative deprivation, operate in a similar way and explain intergroup processes across countries. But again, more finely grained analyses showed *how* the social context affects the amount of negative intergroup attitudes by influencing the social psychological mechanisms.

Two of the authors of this paper (Uli Wagner and Andreas Zick) have collaborated with Thomas Pettigrew for almost 20 years. We started working together on a project investigating xenophobia in Western Europe. The project was based on the 1988 Eurobarometer data (Eurobarometer 30), an annual survey in Western Europe (see Pettigrew et al., 1998). We were impressed and strongly influenced by Pettigrew's ability to combine the available survey data with social and political background information regarding different countries. Furthermore, he strongly promoted the societal consequences of the study's findings. Pettigrew was and is clearly interested in the *practical implications* of scientific results for the improvement of inter-group relations—a position contrary to the typical academic stance of keeping science and politics apart. And, in his practical and political interests, he has never been "neutral." He was always sympathetic to the position of the weaker members of society, in many cases of the powerless ethnic minorities and immigrant groups in Western Societies. This might also explain why he showed such a great interest in top-down processes, that is how social structure at the macrolevel influences behavior and attitudes at the individual level (Pettigrew, 1996; 2006).

Our work with Pettigrew since the early 1990s has involved exploiting rich survey data from Germany and Europe. In particu-lar, our research has focused on the role of intergroup contact in explaining intergroup attitudes (e.g., Pettigrew, Christ, Wagner, & Stellmacher, 2007; van Dick et al., 2004; Wagner, van Dick, Pettigrew, & Christ, 2003; Wagner, Christ, Pettigrew, Stellmacher, & Wolf, 2006). In this chapter, we will present some of our recent research, in large parts results emerging from direct collaboration with Pettigrew. Much of this research is based on data of the project "Group-Focused Enmity," a combination of an annual representative German survey and a panel (Heitmeyer, 2007).

First, we present evidence showing that a higher proportion of minor-ities increases intergroup contact which in turn contributes to a decrease in prejudice. We will also show that, if we consider the per-centage of minorities *in respondents' immediate environment*, higher proportions of ethnic minorities is not associated with stronger feel-ings of intergroup threat. In contrast, analysis across the countries in Europe shows a positive correlation between the percentage of ethnic minorities *in the country* and level of prejudice displayed by the countries' majority group. In the second part of the chapter, we discuss how country-level effects of ethnic composition are likely to be mediated by a different process, namely media influences. As an example, we will present preliminary results supporting the idea that media coverage of the immigration issue induces negative attitudes towards immigrants. This effect exists primarily among respondents who have not had contact with minorities, again underlining the importance of considering cross-level interactions.

We will focus on the attitudes of indigenous Germans toward immigrants and ethnic minorities living in Germany. Due to very restric-tive policies, most ethnic minority members in Germany do not pos-sess German citizenship, even if they were born in Germany or have lived there for decades. As a result, most immigrants have an insecure residential status in Germany, having no right to vote and restricted access to unemployment grants. The proportion of immigrants in Germany is about 9% of the population or almost 7.3 million people (Statistische Ämter des Bundes und der Länder, 2005), with the largest immigrant group coming from Turkey (26%).

Minority Proportion, Contact and Prejudice

Many politicians, in Germany and elsewhere, support their demands for policies restricting immigration by arguing that an increase in the proportion of ethnic minorities would reduce their acceptance by members of the host society. Some politicians even claim that there is a particular threshold—a certain number or proportion of minority members that would exceed the capacity to integrate minorities into the host society. The naïve theoretical background of this political argument is close to threat theory (Esses, Jackson, & Amstrong, 1998; Stephan & Renfro, 2002): According to threat theory, an increase in the proportion of ethnic minorities threatens the majority's status (Blalock, 1967) and as a consequence leads to an increase in prejudice (Blumer, 1958; Bobo, 1999).

There is also an alternative consequence of an increase in the proportion of ethnic minorities: It offers more opportunities for intergroup contact (Stein, Post, & Rinden, 2000). Numerous studies have shown that intergroup contact is capable of reducing intergroup prejudice (Pettigrew & Tropp, 2006), particularly when certain facilitating factors such as common goals, cooperation, equal status, and institutional support are given (Allport, 1954). Thus, if one takes the contact hypothesis into account, it seems plausible that a higher proportion of ethnic minorities could reduce ethnic prejudice. Evidently, this prediction—derived from the contact hypothesis—seems at odds with assumptions of threat theory and political proclamations.

As a first indirect test of the effect of the proportion of ethnic minorities on ethnic prejudice, we examined whether differences in ethnic prejudice between East and West Germany can be explained by differences in intergroup contact (Wagner et al., 2003). In the late 1980s, socialist countries in Eastern Europe imploded. One consequence of this was the reunification of the formerly divided Germany in October 1990. Shortly after reunification, the new German state became infamous for a wave of hate crime attacks on ethnic minorities (Wagner & Zick, 1998; Zick, Wagner, van Dick, & Petzel, 2001). Official statistics show that the number of such violent acts against ethnic minorities is much greater in East Germany, the former German Democratic Republic, than in West Germany (formerly the Federal Republic of Germany). This trend is supported by results from survey studies, which consistently reveal higher ethnic prejudice levels in East than in West Germany (see Wagner et al., 2003).

To understand the proximal processes that help explain the difference in ethnic outgroup derogation between East and West Germany, it is important to note that the number of ethnic minorities in East Germany is substantially lower than in the West. In 2005, the percentage of ethnic minorities was 2.4% in the East and 10.1% in the West (Statistische Ämter des Bundes und der Länder, 2005). This difference mainly reflects the more restrictive immigration policy in the former Democratic Republic of Germany (cf. Poutrus, Behrends, & Kuck, 2000) and of the rural character of East Germany. The lower numbers and proportion of ethnic minorities imply fewer opportunities for contact with ethnic minorities for the German majority population in East Germany. It is, therefore, reasonable to assume that East Germans, compared to West Germans, have less direct contact with ethnic minority members in their neighborhoods, at work, or in schools, which in turn results in less intimate or important contacts, such as interethnic friendships. We hypothesized, therefore, that the higher levels of ethnic prejudice in East Germany compared to West Germany are due to differences in the number and proportion of ethnic minorities, mediated (i.e., explained) by differential opportunities for intergroup contact and differences in intimate and important intergroup encounters.

We tested this hypothesis using three surveys (Wagner et al., 2003). In Figure 13.1, the results of our third study, based on a sample of 769 East and West German school students of German origin (mean age of 15.5 years, range 14 to 18), are summarized. The simple correlation between region of origin (1 = West Germany, 2 = East Germany) and ethnic prejudice was $r = .23$. However, as shown in Figure 13.1, this correlation is completely mediated by intergroup contact. The two other surveys delivered similar results. Thus, Wagner et al. (2003) showed that differences in prejudice between West and East Germany can be traced back to differences in objective living conditions, i.e. the objectively defined proportions of ethnic minorities in different parts of Germany. In addition, the study demonstrates, based on contact theory, that this covariation can be understood as a consequence of intergroup contact.

In a second survey-based study Wagner et al. (2006) used a recent German probability phone survey (N = 2,722) of the German adult

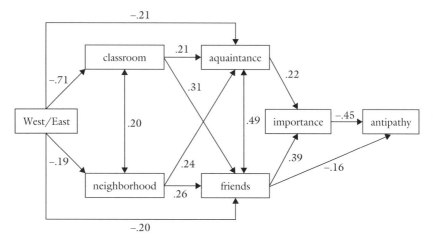

Figure 13.1 Intergroup contact as mediator of effects of region of origin (West vs. East Germany) on ethnic prejudice.
Notes: N = 764, $x^2(7)$ = 17.68, p < .01, CFI = .99, RMSEA = .05; All paths are significant.
Source: Wagner et al. (2003; Study 3) with permission.

population (the 2002 Group Focused Enmity survey; see Heitmeyer, 2002). The survey data include district codes that indicate the location of residence for each respondent. A district is an administrative unit of about 50,000 inhabitants (see Wagner et al., 2006). The district codes allowed us to match objective statistical data, such as the proportion of ethnic minorities in the district to the interview data including measures of prejudice and other attitudes. First of all, multilevel analyses showed that the proportion of ethnic minorities in the district and the district inhabitants' prejudice are negatively correlated. In addition, we did not find any indication of a curvilinear relationship between the proportion of ethnic minorities and ethnic prejudice. Thus, we found no indication of any threshold which, if exceeded, would lead to an increase in prejudice. Finally, and in accordance with the findings from Wagner et al. (2003), parts of the negative covariation of ethnic minority proportion and ethnic prejudice were mediated, i.e., explained, by direct contact experiences (e.g., cross-group friendships), again supporting the contact hypothesis.

Our results contradict some findings of research on the relationships between ethnic prejudice and proportion of ethnic minorities in the United States. Some of these studies show a positive covariation between the proportion of ethnic minorities and majority members' ethnic prejudice and discrimination (e.g., Pettigrew & Campbell, 1960; Pettigrew & Cramer, 1959; Quillian, 1995; 1996; Stein et al., 2000; Wilcox & Roof, 1978). Other studies have shown negative curvilinear relationships such that small or moderate proportions of minorities are negatively correlated with negative attitudes but a higher proportion of minorities correlates positively with prejudice (Forman, 2003; Fossett & Kiecolt, 1989; Taylor, 1998). The differences between our findings and those from the United States may be explained by differences in the historical and current sociostructural context, which include differences in the degree of segregation, absolute numbers of ethnic minorities, and differences in the economic prosperity of the areas under consideration. We assume that the differences between our findings and studies based in the United States might also relate back to differences in the position of power for minorities in Germany and in the United States. As described above, many ethnic minority members in Germany do not possess a permanent residence permit and none of them have a right to vote. Comparatively, minorities in the United States do possess at least formal rights as citizens which may cause the majority to perceive them more as a threat (cf. Wagner et al., 2006).

Intergroup Contact and Threat

Our research program had started from the political claim that intergroup relations would be more problematic if the percentage of ethnic minorities exceeds a certain threshold. To justify those claims, politicians typically refer to threat: A higher proportion of ethnic minorities would pose a threat to the majority. Although we have shown above that a higher proportion of ethnic minorities is actually *negatively* related to ethnic prejudice, we have not yet directly tested the different predictions made by contact theory and threat theory.

A recent study, however, allowed such a direct comparison. This study (Wagner, Christ, & Pettigrew, 2007) was also based on a representative German survey run in 2004 (N = 1,383; see Heitmeyer, 2005 for details). The survey included indicators of intergroup contact and ethnic prejudice and, in addition, measures of group- and individual-levels of realistic and symbolic threat posed by ethnic minorities (cf. Stephan & Renfro, 2002). Replicating the findings of Wagner et al. (2003, 2006), the relationship between the proportion of ethnic minorities at the district level and ethnic prejudice is linear and negative. This covariation is mediated by intergroup contact, i.e.,

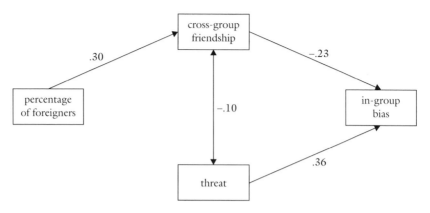

Figure 13.2   Effects of percentage of foreigners living in a district on indigenous population's contact, threat, and ingroup bias.
Notes: N = 1,383, $x^2(2)$ = 0.225, p = .89, CFI = 1.00, RMSEA < .001, SRMR = .003.
Source: Wagner, Christ, & Pettigrew (2007).

cross-group friendships. In Figure 13.2, the results are summarized. In accordance with prior research (e.g., Esses et al., 1998), our results support the assumption that perceived threat also relates to a marked increase in prejudice. Detailed analyses show that this is primarily due to group threat, r (group threat–prejudice) = .65; r (individual threat–prejudice) = .51. Surprisingly, however, perceived intergroup threat did not correlate with the objective proportion of ethnic minorities in the district (see also Semyonov, Rajman Tov, & Schmidt, 2004, for similar results).

Based on these results, we suggest that higher proportions of ethnic minorities do not pose a threat but that the presence of immigrants in the district mainly offers opportunities for intergroup contact. Nevertheless, perceived threat has a strong effect on ethnic prejudice. This data pattern leads to the question about the causes for perceiving an ethnic minority as threatening.

Coenders (2001), as well as Wagner and van Dick (2001), using the same 1996 Eurobarometer data (N = 15,722), have shown a positive correlation of ethnic prejudice and the proportion of ethnic minorities at the level of 15 European countries. This positive covariation contrasts with the negative relationships between proportions of minorities and prejudice found in the German district data. In a further study McLaren (2003) has demonstrated that this positive covariation is at least partially mediated by an increase in threat perceptions. Thus, these patterns of results are in accordance with threat theory.

Negative Political Propaganda

One possible explanation for the contrasting relation between ethnic prejudice and the proportion of ethnic minorities in the studies of Wagner et al. (2003, 2006) on the one hand, and Coenders' (2001) as well as Wagner and van Dick's (2001) findings on the other, may lie in the type and size of the units analyzed. In smaller units, such as districts, an increase in the number of ethnic minority members seems to induce positive contact effects. With units increasing in size, the proportion of ethnic minorities may become more a target of political and media discourse. And these kinds of public debates often emphasize economic and political threats (see Blalock, 1967; Galliker, Herman, Imminger, K., & Weimer, 1998). A public debate regarding the issue of minorities and immigration usually covers a whole country and then reflects in more negative attitudes toward ethnic minorities in general (cf. Maio, Esses, & Bell, 1994; Wagner, Zick, & van Dick, 2002). Thus, when the focus lies on large units such as countries, threat effects may emerge as a result of a third confounding variable, namely negative political propaganda.

Preliminary support for the importance of media influences as a mediator between minority proportion and prejudice in larger units comes from Schlüter (2006). He analyzed ethnic prejudice in Germany between 1990 and 1996, based on data from representative surveys. Schlüter then compared these data on prejudice with results of a content analysis on the coverage of immigration in a prominent German newspaper over the same time period (*Frankfurter Rundschau*, for data analyses see Koopmans & Olzak, 2004). Schlüter found a positive covariation between negative depictions of immigrants in the newspaper and mean prejudice levels in the different surveys. In addition, the relation between negative depictions of immigrants in the media and mean prejudice levels was moderated by respondents' reported intergroup contact. Those German respondents who reported having no contact with immigrants were more strongly influenced by negative newspaper coverage than those who did report having contact with immigrants.

Schlüter's findings accord well with our assumption that ethnic prejudice depends on the general political and societal debate about ethnic minorities in a society, operationalized here as newspaper coverage of the topic. This ideological influence depends, however, on individual variables such as intergroup contact. Accordingly, McLaren (2003) and Wagner and van Dick (2001) demonstrated on the basis of 1997 Eurowide survey data that the positive covariation between ethnic minority proportion in a country and ethnic prejudice is primarily due to those respondents with no or only few contacts to ethnic minorities. However, respondents who reported having cross-group friends were much less affected in their prejudice by the proportion of ethnic minorities in the country. Thus, intergroup contact can apparently serve as a buffer against the effects of negative propaganda described above.

Conclusions and Practical Implications

Which conclusions can be drawn? First of all, intergroup contact works! Although this has been shown in numerous studies before (Pettigrew & Tropp, 2006), it is encouraging to see that, at least in the German context, a higher proportion of ethnic minorities offers more contact opportunities and thus results in more positive intergroup attitudes. This clearly contradicts naïve claims of politicians that a higher proportion of ethnic minorities threatens the majority and leads to more conflict between groups. The findings of Schlüter (2006) give further reason to assume that perceived threat and ethnic prejudice depend on general political and societal debates on the issue of immigration and ethnic minorities: Negative political propaganda and media coverage are related to increased ethnic prejudice. Schlüter's results can also help explain the positive covariation between the proportion of ethnic minorities and ethnic prejudice, on a higher level of analysis, as for example in comparing different European countries (see Coenders, 2001, as well as Wagner & van Dick, 2001). It seems reasonable to assume that with an increase in the proportion of ethnic minorities negative political propaganda and media coverage of the issue also increase. However, additional research comparing the public debate in different countries is needed, to test directly whether media coverage or other forms of public debates are relevant mediators of the positive covariation between the proportion of ethnic minorities and ethnic prejudice in country-level analyses.

Our results clearly support Pettigrew's (1996) call for keeping levels of analysis straight. Phenomena located at different levels have to be recognized, described and methodologically treated differently. Relationships observed on one level of analysis (e.g., the district), can differ from or even contradict processes registered on a higher level (e.g., countries)—as demonstrated above. However, a contextual social psychology not only describes the differences (and similarities) of covariations between variables located at different levels of analysis, it also aims to understand them. This means to consider, theoretically and empirically, mediators located at the same level, but also to incorporate mediators at a lower level, as long as they are theoretically deduced (for details of avoiding fallacies see Pettigrew, 1996, ch. 6). In this sense, we come to the conclusion that size of the geographical region may moderate the relevant mediating processes: In smaller units, intergroup contact mediates the relationship between minority proportion and prejudice, whereas in larger units political and media coverage of the topic of immigration may become more salient, making intergroup threat a more relevant mediator. And finally, processes located at different levels can interact as has been demonstrated by Schlüter (2006), showing that receptivity to political propaganda depends on individual intergroup contact experiences.

Tom Pettigrew's campaign for a contextualized social psychology has important practical consequences. Our results again help to exemplify this. On a political level the message is clear. It is not the objective proportion of ethnic minorities per se that automatically leads to negative intergroup attitudes as asserted by politicians. On the contrary, at least in the German case, the "default option" of an increase in the number of minority members corresponds with an increase in prejudice-reducing contact effects. Whether majority members perceive threat seems to depend on the public discourse, for instance, on public warnings about the negative consequences of immigration for ethnic intergroup relations. Thus, politicians and the media have to be aware of their responsibilities in promoting intergroup prejudice. Heating up the issue by claiming that the threshold of immigration is reached (such as "the boat is full" campaigns) will foster intergroup conflict and should thus be avoided.

If we consider our results in light of the aim to reduce and prevent prejudice, an increasing number of ethnic minorities can also be seen as an opportunity instead of a burden. Evaluation of prevention programs conducted in schools, for example, show that particularly those programs that are based on improving intergroup contact and cooperation proved to be effective (e.g., Stephan, 1999; Wagner, Christ, & Van Dick, 2002). These programs not only help overcome prejudice, they also make a significant contribution to broadening the majority members' horizon, as described by Pettigrew in his concept of deprovincialization (Pettigrew, 1997, 1998; see also Brewer, this volume). Regarding our results as well as the many positive evaluations of intergroup contact programs in schools, one could also feel regret for those schools that do not have such opportunities, because they only have a few, or no, minority students. Still, context variables are of importance here, too: Cooperative education programs need the appropriate levels of economic and material support. And, as school representatives, students and parents can contribute not only to a climate of fear and rejection against minorities, but they can also produce the opposite effect.

References

Allport, G. W. (1954). *The nature of prejudice*. Reading, MA: Addison-Wesley.

Blalock, H. M. (1967). Percent non-white and discrimination in the South. *American Sociological Review, 22,* 677–682.

Blumer, H. (1958). Racial prejudice as a sense of group position. *Pacific Sociological Review, 23,* 3–7.

Bobo, L. (1999). Prejudice as group position: Microfoundations of a sociological approach to racism and race relations. *Journal of Social Issue, 55,* 445–472.

Coenders, M. (2001). *Nationalistic attitudes and ethnic exclusionism in a comparative perspective. An empirical study of attitudes toward the country and ethnic immigrants in 22 Countries.* Nijmegen, Holland: KUN.

Esses, V. M., Jackson, L. M., & Amstrong, T. L. (1998). Intergroup competition and attitudes towards immigrants and immigration: An instrumental model of group conflict. *Journal of Social Issues, 54,* 699–724.

Forman, T. (2003). *From pet to threat? Minority concentration, school racial context and white youths' racial attitudes.* Unpublished manuscript, University of Illinois at Chicago.

Fossett, M. A., & Kiecolt, K. J. (1989). The relative size of minority population and white racial attitudes. *Social Science Quarterly, 70,* 820–835.

Galliker, M., Herman, J., Imminger, K., & Weimer, D. (1998). The investigation of contiguity: Co-occurrence analysis of print media using CD-ROMs as a new data source, illustrated by a discussion on migrant delinquency in a daily newspaper. *Journal of Language and Social Psychology, 17,* 200–219.

Heitmeyer, W. (2002). Gruppenbezogene Menschenfeindlichkeit. Die theoretische Konzeption and erste empirische Ergebnisse [Group focused enmity. The theoretical conception and first empirical results]. In W. Heitmeyer (Ed.), *Deutsche Zustände. Folge 1* [German states. Sequel 1] (pp. 15–34). Frankfurt: Suhrkamp.

Heitmeyer, W. (2005). Gruppenbezogene Menschenfeindlichkeit. Die theoretische Konzeption und empirische Ergebnisse aus den Jahren 2002, 2003, und 2004 [Group focused enmity. The theoretical conception and empirical results from the years 2002, 2003, and 2004]. In W. Heitmeyer (Ed.), *Deutsche Zustände. Folge 3* [German states. Sequel 3] (pp. 13–36). Frankfurt: Suhrkamp.

Heitmeyer, W. (Ed.) (2007). *Deutsche Zustände. Folge 5* [German states. Sequel 5]. Frankfurt: Suhrkamp.

Koopmans, R., & Olzak, S. (2004). Discursive opportunities and the evolution of Right-Wing violence in Germany. *American Journal of Sociology*, *110*, 198–230.

Maio, G. R., Esses, V. M., & Bell, D. W. (1994). The formation of attitudes toward new immigrant groups. *Journal of Applied Social Psychology*, *24*, 1762–1776.

McLaren, L. M. (2003). Anti-immigrant prejudice in Europe: Contact, threat perception, and preferences for the exclusion of migrants. *Social Forces*, *81*, 909–936.

Pettigrew, T. F. (1958). Personality and socio-cultural factors in intergroup attitudes: A cross-national comparison. *Journal of Conflict Resolution*, *2*, 29–42.

Pettigrew, T. F. (1959). Regional differences in anti-negro prejudice. *Journal of Abnormal and Social Psychology*, *59*, 28–36.

Pettigrew, T. F. (1991). Toward unity and bold theory: Popperian suggestions for two persistent problems of social psychology. In C. W. Stephan, W. Stephan, & T. F. Pettigrew (Eds.), *The future of social psychology* (pp. 13–27). Springer, New York.

Pettigrew, T. F. (1996). *How to think like a social scientist*. New York: HarperCollins.

Pettigrew, T. F. (1997). Generalized intergroup contact effects on prejudice. *Personality and Social Psychology Bulletin*, *23*, 173–185.

Pettigrew, T. F. (1998). Intergroup contact theory. *Annual Review of Psychology*, *49*, 65–85.

Pettigrew, T. F. (2006). The advantage of multilevel approaches. *Journal of Social Issues*, *62*, 615–620.

Pettigrew, T. F., & Campbell, E. Q. (1960). Faubus and segregation: An analysis of Arkansas voting. *Public Opinion Quarterly*, *24*, 436–447.

Pettigrew, T. F., Christ, O., Wagner, U., & Stellmacher, J. (2007). Direct and indirect intergroup contact effects on prejudice: A normative interpretation. *International Journal of Intercultural Relations*, *31*, 411–425.

Pettigrew, T. F., & Cramer, M. R. (1959). The demography of desegregation. *Journal of Social Issues*, *15*, 61–71.

Pettigrew, T. F., Jackson, J. S., Ben Brika, J., Lemaine, G., Meertens, R. W., Wagner, U., et al. (1998). Outgroup prejudice in Western Europe. In W. Stroebe & M. Hewstone (Eds.), *European Review of Social Psychology* (Vol. 8) (pp. 241–273). Chichester: Wiley.

Pettigrew, T. F., & Tropp, L. R. (2006). A meta-analytic test of intergroup contact theory. *Journal of Personality and Social Psychology*, *90*, 751–783.

Poutrus, P. G., Behrends, J. C., & Kuck, D. (2000). Historische Ursachen der Fremdenfeindlichkeit in den neuen Bundesländern [Historical causes of hostility against foreigners in the Federal Republic of Germany]. *Aus Politik und Zeitgeschichte*, *39*, 15–21.

Quillian, L. (1995). Prejudice as a response to perceived group threat: Population composition and anti-immigrant and racial prejudice in Europe. *American Sociological Review*, *60*, 586–611.

Quillian, L. (1996). Group threat and regional change in attitudes toward African-Americans. *American Journal of Sociology*, *102*, 816–860.

Schlüter, E. (2006, March). *Was erklärt fremdenfeindliche Einstellungen? Modellierung von Kontext- und individuellen Prädiktoren im Zeitverlauf* [*What explains hostility against foreigners? Modelling of context- and individual predictors over time*]. Paper presented at the colloquium of the Graduate School "Group Focused Enmity," University of Marburg, Germany.

Semyonov, M., Rajman R., Tov, A. Y., & Schmidt, P. (2004). Population size, perceived threat and exclusion: A multiple indicator analysis of attitudes toward foreigners in Germany. *Social Science Research*, *33*, 681–701.

Stastische Ämter des Bundes und der Länder (2005). *Auslaendische Bevoelkerung* [Foreign population]. Retrieved June 12, 2006, from http://www.statistik–portal.de/Statistik-Portal/de_jb01_jahrtab2.asp

Stein, R. M., Post, S. S., & Rinden, A. L. (2000). Reconciling context and contact effects on racial attitudes. *Political Research Quarterly*, *53*, 285–303.

Stephan, W. G. (1999). *Reducing prejudice and stereotyping in schools*. New York: Teachers College Press.

Stephan, W. G., & Renfro, C. L. (2002). The role of threat in intergroup relations. In D. M. Mackie & E. R. Smith (Eds.) *From prejudice to intergroup emotions. Differential reactions to social groups* (pp. 191–207). New York and Hove: Psychology Press.

Taylor, M. C. (1998). How white attitudes vary with the racial composition of local populations: Numbers count. *American Sociological Review*, *63*, 512–535.

van Dick, R., Wagner, U., Pettigrew, T. F., Christ, O., Wolf, C., Petzel, T., et al. (2004). The role of perceived importance in intergroup contact. *Journal of Personality and Social Psychology*, *87*, 211–227.

Wagner, U., Christ, O., & Pettigrew, T. F. (2007). *Contact and threat effect of prejudice against immigrants*. Unpublished manuscript, Philipps-University Marburg, Germany.

Wagner, U., Christ, O., Pettigrew, T. F., Stellmacher, J., & Wolf, C. (2006). Prejudice and minority proportion: Contact instead of threat effects. *Social Psychology Quarterly*, *69*, 380–390.

Wagner, U., Christ, O., & van Dick, R. (2002). Die empirische Evaluation von Präventionsprogrammen gegen Fremdenfeindlichkeit [The empirical evaluation of primary prevention programs of hostility against foreigners]. *Journal für Konflikt- und Gewaltforschung*, *4*, 101–117.

Wagner, U., & van Dick, R. (2001). Fremdenfeindlichkeit "in der Mitte der Gesellschaft": Phänomenbeschreibung, Ursachen, Gegenmaßnahmen

[Prejudice "in the center of Society": Description of phenomena, causes, interventions]. *Zeitschrift für Politische Psychologie*, 9, 41–54.

Wagner, U., van Dick, R., Pettigrew, T. F., & Christ, O. (2003). Ethnic prejudice in East and West Germany: The explanatory power of intergroup contact. *Group Processes and Intergroup Relations*, 6, 23–37.

Wagner, U., & Zick, A. (1998). Ausländerfeindlichkeit, Vorurteile und diskriminierendes Verhalten [Anti-alien feeling, prejudice and discrimination]. In H. W. Bierhoff & U. Wagner (Eds.), *Aggression und Gewalt* [Aggression and violence] (pp. 145–164). Stuttgart, Germany: Kohlhammer.

Wagner, U., Zick, A., & van Dick, R. (2002). Die Möglichkeit interpersonaler und massenmedialer Beeinflussung von Vorurteilen [The possibility of interpersonal and mass-media influences on prejudice]. In K. Boehnke, D. Fuss, & J. Hagan (Eds.), *Jugendgewalt und Rechtsextremismus* [*Youth violence and right wing extremism*] (pp. 225–237). Weinheim: Juventa.

Wilcox, J., & Roof, W. C. (1978). Percent black and black-white status inequality: Southern versus Northern patterns. *Social Science Quarterly*, 59, 421–434.

Zick, A., Wagner, U., van Dick, R., & Petzel, T. (2001). Acculturation and prejudice in Germany: Perspectives of majority and minority. *Journal of Social Issues*, 57, 541–557.

14

Positive Intergroup Relations

From Reduced Outgroup Rejection to Outgroup Support

Kai J. Jonas and Amélie Mummendey

Social psychological research on the attitudes and behavior of social groups has focused extensively on negative intergroup relations (e.g., prejudice and its determinants). Given the pervasiveness and cost of this societal problem, it is not surprising that researchers feel motivated to look for the causes and functions of negative intergroup processes such as ingroup favoritism, outgroup derogation, and intergroup conflict. Understanding and explaining problematic group relations can provide knowledge and tools for diminishing conflict and prejudice. In their comprehensive analysis, Stephan and Stephan (2001) list among others, intergroup communication, mediation, and conciliation, as useful techniques for reducing intergroup conflict. A structural variable, namely the existence of a superordinate goal or common identity, also has long'been known to be effective. Sherif's summer camp studies (Sherif, Harvey, White, Hood, & Sherif, 1961) illustrated this effect, and the recent work by Hornsey and Hogg (2000) emphasizes the importance of retaining clear group boundaries and introducing a superordinate category to achieve balanced and harmonious intergroup relations.

Perhaps the most prominent of the models associated with improving intergroup relations is the contact hypothesis (Allport, 1954). If one seeks to name current scholars whose academic endeavors are closely linked to the topic of intergroup relations and the reduction of prejudice, the name of Thomas Pettigrew is inextricable. His seminal work on the contact hypothesis, and in a larger framework, the reduction of prejudice, not only represents one of the most impressive research programs in social psychology, but also has the shape and form of a conviction for life. His work has influenced the thinking of many colleagues, and to no great surprise, ours too.

Given the extensive literature on weakening negative processes and reducing prejudice, we suggest that it may be time to focus more explicitly on how to cultivate positive relations between social groups and their members. Negative intergroup relations typically involve negative judgments, attitudes, and behaviors toward outgroups that are easy to detect, or on a more complex level, those that appears to be positive, but are in fact intended to exploit the outgroup for the benefit of the ingroup. We define positive intergroup relations as judgments (e.g., expressions of appreciation, attraction, admiration and warm emotions), attitudes, and behavior between groups that are intended to reach or maintain a mutual, and positively perceived relationship; as such, the purpose of the interaction is to promote positive intergroup relationships, rather than improve a poor existing relationship, or to ameliorate conflict. We acknowledge that positive behavior of one group towards the other may be perceived as negative, given a divergence of perspectives. Thus, the definition of what constitutes "positive intergroup relations" is clearly not straightforward, and more work in this area is needed.

In this chapter, we summarize research findings with the goal of furthering this line of inquiry. Here, we do not consider the reduction of prejudice or the resolution of conflict, but the establishment of positive relations early on in the history of intergroup interaction. We consider this approach to be important because, as intergroup researchers, we often settle for the improvement of intergroup relations (which is difficult enough), but tend to neglect the potential for establishing positive relations at the outset of contact between two groups. Moreover, we believe this approach is fruitful because intergroup relations are not always determined by conflict, and because by analyzing determinants of positive relations, we can learn how further to promote positive relations between groups.

With the abundance of research on outgroup derogation one starts to wonder whether positive intergroup relations actually exist. However, there are several examples of positive relations between groups, some not analyzed beyond the descriptive level, and some already scientifically analyzed. Pertaining to the latter, Varshney's (2002) analyses of conflict-free societal realms in India (that are in many other cases characterized by ethnic or caste violence), offer an excellent example of positive intergroup relations. On the more descriptive level, the 2006 World Soccer Championships in Germany also provide an example of how many groups, fans and teams can celebrate peacefully while simultaneously competing with each other. We can also borrow evidence from the field of interpersonal relations, where an abundance of research describes the determinants and processes of positive relations between individuals (Gable & Reis, 2006) and mutual support (for a summary, see Clark & Grote, 2003). We believe it is necessary to analyze carefully cases of positive attitudes and behavior between groups in their own right. Intergroup relations can benefit from these analyses, and perhaps might even be "designed" to ensure a positive character.

Contexts That Can Promote Positive Intergroup Relations

When gathering evidence for the potential of positive intergroup relations one has to be vigilant about the contexts in which group relations occur. In some cases, it may be that what appear to be positive relations between different groups actually take place in social contexts in which only *one* group identity is salient. This may be explained by processes of recategorization referred to in the common ingroup identity model (Gaertner & Dovidio, 2000), or by processes where several identities are present but one (superordinate) category unifies the subcategorizations, such as the dual identity model (González & Brown, 2006), the ingroup projection model (Wenzel, Mummendey, & Waldzus, 2003), or by processes of "deprovincialization," as described by Pettigrew (1997). Furthermore, there is evidence from intergroup contact research (Brown & Hewstone, 2005), that salient group memberships, in the context of mutual distinctiveness, can lead to the generalization of positive intergroup contact effects.

In addition, findings from social cognitive research point to the possibility that, in certain contexts, intergroup behavior can commence positively. For example, Moskowitz, Gollwitzer, Wasel, & Schaal (1999) describe chronic egalitarianism as an individual characteristic for prejudice-free attitudes, and a group of chronic egalitarians could be internally motivated to maintain positive relations in the intergroup context (see also Devine, Plant, & Buswell, 2000). Similarly, it is known from research on automatic behavior that over-learned positive responses towards categories can be automatically activated by mere priming (Jonas & Sassenberg, 2006), and this underlines the notion that outright positive intergroup behavior is possible. Linking this approach (category activation via priming) to intergroup relations reveals the benefits of having salient categorizations for promoting positive behavior towards groups. Recent evidence from research on automatic behavior has shown that responses (i.e., denoting response behavior targeted at these groups and not behavior that is in fact imitating stereotypical behavior of the group) to clearly differentiated social categories are automatically activated, and that these responses can be very positive and supportive in their nature. Jonas and Sassenberg have shown that a salient intergroup context functions as a moderator for these effects (i.e., whether response or imitation behavior is being activated). Given less salient group boundaries, imitative behavior is shown, whereas clear salient group boundaries (i.e., intergroup differentiation) lead to the activation of responses. In some cases, these responses can take the form of outright positive behavior such as helping (Jonas & Sassenberg, 2006, Study 3). Thus, positive behavior toward an outgroup may not necessarily occur naturally on the automatic level, but salient group boundaries have the potential to promote such positive behavior.

We, therefore, conclude that blurred intergroup boundaries or superordinate categorizations are not necessary preconditions (and are indeed sometimes not even adequate) for positive intergroup relations, and that maintaining salient group differences in the intergroup context can in appropriate circumstances provide a basis for such positive relations.

Examples of Positive Intergroup Relations

In the following we describe examples of positive intergroup relations that can point to fruitful paths for further research and help us to become aware of some limiting conditions, as well.

Outgroup Support

The simple hypothesis, that outgroup support may occur under the right circumstances was tested in a series of experiments by Fuchs-Bodde (2005), of which we describe one in detail. This research sought to determine conditions under which outgroup support is possible. Based on previous research in intergroup relations (Mummendey, Klink, Mielke, Wenzel, & Blanz, 1999), it was anticipated that these conditions could be created when the comparison dimension in a close intergroup relation context is of low relevance. Of course, these intergroup context characteristics seem close to a "basking in reflected glory" approach (Cialdini et al., 1976) which we describe below, but are limited here to mere measurement of outgroup support. In a 2 × 2 Design (*intergroup relation*: close vs. not close, and *relevance of comparison dimension*: high vs. low) 55 psychology students served as participants. As context relevant groups, psychology and medical students were used. In one condition the group relation was described as close, strongly interrelated, and in the other condition as the opposite of this. The relevance of the comparison dimension was operationalized as either regarding psychotherapy (high) or cancer therapy (low) from the perspective of psychologists. To induce inferiority for psychology students, a fictitious university ranking was presented in which their home university was rated extremely well, but mostly due to the academic performance of the medical department and not the psychology department. For the dependent measure, a scale assessing outgroup support on resource dimensions was employed (7-item Likert scale, higher values denoting more outgroup support). The results show the desired contrast coding effect $F(1,51) = 5.09$, $p = .028$, $\eta^2 = .091$, with all other contrasts being nonsignificant. In line with our contentions, outgroup support was highest in the condition with low comparison relevance, and in the context of a close group relation. For a distribution of means and standard errors, see Figure 14.1. In other words, the data show that outgroup support is possible when two distinct groups are seen as close to each other, and when the context of comparison allows for the support of an outgroup by members of the group for whom the comparison dimension is less important. Taken together, we interpret these findings as offering very basic support for the possibility of framing contexts to achieve positive intergroup relations. Of course, richer social contexts will probably increase the complexity of the relationships and introduce possible limiting conditions. We turn to such contexts in the examples described below.

		Relevance of comparison dimension	
		low	high
Group closeness	*not close*	4.94 (.68)	5.07 (1.21)
	close	5.64 (.92)	4.71 (.96)

Figure 14.1   Means and standard errors (in brackets) of outgroup support, as a function of group closeness and comparison relevance.

Group-Based Helping

A helping relation is characterized by a helpee (in need, and without sufficient resources to resolve the situation alone), and a helper (who has sufficient resources to provide the necessary help). Though help-ing is often construed in terms of interpersonal relationships, it is also a behavior that is driven by group membership, or interactions between groups. Ingroup members are typically more likely to receive help (Levine, Prosser, Evans, & Reicher, 2005; Levine & Thompson, 2004), but members of different groups may also offer and receive help from each other (Nadler, 2002; Nadler & Halabi, 2006). For example, countries may give help to other countries after natural disasters, and members of humanitarian organizations (e.g., Rotary International, Médecins Sans Frontières, Habitat for Humanity) help members of disadvantaged groups. It is noteworthy that prior positive intergroup relations can, but do not necessarily have to exist to encourage helping behavior. In general, research on helping behavior has shown that not only groups or categories matter when it comes to the decision about who is worth helping, but that specific relations of intergroup helping may further promote the behavior (Laner, Benin, & Ventrone, 2001).

Additionally, though we might assume that intergroup help would be free of relational animosities, from the perspective of the helpee (Schneider, Major, & Luhtanen, 1996), interpretations of help given by other groups may depend on perceived group status and identification, thereby limiting the potential that the help offered by a group will encourage positive intergroup relations. For example, Nadler and Halabi (2006) showed that high identifiers are reluctant to receive help from a high status outgroup (Studies 1–3), and that dependency-oriented help in unstable status relations is considered the most problematic to receive (Study 4). Nadler (2002) also found evidence that receiving help from a high power group can be judged as a social dominance endorsement, or in the case where help is refused, as a challenge to the relation. Of course, this only holds if the status difference is seen as illegitimate from the perspective of the helpee group.

Considering these examples, we conclude that intergroup help can qualify in some cases as an example of positive intergroup relations in action, or at least as outgroup support. Nonetheless, since helping is based on clear differences in resources available to the interacting groups, as well as differences in power and status, not all forms and contexts of helping are perceived to be positive by all parties involved. These results point to the necessity of further research to determine the form, context, and determinants of "true" intergroup help, i.e., help that is not judged as beneficial for the helping group, or manifesting an illegitimate social structure from the perspective of the group that is being helped. More work is also needed to explore the different forms and directions of causal relationships that underlie intergroup help, as helping can be seen as an outcome of previously existing positive intergroup relations, or as an indicator of the potential for future positive intergroup relations.

Basking in Reflected Glory (BIRG)

In this section, we argue that positive intergroup relations may be promoted further by the BIRG mechanism put forward by Cialdini et al. (1976) and Tesser (1988) in the interpersonal domain. BIRG denotes an increase in self-esteem (glory) due to associating oneself with the success of another individual or group. According to Tesser (1988), a basking mechanism should occur when relations are close, yet the comparison dimension is less relevant for the inferior individual.

We believe this mechanism (BIRG) can be a particularly useful framework for understanding determinants of positive intergroup relations. One determinant involves the case when two groups are in close relation (e.g., seeing each other as similar, are spatially and temporally close), and their respective identities are salient in the situation. The second determinant can be described as a low relevance of the comparison condition for the subordinate group. If one group is of lower status or power compared to another, the inferior group can simply accept the fact that it is not equivalent to the superior group on a given comparison dimension. In such cases we would expect no outgroup support effect from the inferior group's point of view. Yet, in the case of specific determinants, the subordinate group should be able to judge that it is inferior, but that the close position to the outgroup is a potential gain for itself. The subordinate ingroup should be willing to support the superior outgroup, because they can "bask in the reflected glory" of the outgroup. To test this proposal empirically, both outgroup support and positive affect on the part of the ingroup (the basking in reflected glory effect) need to be measured. Taken together, we would expect the most outgroup support from the subordinate group when the level of interaction of the groups is high, and the relevance of the comparison dimension is low, compared to all other combinations of these determinants. Yet, even this BIRG approach immediately reveals a limiting condition. Even with salient group boundaries, there is a binding force given by means of a common larger categorization that is accessible for both groups.

Intergroup Contact

Research on the intergroup contact hypothesis is backed by an impressive meta-analytic integration of empirical findings (Pettigrew & Tropp, 2006) as well as a theoretical integration (Brown & Hewstone, 2005). Intergroup contact bears the potential for a very high degree of variability in terms of its outcomes, which can vary from a rather positive judgment of outgroups, to clear, positive behavior towards the outgroup. In addition, there may or may not be a joint task or goal, which has been described as one variable that can facilitate the success of contact (Pettigrew & Tropp, 2006). Thus, it is quite hard to determine where each example listed below fits, since the character of the field studies, and the sometimes protracted conflicts show a considerable variance in themselves.

Studies within the intergroup contact framework that actually show positive behavior and outgroup support beyond a (mere) reduction of outgroup derogation are rare. The reduction of prejudice and outgroup devaluation, and changes in stereotype content are seen as central concerns—and surely are—for the development of less problematic group relations. Few studies can be identified that go beyond these dependent variables. On the level of positive behavior, strong support for our argument comes from Malhotra and Liyanage (2005), who can provide evidence from their study, a peace workshop situated in Sri Lanka, during a period of ethnic conflict. Participants of these peace workshops, compared to two control groups, donated more money to help poor children of the "other" ethnicity, even after one year had elapsed. In the context of heterosexual and gay and lesbian relationships, contact has also been shown to lead to closer relationships and true friendships among members of opposite sexual orientation groups, using one year cross wave analyses (Herek & Capitanio, 1996). Similar to these clearly positive intergroup effects, other findings of attitudinal support point to an improved evaluation of outgroups and a general openness to other cultures (Eller & Abrams, 2004; Nesdale & Todd, 2000). However, we believe it is important to note that the four studies described above are all field studies and that the effects they report are still to be put to rigorous test in laboratory research.

There is also evidence for contact effects in relation to the valuing of diversity and having a positive orientation toward outgroups (see Molina, Wittig, & Giang, 2004; Tropp & Bianchi, 2006; van Dick et al. 2004). Valuing diversity, as a concept, connotes a willingness to construct a joint or at least blurred superordinate category, since a single group cannot be diverse in itself on the group level. We, therefore, consider the value of diversity, and/or openness to other cultures and the evaluation of uninvolved groups as a rather rudimentary condition for positive outgroup relations or outgroup support.

Moreover, we conclude from this research, and the findings reported above in the field of intergroup help, that constituting and maintaining positive intergroup relations works differently for high status/power or majority members than for low status/power or minority members (see also Dovidio, Gaertner, Saguy, & Halabi, this volume; Tropp & Bianchi, 2007). Such findings suggest that the low status group is likely to be more sensitive to explicit group boundaries and differences. In this case, one may be tempted to propose a superordinate category as the solution. Thus it is of core interest to consider how group boundaries are maintained or if they are given up for the (positive) sake of a superordinate or joint categorization (see also Hornsey & Hogg, 2000).

Joint Goals

A cluster of positive intergroup relations characterized by a current and salient task, an explicit structure between the groups, and actual joint behavior, can be described as being determined by a joint goal. Many examples for such goal-driven intergroup relations can be found in political alliances, coalitions to form a government and to maintain power (Nownes, 2000), alliances in wars to fight external enemies, and mergers of companies or institutions. All of these examples are characterized by the fact that there is joint goal attainment (i.e., the source of the positive intergroup relations), agreed upon by both groups. Still, this common ground may be disrupted or abandoned when the goal cannot be reached, or when the equilibrium of relations between partners is changing. This can especially be the case in merger contexts, where presumed equal status may be desired, but unclear, and/or the groups may adopt different viewpoints regarding their statuses (Giessner, Viki, Otten, Terry, & Täuber, 2006; Giessner & Mummendey, 2007; Haunschild, Moreland, & Murrell, 1994; Worchel, Andreoli, & Folger, 1977). One might object that the research in focus here only contains contexts involving superordinate categorization, such that two independent groups are given up for the sake of a coalition, alliance, or merger. However, a lay analysis of political coalition processes could reveal that groups continuously struggle to maintain their ingroup identity, especially the weaker, low status partner. In sum, we believe this field of research to be important as an example of positive intergroup relations and outgroup support, yet we conclude that these types of relations and support are probably in many cases determined by functional considerations as to why the cooperation is feasible for both groups.

Competition

A final type of intergroup relation that bears mentioning is group competition. One might wonder whether outgroup support or positive intergroup behavior can take place in the context of competition. We think in particular of cases where there is a nested positive-negative interdependence (i.e., a mixed-motive) between the groups. This nested positive-negative interdependence appears to be rooted in a simultaneous superordinate and subgroup categorization (Turner, 2005). On a superordinate level, groups are in positive inter-dependence to actually allow for a competitive relation on a subgroup level. Contexts for such a complex intergroup situation can be found in team sports. In order for social comparison between the subgroups to be enacted, an outgroup has by definition to be available. Outside the actual competition, sport team members treat their rival team affably, for instance hosting them, offering them accommodation and refreshments. Or, in stadium announcements, both teams are treated equally, since blatant ingroup favoritism could lead to the "rival" team deciding not to compete. In other words, a negative interdependence is embedded in a positive interdependence, and the combination suggests positive intergroup relations. Specific to this context is an unstable but legitimate status, on the competitive level, and an assumed status equality on the superordinate level. To our knowledge there is presently little research tackling this complex "janus face" of intergroup relations, a rare exception being the work of Simon and Oakes (2006).

Summary

We have given a description of existing and proposed research on positive intergroup relations and outgroup support. Based on the notion that groups need to maintain their distinctiveness, we reviewed various examples of research in the light of determinants of relations that commence positively. We believe it is necessary to differentiate whether support for the outgroup is actually real support, or if it is mainly driven by a motivation to maintain ingroup-favoring biases or ingroup distinctiveness. On the other hand, outgroup support is possible when the outgroup is not merely an outgroup anymore, but also an ingroup based on a superordinate categorization. Put differently, positive intergroup relations and outgroup support on the subgroup level can be driven by an overarching salient superordinate categorization. On the level of empirical evidence, our review of the research suggests that there is no single, guaranteed pathway for the ambitious aim of achieving and maintaining positive intergroup relations or outgroup support. Research in the helping and contact domains shows that there are determinants of intergroup contexts that may lead to outgroup relations that are patronizing. Basking in reflected glory mechanisms are, given a clear set of determinants, possible, but vulnerable processes. The same holds for our other examples in the cooperation domain. Thus, future research needs to explore further these boundary conditions to understand how applications of intergroup contact can promote positive outcomes.

We consider the significance of a superordinate joint categorization as our core message. Contrary to subgroup-focused political approaches such as "color consciousness," we believe that a sole subgroup categorization may not be the most effective path for positive intergroup relations or outgroup support. Instead, the most promising effects in terms of explicitly positive attitudes and behavior towards outgroups are shown when a superordinate grouping that includes the ingroup and outgroup is accessible. This might refer to cases of mere salience of the superordinate group, in which both subgroups are "dissolved" by recategorization. Alternately, salience of the superordinate group might add a simultaneously salient distinction between ingroup and outgroup on the subgroup level. All promising examples of positive effects we have identified in our review work with a "categorical parenthesis," either as a clear and only superordinate categorization (as suggested in the common ingroup identity model by Gaertner & Dovidio, 2000) or as an accessible comparison dimension, provided by a superordinate group, and on which the similarity of the subgroups can be assured.

Overall, then, an accessible superordinate category working as a backdrop may be judged a precondition not only for positive but also for negative intergroup relations. For the positive domain, we presented evidence that a reference to a superordinate category is necessary to ensure, for example, that intergroup help is accepted. But also within the domain of negative intergroup relations, explanations like that offered by the ingroup projection model (Wenzel et al., 2003) draw heavily on the notion of joint categorization. In this model, the superordinate category is used to derive and determine prescriptive norm violations. In the research we presented here, the superordinate category is needed to fuel joint efforts, helping, basking mechanisms, or the possibility to cooperate and compete. In sum, to understand how positive intergroup relations and true outgroup support may be achieved we should consider widening the limited perspective on one single level of intergroup relations to incorporate multilevel characteristics of categorization. This may be the route to a more promising analysis of intergroup processes.

References

Allport, G. W. (1954). *The nature of prejudice.* Reading, MA: Addison-Wesley.

Brown, R., & Hewstone, M. (2005). An integrative theory of intergroup contact. In M. Zanna (Ed.), *Advances in experimental social psychology* (Vol. 37) (pp. 255–343). San Diego, CA: Academic Press.

Cialdini, R. B., Borden, R. J., Thorne, A., Walzer, M. R., Freeman, S., & Sloan, L. R. (1976). Basking in reflected glory: Three (football) field studies. *Journal of Personality and Social Psychology, 34*, 366–375.

Clark, N. K., & Grote, M. S. (2003). Close relationships. In T. Millon & M. J. Lerner (Eds.), *Handbook of psychology: Personality and social psychology* (Vol. 5) (pp. 447–461). Hoboken, NJ: Wiley.

Devine, P. G., Plant, E. A., & Buswell, B. N. (2000). Breaking the prejudice habit: Progress and obstacles. In S. Oskamp (Ed.), *Reducing prejudice and discrimination* (pp. 185–208). Mahwah, NJ: Erlbaum.

Eller, A., & Abrams, D. (2004). Come together: Longitudinal comparisons of Pettigrew's reformulated intergroup contact model and the Common Ingroup Identity Model in Anglo-French and Mexican-American contexts. *European Journal of Social Psychology, 34*, 229–256.

Fuchs-Bodde, K. (2005). *Bereitschaft zur Unterstützung der Fremdgruppe als Folge von Basking in Reflected Glory zwischen Gruppen* [Willingness to support an outgroup as a consequence of basking in reflected glory between groups]. Unpublished doctoral dissertation, University of Jena.

Gable, S. L., & Reis, H. T. (2006). Intimacy and the self: An iterative model of the self and close relationships. In P. Noller & J. A. Feeney (Eds.), *Close relationships: Functions, forms and processes* (pp. 211–225). Hove: Psychology Press.

Gaertner, S., & Dovidio, J. (2000). *Reducing intergroup bias: The common ingroup identity model.* Philadelphia, PA: Psychology Press.

Giessner, S. R., & Mummendey, A. (2007). *United we win, divided we fail? Effects of cognitive merger representations and performance feedback on merging groups.* Manuscript submitted for publication.

Giessner, S. R., Viki, G. T., Otten, S., Terry, D. J., & Täuber, S. (2006). The challenge of merging: Merger patterns, pre-merger status and merger support. *Personality and Social Psychology Bulletin, 32,* 339–352.

González, R., & Brown, R. (2006). Dual identities in intergroup contact: Group status and size moderate the generalization of positive attitude change. *Journal of Experimental Social Psychology, 42,* 753–767.

Haunschild, P. R., Moreland, R. L., & Murrell, A. J. (1994). Sources of resistance to mergers between groups. *Journal of Applied Social Psychology, 24,* 1150–1178.

Herek, G. M., & Capitanio, J. P. (1996). "Some of my best friends": Intergroup contact, concealable stigma, and heterosexuals' attitudes toward gay men and lesbians. *Personality and Social Psychology Bulletin, 22,* 412–424.

Hornsey, M. J., & Hogg, M. A. (2000). Assimilation and diversity: An integrative model of subgroup relations. *Personality and Social Psychology Review, 4,* 143–156.

Jonas, K. J., & Sassenberg, K. (2006). Knowing how to react. Automatic response priming from social categories. *Journal of Personality and Social Psychology, 90,* 709–721.

Laner, M. R., Benin, M. H., & Ventrone, N. A. (2001). Bystander attitudes towards victims of violence: Who's worth helping? *Deviant Behavior, 22,* 23–42.

Levine, M., Prosser, A., Evans, D., & Reicher, S. (2005). Identity and emergency intervention: How social group membership and inclusiveness of group boundaries shape helping behavior. *Personality and Social Psychology Bulletin, 31,* 443–453.

Levine, M., & Thompson, K. (2004). Identity, place and bystander intervention: Social categories and helping after natural disasters. *The Journal of Social Psychology, 144,* 229–245.

Malhotra, D., & Liyanage, S. (2005). Long-term effects of peace workshops in protracted conflicts. *Journal of Conflict Resolution, 49,* 908–924.

Molina, L. E., Wittig, M. A., & Giang, M. T. (2004). Mutual acculturation and social categorization: A comparison of two perspectives on intergroup bias. *Group Processes and intergroup Relations, 7,* 239–265.

Moskowitz, G. B., Gollwitzer, P. M., Wasel, W., & Schaal, B. (1999). Preconscious control of stereotype activation through chronic egalitarian goals. *Journal of Personality and Social Psychology, 77,* 167–184.

Mummendey, A., Klink, A., Mielke, R., Wenzel, M., & Blanz, M. (1999). Socio-structural characteristics of intergroup relations and identity management strategies: Results from a field study in East Germany. *European Journal of Social Psychology, 29*, 259–285.

Nadler, A. (2002). Inter-group helping relations as power relations: Maintaining or challenging social dominance between groups through helping. *Journal of Social Issues, 58*, 487–502.

Nadler, A., & Halabi, S. (2006). Intergroup helping as status relations: Effects of status stability, identification, and type of help on receptivity to high-status group's help. *Journal of Personality and Social Psychology, 91*, 97–110.

Nesdale, D., & Todd, P. (2000). Effect of contact on intercultural acceptance: A field study. *International Journal of Intercultural Relation, 24*, 341–360.

Nownes, A. J. (2000). Interest group conflict, alliances, and opposition: Evidence from three states. *The Social Science Journal, 37*, 231–244.

Pettigrew, T. F. (1997). The affective component of prejudice: Empirical support for the new view. In S. A. Tuck & J. K. Martin (Eds.), *Racial attitudes in the 1990s: Continuity and change* (pp. 76–90). Westport, CT: Praeger.

Pettigrew, T. F., & Tropp, L. R. (2006). A meta-analytic test of intergroup contact theory. *Journal of Personality and Social Psychology, 90*, 751–783.

Schneider, M. E., Major, B., & Luhtanen, R. (1996). Social stigma and the potential costs of assumptive help. *Personality and Social Psychology Bulletin, 22*, 201–209.

Sherif, M., Harvey, O. J., White, B. J., Hood, W. R., & Sherif, C. W. (1961). *Intergroup conflict and cooperation: The Robbers Cave experiment*. Norman, OK: University of Oklahoma Book Exchange.

Simon, B., & Oakes, P. (2006). Beyond dependence: An identity approach to social power and domination. *Human Relations, 59*, 105–139.

Stephan, W. G., & Stephan, C. W. (2001). *Improving intergroup relations*. Thousand Oaks, CA: Sage.

Tesser, A. (1988). Toward a self-evaluation maintenance model of social behavior. In L. Berkowitz (Ed.), *Advances in experimental social psychology* (Vol. 21) (pp. 181–227). New York: Academic Press.

Tropp, L. R., & Bianchi, R. A. (2006). Valuing diversity and interest in intergroup contact. *Journal of Social Issues, 62*, 533–552.

Tropp, L. R., & Bianchi, R. A. (2007). Interpreting references to group membership in context: Feelings about intergroup contact depending on who says what to whom. *European Journal of Social Psychology, 37*, 439–451.

Turner, J. C. (2005). Explaining the nature of power: A three-process theory. *European Journal of Social Psychology, 35*, 1–22.

van Dick, R., Wagner, U., Pettigrew, T. F., Christ, O., Wolf, C., Petzel, T., et al. (2004). The role of perceived importance in intergroup contact. *Journal of Personality and Social Psychology, 87*, 211–227.

Varshney, A. (2002). *Ethnic conflict and civic life*. New Haven, CT: Yale University Press.

Wenzel, M., Mummendey, A., & Waldzus, S. (2003). The ingroup as pars pro toto: Projection from the ingroup onto the inclusive category as a precursor to social discrimination. *Personality and Social Psychology Bulletin, 29*, 461–471.

Worchel, S., Andreoli, V. A., & Folger, R. (1977). Intergroup cooperation and intergroup attraction: The effect of previous interaction and outcome of combined effort. *Journal of Experimental Social Psychology, 13*, 131–140.

Part V

Intergroup Relations as a Commitment to Social Change

15

Feeling Relative Deprivation

The Rocky Road from Comparisons to Actions

Heather Smith and Iain Walker

Social scientists have employed the concept of relative deprivation (RD) to explain phenomena ranging from poor physical health (Adler & Snibbe, 2003) to participation in collective protest (Walker & Mann, 1987) and susceptibility to terrorist recruitment (Moghaddam, 2005). RD is a "model social psychological concept" because it outlines how subjective interpretations of one's circumstances (created by larger institutional and cultural forces) lead to strong feelings and behavioral reactions (Pettigrew, 2002, p. 352).

We attribute the longevity of the RD concept, in part, to Thomas Pettigrew's skillful integration (1967; 1978; 2002) of the concept with larger theoretical frameworks and themes, and his use of the concept to understand major social problems. As Pettigrew taught us, it is not helpful to develop complex theories isolated from other theoretical developments, and perhaps more importantly, social problems. Instead, he viewed RD as a tool that could advance social scientists' thinking about the complex contribution of social identification and comparisons to people's attitudes and behavior. Rather than investing in a single tool or concept, Pettigrew always keeps his eye on the larger question, whether it is explaining and predicting prejudice, or the focus of this chapter, people's willingness to (collectively) challenge injustice.

Samuel Stouffer, one of Pettigrew's graduate school mentors, coined the term *relative deprivation* to describe unexpected relationships that emerged from surveys of World War II soldiers (Stouffer, Suchman, DeVinney, Starr, & Williams, 1949). Readers familiar with

Pettigrew's contributions to social psychology will recognize Stouffer's strong influence—in Pettigrew's adoption of the RD construct, expert use of large-scale national survey data, and more recent use of meta-analysis.

In this chapter, we build upon the "lessons learned" from RD research listed by Pettigrew (2002) to suggest a more complex and useful framework for understanding collective challenges to injustice. We begin with a discussion of social comparisons and argue that we need to investigate the circumstances under which people reframe disadvantageous inter*personal* comparisons as disadvantageous inter*group* comparisons. Next, we suggest the value in specifying emotional reactions that mediate the relationship between disadvantageous intergroup comparisons and collective action. Finally, we consider why one particular emotional reaction, group-based anger, does not always lead to collective protest.

Group Relative Deprivation

One of the most important conceptual distinctions within RD theory is the distinction between individual and group relative deprivation (Walker & Smith, 2002). Individual relative deprivation (IRD) includes perceived undeserved individual disadvantage and associated emotions. Group relative deprivation (GRD) includes perceived undeserved collective disadvantage and associated emotions. Compared to IRD, GRD more reliably predicts political protest and active attempts to change the social system (Walker & Smith, 2002). Data from field studies and laboratory experiments (Leach, Iyer, & Pedersen, 2007; Mummendy, Kessler, Klink, & Mielke, 1999; van Zomeren, Spears, Fischer, & Leach, 2004; Wright, Taylor, & Moghaddam, 1990a) show that people will react to group disadvantages that they view as unfair with anger and resentment. Feelings of anger and resentment, in turn, increase people's willingness to engage in collective protest. This research suggests that the road to collective action is relatively straightforward. If people make a disadvantageous intergroup comparison, they will feel angry. If they feel angry, they will protest. But as we outline below, the road to collective action may not be so smooth.

Social Comparisons

Who compares to whom remains a key issue for RD models. Although intergroup comparisons are linked to collective behavior

(Smith & Ortiz, 2002), these comparisons appear to be rare (Smith & Leach, 2004). When university students reported their most recent social comparison after they received a random signal, over 60% of the reported comparisons were to another person and less than 10% were comparisons in which they thought of themselves as a group representative in comparison to an outgroup.

Students' comparison choices most likely reflect Western political and cultural contexts. University students may have reported frequent interpersonal comparisons because of the traditional academic emphasis on individual achievement and effort or general cultural and political support for meritocratic beliefs (Foster & Tsarfati, 2005; Major, Quinton, & McCoy, 2002). Similar comparison processes may explain why subjective social status consistently predicts self-reported physical health even after controlling for objective measures of education, income, occupation and health risks (Ostove, Adler, Kuppermann, & Washington, 2000). When people believe that they are worse off than a peer, it can increase stress, anxiety, or depression—and subsequently influence physical health (Walker & Mann, 1987). If people can attribute their negative outcomes to group-based discrimination, they report less psychological distress (Branscombe, Schmitt, & Harvey, 1999; Foster & Tsarfati, 2005; Tougas, Rinfret, Beaton, & de la Sablonnière, 2005).

If a negative comparison is framed in intergroup terms, the ingroup can serve as a source of emotional or instrumental support and provide social validation for one's perceptions (see Major et al., 2002). People also might be more willing to debate and protest their disadvantage when framed in intergroup terms (Walker & Mann, 1987). But without ideological help or encouragement, intergroup comparisons will be rare in individualistic cultures. In fact, some researchers argue that unions and other social movement organizations do just that—encourage their members and constituents to view interpersonal differences in salaries, for example, as intergroup differences (Drury & Reicher, 2005; Simon & Klandermans, 2001).

However, we should not oversell the benefits of group-based interpretations of personal negative outcomes, as we may be replacing one problematic relationship with another (see Foster & Tsarfati, 2005). In one case, we may interpret personal negative outcomes as the product of unfair systems, such that we would feel good but not try particularly hard. In the other case, we may ignore obvious inequity, where we would try to achieve personal success but report poor self-image. Also, we should not pretend that group-based interpretations will protect people from the health consequences of disadvantage or deprivation. Interpreting one's subjective social status as a product of individual ability or effort may increase anxiety and/or depression, but interpreting one's subjective social status as a product of group discrimination may increase anger and hostility. Both hostility and depression are linked to declines in physical health (Taylor, 2002). These different paths may explain why both GRD and IRD lead to subsequent decreases in self-esteem, life quality, and increased depressive symptoms (Schmitt, 2006).

Relationships Between IRD and GRD

The distinction between intergroup and interpersonal comparisons reflects the traditional treatment of IRD and GRD as two independent levels of analysis (Ellemers, 2002; Smith & Ortiz, 2002). If we treat IRD and GRD as orthogonal constructs (Vanneman & Pettigrew, 1972), we can distinguish among people who experience "double deprivation," GRD coupled with personal advantage, IRD coupled with group advantage and "double gratification." Some researchers suggest that the "doubly deprived" will be the most motivated to challenge the system (Foster & Matheson, 1995; Vanneman & Pettigrew, 1972). Other researchers suggest that the group deprived but personally advantaged will have the personal resources to lead collective challenge (Pettigrew, 1978). Still others suggest that personal fortune can compensate for group deprivation and vice versa (Zagefka & Brown, 2006). For example, when participants were given feedback that their group had been collectively disadvantaged but they personally enjoyed an advantage, they reported more satisfaction and fairness, not less (Smith, Spears, & Oyen, 1994). The knowledge that their ingroup was disadvantaged made their personal reward that much sweeter.

Although treating GRD and IRD as orthogonal constructs leads to provocative hypotheses, the data suggest that IRD and GRD are consistently positively correlated (Pettigrew, 2002). Tougas and her colleagues (Tougas & Beaton, 2002; Tougas et al., 2005) argue for a "spill-over" effect in which high levels of IRD increase feelings of GRD. GRD, in turn, mediates the effects of IRD on collective action and prejudice. However, a full understanding of the relationship between GRD and IRD must distinguish between interpersonal comparisons to ingroup and outgroup members (Smith & Ortiz, 2002). We believe that people's comparisons to a target identified as an outgroup member may be an important developmental stage between comparisons to targets identified as ingroup members and intergroup comparisons.

Shared social categories, even if not explicitly acknowledged, shape people's interpersonal comparison choices and interpretations. For example, men and women preferred same sex comparisons even when opposite sex comparisons were more relevant or informative (Major et al., 2002). Even when the local environment "imposes" more cross group comparisons, people may discount their relevance (Leach & Smith, 2006). Ethnic minority students recorded many more comparisons to ethnic majority targets than to ethnic minority targets, but only comparisons to other ethnic minority targets shaped how they felt. This "ingroup primacy" effect (Zagefka & Brown, 2006) might explain why disadvantaged group members report relatively high self-esteem despite their disadvantages or discrimination (Crocker, Major, & Steele, 1998).

However, most of us belong to multiple social categories—and even if gender and ethnicity provide primary reference groups—shared occupations or neighborhoods also create relevant reference groups (Gartrell, 2002). We think that these overlapping social categories or reference groups are crucial for fostering the types of comparisons that lead to group-based interpretations of deprivation (see Davis, 1959; Wenzel, 2004). We expect people like us (e.g., those who share the same social category) to receive similar treatment and outcomes. For example, imagine that I compare myself with a particular, better paid outgroup member because we share a common occupational category. When I discover the inequity, I am motivated to look for explanations—including our different social category memberships within the common reference group. For example, East Germans who reported more identification with Germany, as a whole, viewed their own group as more deprived. In this context, Germany represented a superordinate category in which East Germans and West Germans should be entitled to equal treatment and outcomes (Schmitt, 2006); the deprivation faced by East Germans violated the expectation that all Germans should enjoy similar outcomes.

Of course, suggesting that the "personal can become political" is not a new idea. Group consciousness models (e.g., Foster & Tsarfati, 2005) and others describe "a-ha" moments in which members of disadvantaged groups discover that their individual effort and ability do not always lead to individual success. We suggest that interpersonal comparisons to outgroup members can lead to these "a-ha" moments that move people to a group-based interpretation of their disadvantage. However, as we discuss later, it is not wise to anchor models of collective challenge with single comparisons or moments of insight. Instead, it may be multiple and consistent inequitable comparisons that create the necessary motivation for collective challenge.

Emotions

Many researchers identify disadvantageous intergroup comparisons as the cognitive part of RD, and argue that it is the affective reaction to these comparisons that drives collective attitudes and action (Walker & Smith, 2002). However, the general negative affect measures (occasionally) used in RD research can be parsed into distinct emotions with different antecedents and action tendencies (Frijda, 1993; Roseman, Spindel, & Jose, 1990). For example, anger typically leads to confrontation or aggression, sadness to withdrawal, and fear to escape (Frijda, 1993).

If we specify emotional reactions, we should ask whether RD always or only elicits anger. People can recognize an illegitimate group disadvantage but feel sad or anxious about it (Smith, Cronin, & Kessler, 2006). Alternatively, disadvantageous intergroup comparisons could be associated with equally potent but different moral emotions such as contempt or disgust (Rozin, Lowery, & Imada, 1999; van Zomeren & Lodewijkx, 2005).

We also might question whether anger is the only emotion that mediates the relationship between GRD and collective action. In his social-psychological analysis of the Holocaust, Glick (2002) proposes an ideological model of scapegoating in which group members interpret collective social or economic frustrations as caused by a particular outgroup. He argues that the chosen outgroups often are the target of "envious" prejudice in which the outgroup's success or competence is viewed with "envy, fear, resentment and hostility." It seems entirely possible that a dominant group's hostile collective behavior (e.g., Kristalnacht) could reflect fear and anxiety (as well as anger).

To distinguish when people might feel sad, fearful, or angry about the same intergroup comparison, we must identify other situational factors or appraisals that shape people's emotional experiences. In their model for understanding the experience of relative privilege (the "flip side" of RD), Leach, Snider, and Iyer (2002) propose four dimensions; self/other focus, legitimacy, stability, and perceived control, that distinguish specific emotional reactions to privilege. For example, advantaged group members who focus on the situation for the disadvantaged, believe the situation is illegitimate, and have some collective control, will feel outraged. If they focus on the disadvant-aged, have some collective control, but feel the situation is legitimate, they will report indignation. Legitimacy and stability also represent two of the three characteristics of intergroup relationships proposed by social identity theorists to be relevant to collective action. As out-lined by Tajfel (1982), disadvantaged group members are most likely to pursue collective action when they believe that group boundaries are impermeable and relationships between the advantaged and dis-advantaged groups are unstable and illegitimate. An integration of these two perspectives with (individual) RD models indicates at least three appraisals; legitimacy, stability, and responsibility for the deprivation, that in conjunction with disadvantageous intergroup comparisons create group-based anger and support for collective action.

RD models suggest that legitimacy judgments or appraisals shape emotional reactions indirectly (Smith & Kessler, 2003). Because a disadvantage that is produced by a legitimate process is unlikely to be viewed as unfair, people who believe negative discrepancies to be justified or legitimate should not be angry, even though they recognize their disadvantage (Ellemers, 2002; Folger, 1987). However, people who believe that the disadvantage is the product of an illegitimate process should feel angry and frustrated (van Zomeren et al., 2004). Most important, appraisals of legitimacy appear to move people from a focus on those who have what they desire and feelings of envy to a focus on how outcomes are distributed and resentment. Our argument parallels the social identity proposal that judgments of illegitimacy will move people from individual normative reactions (designed to improve one's own position and acceptable within the larger system) to collective non-normative reactions (designed to improve the group's position and unacceptable within the larger system; see Wright et al., 1990a; Wright & Tropp, 2002).

A second appraisal common to almost all RD models is the perceived stability of the deprivation (Smith & Kessler, 2003). When people see little possibility for change, they are more likely to feel depressed rather than angry. In contrast, if circumstances might change, they will feel angry (Folger, 1987; Mummendey et al., 1999). Stability, as we define it, represents the possibility of change even if people do nothing (see Folger, 1987; Mummendey et al., 1999). This definition captures feasibility (that is, the perceived likelihood that people believe they might get what they feel they deserve in the future, Crosby, 1976; Runciman, 1966) or the likelihood of ameliora-tion (Folger, 1987). Interestingly, laboratory participants' ratings of future success and their feelings of frustration and resentment separately predicted their behavioral reactions to deprivation (Wright, Taylor, & Moghaddam, 1990b). Similarly, university faculty members' ratings of situation stability predicted sadness but not anger or protest (Smith et al., 2006).

Judgments of responsibility for negative events are central appraisal dimensions for most conceptualizations of anger (Averill, 1983; Weiner, 1995), but are included in only two models of (individual) RD (Crosby, 1976; Walker, Wong, & Kretzschmar, 2002). However, it is difficult to see how collective protest could occur without people attributing responsibility for their deprivation to dominant outgroups and/or systems. Appraisals of responsibility may shape the emotional experience in two ways. First, it may move the focus from the self to another person, group, or system. If people view themselves or the situation (e.g., bad luck, fate) as responsible for a negative outcome, they report sadness and depression (Frijda, 1993; Roseman et al., 1990; Weiner, 1995). However, if they attribute a negative event to discrimination by another person or group, they are angry (Major et al., 2002). Attributions of intention and blame might be even more important than attributions of responsibility. Although attributions of responsibility and blame often are highly correlated, if people do not believe that the responsible agent intended the harm, they are less likely to blame him or her (Tyler, Boeckmann, Smith, & Huo, 1997). Indeed, within the retributive justice research tradition, blame is more closely associated with moral outrage than is responsibility.

Notice that in this approach, we treat appraisals of responsibility and intention independently of disadvantageous comparisons. Often, however, people view the comparison group as the agent responsible for the deprivation (Glick, 2002). Not only did Germans view Jews as more privileged, they viewed them as responsible for their own deprivation (Glick, 2002). However, if we distinguish comparison groups from agents of deprivation, it enables us to view group deprivation as part of a larger power struggle in which other groups must choose to side with or against their group (Simon & Klandermans, 2001). The important question is *when* will people shift their focus from the outcomes they deserved (and someone else has) to the system that produced the inequities.

Action

Support for, or participation in, collective action is just one of many possible responses to feeling deprived (Crosby, 1976; Folger, 1987;

Wright et al., 1990a). Importantly, direct confrontations of injustice are risky and rare (Tyler et al., 1997). When people challenge injustice, they risk adopting the role of "victim," "whistle-blower" and any associated negative stereotypes, and they often must confront a more powerful authority (Leach et al., 2002; Tyler et al., 1997). Therefore, it is not surprising that inaction (and verification of one's interpretation) is the most common response to injustice (Tyler et al., 1997).

Nor is it surprising, given the risks involved in confrontation of injustice, that most models of reactions to injustice include some sort of cost–benefit analysis (Tyler et al., 1997). As documented by Martin (1986), if people feel resources are available to support political action, they are more likely to participate—regardless of how deprived they feel. In fact, for many years, resource mobilization theory (Klandermans, 1997) was sociologists' preferred explanation for collective protest. More recently, van Zomeren and colleagues (2004) proposed a dual pathway model for understanding coping with disadvantage. One path, presented as emotion-based coping, describes collective protest as the product of group-based anger and perceptions of injustice. The other path, presented as problem-based coping, describes collective protest as the product of perceived group efficacy (defined as the group's ability to change the situation). Although some research suggests that perceived efficacy influences anger (Frijda, 1993; Roseman et al., 1990), more recent research suggests that efficacy and cost–benefit analysis independently contribute to collective action. Finally, some researchers (Azzi, 1998; Van Zomeren et al., 2004) suggest that it is not just group efficacy that matters, but participative efficacy—the belief that without one's participation, collective success is unlikely. The key question, then, is whether people feel that they can do something to change the situation, as opposed to feeling that the situation will improve without intervention.

Of course, a full understanding of collective action requires us to shift our focus from the willingness to act to actual participation. This requires a closer consideration of differences among types of collective action. For example, political scientists distinguish between conventional (normative) and unconventional (non-normative) behavior (Herring, 1989; Walker et al., 2002). Conventional action refers to such institutionalized activities as writing letters to public officials, participating in legal demonstrations and rallies, and signing petitions. Unconventional action includes such illegal or violent activities as damaging property and blocking roads illegally. Not only might legitimacy determine whether people react to undeserved negative outcomes with anger, sadness, or fear, it might constrain the behavioral reaction of people who are upset (Drury & Reicher, 2005). It is quite possible that people can view the process that produced the inequity as illegitimate and simultaneously view any collective protest against the inequity as also illegitimate. In other words, a preference for nonnormative behavior might require more than the perception that the intergroup relationships are illegitimate.

It is tempting to treat the experience of RD as a discrete event and, depending upon the situation and their personal beliefs, people chose among a repertoire of possible responses. But as epidemiological research (Ostrove, Adler, Kuppermann, & Washington, 2000; see Adler & Snibbe, 2003) eloquently documents, the effects of deprivation and injustices often are cumulative. In fact, health researchers describe a "weathering effect" in which the effects of social inequality on health increase as people get older (Geronimus, Hicken, & Keene, 2006). Although recent models of collective action (Glick, 2002; Moghaddam, 2005) focus on the extent to which particular injustices or deprivation are shared, it seems equally important to consider the cumulative effects of deprivation, bringing us back to RD theorists' early interest in patterns of deprivation over time (see Davies, 1962; Gurr, 1970). The possible contribution of cumulative injustice reminds us that what looks like inaction can range from "passive acceptance of the ingroup's low status position, to efforts to revise one's understanding of the ingroup's status, to hopeful patience that the ingroup's situation will soon improve, to angry resignation" (Wright & Tropp, 2002, p. 204).

In one of the few developmental approaches to cumulative injustice, Taylor and Moghaddam (1994) propose that once people recognize a persistent ingroup disadvantage, they evaluate how easy it is to move to a different, more advantaged group. Even if the possibility of movement is incredibly small (e.g., a few tokens can move up the ladder), people tend to adopt individual mobility beliefs, distance themselves from their group, and focus on individual solutions (Wright & Tropp, 2002). If movement is impossible (e.g., due to psychological connections to the disadvantaged group or structural barriers), people will adopt social change beliefs centered on group-based entitlements and discrimination. Although researchers have identified victims' perceptions of the pervasiveness and stability of their disadvantage as important factors for predicting their reactions (Branscombe et al., 1999; Foster & Tsarfati, 2005; Major et al., 2002), these types of developmental approaches to cumulative injustices are rare (Moghaddam's (2005) staircase to terrorism is an exception).

Causal Model

Relative deprivation models imply a causal argument in which cognitive appraisals lead to different emotional reactions which, in turn, lead to different action tendencies. Although evidence supports some of these causal relationships (van Zomeren et al., 2004), there is also evidence for the opposite causal paths. For example, priming anger shapes attributions of fairness, legitimacy, and responsibility (Goldberg, Lerner, & Tetlock, 1999; Lerner & Keltner, 2001).

Many RD models also assume that greater identification with one's disadvantaged group will increase one's sensitivity to GRD (Smith & Ortiz, 2002). Again, some evidence supports this assumption (Smith & Leach, 2004; Tropp & Wright, 1999), but other research does not (Zagefka & Brown, 2006). We think that these patterns may depend upon the content of the collective representations associated with particular group memberships. We imagine that politicized collective identification (Kelly & Breinlinger, 1996; Simon & Klandermans, 2001) will promote intergroup comparisons whereas non-politicized collective identities will not; this distinction parallels evidence that an interest in equity and justice promotes intergroup comparisons whereas an interest in self-enhancement does not (Zagefka & Brown, 2006).

However, even if identification with the deprived group does not increase frequency or sensitivity to intergroup comparisons, group identification does shape people's reactions. In comparison to low identifiers, high identifiers are: (1) less likely to try to escape a disadvantaged group even if they can (Ellemers, 2002); (2) less sensitive to differences in group efficacy (van Zomeren et al., 2004); and (3) more likely to use anger strategically (van Zomeren et al., 2004). Further, people who endorse more politicized collective identities (in which they view their group as engaged in a power struggle with another group), or who identify as activists, are much more likely to participate in collective protest (Simon & Klandermans, 2001).

Finally, we can question whether disadvantaged group comparisons and associated anger lead to collective protest or whether collective protest increases the likelihood of these experiences. Above, we alluded to the rhetorical role of unions and social movements in framing inequities as group based. More recently, van Zomeren, Spears and Leach (2006) show how highly identified members of disadvantaged groups will use anger to increase ingroup support for collective challenge. Also, if feelings of ingroup pride, happiness and anger toward an outgroup increase ingroup identification (Kessler &

Hollbach, 2005), it seems plausible that participation in collective action will motivate further protest. Social movement participation can increase feelings of empowerment, pride in one's group, and interpersonal connections to others as well as offer more arguments to support collective challenges to injustice (Drury & Reicher, 2005). Similarly, Glick (2002) draws upon classic cognitive dissonance research to suggest how initial commitment to collective action can lead to further and more difficult action.

Conclusions

Group-based interpretations of deprivation are neither better nor worse than individual-based interpretations. Although the former might motivate collective challenges to the system, the later might motivate personal effort. But in contrast to early formulations of RD, the road from group deprivation to anger to collective protest appears to be long and rocky. Group deprivation must combine with several different situational appraisals to produce anger, and only under some circumstances, does anger lead to collective action. Most importantly, not all deprivation consequences are "seen." Disadvantageous social comparisons appear to be closely linked to differences in *physical* health. Further, collective action is not the only way to undermine a system (individual retaliation, lack of commitment and professional withdrawal all can be effective). Collective action is rare, risky and often limited to a very small percentage of the people who might be mobilized to participate (Klandermans, 1997). Just because we do not see large and constant forms of protest does not mean people do not feel group deprived and angry. In fact, the absence of collective challenge may mask the cumulative and frustrating consequences of both individual and group relative deprivation.

References

Adler, N. E., & Snibbe, A. C. (2003). The role of psychosocial processes in explaining the gradient between socioeconomic status and health. *Current Directions in Psychological Science, 12*, 119–123.

Averill, J. R. (1983). Studies on anger and aggression: Implications for theories of emotion. *American Psychologist, 38*, 1145–1160.

Azzi, A. (1998). From competitive interests, perceived injustice, and identity needs to collective action: Psychological mechanisms in ethnic nationalism.

In C. Dandeker (Ed.), *Nationalism and violence* (pp. 73–138). New Brunswick, NJ: Transaction.

Branscombe, N. R., Schmitt, M. T., & Harvey, R. D. (1999). Perceiving pervasive discrimination among African Americans: Implications for group identification and well-being. *Journal of Personality and Social Psychology*, *77*, 135–145.

Crocker, J., Major, B., & Steele, C. (1998). Social Stigma. In D. Gilbert, S. T. Fiske, and G. Lindzey (Eds.), *Handbook of social psychology* (4th ed.) (pp. 504–553). New York: McGraw Hill.

Crosby, F. (1976). A model of egotistical deprivation. *Psychological Review*, *83*, 85–113.

Davies, J. (1962). Toward a theory of revolution. *American Sociological Review*, *27*, 5–18.

Davis, J. A. (1959). A formal interpretation of the theory of relative deprivation. *Sociometry*, *22*, 280–296.

Drury, J., & Reicher, S. (2005). Explaining enduring empowerment: A comparative study of collective action and psychological outcomes. *European Journal of Social Psychology*, *25*, 25–58.

Ellemers, N. (2002). Social identity and relative deprivation. In I. Walker & H. J. Smith (Eds.), *Relative deprivation: Specification, development and integration* (pp. 239–264). New York: Cambridge University Press.

Folger, R. (1987). Reformulating the preconditions of resentments: A referent cognitions model. In J. Masters & W. Smith (Eds.), *Social Comparison, Social Justice and Relative Deprivation* (pp. 76–85). Hillsdale, NJ: Erlbaum.

Foster, M. D., & Matheson, K. (1995). Double relative deprivation: Combining the personal and political. *Personality and Social Psychology Bulletin*, *21*, 1167–1177.

Foster, M. D., & Tsarfati, E. M. (2005). The effects of meritocracy beliefs on women's well-being after first-time gender discrimination. *Personality and Social Psychology Bulletin*, *31*, 1730–1738.

Frijda, N. H. (1993). The place of appraisal in emotion. *Cognition and Emotion*, *7*, 357–387.

Gartrell, C. D. (2002). The embeddedness of social comparison. In I. Walker & H. J. Smith (Eds.), *Relative deprivation: Specification, development and integration* (pp. 164–184). New York: Cambridge University Press.

Geronimus, A. T., Hicken, M., & Keene, D. (2006). "Weathering" and age patterns of allostatic load scores among Blacks and Whites in the United States. *American Journal of Public Health*, *96*, 826–833.

Glick, P. (2002). Sacrificial lambs dressed in wolves' clothing: Envious prejudice, ideology and the scapegoating of Jews. In L. S. Newman & R. Erber (Eds.), *Understanding genocide: The social psychology of the Holocaust* (pp. 113–142). Oxford: Oxford University Press.

Goldberg, J. H., Lerner, J. S., & Tetlock, P. E. (1999). Rage and reason: The psychology of the intuitive prosecutor. *European Journal of Social Psychology, 29,* 781–795.

Gurr, T. (1970). *Why men rebel.* Princeton, NJ: Princeton University Press.

Herring, C. (1989). Acquiescence or activism? Political behavior among the politically alienated. *Political Psychology, 10,* 135–153.

Kelly, C., & Breinlinger, S. (1996). *The social psychology of collective action.* London: Taylor and Francis.

Kessler, T., & Hollbach, S. (2005). Group-based emotions as determinants of ingroup identification. *Journal of Experimental Social Psychology, 41,* 677–685.

Klandermans, B. (1997). *Principles of movement participation.* Oxford: Blackwell.

Leach, C. W., Iyer, A., & Pedersen, A. (2007). Angry opposition to government redress: When the structurally advantaged perceive themselves as relatively deprived. *British Journal of Social Psychology, 46,* 191–204.

Leach, C. W., & Smith, H. J. (2006). By whose standard? The affective implications of ethnic minorities' comparisons to ethnic minority and majority references. *European Journal of Social Psychology, 36,* 747–760.

Leach, C. W., Snider, N., & Iyer, A. (2002). "Poisoning the consciences of the fortunate": The experience of relative advantage and support for social equality. In I. Walker & H. J. Smith (Eds.), *Relative deprivation: Specification, development and integration* (pp. 136–163). New York: Cambridge University Press.

Lerner, J. S., & Keltner, D. (2001). Fear, anger, and risk. *Journal of Personality and Social Psychology, 81,* 146–159.

Major, B., Quinton, W. J., & McCoy, S. K. (2002). Antecedents and consequences of attributions to discrimination: Theoretical and empirical advances. *Advances in Experimental Social Psychology, 34,* 251–330.

Martin, J. (1986). The psychology of injustice. In J. Olson, C. P. Herman, and M. Zanna (Eds.), *Relative deprivation and social comparison: The Ontario Symposium* (Vol. 4) (pp. 217–242). Hillsdale, NJ: Lawrence Erlbaum.

Moghaddam, F. M. (2005). The staircase to terrorism: A psychological exploration. *American Psychologist, 60,* 161–169.

Mummendey, A., Kessler, T., Klink, A., & Mielke, R. (1999). Strategies to cope with negative social identity: Predictions by social identity theory and relative deprivation theory. *Journal of Personality and Social Psychology, 76,* 229–245.

Ostrove, J. M., Adler, N. E., Kuppermann, M., & Washington, A. E. (2000). Objective and subjective assessment of socioeconomic status and their relationship to self-rated health in an ethnically diverse sample of pregnant women. *Health Psychology, 19,* 613–619.

Pettigrew, T. F. (1967). Social evaluation theory: Convergences and applications. In D. Levine (Ed.), *Nebraska Symposium on Motivation* (Vol. 15) (pp. 241–311). Lincoln, NE: University of Nebraska Press.

Pettigrew, T. F. (1978). Three issues in ethnicity: Boundaries, deprivations and perceptions. In J. M. Yinger & S. J. Cutler (Eds.), *Major social issues* (pp. 25–49). New York: Free Press.

Pettigrew, T. F. (2002). Summing up: Relative deprivation as a key social psychology concept. In I. Walker, I. & H. J. Smith (Eds.), *Relative deprivation: Specification, development and integration* (pp. 351–373). New York: Cambridge University Press.

Roseman, I. J., Spindel, M. S., & Jose, P. E. (1990). Appraisals of emotion-eliciting events: Testing a theory of discrete emotions. *Journal of Personality and Social Psychology, 59*, 899–915.

Rozin, P., Lowery, L., & Imada, S. (1999). The CAD triad hypothesis: A mapping between three moral emotions (contempt, anger, disgust) and three moral codes (community, autonomy, divinity). *Journal of Personality and Social Psychology, 76*, 574–586.

Runciman, W. G. (1966). *Relative deprivation and social justice: A study of attitudes to social inequality in twentieth-century England.* Berkeley, CA: University of California Press.

Schmitt, M. (2006). *Longitudinal effects of fraternal deprivation and individual life quality on well-being and protest.* Unpublished manuscript, University of Koblenz-Landau.

Simon, B., & Klandermans, B. (2001). Politicized collective identity: A social psychological analysis. *American Psychologist, 56*, 319–331.

Smith, H. J., Cronin, T., & Kessler, T. (2006). *Anger, fear or sadness: Faculty members' emotional reactions to group relative deprivation.* Unpublished manuscript, Sonoma State University.

Smith, H. J., & Kessler, T. (2003). Group-based emotions and intergroup behavior: The case of relative deprivation. In L. Z. Tiedens & C. W. Leach (Eds.), *The social life of emotions* (pp. 43–63). New York: Cambridge University Press.

Smith, H. J., & Leach, C. W. (2004). Group membership and everyday social comparison experiences. *European Journal of Social Psychology, 34*, 297–308.

Smith, H. J., & Ortiz, D. J. (2002). Is it just me?: The different consequences of personal and group relative deprivation. In I. Walker & H. J. Smith (Eds.), *Relative deprivation: Specification, development and integration* (pp. 91–115). New York: Cambridge University Press.

Smith, H. J., Spears, R., & Oyen, M. (1994). People like us: The influence of personal deprivation and salience of group membership on justice evaluations. *Journal of Experimental Social Psychology, 30*, 277–299.

Stouffer, S. A., Suchman, E. A., DeVinney, L. C., Starr, S. A., & Williams, R. M. (1949). *The American soldier: Adjustment to army life* (Vol. 1). Princeton, NJ: Princeton University Press.

Tajfel, H. (1982). *Social identity and intergroup relations.* Cambridge: Cambridge University Press.

Taylor, D. M., & Moghaddam, F. M. (1994). *Theories of intergroup relations: International social psychological perspectives* (2nd ed.). Westport, CT: Praeger Publishers.

Taylor, S. E. (2002). *Health psychology* (5th ed.). New York: McGraw Hill.

Tougas, F., & Beaton, A. M. (2002). Personal and group relative deprivation: Connecting the I to the We. In I. Walker & H. J. Smith (Eds.), *Relative deprivation: Specification, development, and integration* (pp. 119–135). New York: Cambridge University Press.

Tougas, F., Rinfret, N., Beaton, A. M., & de la Sablonnière, R. (2005). Policewomen acting in self-defense: Can psychological disengagement protect self-esteem from the negative outcome of relative deprivation? *Journal of Personality and Social Psychology, 88,* 790–800.

Tropp, L. R., & Wright, S. C. (1999). Ingroup identification and relative deprivation: An examination across multiple social comparisons. *European Journal of Social Psychology, 29,* 707–724.

Tyler, T. R., Boeckmann, R. J., Smith, H. J., & Huo, Y. J. (1997). *Social justice in a diverse society.* Denver, CO: Westview Press.

van Zomeren, M., & Lodewijkx, H. F. M. (2005). Motivated responses to "senseless" violence: Explaining emotional and behavioural responses through person and position identification. *European Journal of Social Psychology, 35,* 755–766.

van Zomeren, M., Spears, R., Fischer, A. H., & Leach, C. W. (2004). Put your money where you mouth is! Explaining collective action tendencies through group-based anger and group efficacy. *Journal of Personality and Social Psychology, 87,* 649–664.

van Zomeren, M., Spears, R., & Leach, C. W. (2006). *The power of the audience: Strategic expression of group-based anger and action readiness.* Manuscript submitted for publication.

Vanneman, R. D., & Pettigrew, T. F. (1972). Race and relative deprivation in the urban United States. *Race, 13,* 461–485.

Walker, I., & Mann, L. (1987). Unemployment, relative deprivation and social protest. *Personality and Social Psychology Bulletin, 13,* 275–283.

Walker, I., & Smith, H. J. (Eds.) (2002). *Relative deprivation: Specification, development and integration.* New York: Cambridge University Press.

Walker, I., Wong, N. K., & Kretzschmar, K. (2002). Relative deprivation and attribution: From grievance to action. In I. Walker & H. J. Smith (Eds.), *Relative deprivation: Specification, development and integration* (pp. 288–312). New York: Cambridge University Press.

Wenzel, M. (2004). A social categorisation approach to distributive justice. *European Review of Social Psychology, 15,* 219–257.

Weiner, B. (1995). Inferences of responsibility and social motivation. In M. P. Zanna (Ed.), *Advances in Experimental Social Psychology, 27,* 1–47.

Wright, S. C., & Tropp, L. R. (2002). Collective action in response to disadvantage. In I. Walker, & H. J. Smith (Eds.), *Relative deprivation:*

Specification, development and integration (pp. 200–238). New York: Cambridge University Press.

Wright, S. C., Taylor, D. M., & Moghaddam, F. M. (1990a). Responding to membership in a disadvantaged group: From acceptance to collective protest. *Journal of Personality and Social Psychology, 58,* 994–1003.

Wright, S. C., Taylor, D. M., & Moghaddam, F. M. (1990b). The relationships of perceptions and emotions to behavior in the face of collective inequality. *Social Justice Research, 4,* 229–250.

Zagefka, H., & Brown, R. (2006). Predicting comparison choices in intergroup settings: A new look. In S. Guimond (Ed.), *Social comparison and social psychology: Understanding cognition, intergroup relations and culture* (pp. 99–126). Cambridge UK: Cambridge University Press.

16

Bridging Individual and Social Change in International Conflict

Contextual Social Psychology in Action

Herbert C. Kelman

I first met Thomas Pettigrew nearly 50 years ago. We were introduced to each other by Gordon Allport at a conference on race relations in Washington. As I recall, Allport said words to the effect: "You fellows should get to know each other." He referred in part to the fact that Tom and I were soon to become colleagues in the Department of Social Relations at Harvard University. But I am sure he also sensed that, despite the differences in our personal backgrounds, we shared fundamental interests and values. He was of course right. Before the conference was over, we had bonded and we have been close professional colleagues and personal friends ever since. I can safely say that we have always been on the same side of the issue—whether it involved academic, national, or international politics.

Pettigrew and I—partly through our many conversations during those early years at Harvard—have evolved a common view (indeed, a common vision) of social psychology. He has called this approach to the discipline *contextual social psychology* (Pettigrew, 1991), and I have readily signed on to this designation. Contextual social psychology analyzes the actions and interactions of individuals in their societal and organizational context. This perspective on social psychology, at least in Pettigrew's and my own practice, has several corollaries: It views social psychology as an interdisciplinary endeavor and, indeed, anchors the field in its two parent disciplines, psychology and sociology, and bridges their respective levels of analysis; it relies on a multiplicity of methods; it engages in social psychology as a cross-cultural, international enterprise; it places applied research and practice based on social-psychological principles at the center of the agenda, along with basic and theory-driven research; it gives special emphasis to applications of research to social issues and to its relevance to social policy and social movements; and it is sensitive to the social and ethical consequences of the processes and products of our research.

Pettigrew and I co-authored one early article (Kelman & Pettigrew, 1959)—a polemical piece criticizing the false dichotomy between psychological and sociological approaches to the study of prejudice. Otherwise, each of us went in his own direction, with Pettigrew's work focusing on race relations and mine increasingly on international relations, though we shared an abiding interest in ethnic conflict. We stayed in touch with each other's work throughout. Pettigrew's research and advocacy in race relations were of great interest to me, in view of my active involvement in the early decades of the American civil rights movement, and I closely followed his theoretical writings on such issues as relative deprivation and the contact hypothesis. He, in turn, closely followed my early work on processes of social influence and my later work on conflict resolution in the Middle East. He gave a special vote of confidence to my efforts in that field when he encouraged his son, Mark, who was an undergraduate at Harvard University at the time, to take my graduate seminar on "International Conflict: Social-Psychological Approaches." This course included a problem-solving workshop on the Israeli–Palestinian conflict, in which the students participated as apprentice members of the third party. Mark has since gone on, by the way, to complete his doctoral work in Middle Eastern Studies and to teach in that field.

The problem-solving workshops in conflict resolution, which are very much in the spirit of contextual social psychology, are the topic of this chapter in honor of Tom Pettigrew. The chapter is based on a talk I presented at the 2003 meeting of the Society of Experimental Social Psychology—a talk for which Tom Pettigrew, along with Marilynn Brewer, served as discussants.

Interactive Problem Solving

Since the early 1970s, my colleagues and I have been developing and applying an unofficial, academically based, third-party approach to the resolution of international and intercommunal conflicts. The work derives from the pioneering efforts of John Burton (1969, 1979; see also Kelman, 1972), but our practice—and our theory of practice—are explicitly anchored in social-psychological principles. I have used the term *interactive problem solving* (Kelman, 1986, 1998a, 2002) to describe the approach, which finds its fullest (though not its sole) expression in problem-solving workshops. My students and associates have applied the approach, or variants of it, to a number of protracted conflicts between identity groups around the world. My own primary focus over the years has been on the Israeli–Palestinian conflict (Kelman, 1979, 1995, 1997, 1998b, 2005a).

The practice of interactive problem solving is informed by a set of social-psychological assumptions about the nature of international conflict and conflict resolution, which enter into our formulation of the structure, the process, and the content of problem-solving workshops. What makes interactive problem solving quintessentially social-psychological in its orientation is its goal of promoting change in individuals—through face-to-face interaction in small groups—as a vehicle for change in larger social systems: in the national policies and the political cultures that maintain the conflict system. In other words, the *microprocess*, best exemplified by problem-solving workshops, is intended to produce changes in the *macroprocess* of conflict resolution, including the official negotiations and the peace process as a whole.

The microprocess relates to the macroprocess in two ways. First and foremost, it provides inputs into the larger process. The challenge here is to identify the appropriate points of entry: those points in the larger process where contributions from problem-solving workshops, and from a social-psychological analysis, can be particularly useful. Second, the microprocess can serve as a metaphor for what happens—or, at least in my view, ought to happen—at the macrolevel. Let me comment briefly on interactive problem solving as a metaphor for the macroprocess, before turning to a description of the microprocess of problem-solving workshops and a discussion of their potential impact on the macroprocess—which is the central theme of this chapter.

The three components of the term interactive problem solving suggest what, I propose, happens or ought to happen in the larger process. First, the conflict needs to be treated as a *problem* shared by the parties—a problem in their relationship, which has become completely competitive, to the point that each, in pursuit of its own needs and interests, threatens and undermines the other's needs and interests and seeks to destroy the other. Second, the conflict resolution process needs to search for a *solution* to the problem: one that addresses the underlying causes of the conflict, i.e., the unfulfilled or threatened needs of both parties, particularly their needs for security, identity, autonomy, justice, and recognition, and that ultimately leads to a transformation of their relationship. Finally, the term *interactive* refers to the proposition that the task of solving the problem presented by the conflict is best achieved through direct interaction, in which the parties are able to share their differing perspectives and learn how to influence each other by way of responsiveness to the other's needs and concerns.

This view of the macroprocess of conflict resolution suggests some of the key components of the process, which must take place somewhere in the larger system. The parties must undertake efforts: (1) *to identify and analyze the problem*, with a focus on each side's fundamental needs and fears as seen within its own perspective, and on the escalatory dynamics of conflict interactions; (2) *to engage in joint shaping of ideas for a mutually acceptable solution*, i.e., a process of "prenegotiation" that includes exploration of options, reframing of issues to make them more conducive to negotiation, and generation of creative ideas for a constructive and durable resolution of the conflict; (3) *to influence each other by being responsive to the other's needs and fears*, relying on the use of positive incentives, including mutual reassurance that it is safe to enter into negotiations and mutual enticement through the promise of attractive gains; and (4) *to help create a supportive political environment for negotiations*, marked by a sense of mutual reassurance, which depends on each side's conviction that the other is sincere in its commitment to negotiating a peaceful solution, and by a sense of possibility—the sense that, even though negotiations may be difficult and risky, it is possible to find a mutually satisfactory solution.

Problem-solving workshops and related activities seek to provide special opportunities for these kinds of processes to occur. They represent a microprocess that is specifically designed to insert into the macroprocess—in a modest but systematic way—the components of conflict resolution that I have outlined. One can think of problem-solving workshops as workshops in the literal sense of the term, like a carpenter's or an artisan's workshop: a specially constructed space, in which the parties can engage in a process of exploration, observation, and analysis, and in which they can create new products for export, as it were. The products in this case take the form of new ideas and insights that can then be fed into the political debate and the decision-making process within the two societies.

My conception of the problem-solving workshop, incidentally, also reflects my experience as an experimental social psychologist. Like a social-psychological experiment, the workshop creates a microcosm and a working model of the real world in a relatively isolated, self-contained, and controlled laboratory setting, in which some of the forces that operate in the larger system (or the real world) can be activated, observed, and analyzed. Workshops—unlike experiments—are not simulations of the real world: They involve real members of the conflicting parties engaged in a very real and often consequential interaction around the issues in conflict—but in a setting that makes joint exploration and analysis possible. Good conflict resolution practitioners, like good experimenters, know that the microcosm they have constructed is not the real world and that the contribution of their work to understanding and changing the real world ultimately depends on systematic attention to how the products of the laboratory interaction are generalized and transferred to the larger system.

Workshops are not negotiating sessions. They are not intended to substitute for negotiations or to bypass negotiations in any way. Negotiations can be carried out only by officials who are authorized to conclude binding agreements, and workshops, by definition, are unofficial and non-binding. But it is precisely their non-binding character that represents their unique strength. They provide an opportunity for the kind of exploratory interaction that is very difficult to achieve in the context of official negotiations. While workshops are not negotiations, they are an integral part of the larger negotiation process, relevant at all stages of the process: the pre-negotiation stage, where they contribute to helping the parties move toward the negotiation table; alongside of negotiations, where they can help to frame issues that are not yet on the table in ways that are conducive to successful negotiation; in the inevitable periods of setback, stalemate, or breakdown of negotiation, where they can contribute to creating momentum and reviving the sense of possibility; and, finally, at the postnegotiation stage, where they can contribute to resolving problems of implementation of the negotiated agreements, as well as to the postconflict process of peace building and reconciliation and to transforming the relationship between the former enemies.

Israeli–Palestinian Workshops

Our Israeli–Palestinian workshops until 1991 were all obviously in the prenegotiation phase. Moreover, until 1990, all of our workshops were one-time, self-contained events, usually consisting of separate pre-workshop sessions (of 4–5 hours) for each party and two-and-a-half days (often over a weekend) of joint meetings. Some of the individual participants in these workshops took part in more than one such event, but each group as a whole met only for this one occasion. It was not until 1990 that Nadim Rouhana and I organized our first continuing workshop: a group of influential Israelis and Palestinians who participated in a series of meetings over a three-year-period (Rouhana & Kelman, 1994).

To give some indication of what happens at workshops and of the principles that govern them, I briefly describe a typical one-time workshop between Israelis and Palestinians. There are, understandably, important differences between one-time and continuing workshops. There is also considerable variation among one-time workshops, depending on the nature of the participants, the occasion for convening them, the specific purposes, the setting, and other considerations. But, despite such variations, there is a set of key principles that apply throughout and that can be gleaned from the description of an ideal-type one-time workshop.

The typical workshop participants are politically involved and, in many cases, politically influential members of their communities. However, with occasional exceptions, they have not been current officials. Participants have included parliamentarians, leading figures in political parties or movements, former military officers or government officials, and journalists or editors specializing in the Middle East. Many of the participants have been academics who are important analysts of the conflict for their societies and some of whom have served in advisory, official, or diplomatic positions and are likely to do so again in the future. We look for participants who are part of the mainstream of their societies and close to the center of the political spectrum. But they have to be interested in exploring the possibilities of a negotiated solution and willing to sit with members of the other society as equals.

The number of participants has varied; our workshops generally include three to six members of each party, as well as a third party of two to four members. On several occasions, we have arranged one-on-one meetings between high-level participants—one Israeli and one Palestinian—who preferred to meet in complete privacy. We have also organized a series of 15 workshops over the years in conjunction with my graduate seminar on international conflict, in which the size of the third party was much larger than usual, because the seminar participants were integrated into the third party in a way that both preserved the integrity of the process and gave the students the opportunity to gain first-hand experience with the model.

The academic setting is an important feature of our approach. It has the advantage of providing an unofficial, private, non-binding context, with its own set of norms to support a type of interaction that departs from the norms that generally govern interactions between conflicting parties. The countervailing norms of our setting both free and require participants to interact in a way that deviates from the conflict norms: The fact that the discussions are noncommittal—"just academic"—makes it relatively safe to do so; the fact that the third party "owns" the setting gives us some authority to prescribe the nature of the interaction.

The third party in our model plays a strictly facilitative role. We do not propose solutions, nor do we participate in the substantive discussions. We do not give advice, take sides, evaluate the ideas presented, or arbitrate between different interpretations of historical facts and international law. Our task is to create the conditions that allow ideas for resolving the conflict to emerge out of the interaction between the parties themselves. Nevertheless, the role of the third party is important. We select and brief the participants, set and enforce the ground rules, and propose the main lines of the agenda. We serve as a repository of trust for the parties who, by definition, do not trust each other: They feel safe to come to the workshop because they trust the third party and rely on it to make sure that confidentiality is maintained and their interests are protected. Finally, the third party moderates the discussion and makes a variety of interventions: content observations, which often take the form of summarizing, highlighting, asking for clarification, or pointing to similarities and differences between the parties; process observations, which suggest how interactions within the group may reflect the dynamics of the conflict between the two societies; and occasional theoretical observations, which offer concepts that might be useful in clarifying the issues under discussion.

Workshop Ground Rules and Agenda

The central ground rule of problem-solving workshops is the principle of *privacy and confidentiality*, which stipulates that whatever is said in the course of a workshop cannot be cited for attribution outside of the workshop setting by any participant, including the third party. To support this ground rule, the typical workshop has no audience, no publicity, and no formal record. To ensure privacy, we have no observers in our workshops; the only way our students were able to observe the process was by being integrated into the third party and accepting the discipline of the third party. To ensure confidentiality, we do not tape workshop sessions, which leaves us only the written notes as our source of data for discourse analysis and other types of research.

In the early years of our Israeli–Palestinian work, confidentiality was particularly important for the protection of our participants, because merely meeting with the other side exposed them to political and, at times, legal or physical risks. It is equally important, however, for the protection of the process we are trying to promote. It enables participants to engage in the kind of interaction that workshops require, as spelled out in three ground rules governing the interaction process: Participants are asked to *focus on each other*, rather than on their constituencies, on an audience, on third parties, or on the record—to listen to the other, with the aim of understanding the other's perspective, and to address the other, with the aim of making their own perspective understood; to *engage in a discourse that is analytical* rather than polemical in nature, enabling them to gain an understanding of each other's needs, fears, concerns, priorities, and constraints, and to develop insight into the escalatory dynamics of the conflict; and to interact in a way that increasingly takes on a *problem-solving mode*, in contrast to the adversarial mode that usually characterizes conflict interactions—to treat the conflict as a shared problem, requiring joint efforts to find a mutually satisfactory solution, rather than try to determine who is right and who is wrong on the basis of historical or legal argumentation.

Three additional ground rules govern the interaction. First, in a workshop, unlike a negotiating session, there is *no expectation that participants will reach an agreement*. If they come away with a better understanding of the other side's perspective, of their own priorities, and of the dynamics of the conflict, the workshop will have fulfilled its purpose. It should be noted, however, that in some of our workshops, participants—either by their own choice or by initial design—worked on the production of joint documents. A Joint Working Group on Israeli–Palestinian Relations that I co-chaired with Nadim Rouhana between 1994 and 1999 was specifically designed to produce joint concept papers on issues in the permanent-status negotiations (Kelman, 1998b). Second, despite important asymmetries between the parties, which must be taken into account in the workshop discussions, there is full *equality in the workshop setting* in the sense that each party has the same right to serious consideration of its needs, fears, and concerns in the search for a mutually satisfactory solution. Finally, the third party performs a *facilitative role*, as described above.

One of the tasks of the third party is to set the agenda for the discussion. In some cases, a workshop may be devoted to a specific substantive theme, as was the case in a 2002 workshop for Israeli and Palestinian journalists, which focused on the role of the media in the escalation and de-escalation of the conflict. However, in the typical one-time workshop, the agenda is relatively open and unstructured, as far as the substantive issues under discussion are concerned. But the way in which these issues are approached and the order of discussion are structured so as to facilitate the kind of discourse that the ground rules seek to encourage. After personal introductions around the table, a review of purposes, procedures, and ground rules, and an opportunity for the participants to ask questions about these, we generally proceed with a five-part agenda.

The first discussion session is devoted to an *exchange of information* between the two sides, which serves primarily to break the ice and to set the tone for the kind of discourse we hope to generate. Each party is asked to talk about the situation on the ground and the current mood in its own community, about the issues in the conflict as seen in that community, about the spectrum of views on the conflict and its resolution, and about members' own positions within that spectrum. This exchange provides a shared base of information and sets a precedent for the two sides to deal with each other as mutual resources, rather than solely as combatants.

The core agenda of the workshop begins with a *needs analysis*, in which each side is asked to talk about its fundamental needs and fears—needs that would have to be satisfied and fears that would have to be allayed if a solution is to be acceptable in its society. Participants are asked to listen attentively and not to debate or argue about what the other side says, although they are invited to ask for elaboration and clarification. The purpose of this second phase of the proceedings is to help each side understand the basic concerns of the other side from the other's perspective. We check the level of understanding by asking each side to summarize the other's needs, as they have heard them. Each side then has the opportunity to correct or amplify the summary that has been presented by the other side.

Once the two sides have come to grasp each other's perspective and understand each other's needs as well as seems possible at that point, we move on to the next phase of the agenda: *joint thinking about solutions to the conflict*. We discourage the participants from proposing solutions in the previous phase of the agenda because we want ideas for solution to be anchored in the problem—i.e., to address the parties' unfulfilled and threatened needs that emerged from the needs analysis. In the joint thinking phase we ask the parties to generate ideas for the overall shape of a solution to the conflict, or to particular issues within the conflict, that are responsive to the fundamental needs and fears of both parties, as presented in the preceding phase. They are given the difficult assignment of thinking of solutions that respond, not only to their own side's needs and fears (as they would in a bargaining situation), but simultaneously to the needs and fears of *both* sides.

Once the parties have achieved some common ground in generating ideas for solutions that would address the fundamental needs and fears of both sides, we turn to a *discussion of the political and psychological constraints* within their societies that stand in the way of such solutions. Discussion of constraints is an extremely important part of the learning that takes place in workshops, but we try to discourage such discussion until the parties have gone through the phase of joint thinking, because a premature focus on constraints is likely to inhibit the creative process of generating new ideas.

Finally, to the extent that time permits, we ask the participants to engage in another round of joint thinking, this time about *ways of overcoming the constraints* against integrative, win–win solutions to the conflict. In this phase of the workshop, participants try to generate ideas for steps that they personally, their organizations, or their governments can take—separately or jointly—in order to overcome the constraints that have been identified. Such ideas may focus, in particular, on steps of mutual reassurance—in the form of acknowledgments, symbolic gestures, or confidence-building measures—that would make the parties more willing and able to take the risks required for innovative solutions to the conflict.

In a volume dedicated to Tom Pettigrew, a question that naturally arises concerns the relationship of interactive problem solving to intergroup contact theory, to which Pettigrew has made—and continues to make—major contributions (e.g., Pettigrew, 1998; Pettigrew & Tropp, 2006). In contrast to the typical structured contact situation, the purpose of problem-solving workshops is not to promote interaction between members of different groups as a vehicle for changing mutual attitudes and reducing intergroup prejudice. Rather, the purpose of the ground rules and agenda that I have outlined is to promote a particular kind of interaction between members of conflicting groups, conducive to the development of new insights and ideas for resolving their conflict, which can in turn influence public opinion and the policy process within their societies. Yet, achieving that purpose clearly calls for changes in participants' attitudes toward the other group—particularly for recognition of the other's openness to a peaceful resolution of the conflict and trust in the other's intentions.

It is interesting, in this connection, that the context, ground rules, and agenda of problem-solving workshops reflect the four conditions of Allport's (1954) original contact hypothesis (as summarized by Pettigrew, 1998, and Pettigrew & Tropp, 2006): equal status, common goals, intergroup cooperation, and authority sanction. Equality in the setting is one of our central ground rules and is stressed in the recruitment and briefing of participants. The common goals of the participants follow directly from the view of the conflict as a shared problem whose solution requires their joint efforts. The participants are interdependent in their cooperative work, because they must rely on each other for information about and insight into the other's situation and perspective so that they can arrive at ideas for resolving the conflict that are responsive to both sets of needs. Finally, the academic auspices of our work give the third party the authority to provide an alternative set of norms for the interaction, in place of the norms that typically govern interactions between parties in conflict, and to serve as a repository of trust for parties that view each other with suspicion.

Change and Transfer

Problem-solving workshops have a dual purpose. First, they seek to produce change in the particular individuals sitting around the workshop table—to enable them to acquire new insights into the conflict and new ideas for resolving it and overcoming the barriers to a nego-tiated solution. However, these changes at the level of individual participants are not ends in themselves, but vehicles for promoting change at the policy level. Thus, the second purpose of workshops is to maximize the likelihood that the new insights and ideas developed by workshop participants will be fed back into the political debate and decision-making procedures in their respective societies.

Clearly, this model is not based on the simple assumption that the aggregation of changes in individuals in the course of workshops even-tually adds up to changes in the conflict system. Rather, the purpose of workshops is to create *inputs* into the larger process—in the form of new understandings, insights, ideas, and proposals for resolving the conflict that can be injected into the political culture, the political debate, and the decision-making process in each society. This is why it is important to differentiate the purpose of facilitating changes in the individual participants from the purpose of transferring these changes into the policy process. Individual change does not automatically and as a matter of course translate into social change. The effect of individual change on social change has to be understood in the light of how changes in individuals enter into social-system processes and play themselves out in interaction with other forces that characterize the larger system.

In keeping with this view, the contribution of the microprocess of problem-solving workshops to macrolevel change depends not only on what happens in the workshop itself—i.e., how effective it is in producing change in the individual participants—but on the place of the workshop program on the larger political map and its relationship to other societal processes. Several features of a workshop program may enhance its contribution to the macroprocess—or, more precisely, to the transfer of workshop products into the policy process: (1) microlevel changes resulting from workshops may have a *cumulative effect*, insofar as they are part of a range of activities within and between the two societies that interact with each other and build on each other, gradually penetrating the political cultures; (2) workshops are most likely to contribute to the macroprocess if they have built-in *multiplier effects*, best exemplified in our work by the recruitment of participants who are credible political influentials within their own societies—individuals situated in positions that enable them to influence public opinion, political action, and/or decision making; (3) depending on the nature of the participants, workshops and related microlevel activities may also have *demonstration* or *legitimation effects*, demonstrating—or at least suggesting—that serious negotiations may indeed be possible and peaceful relations attainable, and helping to make interactions across the conflict lines legitimate; and finally, (4) the impact of unofficial, microlevel activities on the larger process depends on their *complementarity* with the entire range of other activities that constitute a peace process, from the official negotiations themselves to public education and grassroot efforts in promoting peace and intercommunal cooperation.

Apropos of my earlier analogy with the social-psychological experiment, these same four features—though with different specific manifestations—apply to the relationship between the microprocess of the laboratory and the real-life situations to which we seek to generalize experimental findings. Our ability to generalize is enhanced by the *cumulative effect* of a series of interconnected and yet diverse studies within and across experimental programs; by built-in *multiplier effects*, such as the heterogeneity of a research program's samples, experimental situations, and response measures; by the use of experiments primarily as *demonstrations* that certain relationships are possible, leaving it to other types of research to explore the contexts and conditions under which these relationships may manifest themselves; and by the *complementarity* of experimental findings with findings generated by other methods, as in the use of "methodological triangulation" (Campbell & Fiske, 1959).

The dual purpose of problem-solving workshops presents one of the greatest challenges to the theory and practice of interactive problem solving: how to structure workshops so that new insights and ideas are likely to be both generated in the course of the interaction and transferred to the policy process. What is particularly challenging, to both theory and practice, is that the requirements for maximizing change in the workshop itself may be not only different from, but often contradictory to the requirements for maximizing the transfer of that change into the political process—just as the requirements for establishing a causal relationship in the laboratory and for ensuring the generalizability of that relationship, i.e., for internal and external validity (Campbell, 1957), may well be contradictory. I have described this issue as the *dialectics of interactive problem solving* (Kelman, 1979). One of the most challenging tasks in designing workshops is to navigate these dialectics—to create the proper balance between an array of contradictory requirements.

The best example of these dialectics is provided by the selection of participants. To maximize transfer into the political process, we might prefer official participants, who are close to the decision-making apparatus and thus in a position to apply directly what they have learned. But to maximize change, we might prefer participants who are removed from the decision-making process and therefore less constrained in their interactions and freer to play with ideas and explore hypothetical possibilities. To balance these contradictory requirements, we look for participants who are not officials, but politically influential. They are thus more free to engage in the process but, at the same time, their positions within their societies ensure that any new ideas they develop can have an impact on the thinking of decision makers and the public at large.

Another example of the dialectics of workshops is the degree of trust and cohesiveness that we try to engender in the group of participants. Adequate levels of interpersonal trust and group cohesiveness are important to the effective interaction among the participants. But if the workshop participants become too trusting and the group becomes too cohesive, they may lose credibility and political effectiveness in their own communities and thus inhibit the transfer of workshop insights into the policy process. To balance these two contradictory requirements, we aim for the development of *working trust* and an *uneasy coalition*—two concepts, elaborated over the years, that have become central to the theory and practice of interactive problem solving.

In view of the dialectics of interactive problem solving, we aim to foster *working trust* among workshop participants, in contrast to trust based on interpersonal closeness (Kelman, 2005b). In the relationship between parties engaged in an existential conflict, I maintain, it is neither possible, nor necessary, nor even entirely desirable to create the kind of trust that develops from personal relationships, friendship, or shared values. The working trust we hope to generate is trust in the other side's seriousness and sincerity in the quest for peace—in their genuine commitment, largely out of their own interests, to finding a mutually acceptable accommodation. An interesting paradox is that this kind of trust among adversaries increases to the extent each is convinced that the other is moving in a conciliatory direction *out of their own interests.* This contrasts with the finding from research on persuasive communication that the trustworthiness of communicators declines if they are seen as having a personal interest in promoting a particular point of view. In our situation, self-interest provides the strongest evidence of the seriousness and sincerity of the other's intentions.

Working trust, however, can develop only if the parties are convinced that the other's pursuit of accommodation, though interest-driven, is genuine: that it represents a strategic choice, not just a tactical maneuver. This is the basis on which, I believe, working trust developed between Rabin and Arafat after the Oslo agreement—a trust that eroded with Rabin's assassination. At later stages of conflict resolution, as a set of shared interests becomes defined, working trust and interpersonal trust may merge. But at earlier stages, the attempt to go beyond working trust is not only unrealistic, but may also be counterproductive because it may undermine the credibility of participants in their own community and thus their ability to transfer their insights to the larger process and to influence public opinion and policy decisions.

Turning to the concept of the *uneasy coalition* (Kelman, 1993), I have conceived of problem-solving workshops and related activities as part of a process of building coalitions between those elements on the two sides that are interested in exploring the possibilities of a negotiated solution. Because this coalition cuts across a very basic conflict line—a line that divides people along their core identities—it is almost by definition an uneasy coalition. The uneasiness of the coalition has the consequence of feeding mutual distrust and often complicating coalition work. This uneasiness, however, is not only an inevitable reality (insofar as coalition members are bona fide representatives of their national groups, as they must be to contribute to change), but also a necessity—primarily, for present purposes, because of the reentry problem and the transfer of change. A workshop group that becomes overly cohesive may undermine the ultimate purpose of the enterprise: to have an impact on the political process within the two societies. Workshop participants (and, of course, negotiators) who develop a close identification with their counterparts on the other side and express trust in them violate a powerful group norm in a situation of protracted conflict. They thus run the risk of becoming alienated from their own co-nationals, losing their credibility at home, and hence forfeiting their political effectiveness and their ability to promote a new consensus within their own communities. Therefore, the most effective overall relationship between participants is best described as an uneasy coalition—sufficiently cohesive so that the members can interact productively (which is a requirement for *change*), but not so cohesive that they lose credibility and political effectiveness in their own communities (which is a requirement for *transfer*).

In sum, one of the challenges for our work is to create an atmosphere in which participants can begin to humanize and trust each other and to develop an effective collaborative relationship, without losing sight of their separate group identities and the conflict between their communities.

Conclusion

A central characteristic of our work in conflict resolution has been its pursuit of a scholar–practitioner model, very much in the Lewinian tradition of action research. In keeping with this orientation, the two major tasks on our agenda at this point are: (1) to develop appropriate ways of evaluating the effectiveness of interactive problem solving and related approaches to conflict resolution through systematic research; and (2) to adapt the approach to the requirements of changing political circumstances, such as those that characterize the Israeli–Palestinian conflict today.

Scholar-practitioners in the field of conflict resolution, including a number of my former students, are increasingly undertaking the task of evaluation research. The dual purpose of interactive problem solving workshops presents a special challenge to their evaluation. The standard, experimental or quasi-experimental model of evaluation is not applicable here because the focus is not the effectiveness of a specifically targeted social program, but the impact of a social movement designed to interact with other events and experiences to produce a change in political culture. I have argued (Kelman, in press) that evaluation of interactive problem solving requires the gradual accumulation of pieces of evidence in support of its underlying assumptions and have proposed two models of evaluation that follow this strategy: the "links-in-the chain" model identifies and tests each of the steps in the process of interactive problem solving that are presumed to account for its effectiveness, starting with the microprocess of workshops and ending with the macroprocess of conflict resolution; and the experimental model calls for systematic tests of some of the assumptions of the approach in settings that may be quite different from problem-solving workshops (though they may include analogs and simulations of such workshops).

As for adapting the approach to the requirements of changing political circumstances, I proposed above that interactive problem solving is potentially relevant at all stages of a peace process. However, at different stages of the process, the precise agenda and procedures of problem-solving workshops may have to be modified in order to be relevant to the political necessities and possibilities of the moment—as long as they remain consistent with the underlying logic of the approach. Thus, in the period following the 1993 Oslo agreement between Israel and the Palestine Liberation Organization—in contrast with our earlier practice—our Joint Working Group on Israeli–Palestinian Relations was specifically devoted to producing and disseminating joint concept papers on issues left to be resolved in final-status negotiations. In the current phase of the Israeli–Palestinian conflict, which is marked by the breakdown of once promising negotiations, a central task for interactive problem solving is to help rebuild public trust in the availability of a credible negotiating partner on the other side. To that end, it is important to frame a final agreement in terms of a principled peace, embodying a historic compromise in the form of a solution that enables each people to express its national identity in its own state within the shared land. Such a framework can mobilize wide public support for negotiations by reassuring the two publics that a negotiated agreement is not jeopardizing their national existence and that it offers a vision of a mutually beneficial common future. Interactive problem solving is well suited to constructing such a framework since it represents a joint process, in which each side can acknowledge and accommodate the other's identity in a context in which the core of its own identity is affirmed.

References

Allport, G. W. (1954). *The nature of prejudice.* Cambridge, MA: Addison-Wesley.

Burton, J. W. (1969). *Conflict and communication: The use of controlled communication in international relations.* London: Macmillan.

Burton, J. W. (1979). *Deviance, terrorism and war: The process of solving unsolved social and political problems.* New York: St. Martin's Press.

Campbell, D. T. (1957). Factors relevant to the validity of experiments in social settings. *Psychological Bulletin, 54,* 297–312.

Campbell, D. T., & Fiske, D. W. (1959). Convergent and discriminant validation by the multitrait-multimethod matrix. *Psychological Bulletin, 56,* 81–105.

Kelman, H. C. (1972). The problem-solving workshop in conflict resolution. In R. L. Merritt (Ed.), *Communication in international politics* (pp. 168–204). University of Illinois Press, Urbana.

Kelman, H. C. (1979). An interactional approach to conflict resolution and its application to Israeli–Palestinian relations. *International Interactions, 6,* 99–122.

Kelman, H. C. (1986). Interactive problem solving: A social-psychological approach to conflict resolution. In W. Klassen (Ed.), *Dialogue toward interfaith understanding* (pp. 293–314). Tantur/Jerusalem: Ecumenical Institute for Theological Research.

Kelman, H. C. (1993). Coalitions across conflict lines: The interplay of conflicts within and between the Israeli and Palestinian communities. In S. Worchel & J. A. Simpson (Eds.), *Conflict between people and groups* (pp. 236–258). Chicago: Nelson-Hall.

Kelman, H. C. (1995). Contributions of an unofficial conflict resolution effort to the Israeli–Palestinian breakthrough. *Negotiation Journal, 11,* 19–27.

Kelman, H. C. (1997). Group processes in the resolution of international conflicts: Experiences from the Israeli–Palestinian case. *American Psychologist, 52,* 212–220.

Kelman, H. C. (1998a). Interactive problem solving: An approach to conflict resolution and its application in the Middle East. *PS: Political Science and Politics, 31,* 190–198.

Kelman, H. C. (1998b). Social-psychological contributions to peace-making and peacebuilding in the Middle East. *Applied Psychology: An International Review, 47,* 5–28.

Kelman, H. C. (2002). Interactive problem solving: Informal mediation by the scholar-practitioner. In J. Bercovitch (Ed.), *Studies in international mediation: Essays in honor of Jeffrey Z. Rubin* (pp. 167–193). New York: Palgrave Macmillan.

Kelman, H. C. (2005a). Interactive problem solving in the Israeli-Palestinian case: Past contributions and present challenges. In R. J. Fisher (Ed.), *Paving the way: Contributions of interactive conflict resolution to peacemaking* (pp. 41–63). Lanham, MD: Lexington Books.

Kelman, H. C. (2005b). Building trust among enemies: The central challenge for international conflict resolution. *International Journal of Intercultural Relations, 29,* 639–650.

Kelman, H. C. (in press). Evaluating the contributions of interactive problem solving to the resolution of ethnonational conflicts. *Peace and Conflict: Journal of Peace Psychology, 14.*

Kelman, H. C., & Pettigrew, T. F. (1959). How to understand prejudice. *Commentary, 28,* 436–441.

Pettigrew, T. F. (1991). Toward unity and bold theory: Popperian suggestions for two persistent problems of social psychology. In C. W. Stephan, W. G. Stephan, & T. F. Pettigrew (Eds.), *The future of social psychology* (pp. 13–27). New York: Springer-Verlag.

Pettigrew, T. F. (1998). Intergroup contact theory. *Annual Review of Psychology, 49,* 65–85.

Pettigrew, T. F., & Tropp, L. R. (2006). A meta-analytic test of intergroup contact theory. *Journal of Personality and Social Psychology, 90,* 751–783.

Rouhana, N. N., & Kelman, H. C. (1994). Promoting joint thinking in international conflict: An Israeli–Palestinian continuing workshop. *Journal of Social Issues, 50*(1), 157–178.

17

School Desegregation Research

Outcomes, Historical Trends, and Issues Affecting its Usefulness in Policy and Practice

Janet Ward Schofield

Research on intergroup relations occupies a special place in social psychology. First, it has an unusually long and rich history, going back well over half a century. Second, it is still one of the major areas of theoretical and empirical work in the discipline, as evidenced by the vigor of research on stereotypes, ingroup bias, and implicit attitudes. Third, it deals with one of the most fundamental problems of our times. Specifically, it has often been said that the central problem of the twentieth century was the "color line" (DuBois, 1903) and the issue of how to build constructive and peaceful relations between those with different backgrounds and beliefs remains one of the world's most intractable problems.

Tom Pettigrew also occupies a special place on the field of social psychology, as a scholar who has both passionately and productively studied intergroup relations during the past 50 years and as one who has labored to highlight the implications of work on this topic for policy. (See, for example, US Commission on Civil Rights, 1967). This chapter discusses some of the ways in which Pettigrew's work influenced my research and summarizes some of the most important findings of that research. In addition, it addresses an issue both important to social psychology and pertinent to Tom's legacy—the issue of problems that need to be addressed in order to effectively foster a link between social psychological research on intergroup relations and policy in this area.

Distinction between Desegregation and Integration

Pettigrew's (1969) paper, "Racially Separate or Together" offered an incisive and compelling analysis of the social costs of racial segregation, including the way in which forced segregation can lead individuals to come to prefer continued voluntary segregation. It also built on Allport's (1954) earlier work by pointing out that although a social psychological analysis of segregation suggested that it was conducive to increased intergroup stereotyping and tension, contact does not automatically lead to improved intergroup relations. Pettigrew also introduced a crucial distinction between desegregation and integration, using the term *desegregation* to refer to situations in which previously segregated groups are brought into contact with each other in milieus in which a legacy of inequality, including intergroup tension, still influences interaction patterns. In contrast, he used the term *integration* to refer to situations characterized by the structural conditions highlighted by Allport (1954), including equal status, an emphasis on cooperation, and the support of relevant authorities for positive intergroup relations (Pettigrew, 1971), as likely to lead to improved relations between groups. This distinction fundamentally influenced my work for decades, as did the potential for constructive social change embodied in Pettigrew's policy-related work.

Social Processes in Racially-Mixed Schools

Consistent with Pettigrew's (1971) call to study more deeply the situational factors that influence the outcomes of intergroup contact, I conducted a 4-year longitudinal study designed to illuminate the social processes occurring in a "model" racially-mixed school in order to better understand the development of intergroup relations between two cohorts of White and African American middle school children (Schofield, 1989). The research site was selected to allow study of how intergroup relations evolved in a school that tried to provide an integrated environment. This project was the beginning of over a decade of work in that school.

The outcomes of that work, which included experimental, quasi-experimental, and quantitative observational studies, as well as sociometric and qualitative research, were numerous. Some of the most important ideas suggested by that research (Schofield, 1989) are that: (1) intergroup attitudes and behaviors can be quite situation specific, even within the relatively homogeneous confines of the school environment; (2) members of different racial groups may have quite different views regarding how well members of those groups get along with each other; (3) different variables appear to influence positive and negative intergroup behaviors; (4) intergroup behaviors and stereotypes may simultaneously change in different directions; (5) race relations may be quite profoundly influenced by gender; (6) institutions adopting a "colorblind" perspective may inadvertently ignore or even reinforce malleable intergroup disparities (Schofield, 2006); and (7) that resegregation, flowing from both policy decisions and social processes, is often a major problem within racially-mixed institutions (Sagar & Schofield, 1984).

Pettigrew's emphasis on the importance of intergroup contact and his distinction between desegregation and integration not only influenced the general topic of this research program and the school environment selected for study. His work also influenced many individual pieces of research. For example, consistent with Pettigrew's emphasis on the importance of the conditions under which intergroup contact occurs, I compared the development of intergroup friendships in this school's seventh grade, which came close to meeting the conditions necessary for integration, to the development of such friendships in its eighth grade, which clearly did not. Consistent with theoretical expectations, intergroup friendships increased in the seventh grade and declined in eighth grade (Schofield, 1979; Schofield & Sagar, 1977). Importantly, students who had entered the school as seventh-graders, and thus had experienced the positive contact conditions there, nonetheless had more intergroup friendships in eighth grade than did those who entered the school as eighth-graders when it first opened and who, for that reason, had not experienced an integrated school environment as seventh-graders (Schofield, 1979).

Assessing the Results of and Trends in Desegregation Research

During the 1970s and 1980s, a substantial body of research on the impact of school desegregation emerged. This set the stage for a number of reviews on: (1) the impact of desegregation on academic achievement (Schofield, 1995a); (2) the impact of desegregation on intergroup relations (Schofield, 1978; 1991; 1995a); and (3) policies and practices likely to improve intergroup relations in racially-mixed schools (Schofield, 2004; Schofield & Eurich-Fulcer, 2001; Schofield & Sagar, 1983). My review of the first of these issues concluded, consistent with earlier reviews (Cook et al., 1984), that desegregation appears to have a modest positive impact on African-American students' achievement, while having no consistent measurable impact on that of White students (Schofield, 1995a). That same review concluded that although the impact of desegregation on near-term racial attitudes varies from positive to neutral to negative, racially-mixed schooling has quite important positive long-term consequences for intergroup relations.

Quite a bit has also been learned about how schools can promote positive intergroup relations, which I have synthesized in several papers (Schofield, 2001; 2004; Schofield & Eurich-Fulcer, 2001). For example, school-based studies provide clear support for Allport's contention that cooperation aimed at achieving common goals is conducive to improved intergroup relations (Slavin, 1995). My work also enhances understanding of factors underlying Pettigrew and Tropp's (2006) recent finding that institutional support appears to be especially important in facilitating positive outcomes from intergroup contact by delineating four specific mechanisms (enabling, modeling, sensitizing, and sanctioning) through which school authorities may influence intergroup outcomes (Schofield, 1995b; 2004).

My work also highlights the potentially negative consequences of adopting the colorblind perspective in racially-mixed schools. Specifically, it suggests that although this perspective sometimes reduces the potential for overt conflict and minimizes discomfort and embarrassment, it often leads to failure to capitalize on the potential educational benefits of diversity (Schofield, 2000). In addition, the colorblind perspective frees aversive racists (Dovidio & Gaertner, 1998) to act in a discriminatory way by helping to remove race from conscious consideration. Furthermore, it tends to make policies and practices that are not overtly discriminatory, but which nonetheless disadvantage minority group students, more acceptable because it makes consideration of their impact of the members of different groups illegitimate. More recent experimental work reinforces the conclusion that the colorblind perspective can have negative consequences (Norton, Sommers, Apfelbaum, Pura, & Ariely, 2006; Richeson & Nussbaum, 2004).

Conducting reviews of research on school desegregation led to the observation (see Figure 17.1) that both the quantity and the nature of research on its outcomes changed markedly over time (Schofield,

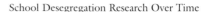

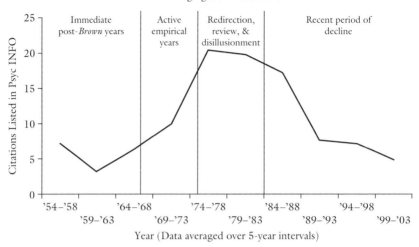

Figure 17.1   School desegregation research over time.
Source: Reprinted with permission of the American Psychological Association from Schofield, J. W., & Hausmann, L. R. M. (2004). School desegregation and social science research. *American Psychologist, 59*, 538–546.

1991; Schofield & Hausmann, 2004a). Consistent with Pettigrew's much earlier observations of the situation (Pettigrew, 1961), we concluded that during the immediate post-Brown period (1954–1967) very little psychological research was conducted on school desegregation, at least partly because school desegregation was slow getting underway, due to widespread resistance to it on the part of Whites. A sharp increase in such research occurred in the later 1960s and early 1970s, with many studies exploring the impact of desegregation on academic achievement and intergroup relations.

Research on desegregation continued apace between the mid-1970s and mid-1980s, although changes in the nature of this work led us to characterize this as a time of redirection, review, and disillusionment (Schofield, 1991, Schofield & Hausmann, 2004a). Specifically, a greater proportion of the studies used qualitative methods to examine the structure and culture of desegregated schools and how students reacted to these environments. More attention was also devoted to illuminating the aspects of racially-mixed schooling responsible for different social and academic outcomes. Finally, more effort was devoted to developing and testing specific approaches to producing positive change through intergroup contact in racially-mixed schools.

By the beginning of this period, enough research had been conducted to create a fertile environment for reviews of the impact of desegregation on student outcomes. Such reviews highlighted methodological and conceptual problems in the existing research, many of which were extremely difficult if not impossible to overcome. For example, students in segregated schools could not serve as members of control groups for longitudinal studies of change in intergroup behavior in desegregated school because there was no opportunity for intergroup behavior in such schools. The previously mentioned conclusions of such work, including the modest impact of desegregation on African-American achievement and the mixed findings regarding its near-term effects on attitudes, were discouraging to many who felt the documented benefits of desegregation were small compared to the financial and other costs of achieving it in many school districts.

After this period, research on desegregation declined sharply in the mid-1980s, and it has stayed at a generally low level, rather like that in the immediate post-Brown period, during the past two decades. Numerous factors discussed in detail elsewhere (Schofield & Hausmann, 2004b) contributed to this, including the broader societal retreat from the policy of school desegregation (Orfield & Eaton, 1996) and the growing belief on the part of Whites that African American's no longer suffer from discrimination (Schuman & Krysan, 1999).

The Intersection of Intergroup Relations Research and the World of Policy and Practice

Intergroup relations research generally, and desegregation research in particular, is often said to exemplify the way in which social psychology can substantially influence policy and practice (Pettigrew, 2001; Zimbardo, 2004). One of the earliest and most notable examples of such influence was the Supreme Court's citation of Kenneth and Mamie Clark's work in footnote 11 of the *Brown vs Board of Education* case, the first time that social science data was ever explicitly cited by the Supreme Court. Cooperative learning, an approach used in many U.S. elementary schools, is a clear example of the way in which the work of social psychologists studying intergroup relations has had substantial impact on educational practice, although such practices are often implemented in ways that do not fully reflect existing theory and research (Antil, Jenkins, Wayne, & Vadasy, 1998; Huberman, 1994).

As these two very disparate examples suggest, the kind of policy and practice involvement that social psychologists working in the same general area can have varies dramatically. Indeed, as APA's Task Force on Psychology and Public Policy (1986) points out, psychologists serve in policy-related roles as different as expert witness, administrator in a human service organization, evaluation researcher, and consultant. Furthermore, as that task force also highlighted, psychologists may participate at points in the policy process ranging from very early stages, such as problem identification, to much later stages, such as assessing program or policy impact. Finally, of course, psychologists can try to influence policies as citizens as well as in their roles as scholars and scientists (Suedfeld & Tetlock, 1992).

Over 30 years as a researcher on school desegregation have provided me with the opportunity to become involved in a multitude of ways with related policy and practice issues. These range from co-leading a day-long workshop for a dozen U.S. Senators and Congressional Representatives, to providing advice to the staff of state and federal legislators, to helping prepare statements submitted by various professional groups on research pertinent to Supreme Court cases, to participating in TV and radio programs on race relations in schools, to leading teacher workshops in school districts in numerous states.

As these examples illustrate, the potential contributions of intergroup relations researchers to policy and practice differ not only in the ways discussed earlier but also with regard to other dimensions likely to influence the issues such work raises, including: (1) whether the aim is to effect legislation, judicial decision-making, government agency actions, public opinion, or school-level practice; (2) whether the input provided is requested by those receiving it; and (3) whether the goal is to serve an "enlightenment function" (Weiss, 1979) by providing concepts and distinctions that enrich policy-makers' and practitioners' understandings of a problem or to suggest specific solutions to perceived problems.

Issues that Impede Effective Involvement of Intergroup Researchers in Policy and Practice

The remaining portion of this chapter discusses several issues that have surfaced repeatedly in my policy- and practice-related work as a university-based scholar engaged in research relevant to a controversial policy issue. In many cases, no ready solution for dealing with such issues is available. Yet, highlighting the nature of such issues and delineating some of the possible ways of responding to them is a step toward developing ways to deal with them more effectively.

Giving Social Psychology Away: A Low Priority in Social Psychology

There have long been calls for social psychology to contribute not only to increasing knowledge, but also to making that knowledge available in useful forms to policy makers, practitioners, and the public (Miller, 1969). Kurt Lewin's famous dictum, "There is nothing as practical as a good theory," embodies the belief underlying such calls, as have the activities of the Society for the Psychological Study of Social Issues for more than 70 years.

However, social psychology, as a discipline, is not structured in a way that reflects much institutional valuation of such activities. To a considerable extent, this reflects the fact that most social psychologists work in academic environments, which typically value theoretical work and empirical research designed to advance theory more highly than applied or policy-oriented work. A failure to value communicating with the broader public has characterized university-based psychologists for decades (Gergen, 1995; Gutek, 1998). Indeed, Rozin (2006) suggests that decisions about what graduate programs universities will provide reflect academic disciplines' devaluation of applied work, with prestigious private universities being less likely to have graduate programs in applied psychology than their high-ranking public peers, presumably because they are freer to focus on what academics themselves value.

Voices advocating more attention to influencing those outside of our discipline can still be heard. For example, Sommer (2006) has argued that researchers should engage in dual dissemination, writing accessible reports for larger audiences as well as journal articles, and has offered practical suggestions about how this goal can be achieved. Research demonstrating that policy makers prefer reports presented in formats familiar to them, and that they use such work more than research that is presented in a less accessible format, supports this suggestion (Landry, Lamari, & Amara, 2003; Rich & Oh, 1993). However, generally speaking, universities do not reward the publication of articles in non-scholarly venues, and scholars sometimes even fear the disapprobation of their peers for such work (Sommer, 2006).

The relative lack of valuation of policy- and practice-related activities often found among social psychologists is also clearly reflected in the professional journals and societies that we as a discipline control.

For example, researchers quite rarely seriously discuss the practical or policy implications of their work in journal articles (Stephan, 2006). This is striking in light of the fact that discussion of a study's implications for further research is an expected part of virtually any journal article (APA, 2001). Further signaling the field's general lack of interest in promoting and recognizing policy-related research (Frey, 2006), not a single one of the ten awards given annually by the Society for Personality and Social Psychology and the Society of Experimental Social Psychology honors contributions related to "giving (social) psychology away," to use George Miller's (1969) very apt term. It should come as little surprise to psychologists that activities that employing institutions, major journals, and disciplinary societies generally do not strongly reinforce will not be given high priority.

The negative practical consequences of detachment from the problems of the world around us are clear in developments over the past several years regarding funding for social psychological and other research (Martin, 2003). The low priority given to bridging the gap between research, policy, and practice also has major intellectual consequences. For example, greater interest in the implications of research for policy and practice would, I contend, put more of the "social" back in social psychology. The field of social psychology has made tremendous strides in recent decades, building on the contributions of cognitive psychology. However, it has made much less progress when we move to levels of analysis above that of the individual or the dyad. Progress in such areas is hard to make for a discipline with experimentation as its methodological gold standard. However, given how exquisitely sensitive individuals are to their social contexts, and the development of increasingly powerful statistical techniques helpful in parsing out the impact of group- and organizational-level effects, the time seems ripe to focus effort on theoretical and empirical work illuminating the effect of complex social contexts on individual and group functioning. Enhanced interest in policy- or practice-related work is likely to bring such issues to the fore, because understanding group- and organizational-level effects is likely to be important in such work.

Giving Psychology Away: Difficulties in Assessing and Valuing Impact

There are widely accepted, although admittedly imperfect, markers of the quality of intellectual work in social psychology, such as the prestige and impact factor of the journal in which a paper is published, or the frequency of a paper's citation in the body of work included in the data bases providing citation counts. If social psychologists were to begin to value using their knowledge to influence policy and practice, the question of how to assess the quality or value of such activities would logically arise. Both judgments regarding the *extent* of such work's impact and regarding whether that impact is *positive, neutral* or *negative* are often difficult to make.

Of course, there are cases in which rough measurement and valuation of the quality of work related to policy or practice is not particularly difficult. Specifically, it is not too difficult when social psychological theory and research lead to specific practices that have demonstrable outcomes that are generally valued. This is particularly true when one has some way of tracking how widely used such practices become. However, even in such relatively easy cases, making judgments about how to value such work is more complex than it might first appear to be. For example, cooperative team learning strategies like the Jigsaw Classroom are specific practices with a demonstrable outcome that is generally valued, raising academic achievement for low achievers (Aranson, Blaney, Stephan, Rosenfield, & Sikes, 1977; Slavin, 1995). However, overall judgments about the value of developing such practices would clearly be influenced by whether and how much another of its demonstrated outcomes, the building of intergroup friendships, is valued. Furthermore, such judgments would also most likely be influenced by the conditions under which the effects of cooperative team learning programs were measured. For example, their positive impact is likely to appear greater when they are implemented and evaluated under the knowledgeable and watchful eye of those who developed these approaches than when cooperative learning becomes widely diffused and hence implemented by those not as familiar with the thinking underlying such practices.

In a great many cases, judgment of the impact and the value of activities designed to inform policy and/or practice are extraordinarily difficult to make. How one can compare the "value" of: (1) a morning's workshop introducing 50 teachers to the Jigsaw Classroom; (2) a 10 minute television interview on how to improve intergroup relations reaching millions of viewers; and (3) a contribution to a professional association's statement on research pertinent to a Supreme Court case, even assuming all of these activities are equal in the scientific merit of the input and the material's pertinence to the policy or practice issue at hand? Providing a definitive answer to this question is most likely impossible. But devoting some thought to the issue would be useful if we are really to make progress in figuring out how to take informed steps toward valuing the policy- and practice-related work of social psychologists.

At a minimum, we might do well to make use of the work of scholars of knowledge utilization to begin to ascertain how to address such issues productively. For example, building on earlier work by Knott and Wildavsky (1980), Landry, Amara, & Lamani (2001) discuss a multistep "ladder" of increasing impact beginning at the bottom, with the mere act of transmitting research results to policy makers or practitioners, and rising all the way to cases in which research shapes specific implemented activities. The intermediate rungs on the ladder begin with modest things like "research was read and understood by policy makers/practitioners," and progress nearer the top of the ladder to cases in which research actually influenced decisions. Factors such as the number of individuals potentially influenced and the importance of the policy area involved could also be considered in assessing the value of practice- or policy-oriented work. (Of course, judgments about the importance of policy areas are value-laden, but rough distinctions may be possible. For example, most people would probably agree that policies related to reducing the achievement gap between majority and minority students have more potential importance than those relating to the basis on which universities make roommate assignments.) Being realistic, perhaps such refinements are not necessary at this stage and just moving toward explicitly valuing policy- and/or practice- related activities as part of a faculty member's work would be an important step, since both research and common sense support the conclusion that career rewards for policy- and practice-related work will encourage it (Huberman, 1994).

Giving Psychology Away: Understanding Factors Related to Research Utilization

The field of knowledge utilization also provides some guidance about how to raise the probability that research will be of use to policy makers and practitioners. Although space constraints preclude extended discussion of this literature, it is worth noting that characteristics enhancing use of research include such things as its focus on the user's needs and the degree to which policy makers perceive the research as relevant to the issues at hand (Amara, Ouimet, & Landry, 2004). Other factors, such as the existence of social and organizational mechanisms linking researchers to policy makers, also appear to play an important role (Dunn, Holzner, & Zaltman, 1980).

Knowledge utilization research also suggests the necessity for understanding the research utilization process if efforts to connect with policy are to be effective. For example, models that assume that research flows from its producers to policy makers, who typically use specific studies to shape specific decisions, are naïve and over-simplified because timing, cultural issues, social relationships, power relationships, and many other factors influence knowledge use (Backer, 1991). Further, even the concept of use itself is complex, including impacts ranging from the provision of new perspectives to the adoption of entire programs (Weiss, 1991).

Underutilization of Disciplinary Knowledge

Although research suggests that being aware of the perspectives of policy makers is important in making research useful to them (Huberman, 1994), a problem that has significantly impeded the usefulness of desegregation research for policy and practice is that researchers have typically used policy makers' definitions of desegregation. Thus, in conducting research on racially-mixed schools, conceptual distinctions provided by contact theorists such as Pettigrew were often ignored (Schofield, 1991). For example, a huge range of situations characterized as desegregated by the courts and policy makers were treated by researchers as if they were the examples of the same phenomenon. Too often, little attention was paid to aspects of the situations that existing theory suggested would strongly influence their outcomes. Thus researchers, following the lead of policy makers, have typically lumped together—under the term *desegregation*—both voluntary transfer programs involving very small numbers of minority students undertaken by predominately White suburban schools and court-ordered programs that many administrators and teachers in large urban school systems with substantial minority group enrollments resisted (St. John, 1975). Furthermore, the information needed to group schools according to factors that theory suggests are likely to influence outcomes is not even provided in many papers, so meta-analytic work exploring the differential impact of various kinds of desegregation has been impeded (Schofield, 1991).

Lack of attention to differences between desegregated situations likely to affect their outcomes has not only made it more difficult to accumulate knowledge over time. It has impeded our ability to provide pertinent information to policy makers concerned with the likely outcomes of particular kinds of desegregated situations. So, for example, although reviews have concluded that desegregation overall is associated with certain outcomes, that is much less useful than more differentiated knowledge about the likely effects of different kinds of desegregated situations. Thus, failure to make consistent use of the conceptual tools provided by our discipline may not only impede researchers' contributions to the development of knowledge, but may also lessen the usefulness of this research to policy and practice. Although recent meta-analytic work (Pettigrew & Tropp, 2006; Tropp & Prenovost, 2008) has been able to draw some useful conclusions about how various aspects of desegregated schools relate to their impact on students, progress in this area would have occurred faster and gone farther if researchers had paid more attention to the conceptual distinctions provided decades ago by contact theory.

The Tension Between Scientific Caution and Policy Makers' Desire for Actionable Certainty

As Campbell (1969) pointed out, policy makers tend to advocate specific courses of action as if they are certain to be the right ones because otherwise it is hard to garner the necessary support for the expenditure of resources. Furthermore, policy makers frequently find it difficult to make use of knowledge presented with hedges and qualifications. Thus, there is often pressure on those working with policy makers to provide rather simple definitive statements regarding what is known. Issues regarding the appropriate use of knowledge are even more prevalent and extreme when scientists serve as expert witnesses or try to influence legal decisions through other means because the adversarial nature of the judicial system is conductive to the overstatement of evidence, the ignoring of qualifications regarding what is known, and the like. The special issues in such cases are discussed in Chesler, Sanders, & Kalmuss (1988) and Wolf (1981).

Yet, in spite of strong pressures for certainty, scientists attempting to influence policy on the basis of their knowledge of relevant research have good reason to be cautious, especially if they recommend a particular course of action. In fact, Suedfeld and Tetlock (1992) suggest that when scientists take a position on policy based on their professional expertise they should employ an even more rigorous standard of evidence than they do when presenting research within the scientific community for a variety of reasons, including the fact that policy-related work often involves a leap from the laboratory to the field where both the environment and the individuals involved may be quite different from those participating in the relevant research.

In addition, nuances often get ignored by policy makers, possibly because they provide politically useful ammunition for those preferring other courses of action.

One not very satisfactory solution to such problems and tensions is for researchers to do their best to convey accurately the state of existing knowledge about a particular issue and then to lay responsibility on others for appropriate use of this information. A useful supplement to this approach, which may or may not be possible to achieve in specific cases, is to negotiate mechanisms to mitigate either inadvertent or intentional inappropriate use of scientific input, such as an agreement that allows researchers to review and make changes in documents reflecting their input.

Increasingly Complex Statistical Tools Create Communication and Usage Issues

The past several decades have seen important developments in the statistical tools available to and increasingly employed by social scientists, including mediational analysis and hierarchical linear modeling. Such developments allow us to ask new questions and to explore old questions more powerfully than was previously possible. However, the increasingly common use of such tools also makes it harder for those without advanced statistical training, including most people in the world of policy and practice, to understand the basis for various conclusions.

In my experience, the one major exception to this generalization (i.e., that the use of increasingly sophisticated statistical methods makes it more difficult for those involved in policy and practice to understand the results of scientific work) is the use of meta-analysis, which can be understood relatively easily at the conceptual level by policy makers even if the details that determine the quality of a specific meta-analysis are not fully appreciated.

When complex statistical techniques are involved, it is often possible to find ways to explain the basic idea underlying them in a straightforward way and to focus on the substance of the findings. However, when the outcomes of various studies are not consistent and methodological or statistical issues appear likely to account for variation in the conclusions drawn, the situation becomes more difficult. In such cases, it may well be necessary to go beyond presenting the substantive "bottom line" and to help clarify the statistical or methodological issues likely to contribute to the inconsistency in results. However, such efforts may well not be particularly successful, especially when the policy debate is highly politicized.

In such cases, research is especially likely to be used to support a previously determined preference rather than to inform or influence a decision (Amara et al., 2004).

A Concluding Note on Giving Social Psychology Away

Numerous factors discussed above pose obstacles to giving social psychology away. Yet, the goal of finding ways to make effective use of social psychological knowledge in relevant areas of policy and practice remains an important one. In the long run, greater emphasis on producing knowledge that is likely to be of use and more attention to thinking hard about the implications of basic research seem likely to garner broader interest in and financial support for social psychology as well as to enrich it intellectually.

References

Allport, G. W. (1954). *The nature of prejudice*. Garden City, NJ: Doubleday.

Amara, N., Ouimet, M., & Landry, R. (2004). New evidence on instrumental, conceptual, and symbolic utilization of university research in government agencies. *Science Communication*, *26*, 75–106.

American Psychological Association (2001). *Publication manual* (5th ed.). Washington, DC: American Psychological Association.

Antil, L. R., Jenkins, J. R., Wayne, S. K., & Vadasy, P. F. (1998). Cooperative learning: Prevalence, conceptualizations, and the relation between research and practice. *American Educational Research Journal*, *35*, 419–454.

Aronson, E., Blaney, N. T., Stephan, S., Rosenfield, D., & Sikes, J. (1977). Interdependence in the classroom: A field study. *Journal of Educational Psychology*, *69*, 121–128.

Backer, T. E. (1991). Knowledge utilization: The third wave. *Knowledge: Creation, Diffusion, Utilization*, *12*, 225–240.

Campbell, D. T. (1969). Reforms as experiments. *American Psychologist*, *24*, 409–429.

Chesler, M. A., Sanders, J., & Kalmuss, D. S. (1988). *Social science in court: Mobilizing experts in the school desegregation cases*. Madison, WI: University of Wisconsin Press.

Cook, T., Armor, D., Crain, R., Miller, N., Carlson, M., Stephan, W. G., et al. (1984). *School desegregation and Black achievement*. Washington, DC: National Institute of Education, US Department of Education.

Dovidio, J. F., & Gaertner, S. L. (1998). On the nature of contemporary prejudice: The causes, consequences, and challenges of aversive racism.

In J. L. Eberhardt & S. T. Fiske (Eds.), *Confronting racism: The problem and the response* (pp. 3–32). Thousand Oaks, CA: Sage.

DuBois, W. E. B. (1903). *The souls of Black folk.* Chicago: McClurg and Company.

Dunn, W. N., Holzner, B., & Zaltman, G. (1980). The two communities metaphor and models of knowledge use. *Knowledge: Creation, Diffusion, Utilization, 1,* 515–536.

Frey, B. S. (2006). Giving and receiving awards. *Perspectives on Psychological Science, 1,* 377–388.

Gergen, K. J. (1995). Postmodern psychology: Resonance and reflection. *American Psychologist, 50,* 394.

Gutek, B. (1998). Report from the President. *SPSSI Newsletter, 205,* 1–2.

Huberman, M. (1994). Research utilization: The state of art. *Knowledge and Policy, 7,* 13–33.

Knott, J., & Wildavsky, A. (1980). If dissemination is the solution, what is the problem? *Knowledge: Creation, Diffusion, Utilization, 1,* 537–578.

Landry, R., Amara, N., & Lamari, M. (2001). Climbing the ladder of research utilization: Evidence from social science research. *Science Communication, 22,* 396–422.

Landry, R., Lamari, M., & Amara, N. (2003). Extent and determinants of utilization of university research in public administration. *Public Administration Review, 63,* 191–204.

Martin, B. R. (2003). The changing social contract for science and the evolution of the university. In A. Geuna, A. J. Salter, & W. E. Steinmueller (Eds.), *Science and innovation: Rethinking the rationales for funding and governance* (pp. 7–29). Cheltenham, UK: Edward Elgar.

Miller, G. A. (1969). Psychology as a means of promoting human welfare. *American Psychologist, 24,* 1063–1075.

Norton, M. I., Sommers, S. R., Apfelbaum, E. P., Pura, N., & Ariely, D. (2006). Color blindness and interracial interaction: Playing the political correctness game. *Psychological Science, 17,* 949–953.

Orfield, G., & Eaton, S. E. (1996). *Dismantling desegregation: The quiet reversal of Brown vs. Board of Education.* New York: The New Press.

Pettigrew, T. F. (1961). Social psychology and desegregation research. *American Psychologist, 16,* 105–112.

Pettigrew, T. F. (1969). Racially separate or together. *Journal of Social Issues, 25,* 43–69.

Pettigrew, T. F. (1971). *Racially separate or together?* New York: McGraw-Hill.

Pettigrew, T. F. (2001). Intergroup relations and national and international relations. In R. Brown & S. Gaertner (Eds.), *Blackwell handbook of social psychology: Intergroup processes* (pp. 514–532). New York: Blackwell.

Pettigrew, T. F., & Tropp, L. R. (2006). A meta-analytic test of intergroup contact theory. *Journal of Personality and Social Psychology, 90*(5), 751–783.

Rich, R. F., & Oh, C. H. (1993). The utilization of policy research. In S. Nagel (Ed.), *Encyclopedia of policy studies* (pp. 93–111). New York: Marcel Dekkar.

Richeson, J., & Nussbaum, R. (2004). The impact of multiculturalism versus color-blindness on racial bias. *Journal of Experimental Social Psychology, 40,* 417–423.

Rozin, P. (2006). Domain denigration and process preference in academic psychology. *Perspectives on Psychological Science, 1,* 365–376.

Sagar, H. A., & Schofield, J. W. (1984). Integrating the desegregated school: Problems and possibilities. In D. E. Bartz & M. L. Maehr (Eds.), *Advances in motivation and achievement. A research annual: The effects of school desegregation on motivation and achievement* (pp. 203–241). Greenwich, CT: JAI Press.

Schofield, J. W. (1978). School desegregation and intergroup attitudes. In D. Bar-Tal & L. Saxe (Eds.), *Social psychology of education: Theory and research* (pp. 330–363). Washington, DC: Halsted Press.

Schofield, J. W. (1979). The impact of positively structured contact on intergroup behavior: Does it last under adverse conditions? *Social Psychology Quarterly, 42,* 280–284.

Schofield, J. W. (1989). *Black and white in school: Trust tension or tolerance?* New York: Teachers' College Press.

Schofield, J. W. (1991). School desegregation and intergroup relations: A review of the research. In G. Grant (Ed.), *Review of research in education.* (Vol. 17) (pp. 335–409). Washington, DC: American Educational Research Association.

Schofield, J. W. (1995a). Review of research on school desegregation's impact on elementary and secondary school students. In J. A. Banks & C. A. McGee Banks (Eds.), *Handbook of research on multicultural education* (pp. 597–617). New York: Macmillan.

Schofield, J. W. (1995b). Improving intergroup relations among students. In J. A. Banks & C. A. McGee Banks (Eds.), *Handbook of research on multicultural education* (pp. 635–647). New York: Macmillan.

Schofield, J. W. (2000). The colorblind perspective's impact on intergroup relations. In J. A. Banks & C. A. McGee Banks (Eds.), *Multicultural education: Issues and perspectives* (6th ed.) (pp. 247–267). New York: John Wiley & Sons.

Schofield, J. W. (2001). Maximizing the benefits of a diverse student body: Lessons from school desegregation research. In G. Orfield (Ed.), *Diversity challenged* (pp. 99–109). Cambridge, MA: Harvard Education Publishing Group.

Schofield, J. W. (2004). Fostering positive intergroup relations in schools. In J. A. Banks & C. A. McGee Banks (Eds.), *Handbook of research on multicultural education* (pp. 799–812). New York: John Wiley & Sons.

Schofield, J. W., & Eurich-Fulcer, R. (2001). When and how school desegregation improves intergroup relations. In R. Brown & S. Gaertner (Eds.), *Blackwell handbook of social psychology: Intergroup processes* (pp. 475–494). New York: Blackwell.

Schofield, J. W., & Hausmann, L. R. M. (2004a). School desegregation and social science research. *American Psychologist, 59,* 538–546.

Schofield, J. W., & Hausmann, L. R. M. (2004b). The conundrum of school desegregation: Positive student outcomes and waning support. *Pittsburgh Law Review*, 66, 83–111.

Schofield, J. W., & Sagar, H. A. (1977). Peer interaction patterns in an integrated middle school. *Sociometry*, 40, 130–138.

Schofield, J. W., & Sagar, H. A. (1983). Desegregation, school practices and student race relations. In C. Rossell & W. Hawley (Eds.), *The consequences of school desegregation* (pp. 58–102). Philadelphia, PA: Temple University Press.

Schuman, H., & Krysan, M. (1999). A historical note on Whites' beliefs about racial inequality. *American Sociological Review*, 64, 847–855.

Slavin, R. E. (1995). Cooperative learning and intergroup relations. In J. A. Banks & C. A. McGee Banks (Eds.), *Handbook of research on multicultural education* (pp. 628–634). New York: Macmillan.

Sommer, R. (2006). Dual dissemination: Writing for colleagues and the public. *American Psychologist*, 61, 955–958.

St. John, N. H. (1975). *School desegregation outcomes for children*. New York: John Wiley & Sons.

Stephan, W. G. (2006). Bridging the research-practitioner divide in intergroup relations. *Journal of Social Issues*, 62, 597–605.

Suedfeld, P., & Tetlock, P. E. (1992). Psychologists as policy advocates: The roots of controversy. In P. Suedfeld & P. E. Tetlock (Eds.), *Psychology and social policy* (pp. 1–30). New York: Hemisphere Publishing Corporation.

Task Force on Psychology and Public Policy (1986). Psychology in the public forum. *American Psychologist*, 41, 914–921.

Tropp, L. R., & Prenovost, M. A. (2008). The role of intergroup contact in predicting children's inter-ethnic attitudes: Evidence from meta-analytic and field studies. In S. Levy & M. Killen (Eds.), *Intergroup relations: An integrative developmental and social psychological perspective*. Oxford, UK: Oxford University Press.

US Commission on Civil Rights (1967). *Racial isolation in the public schools*. Washington, DC: Supt. of Documents, U.S. Govt. Printing Office.

Weiss, C. (1991). Policy research as advocacy: Pro and con. *Knowledge & Policy*, 4, 37–56.

Weiss, C. H. (1979). The many meanings of research utilization. *Public Administration Review 39*, 426–431.

Wolf, E. P. (1981). *Trial and error: The Detroit school segregation case*. Detroit, MI: Wayne State University Press.

Zimbardo, P. G. (2004). Does psychology make a significant difference in our lives? *American Psychologist*, 59, 339–351.

Part VI

Final Reflections

18

Reflections on Core Themes in Intergroup Research

Thomas F. Pettigrew

This volume is both a special honor and a genuine surprise. It is a special honor because the many authors are colleagues whom I value as good friends and major contributors to our joint enterprise of social psychology. It is also a surprise, because until now I was unaware I had "a legacy!" Following decades of intergroup research, this volume reassures me that some significant social psychologists have been seriously considering my contentions after all.

However, reflective memory of past events, especially when given the specific assignment by the editors, can (and obviously did) lead to overestimating my influence on the authors' work. In truth, of course, social psychology is a far-flung community of scholars hopefully moving the discipline collectively toward maturity and a greater understanding of social phenomena. We give to, and take from, one another as befits such a collective enterprise.

This view makes obvious one glaring omission in the preceding chapters—namely, there is no mention of the authors' considerable influence on me. It is the academy's best kept secret of how much teachers learn from their students. I followed my mentor's example and encouraged my doctoral students to go in their own chosen directions. Consequently, their work continuously opened up new vistas for me. My doctoral students—from Eliot Smith, Janet Schofield, and Joanne Martin at Harvard to Heather Smith, Iain Walker, and Linda Tropp at the University of California, Santa Cruz—often reversed roles and gave me extensive reading assignments so that I could comment intelligently on their research. My colleagues, too, have influenced me greatly. With their impressive extended contact studies, Steve Wright and Art Aron broadened my views, and everyone else's, on intergroup contact. I enjoyed long discussions at Harvard with Herbert Kelman, my oldest and closest friend in the discipline; often we talked about his incisive views of social psychology. His perspective led directly to my notion of contextual social psychology—little wonder he likes the term! Ulrich Wagner is an old friend and research colleague over the past two decades. Recently, Wagner, together with Rolf van Dick and Oliver Christ, have furthered my interest in and knowledge of structural equation modeling with probability survey data. They also provided me with the opportunity to join them in working with the best probability sample survey data on prejudice I have ever analyzed.

Over my half-century in the field, one observation has especially impressed me about my many friendships with other social psychologists. We often come from vastly different backgrounds and yet have similar views not only about social psychology but the world in general. Kelman and Wagner, for example, could not have had more contrasting early lives than my Scottish-Protestant beginnings in the southern United States. Yet we have trouble finding anything to argue about! This phenomenon suggests that there are strong selection factors operating as to who decides to become a social psychologist as well as some common socializing processes we all go through becoming social psychologists.

In consideration of their influence on me, this chapter elaborates on points raised about my putative "legacy" and considers several core themes that emerge throughout the volume.

The Question of Values in Social Research

Frances Cherry and others in this volume mention my desire to have social psychological findings influence social policy and benefit the victims of prejudice and discrimination. But this aspiration is *not* an attempt to politicize social psychology. It does, however, raise the controversial issue of values in social science. Indeed, the tensions surrounding values are especially acute for specialists in intergroup relations.

The immediate relevance of social science for everyday life necessarily involves values—judgments of right and wrong and "what ought to be." Social scientists are human beings with their own values studying other human beings with their values. So value assumptions, often unrecognized, are embedded in both theory and research. Moreover, social science influences public policy in ways that directly impinge on people's lives. Consequently, social science cannot avoid involving values.[1]

As a University of Virginia undergraduate in 1951, I read Appendix 2 of Gunnar Myrdal's (1944) classic volume, *An American Dilemma*. In "A methodological note on facts and valuations in social science," the Swedish economist maintained that values are inherent in social science. His trenchant analysis was shaped by his earlier incisive rebuke of classical economic theory in which he uncovered its many unstated and value-laden assumptions (Myrdal, 1930). Undoubtedly, Myrdal's position was influenced by his active participation in the major restructuring of Swedish society by the Social Democrats in the 1930s and 1940s (Jackson, 1990).

Myrdal's view is as straightforward as was his personality.[2] Better to be aware of your values, struggle against their biasing effects, and alert your readers to them, he asserts, than to fool yourself and others that you are coldly "objective." "There is no other device for excluding biases in [the] social sciences," Myrdal writes, "than to face the valuations and to introduce them as explicitly stated, specific, and sufficiently concretized value premises." (Myrdal, 1944, p. 1043) I found Myrdal's argument persuasive and realistic, and nothing during the ensuing six decades has dissuaded me.

But there is risk involved in following Myrdal's advice. Those who allege "objectivity" for themselves but who accuse others of bias can exploit such open statements of value premises as "proof" of their claims. These critics are usually politically conservative social scientists who simply refuse to accept that "objectivity" is a never fully attained goal in science, not an assumed state from which to deny bias. Such a self-serving "*pseudo-objective*" stance is a disservice to the discipline, the researchers, their work, and the consumers of their work.

Yet a response from the political left can be just as damaging. "*Ideologists*" substitute strident ideological contentions for serious scholarship. They perceive social science as simply a power game, one won or lost by political means. Theory becomes dogma, and research becomes mere demonstration of ideological assertions. Though I suspect the pseudo-objectivists and the ideologists are less numerous in social psychology than in other social sciences, they do exist. But the political tensions that typically surround intergroup relations cause these two extreme positions to be overrepresented in the study of intergroup relations throughout social science.

On occasion, both pseudo-objectivists and the ideologists have attacked my work as representing the opposite extreme. In turn, the similarities of the two camps impress me. Each justifies its position in part by its opposition to the other. Both are serenely secure in the rectitude of their presumed objectivity or ideologically revealed truth.

As such, these groups deny the vast complexity of the social world and the tentativeness of science.

Both these extreme responses hold that science and values are necessarily in conflict. Donald Campbell (1959) forcefully countered this view. While agreeing with Myrdal that social science can never be value free, he held that strong goal motivation creates more, not less, investment in tracing an accurate map of reality. He pointed to rats in mazes. High hunger levels motivate rapid and accurate, not slow and error-prone, learning of the maze. Goal commitment, Campbell insisted, leads to good science.

The problem lies with *means* commitment—letting the desired ends distort the means. This travesty obviously results in poor science. But what is often overlooked is that means distortion also offers poor support and implementation of one's values. If you feel passionately about intergroup injustice, you should want to understand the true character of the injustice. Effective remedies require an accurate understanding of the problem. Twisting your research to obtain results that simply confirm your preconceived notions will not effectively advance social change. It is here that the Myrdalian struggle against the biasing effects of our values is most relevant.

Critics raise two objections to Myrdal's position. First, what purpose does it serve to be up-front with our value positions—such as publicly advocating racially integrating social institutions in order to achieve more optimal intergroup contact? And does this openness outweigh the obvious risks involved? Besides the ethical reasons for doing so, there are scientific reasons for Myrdal's stance. As the sociology of science makes clear, science is a social enterprise—not an individual endeavor. Significant scientific advances are social products made possible by the work of many people. To further this process, explicit statements of value premises are helpful to those who follow up and expand theoretical and empirical advances. Triangulation with multiple methods gives us greater confidence in research findings. Similarly, agreement among investigators with different value perspectives also provides greater confidence.

A second objection to Myrdal's approach involves a misreading of his stance. Some believe that this view precludes strong social commitment. By maintaining that science and values need not conflict, Myrdal's position explicitly holds that social commitment is not antithetical to scientific advances.

This point is highlighted when social science attempts to influence social policy. Pseudo-objectivists and activists disagree sharply on the standard required before scientific evidence should be used to influence policy. Critics, often defending their political conservatism behind the cloak of supposed "scientific rigor," favor a standard even higher than that for scientific audiences. Those who favor activism, such as Janet Schofield and Susan Fiske, counter that social scientists should "tell what we know" rather than "wait for Godot" (Ellsworth, 1991). Science is open-ended and dynamic; *all* the evidence is never in; *final* conclusions are never reached. Besides, the standards that prevail without social scientific evidence will consist of the untested conventional wisdom of decision-makers (Langenberg, 1991).

Upgrading our Methods

This discussion of values raises the importance of rigorous research methods in the study of intergroup relations—of multimethod replication, longitudinal research, and multilevel analyses. Eliot Smith recalls my delight in finding agreement between experimental and survey findings. Both the subject bias in social psychological experiments and the lack of built-in controls in survey research concern me. Each method corrects in part for the other; so, when their findings coincide, we can be more confident about their validity. Indeed, qualitative data are also invaluable, especially in the early stages of research. The chapter by Gillian Finchilescu and Colin Tredoux provides instructive examples of such work.

As individual investigators, we tend to follow our talents and use just one type of methodological approach. Although I have conducted experiments, I lack the skills of my experimental colleagues to run innovative experiments. My specialty and favorite endeavor is probability survey analysis; indeed, I happily analyze survey data in retirement just as retired postal workers take long walks. But this does not mean that one cannot appreciate the results from other methods. The two best items of the subtle prejudice scale I developed with Roel Meertens (Pettigrew & Meertens, 1995)—tapping the denial of positive emotions to the outgroup—were inspired by the findings of an elegant experiment by Dovidio, Mann, and Gaertner (1989).

Calls for replication across methods to establish "stubborn facts" are, of course, commonplace. Yet such replication is not routinely conducted in social psychology. Schofield's 10-year study of a single racially desegregated school provides a striking exception. And many of this book's chapters employ both experimental and survey research. The chapter by Colette van Laar, Shana Levin, and Jim Sidanius provides an outstanding example of longitudinal research—a rarely employed and badly needed design throughout social psychology. The general failure of intergroup research to follow Sherif's example and conduct longitudinal studies almost certainly means that we have missed detecting key cumulative effects (Pettigrew, 1991).

Multilevel analyses are also needed (Pettigrew, 2006), because intergroup relations are shaped by social institutions, mediated by situations, and experienced by individuals. Social psychology's hesitancy to link intergroup phenomena to social structures has unduly narrowed the discipline's approaches and restricted its influence on social policy. New software makes multilevel research much easier to analyze, and the chapter by Wagner and his colleagues supplies a pointed example of its value.

For the future, I hope that methodological training in social psychology will be broadened to encompass a wide array of methods and that multimethod replication, longitudinal designs, and multilevel analyses will become routine in the social psychology study on intergroup relations.

Innovative Ideas in Social Psychology

Social psychology's unfortunate tendency to place too much of its limited resources into one or two areas—authoritarianism in the 1950s, dissonance and attribution theories in the 1960s, social cognition in the 1970s, etc.—stifles progress. For this reason, I have especially admired those who go their own way and offer new ideas in areas not in fashion. From my own cohort, Robert Abelson, Donald Campbell, Herbert Kelman, and Robert Zajonc offer such role models. In later cohorts, Marilynn Brewer, Susan Fiske, Amélie Mummendey, and Eliot Smith are examples of such unique contributors. Their innovative chapters in this volume illustrate the point.

Kelman's work on the Middle-East conflict offers a rare example of a social psychological intervention into a macrocontext involving intergroup conflict. My son, Mark, now a Middle East specialist and fluent in Arabic, participated in one of Kelman's famous Harvard seminars. He noted a factor that Kelman modestly does not stress. Mark marveled at the way both Israelis and Arabs in the seminar respected and trusted him—the key variable in Tropp's chapter. Unless the leader of the intervention is fully trusted by both sides, such successful intergroup interventions may not be possible.

Marilynn Brewer was as fortunate as I in having a great mentor—Donald Campbell. Ever since her unique book with Campbell on East

African tribal ethnocentrism (Brewer & Campbell, 1976), Brewer has contributed to the study of intergroup relations from all directions. Here she takes a merely descriptive concept, *deprovincialization*, and gives it a rich theoretical grounding in terms of social identity complexity. For the future, as another link with intergroup contact as well as Aron's interpersonal closeness model (Aron et al., 2005), the effects of intergroup friendship on social identity complexity should be tested. Since cross-group friendship has emerged as an optimal form of intergroup contact (Pettigrew & Tropp, 2006), its link with social identity complexity might well prove to be of special theoretical and practical importance.

Though I was impressed with social psychology's cognitive advances in the 1970s—especially as they applied to stereotypes, I was unhappy that the discipline was virtually ignoring affect (e.g., Pettigrew, 1981). Eliot Smith and I had a friendly running argument on this issue. I admired his cognitive findings, but always asked him, "Where does affect fit in? Prejudice involves hate, envy, and a host of other strong emotions. Isn't something being left out of these cognitive analyses?" Now Smith has gone further in emphasizing affect than I ever did in defining prejudice itself as an emotion (Smith, 1993).

In his chapter, Smith describes his recent intergroup emotions theory and the research supporting it. The primary point uncovered in this work is the significance of group-based emotions. His findings link with many of the contentions concerning affect described in other chapters. And analyses with survey data on probability samples of Germans support the theory's predictions (Christ et al., 2008). Moreover, the special importance of group emotions mirrors the central role of collective threat and of group relative deprivation. Group-focused variables repeatedly show their superiority over their individual equivalents in the prediction of prejudice.

Among her many distinctive contributions to the study of intergroup relations, Susan Fiske has also helped to bring emotion back into focus. After making major cognitive advances with her mentor, Shelley Taylor, Fiske helped to return attention to the role of affect in a highly influential article (Abelson, Kinder, Peters, & Fiske, 1982). Now she reports that affect predicts discriminatory behavior better than such cognitive indices as stereotypes. This finding coincides with other intergroup research reported in this volume. Indeed, a spate of additional empirical work using a variety of methods now supports the critical importance of affect for intergroup relations (e.g., Christ et al., 2008; Dijker, 1987; Pettigrew, 1997; Smith, 1993; Stangor, Sullivan, & Ford, 1991).

Like Schofield, Fiske is an effective activist in the policy use of social psychology. Unless you have personally done it, one cannot fully appreciate the difficulties she faced as an expert witness in court. The law's adversarial system conflicts sharply with scientific thinking and logic in many ways. In American courts, at least, getting at the facts is secondary to who wins the argument; and your testimony can be distorted without an adequate opportunity for rebuttal. Moreover, the low legal standards for both evidence and so-called "expert witnesses" surprise social scientists when they first testify (Pettigrew, 1979). Though I testified in numerous school desegregation cases using contact theory, I always found the experience extremely stressful and frustrating. But, unlike many of my cases, Fiske helped to win her famous case involving sexist stereotypes of women and gender discrimination —*Price Waterhouse v. Hopkins* (Fiske, Bersoff, Borgida, Deaux, & Heilman, 1991).

Amélie Mummendey also offers her own unique contributions to intergroup relations theory and research. Her special talent is to detect problems with such popular theories as social identity, point them out, and then supply a deeper theoretical means of handling the issue. Her chapter with Kai Jonas illustrates this talent by considering how positive intergroup relations can arise even from situations generally thought to be conducive to conflict. Under a particular set of conditions—such as with the basking-in-reflective-glory phenomenon, even the triumph of a comparison group can lead to positive intergroup responses. It should be added that Mummendey has also actively pursued the use of social psychology in public policy. She was one of the first West Germans to head up a social psychological program in East Germany after the nation's unification. And, working with Germans from both regions, she turned it into one of the nation's leading centers for the study of intergroup relations at Jena's Schiller University. One could say Mummendey successfully used the principles of optimal intergroup contact within the discipline itself.

The Controversial Role of Relative Deprivation

Samuel Stouffer's (Stouffer, Suchman, DeVinney, Star, & Williams, 1949) concept of relative deprivation (RD) supplies an important predictor for understanding intergroup relations. Heather Smith and Iain Walker provide a concise, up-to-date analysis of this area as it applies to collective protest. But they lack the space to describe the controversies that still surround the concept. Some investigations strongly support RD models—especially group relative deprivation (e.g., Abrams, 1990; Pettigrew, Christ, Wagner, & Stellmacher, 2007; Pettigrew, Christ, et al., in press; Vanneman & Pettigrew, 1972; Walker & Mann, 1987; Walker & Smith, 2001), but others do not (e.g., Gaskell & Smith, 1984; Snyder & Tilly, 1972; Thompson, 1989). In response to these apparent inconsistencies, some sociologists have prematurely dismissed the concept's value (Finkel & Rule, 1986; Gurney & Tierney, 1982; Snyder & Tilly, 1972).

Smith and I propose that the negative RD results are a direct result of inadequate measurement (Smith & Pettigrew, 2007). In particular, we question the use of difference scores to measure respondents' subjective comparisons, the use of only cognitive RD measures without tapping affect, and the use of dissimilar levels of reference for the RD measures and the dependent variables. Our hypothesis is: *the predictive power of RD improves as a direct function of how closely its measurement reflects RD theory.*

We are testing our contentions with separate meta-analytic tests for each of the four types of dependent variables found in the RD literature: collective behavior, attitudes toward outgroups, individually oriented behaviors, and such internal responses as stress and depression. The initial results of these meta-analyses look promising for our hypothesis.

The Importance of Intergroup Contact

My meta-analysis with Linda Tropp analyzed all the relevant studies on intergroup contact we could locate through 2000 (Pettigrew & Tropp, 2006). But this volume describes the many exciting new advances that have been made in this area since 2000. Indeed, the major research programs on intergroup contact are all reported in these pages.

Van Laar, Levin, and Sidanius describe their findings on the most extensive longitudinal study of intergroup contact ever conducted. Their work at UCLA offers a model for future longitudinal studies in this area. Their thorough design allows them to infer causal connections and uncover new findings. It even involved random assignment of student roommates. They show how cumulative and nonrecursive the processes are: cross-ethnic contact leads to more such contact and no contact leads to further avoidance of contact; and contact leads to less prejudice while prejudice leads to less contact. White fraternities and sororities recruit more biased students and further their bias against diversity. Of course, this phenomenon is a function of the anti-diversity norms of these institutions as well as their homogeneous friendship networks.

But, as both the Tropp and the Dovidio, Gaertner, Saguy, and Halabi chapters also note, there are different consequences for majority and minority students. Ever since early studies of desegregated schools in the 1960s, we have known that American minorities carry an extra burden in intergroup institutions. I have studied and written about this extra burden (Pettigrew, 1998a), and my position on this is somewhat different than the one ascribed to me in the chapter by van Laar and her colleagues. Given American demographics and history, some minorities undoubtedly have a special need for separate organizations. But the extent of the minority's burden is also a direct function of how "integrated" the institution is—with "integration" defined in terms of Allport's (1954) conditions for optimal intergroup contact. From this perspective, the need of minority students at UCLA for all-minority organizations partly reflects the university's failure to provide a truly integrated environment.

With ingenious experiments and field studies, John Dovidio and Samuel Gaertner have long been assiduously conducting research to understand "when, how, and for whom contact reduces intergroup bias." Their chapter here draws on this extensive work to investigate further the differential contact processes of minorities and majorities. In particular, they stress the moderating influence of status in the relationship between dual identity and bias.

This finding recalls a conclusion based on the meta-analysis of contact effects (Pettigrew & Tropp, 2006). Allport's (1954) four conditions of optimal contact—equal status, cross-group cooperation, common goals, and authority sanction—have been viewed largely as structural features of the contact situation. But from contrasting status perspectives, the same conditions can be perceived in quite different ways. Thus, a contact situation regarded by majority members as being of equal status might well be viewed by minority members as patronizingly unequal.

Equally tireless, Miles Hewstone and his international coworkers have been conducting surveys and experiments on intergroup contact in Australia, India, Italy, and Northern Ireland. They have concentrated on specifying the mediating and moderating variables that will elucidate just how and when the intergroup contact process operates. In their chapter, they emphasize the importance of cross-group friendship and describe key mediators (anxiety reduction and closeness of friendship ties) and moderators (attitude structure and perceived group typicality). In her chapter, Tropp adds trust as a critical variable both in predicting willingness to have contact and as a mediator for contact's effects.

The many studies of intergroup contact mediation by Hewstone and his colleagues formed much of the basic data for a meta-analytic analysis Tropp and I conducted on three mediators of contact's effect on prejudice (Pettigrew & Tropp, in press). We found empathy to be the most important mediator followed closely by anxiety reduction. The original mediator advanced by Allport (1954) was knowledge of the outgroup gained through contact. While this variable proved to be a minor mediator, it did not approach empathy and anxiety reduction in importance.

These positive effects of direct intergroup contact radiate out beyond the immediate situation. To understand how this secondary effect operates, the Vonofakou et al. and Wright, Aron, and Brody chapters should be read together. Wright and his colleagues describe how they combined intergroup and interpersonal theory to uncover an important new phenomenon—extended contact. (I prefer to call it *indirect contact* in parallel with direct contact.) Their discovery is significant for both theory and practice. Note the manner in which they brought together two levels of analysis and two areas of theory. Their success suggests that Brown and Turner (1981) and Hewstone and Brown (1986) differentiated too sharply between the interpersonal and intergroup levels of analysis (see also Pettigrew, 1986, p. 185). Though we need to keep our levels of analysis straight (Pettigrew, 1996), Wright and his co-authors show that careful investigation into the connections between levels can be especially fruitful.

For practical application and social policy, indirect intergroup contact expands the potential of intergroup contact to improve intergroup relations. But just how indirect contact contributes to change beyond that of direct contact is complex. German surveys found direct and indirect intergroup contact are highly interrelated, and both are negatively related to prejudices against Muslims and resident foreigners (Pettigrew et al., 2007). Direct and indirect contact together enhance the prediction of prejudice, and they are shaped by similar social and personality variables. Their effects are mediated by threat, but here there is a difference. Direct contact is negatively related to both individual and collective threat—consistent with Tropp's analysis. Indirect contact is also negatively related to collective threat but, as Wright holds, only slightly related to individual threat. Clusters of young, urban Germans evinced both direct and indirect contact with foreign residents—offering further support for Wright's emphasis on a normative explanation for their effects.

The Vonofakou et al. chapter uncovers further differences between the effects of the two contact types. It reports direct friendship effects are larger for individuals and outgroups (e.g., the elderly) characterized by "strong emotions." This finding coincides with meta-analytic results (Tropp & Pettigrew, 2005). By contrast, indirect friendship effects are larger for individuals and outgroups (e.g., engineering students) characterized by "elaborated cognitions." Moreover, attitude changes wrought by direct friendship tend to be stronger and less susceptible to change. Vonofakou and her colleagues also found in both Germany and Northern Ireland that indirect contact was most important for those without direct contact. They suggest that indirect contact may be important for preparing people for direct contact experiences. These findings have all been replicated with different German samples (Pettigrew et al., 2007; Wagner, Christ, & Pettigrew, 2007).

Linda Tropp suffered with me through eight long years of work on our meta-analysis of intergroup contact (Pettigrew & Tropp, 2006). It could not have been done without her. In her chapter, Tropp convincingly demonstrates the crucial role of intergroup trust—a theme that joins with many of those of other chapters. The importance of increased intergroup trust suggests it should be made a criterion of successful intergroup contact. Indeed, recent research in South Africa by Justine Burns (2007), an experimental economist, finds that White students from interracial high schools, when compared with White students from all-White high schools, evinced significantly greater trust of Black students.

Intergroup Contact in Action

These advances in contact theory and research are laden with social policy implications. While no one claims intergroup contact is in itself a panacea for intergroup conflict (Hewstone, 2003), it clearly must be part of the solution. Other chapters contribute to our understanding of just how it might operate.

Critics of contact theory often come from and emphasize the tense intergroup conditions in their homelands—South Africa and Northern Ireland (e.g., Dixon, Durrheim, & Tredoux, 2005; McGarry and O'Leary, 1995). Repeated verifications of the theory by Hewstone and his coworkers demonstrate, however, that the process fully operates in Northern Ireland.

But what about the more extreme case of South Africa? The informative chapter by Finchilescu and Tredoux provides an answer. They show that there is a great need to focus upon the factors that inhibit contact. Post-Apartheid research demonstrates that, as in Northern Ireland, interracial contact typically reduces prejudice in South Africa. But, just as in Northern Ireland and the American South, the problem is achieving intergroup contact in the first place. Though this question had been addressed earlier, South African social psychologists have led the way in innovative methods of studying this problem—from filming Durban's beaches from helicopters to observational studies through the night in Cape Town bars.

It is hardly surprising after centuries of racial discrimination and a half-century of Apartheid that racial contact is awkward and avoided. The old norms are fading, but the new norms have yet to be firmly established. In today's South Africa, racial interaction is typically polite and distant. Finchilescu and Tredoux emphasize the central role of metastereotypes: Africans fear Whites view them as inferiors, while Whites fear Africans view them as racists. As Tropp stresses in her chapter, it takes time for trust to develop; and distrust acts as a formidable barrier to intergroup contact.

Threat is also involved, and the Stephan, Renfro, and Davis chapter outlines the discipline's guiding theory in this realm. A critical new component in the revised theory is the distinction between individual and group (or collective) threat. Inspired by Stephan's theory, Wagner's Marburg group and I have found this distinction to be highly useful when studying German attitudes toward resident foreigners. In our analyses, individual threat is mediated by collective threat, and positive intergroup contact significantly reduces both types of threat (Pettigrew et al., 2007; Pettigrew et al., in press).

Schofield's chapter summarizes her extensive research on racially desegregated schools in the US. Her intensive approach is rare in psychological social psychology—long-term, multimethod, and institutionally-grounded. She uncovered both the strengths and weaknesses of interracial contact in a Pittsburgh public school where the authorities had the best of intentions. She was one of the first to stress the negative consequences of so-called "colorblind" approaches—a finding consistent with the Hewstone–Brown (1986) model of group salience. And she lists the many problems with American research on desegregated schools. Recently, Schofield (2006) has written an astute policy-oriented research summary for the German government on intergroup schools.

Like Mummendey, Wagner has been active in advancing social psychology in Germany's public arena and has developed a leading department specializing in intergroup relations research at Marburg's Philipps University. In their chapter, Wagner and his coauthors highlight the mass media's role in shaping intergroup opinions. Of particular interest is their finding that intergroup contact acts as a buffer against negative media effects—an outcome that coincides with the Vonofakou finding that direct contact leads to strong, change-resistant intergroup attitudes.

Summing Up

Thanks to the authors of these chapters, intergroup research has expanded and advanced rapidly in the past two decades. Six inter-related core themes emerge in this new work and are described in this volume. Considered together, these themes provide a changing perspective on intergroup phenomena: (1) multilevel complexity; (2) cumulative, nonrecursive processes; (3) multiple moderators and mediators of effects; (4) intergroup contact effects expand beyond the immediate situation; (5) group, not individual, concerns are of primary importance; and (6) affect is more critical than cognitive processes for many intergroup phenomena. Consider briefly each of these themes in turn.

Multilevel Complexity

For the most part in the twentieth century, intergroup phenomena were studied at only a single level of analysis: discrimination at the societal macrolevel, interaction at the situational mesolevel, and prejudice at the individual microlevel. Recent intergroup research has broken out of this too-simple approach—as demonstrated forcefully throughout this volume. Armed with improved multilevel software for complex analyses, this new work unfolds for us the complexity of intergroup relations. Recall the Wagner et al. chapter's multi-level findings. The population ratio of the outgroup at the macrolevel has contrasting effects at the situational mesolevel and the individual microlevel—greater potential threat coupled with increased opportunities for beneficial intergroup contact. Which process is dominant depends on a host of moderating variables—such as intergroup segregation that reduces the contact effect. Wagner and his colleagues further show that these complex effects will appear differently as a function of the size of the units used in the analysis.

Cumulative, Nonrecursive Processes

Part of this intergroup complexity involves slowly-evolving cumulative effects that often turn out to be nonrecursive. For instance, intergroup contact not only typically reduces prejudice, but prejudice operates to reduce intergroup contact. Schofield noted these intricate processes in her detailed work in a racially desegregated school. Now we have extensive quantitative evidence from the longitudinal UCLA study. Van Laar and her colleagues uncovered numerous cumulative and non-recursive processes. Interethnic contact over the four years of the study led to more such contact; while no intergroup contact led to further intragroup isolation. Moreover, discriminatory institutions, such as all-White fraternities, both attracted bigots and led to further bigotry.

Multiple Mediators and Moderators of Intergroup Effects

Further complexity is introduced when we consider the many mediators and moderators that shape intergroup phenomena. Work on this, led by Hewstone's Oxford University group, has concentrated on how and when intergroup contact influences prejudice. Long lists of mediators and moderators have now been developed, though we are only now starting to understand how these many factors relate to each other. Thus, in addition to empathy and anxiety-reduction, we now know that self-disclosure mediates both direct and indirect contact effects (Turner, Hewstone, & Voci, 2005). Broadened views of the ingroup (Brewer, this volume; Gaertner & Dovidio, 2000; Pettigrew, 1998b), the perceived importance of the contact (Van Dick et al., 2004), the perception of greater outgroup variability (Islam & Hewstone, 1993; Oaker & Brown, 1986; Paolini, Hewstone, Cairns, & Voci, 2004), trust (Tropp, this volume) and threat (Tausch, Hewstone, Kenworthy, Cairns, & Christ, in press; Wagner, Christ, Pettigrew, Stellmacher, & Wolf, 2006) also mediate intergroup contact effects. In addition, group salience effects (Voci & Hewstone, 2003), group status (Dovidio et al., this volume), attitude structure and perceived group typicality (Vonofakou et al., this volume) act as moderators of contact effects.

Intergroup Contact Effects Expand Beyond the Immediate Situation

The positive effects of intergroup contact typically generalize from the participants in the immediate contact situation to the entire groups.

And such contact subtly changes the intergroup norms. Thus, even having ingroup friends with outgroup friends, as in indirect contact, has prejudice-reducing effects.

Group, not Directly Individual, Concerns are of Primary Importance

It is commonly thought that prejudice and discrimination at the individual level of analysis largely involves direct individual threat— how the outgroup's existence and behavior are viewed as threatening the person individually. However, research in many different realms repeatedly suggests that group concerns are generally of greater importance than directly individual concerns. Individual threat is not unimportant, but its effects are often mediated by group threat. Thus, individual threat generally influences prejudice and other intergroup phenomena by increasing group threat.

Previous chapters revealed the power of group concerns in several realms. Group relative deprivation (perceiving one's group as deprived relative to the outgroup) consistently relates more strongly to intergroup prejudice and behavior than individual relative deprivation (perceiving one's self to be deprived relative to the outgroup). Smith's chapter showed the special significance of group-based emotions. And measures of collective threat in surveys typically outweigh comparable measures of individual threat in predicting intergroup prejudice.

Affect is more Critical than Cognitive Processes for many Intergroup Phenomena

Following the "cognitive revolution" in psychology, the study of stereotypes became dominant (see Pettigrew, 1981). But intergroup research since the 1980s has belatedly returned to understanding the central role of emotion in intergroup phenomena. The most important mediators of contact effects—empathy and anxiety-reduction— are affective (Pettigrew & Tropp, in press). And optimal intergroup contact typically reduces the affective components of prejudice more than the cognitive components of prejudice (Tropp & Pettigrew, 2005). Moreover, stereotypes are poor predictors of intergroup behavior. One reason for this finding is that ethnic, racial, and gender stereotypes are deeply imbedded in culture. Those who participate in the general culture cannot escape them. As such, the acceptance of stereotypes tells us much less about individuals than their intergroup emotions.

A Final Word

To close, let me note that my association with the editors and authors of this volume has obviously led to lasting friendships and scholarly influence. I both admire and have been deeply influenced by the theory and research described in these pages. I trust the reader will have also benefited from reading these concise statements of the leading work in the social psychology of intergroup relations. Hopefully, these empirically grounded insights will help shape policy for a world less torn by intergroup strife.

Notes

1   Nor do the natural sciences escape this issue. Consider the complex value concerns raised by atomic energy and DNA research.
2   I had the great opportunity to get to know Myrdal and to teach a seminar with him at the University of California, Irvine in 1976.

References

Abrams, D. (1990). Political identity: Relative deprivation, social identity, and the case of Scottish nationalism. *ESRC 16–19 Initiative: Occasional Papers*.

Abelson, R. P., Kinder, D. R., Peters, M. P., & Fiske, S. T. (1982). Affective and semantic components in political person perception. *Journal of Personality and Social Psychology, 42*, 619–630.

Allport, G. W. (1954). *The nature of prejudice*. Addison-Wesley, Reading, MA.

Aron, A., McLaughlin-Volpe, T., Mashek, D., Lewandowski, G., Wright, S. C., & Aron, E. N. (2005). Including others in the self. *European Review of Social Psychology, 14*, 101–132.

Brewer, M. B., and Campbell, D. T. (1976). *Ethnocentrism and intergroup attitudes: East African evidence*. Beverley Hills, CA: Sage.

Brown, R. J., & Turner, J. C. (1981). Interpersonal and intergroup behaviour. In J. Turner & H. Giles (Eds.), *Intergroup Behaviour*. Oxford, UK: Blackwell.

Burns, J. (2007). *Race and trust in a segmented society*. Paper presented at the Conference on Global Studies of Discrimination, Princeton University.

Campbell, D. T. (1959). *Systematic errors to be expected of the social scientist on the basis of a general psychology of cognitive bias*. Paper presented at the annual meeting of the American Psychological Association, Cincinnati, OH.

Christ, O., Mansel, J., Wagner, U., Asbruck, F., Schulter, E., & Pettigrew, T. F. (2008). *Intergroup emotions as both a cause and a consequence of prejudice*. Manuscript under review.

Dijker, A. J. M. (1987). Emotional reactions to ethnic minorities. *European Journal of Social Psychology, 17,* 305–325.

Dixon, J. A., Durrheim, K., & Tredoux, C. (2005). Beyond the optimal strategy: A "reality check" for the contact hypothesis. *American Psychologist, 60,* 697–711.

Dovidio, J. F., Mann, J., & Gaertner, S. L. (1989). Resistance to affirmative action: The implications of aversive racism. In F. Blanchard & F. Crosby (Eds.), *Affirmative action in perspective* (pp. 83–103). New York: Springer.

Ellsworth, P. C. (1991). To tell what you know or wait for Godot? *Law and Human Behavior, 15,* 77–90.

Finkel, S., & Rule, J. (1986). Relative deprivation and related psychological theories of civil violence: A critical review. *Research in Social Movements: Conflicts and Change, 9,* 47–69.

Fiske, S. T., Bersoff, D. N., Borgida, E., Deaux, K., & Heilman, M. E. (1991). Social science research on trial: Use of sex stereotyping research in *Price Waterhouse v. Hopkins. American Psychologist, 46,* 1049–1060.

Gaertner, S. L., & Dovidio, J. F. (2000). *Reducing intergroup bias: The common ingroup identity model.* Philadelphia, PA: Psychology Press.

Gaskell, G., & Smith, P. (1984). Relative deprivation in White and Black youth: An empirical investigation. *British Journal of Social Psychology, 23,* 121–131.

Gurney, J., & Tierney, K. (1982). Relative deprivation and social movements: A critical look at twenty years of theory and research. *The Sociological Quarterly, 23,* 33–47.

Hewstone, M. (2003). Intergroup contact: Panacea for prejudice? *Psychologist, 16,* 352–355.

Hewstone, M., & Brown, R. (1986). Contact is not enough: An intergroup perspective on the "contact hypothesis." In M. Hewstone & R. Brown (Eds.), *Contact and conflict in intergroup encounters.* Oxford, UK: Blackwell.

Islam, M. R., & Hewstone, M. (1993). Dimensions of contact as predictors of intergroup anxiety, perceived out-group variability, and out-group attitude: An integrative model. *Personality and Social Psychology Bulletin, 19,* 700–710.

Jackson, W. A. (1990). *Gunnar Myrdal and America's conscience: Social engineering and racial liberalism, 1938–1987.* Chapel Hill, NC: University of North Carolina Press.

Langenberg, D. N. (1991). Science, slogans, and civic duty. *Science, 252,* 361–364.

McGarry, J., & O'Leary, B. (1995). *Explaining Northern Ireland: Broken images.* Oxford, UK: Blackwell.

Myrdal, G. (1930). *Vetenskap och politik I nationalekonomien.* Stockholm, Sweden: Kooperativa forbundets bokforlag.

Myrdal, G. (1944). *An American dilemma.* New York, NY: Harper & Row.

Myrdal, G. (1961). *The political element in the development of economic theory.* Cambridge, MA: Harvard University Press.

Oaker, G., & Brown, R. (1986). Intergroup relations in a hospital setting: A further test of social identity theory. *Human Relations, 39,* 767–778.

Paolini, S., Hewstone, M., Cairns, E., & Voci, A. (2004). Effects of direct and indirect cross-group friendships on judgments of Catholics and Protestants in Northern Ireland: The mediating role of an anxiety-reduction mechanism. *Personality and Social Psychology Bulletin, 30,* 770–786.

Pettigrew, T. F. (1979). Tensions between the law and social science: An expert witness view. In *Schools and the Courts: Desegregation* (Vol. 1) (pp. 23–44). Eugene, OR: ERIC Clearinghouse for Educational Management, University of Oregon.

Pettigrew, T. F. (1981). Extending the stereotype concept. In D. L. Hamilton (Ed.), *Cognitive processes in stereotyping and intergroup behavior* (pp. 303–331). Hillsdale, NJ: Erlbaum.

Pettigrew, T. F. (1986). The intergroup contact hypothesis reconsidered. In M. Hewstone & R. Brown (Eds.), *Contact and conflict in intergroup encounters* (pp. 169–195). Oxford, UK: Blackwell.

Pettigrew, T. F. (1991). The importance of cumulative effects: A neglected emphasis of Sherif's work. In D. Granberg & G. Sarup (Eds.), *Social judgment and intergroup relations: Essays in honor of Muzafer Sherif* (pp. 89–103). New York Springer-Verlag.

Pettigrew, T. F. (1996). *How to think like a social scientist.* New York: HarperCollins.

Pettigrew, T. F. (1997). The emotional component of prejudice: Results from Western Europe. In S. A. Tuch and J. K. Martin (Eds.), *Racial Attitudes in the 1990s: Continuity and Change* (pp. 76–90). Westport, CN: Praeger.

Pettigrew, T. F. (1998a). Prejudice and discrimination on the college campus. In J. Eberhardt & S. T. Fiske (Eds.), *Confronting racism: The problem and the response* (pp. 263–279). Thousand Oaks, CA: Sage.

Pettigrew, T. F. (1998b). Intergroup contact theory. *Annual Review of Psychology, 49,* 65–85.

Pettigrew, T. F. (2006). Commentary: The advantages of multi-level approaches. *Journal of Social Issues, 62,* 615–620.

Pettigrew, T. F., Christ, O., Meertens, R. W., Wagner, U., van Dick, R., & Zick, A. (in press). Relative deprivation and intergroup prejudice. *Journal of Social Issues.*

Pettigrew, T. F., Christ, O., Wagner, U., & Stellmacher, J. (2007). Direct and indirect intergroup contact effects on prejudice: A normative interpretation. *International Journal of Intercultural Relations, 31,* 411–425.

Pettigrew, T. F., and Meertens, R. W. (1995). Subtle and blatant prejudice in Western Europe. *European Journal of Social Psychology, 25,* 57–75.

Pettigrew, T. F., & Tropp, L. R. (2006). A meta-analytic test of intergroup contact theory. *Journal of Personality and Social Psychology, 90,* 751–783.

Pettigrew, T. F., & Tropp, L. R. (in press). How does intergroup contact reduce prejudice? Meta-analytic tests of three mediators. *European Journal of Social Psychology.*

Pettigrew, T. F., Wagner, U., & Christ, O. (in press). Who opposes immigration? Comparing German results with those of North America. *DuBois Review.*

Schofield, J. W. (2006). *Migration background, minority-group membership and academic achievement.* Berlin, Germany: Wissenschaftszentrum Berlin.

Smith, E. R. (1993). Social identity and social emotions. Toward new conceptualizations of prejudice. In D. M. Mackie & D. L. Hamilton (Eds.), *Affect, cognition, and stereotyping: Interactive processes in group perception* (pp. 297–315). San Diego, CA: Academic Press.

Smith, H. J., & Pettigrew, T. F. (2007). *Does relative deprivation predict? A meta-analytic critique.* Paper in preparation.

Snyder, D., & Tilly, C. (1972). Hardship and collective violence in France, 1830–1910. *American Sociological Review, 37,* 520–532.

Stangor, C. L., Sullivan, A., & Ford, T. E. (1991). Affective and cognitive determinants of prejudice. *Social Cognition, 9,* 359–380.

Stouffer, S. A., Suchman, E. A., DeVinney, L. C., Star, S. A., & Williams, R. M., Jr. (1949). *The American soldier. Adjustment during army life.* (Vol. 1). Princeton, NJ: Princeton University Press.

Tausch, N., Hewstone, M., Kenworthy, J., Cairns, E., & Christ, O. (2007). Cross community contact, perceived status differences, and intergroup attitudes in Northern Ireland: The mediating roles of individual-level vs. group-level threats and the moderating role of social identification. *Political Psychology, 28*(1), 53–68.

Thompson, J. L. (1989). Deprivation and political violence in Northern Ireland. *Journal of Conflict Resolution, 33,* 676–699.

Tropp, L. R., & Pettigrew, T. F. (2005). Differential relationships between intergroup contact and affective and cognitive dimensions of prejudice. *Personality and Social Psychology Bulletin, 31,* 1145–1158.

Turner, R., Hewstone, M., & Voci, A. (2007). Reducing explicit and implicit prejudice via direct and extended contact: The mediating role of self-disclosure and intergroup anxiety. *Journal of Personality and Social Psychology, 93*(3), 369–388.

Van Dick, R., Wagner, U., Pettigrew, T. F., Christ, O., Wolf, C., Petzel, T., et al. (2004). The role of perceived importance in intergroup contact. *Journal of Personality and Social Psychology, 87,* 211–227.

Vanneman, R. D., & Pettigrew, T. F. (1972). Race and relative deprivation in the urban United States. *Race, 13,* 461–486.

Voci, A., & Hewstone, M. (2003). Intergroup contact and prejudice toward immigrants in Italy: The mediational role of anxiety and the moderational role of group salience. *Group Processes and Intergroup Relations, 6,* 37–54.

Wagner, U., Christ, O., Pettigrew, T. F. (2007). *Direct and extended contact effects on intergroup attitudes: Preconditions, consequences and opportunities.* Paper presented at the annual meeting of the Society for Experimental Social Psychology, Chicago, IL.

Wagner, U., Christ, O., Pettigrew, T. F., Stellmacher, J., & Wolf, H. (2006). Prejudice and minority proportion: Contact instead of threat effects. *Social Psychology Quarterly, 69,* 380–390.

Walker, I., & Mann, L. (1987). Unemployment, relative deprivation, and social protest. *Personality and Social Psychology Bulletin, 13,* 275–283.

Walker, I., & Smith. H. (Eds.) (2001). *Relative deprivation: Specification, development and integration.* New York: Cambridge University Press.

Author Index

Subject Index

Note: page numbers in *italics* refer to an illustration on that page.